Leisure Marketing

Leisure Marketing

A Global Perspective

Susan Horner
John Swarbrooke

AMSTERDAM • BOSTON • HEIDELBERG • LONDON • NEW YORK • OXFORD
PARIS • SAN DIEGO • SAN FRANCISCO • SINGAPORE • SYDNEY • TOKYO

Elsevier Butterworth-Heinemann
Linacre House, Jordan Hill, Oxford OX2 8DP
30 Corporate Drive, Burlington, MA 01803

First published 2005
Reprinted 2006

British Library Cataloguing in Publication Data
A catalogue record for this book is available from the British Library

Library of Congress Cataloguing in Publication Data
A catalogue record for this book is available from the Library of Congress

ISBN 0 7506 5550 X

Typeset by Integra Software Services Pvt. Ltd, Pondicherry, India
Printed and bound in Great Britain

Contents

Preface

This book is designed to offer a truly international perspective on marketing in the diverse field of leisure. It is not simply meant to be a description of the situation in individual countries. Instead it is an attempt to take a supranational view of the subject for we believe leisure is now a truly global phenomenon. However, before we plunge into the debates with which the book is concerned, perhaps we should begin by explaining why we believe there is a need for a book on leisure marketing, in the first place.

First, why leisure? This industry, if single industry it is, has grown dramatically in recent decades. Leisure has been in the vanguard of the development of the modern consumer society. Furthermore, the authors believe that the word 'leisure' is a convenient umbrella term for a range of different sectors or individual industries. However, it is also true that, as the book will show, there are still some major differences between the different sectors of leisure.

Secondly, why marketing? Because marketing is the 'buzz word' of modern management theory and practice, in both the public and private sectors, across the world. The concept of marketing has been broadened to the point where it now appears to encompass most aspects of corporate life. It is particularly appropriate to take a marketing approach when one is looking at service industries like leisure, for it is in such largely modern industries where staff and customers interact on a face-to-face basis, that many modern innovations in marketing have been born.

The book has been designed to be both valuable, and, hopefully, stimulating for a variety of audiences, including:

- undergraduate and postgraduate students on leisure-related courses;
- students on business courses, who have an interest in service industries;
- students following vocational courses, for example GNVQ courses in the UK;
- lecturers who teach on leisure-related courses;
- managers, working for regional, national and international leisure organisations.

This book draws heavily on our 1996 book, *Marketing Tourism, Hospitality and Leisure in Europe*, but it has been substantially modified and updated with the addition of new case studies.

The text is split into a number of sections, as follows:

- Part One provides the context for the book and includes a discussion of the meaning of the terms 'leisure' and 'marketing'.
- Part Two sets out the international dimension of leisure in terms of the supply and demand sides, and the business environment of leisure organisations.

- Part Three applies the Marketing Mix to the field of leisure marketing.
- Part Four looks at the marketing planning process in relation to leisure organisations.
- Part Five looks at how marketing practices and techniques vary between different sectors within the leisure industry from airlines to theatres, destinations to fast-food outlets.
- Part Six looks at topical issues in leisure marketing including quality, ethics and competition.

Throughout the book, the points made are illustrated by a wide range of examples and in Part Nine the authors offer fourteen detailed new case studies on aspects of leisure marketing around the world.

At the end of the book there is a Glossary for those readers who are unfamiliar with some of the terms used.

A number of features have been incorporated in the book to make it easier for the reader to use and to make it a truly interactive text. These include:

- Key concept boxes, at the beginning of each chapter, which inform readers about the main issues they may expect to find covered in the chapter.
- Potential discussion points and/or essay questions are identified at the end of each chapter and case study.
- At the conclusion of each chapter an exercise is provided to help students, individually or in groups, to increase their understanding of key topics covered in the text and to explore how the concepts and models can be applied in practice.

We have endeavoured to write the book in a style that is easy to read and follow, particularly for international readers whose first language is not English. Only such readers can tell us to what extent we have succeeded in this aim.

Throughout the period we have spent writing this book, we have tried to ensure that it did not become insular. We recognise that leisure does not exist in isolation from the rest of modern consumer society. A chapter at the latter end of the book explains this theme further.

In spite of all our efforts we are aware of the limitations of this book. There are not enough pages to fully explain this fascinating and hugely complex subject, and while we have tried to write the book from an international point of view, the fact remains that we are British. Therefore, in spite of all our efforts, it is likely that the book still has an anglocentric flavour.

While all the weaknesses of the book are solely our responsibility, many of its strengths reflect the help and support of many people and organisations. We can only thank a few of them here but the others know who they are and, hopefully, they know how much we appreciate their help.

We would first like to thank Judy Mitchell who has typed every word of the book, quickly and accurately. Her patience and good humour were a constant source of strength to both of us during the months of hard work involved in writing this book.

We must also express our thanks to our many colleagues all over the world who helped with the production of the book, in a number of ways.

It is important for us to place on record our gratitude to our respective parents for all their help and support throughout our lives. We know that without the sacrifices they have made for us, we would never have been in a position to write this book.

Finally, there is the enormous debt which we owe to our son John, who has brought us great joy. He made us laugh at times when writing this book was hard work and he made us see that life is about more than work. This book is dedicated to him.

It only remains now for us to wish you 'happy reading'. If you find this book useful and interesting, then all our efforts will have been worthwhile.

Best wishes

Susan Horner
John Swarbrooke

Part One

Introduction

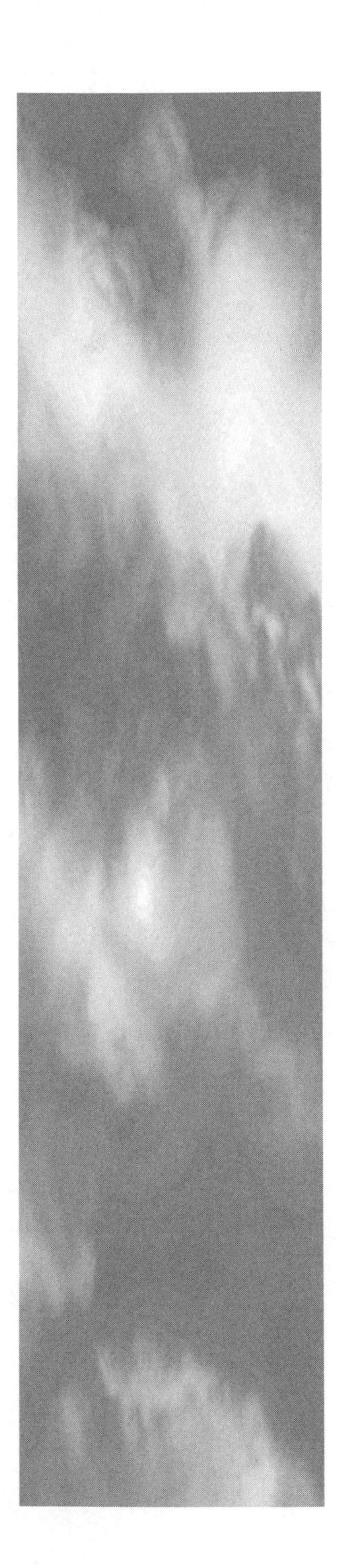

Introduction

This first section of the book sets the scene by answering two questions which are central to the whole book, namely:

Chapter 1 What is marketing?
Chapter 2 What is leisure?

We will look at the marketing concept and examine some current trends and key issues in the theory and practice of marketing.

In this section of the book, the authors will also seek to offer a definition of leisure. They will examine the interrelationship between the different sectors of leisure, and suggest that the distinctions between them are becoming increasingly blurred.

CHAPTER 1

What is marketing?

Key concepts

The main concepts covered in the chapter are:

- The scope and nature of marketing
- Definitions of the marketing concept
- The application of marketing principles to profit-making and nonprofit making organisations
- The differences between strategic and tactical marketing
- Service product marketing in comparison to the marketing of manufactured products.

This chapter introduces the marketing concept. It looks at the historical development of marketing and discusses the application of marketing to different kinds of organisation. The chapter also looks at the marketing function within the context of other management functions. Differences between product marketing and service marketing will be discussed. The chapter will review the reasons why marketing has become a highly fashionable influential subject in all aspects of the economy and society, and review some of the current contemporary marketing issues.

The main points covered in the chapter are as follows:

- introduction to the marketing concept;
- definitions of marketing;
- the historical development of the marketing concept;

- the application of the marketing concept to different kinds of organisation;
- different approaches to the running of business organisations;
- the consequences of an organisation adopting a marketing approach;
- the differences between strategic and tactical marketing;
- marketing and other business functions;
- a review of the differences between product marketing and service marketing;
- contemporary marketing issues.

Introduction to the marketing concept

What does marketing mean? For most people, marketing constitutes selling and promotion. Marketing does involve selling and promotion. If the products, however, have been designed to suit customer wants, selling and promotion will just be the icing on the cake.

The marketing concept is something of an enigma. It is a well-recognised business function in many organisations, but the underlying concept of the marketing philosophy is rarely discussed. The introduction of a marketing department to many organisations involves the appointment of one or a number of personnel who organise promotional materials and nothing more. This, it must be stressed, does not constitute the marketing.

Marketing is concerned with the relationship between buyer and seller, and the transactions involved in bringing this to a satisfactory conclusion. It could be argued that, unlike economics which concentrates on the relationship between supply and demand, marketing relies on the idea that the customer forms the central focus for all people working in the organisation. The application of the marketing concept to an organisation involves putting the customer at the centre of all decision-making processes in the business.

The marketing concept suggests that the overriding inclination of the organisation will be to serve the final customer needs and wants as the main priority. The organisation will seek constantly to find out what the customer want both today and in the future and work tirelessly to produce the products and services that are requested. This may mean that the organisation has to make major shifts in their product and service ranges, and may even involve the organisation moving into new markets and changing fixed asset bases.

These are fundamental problems with the organisation adopting a consumer-led approach. It is often difficult for many people in organisations to see the final customer as being central to their individual roles. Many people in organisations are divorced from the final customers and it is difficult for them to see the logic of introducing the marketing approach.

Some organisations even have difficulty in recognising who the customers are, particularly if the product or service is offered free of charge, or if the organisation supplying it is the sole supplier. This can be particularly prevalent if the organisation has been faced with a buoyant market position where demand outstrips supply. The logic here is that there have always been more customers demanding the products and services on offer, so why bother with any expensive marketing effort? Organisations in this type of market position tend to look to marketing when market conditions become more difficult and customer demand starts to reduce.

The second reason for organisations having difficulty with putting the customer at the centre of the business is the fact that the implication of changing consumer demand on the organisation may be too difficult to cope with. This is particularly apparent if the organisation has long-term investments in fixed assets. The hotel chain with major investments in a group of prestigious hotels, or a theme park owner, faced with changing consumer demands would find it very difficult in the short term to change. The idea of total customer sovereignty, in a business which relies on substantial fixed capital asset, is impossible to implement in the short term.

Organisations often consider their customer wants and needs, but also rely on persuading their customers to buy their existing products and services. The idea of persuasion rather than meeting customer needs and wants represents a totally different approach to the marketing concept. It is this idea of *customer persuasion* or at the most extreme *customer manipulation* which large numbers of the population interpret marketing to be. Marketing is often viewed by the man or woman in the street as aggressive hard selling by unscrupulous persons eager to make themselves vast profits.

The idea that organisations use *customer sovereignty* or *customer manipulation* in the extreme is wrong. It is more likely that the marketing approach can be expressed in terms of a continuum model.

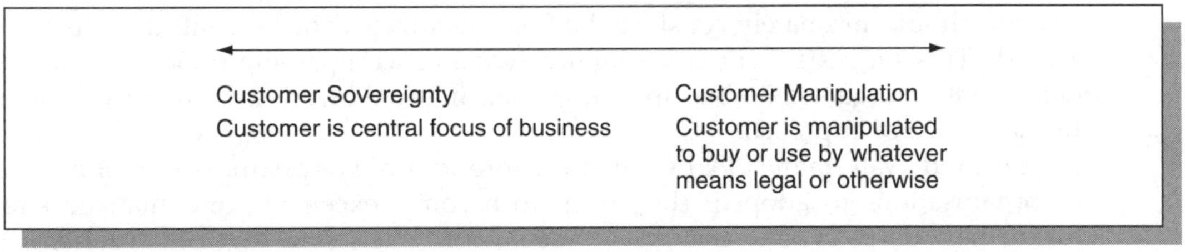

Customer Sovereignty	Customer Manipulation
Customer is central focus of business	Customer is manipulated to buy or use by whatever means legal or otherwise

Figure 1.1 The marketing continuum model

Organisations will tend to fall somewhere in the middle of the continuum, using some market research to find out about customer wants but using some manipulation techniques to increase sales.

Packard (1957) in his book *The Hidden Persuaders*, portrayed a frightening manipulative view of the marketing function. The idea that consumers, including children, could be manipulated by marketing activity to buy products and services was seen by many as a horrifying vision of the marketing profession.

Definitions of marketing

The definitions of marketing demonstrate the different approaches which academics have taken to the marketing philosophy. Marketing has been defined in many different ways, emphasising different points. This is perhaps a reflection of the immature stage of development of the marketing discipline.

Kotler (2003), the American marketing academic, defined marketing as follows:

> A social and managerial process by which individuals and groups obtain what they need and want through creating and exchanging products and values with others.

Levitt (1986) discussed the role of marketing as follows:

> a truly marketing minded firm tries to create value satisfying goods and services that consumers will want to buy.

This definition is useful because it identifies the importance of customer needs and wants as being central to the marketing function. Once the needs and wants have been identified, they must be met by producing goods and services which satisfy them and produce a successful deal for both producer and consumer.

Other academics suggest that the marketing concept can only work if it is embedded in the whole culture of the organisation. The management guru Drucker (1969), for example, considered this view in his definition:

> Marketing is not only much broader than selling, it is not a specialised activity at all. It encompasses the entire business. It is the whole business seen from the point of view of its final result, that is from the customer's point of view. Concerns and responsibilities for marketing must therefore permeate all areas of the enterprise.

This definition suggests that everybody in an organisation involved in the marketing function should ultimately consider the final customer as being central to their activities at work. This suggests that marketing involves an encompassing philosophy which often means that an organisation has to change their internal business culture to accommodate this new form of approach.

Peters and Waterman (1982) were at the forefront of suggesting styles of management for organisations to adopt if they want to become 'excellent', and manage effectively during periods of chaotic change. Kantner (1984) suggested that organisations have to empower individuals to stimulate entrepreneurial spirit and become market leaders. The underlying culture of the organisation needs to facilitate the exchange of goods and services for money or benefits by satisfying the target customers.

The Chartered Institute of Marketing, the professional body for practising marketers in the UK defines marketing as:

> Identifying, anticipating and satisfying customer requirements profitably.

This definition explains how the marketing philosophy is to put the customer as the central focus for business decision-making. The definition has been criticised because of the word 'profitably'. It has been argued that many nonprofit making organisations can use the marketing philosophy to become more effective rather than simply more profitable.

The definition is useful in that it identifies the role of marketing as being identifying the needs and wants of consumers both now and in the future, and then meeting them.

Academics from other European countries also define marketing as the methods which an organisation can employ to result in successful transaction with customers. Lendrevic and Lindon (1990), for example, defined marketing as:

> The assembly of methods and means at the disposal of an organisation, in order to give favourable impressions to the public, to achieve the right objectives.

Table 1.1 summarises the main points which have come out of the definitions so far.

Emphasis	Example
Marketing is about putting the customer at the centre of the business	Kotler Chartered Institute of Marketing
Marketing is about methods which can be used to gain favourable impressions	Lendrevic and Lindon
Marketing is about the way in which the business develops its markets	Levitt
Marketing is about organising the culture of the business to become market- and customer-focused	Peters and Waterman Kantner Drucker

Table 1.1 The main emphasis of the definitions of marketing

The marketing philosophy can therefore be seen to encompass a number of steps which are summarised below in Figure 1.2:

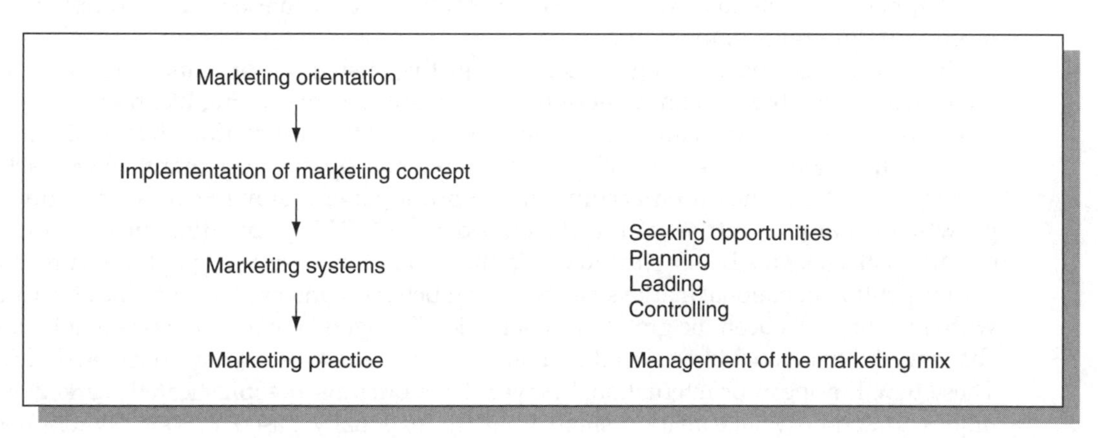

Figure 1.2 The marketing philosophy

The practical application of marketing in business organisations involves an understanding of a number of theoretical disciplines.

The business and management disciplines

An effective marketer must have an understanding of how organisations function and how they become successful. Marketing must be clearly defined within the whole business.

Social and behavioural disciplines

The development and interpretation of a body of knowledge about the customers and their behaviour, both now and in the future, is crucial in marketing.

Methodological disciplines

The collection, analysis and interpretation of marketing data to help in determining marketing programmes is vital.

The historical development of the marketing concept

The marketing concept has been encouraged by the adoption in most parts of the world of capitalist ideas and free market principles. In the UK, for example, the 1980s and 1990s have been the era of the entrepreneur and free enterprise has been encouraged. This has been accompanied with the development of marketing as a business discipline. The beginning of the new millennium has seen the growth in the concept of relationship marketing.

Marketing is not a new phenomenon. It can be argued that marketing is as old as civilisation itself. Early traders were very skilled at marketing in their daily exchanges. Entrepreneurs travelled the world to trade commodities which people wanted to buy.

The rise of industrialisation ushered in a new era of mass-produced products, being marketed to mass audiences, including clothes and cars. Many of the brand names which are now universally recognised symbols of mass marketing, such as Coca-Cola and Heinz, are already decades old.

The early 1950s saw a huge expansion in the supply of goods and services which often outstripped the demand. Most markets became buyer's markets and companies were faced with growing competition.

There have also been changes occurring in the business world more recently, which have encouraged the development of more sophisticated marketing techniques.

The rapid growth in technological innovation over the last century has made the business environment much more challenging and has opened up many new marketing opportunities. This has been accompanied with a general slowing down in population growth in many countries of the developed world. The population in the developed countries has become better educated and therefore more discerning in their purchases.

Competition in national markets has become much more intense and complicated. Coupled with this, there has been the growth of international players in many markets that have often challenged the national players in their markets, which they historically considered very safe. These new European or international players have often used sophisticated marketing techniques to seriously take market share from the nationally based players. Whole national industries have been removed in very short periods of time by this new competitive situation.

This new competitive business situation has meant that it is difficult enough to survive, never mind become successful on a long-term basis. This has meant that a completely new philosophy of business had to develop in which effective and efficient manufacturing processes are not sufficient. The answer to this situation has been suggested to be the application of the marketing concept.

Levitt (1960) was one of the first management theorists to stress the importance of a marketing approach for business organisations and raise the profile of marketing as an academic discipline. In the influential article 'Marketing Myopia' published in the *Harvard Business Review* in the summer of 1960, he argued that an industry should be a 'customer satisfier' rather than a 'goods producer'. He argued that there was a fundamental difference between marketing and selling. Selling focused on the needs of the seller, whereas marketing focused on the needs of the buyer. Marketing, he argued, was concerned with the idea of satisfying the needs of the customer by means of the product and the whole cluster of things associated with creating, delivering and consuming it.

Marketing had been developing in business before this. The original idea of marketing had been developed by the fast moving consumer goods (FMCG) industries, typically in the United States of America from the 1930s onwards.

Proctor and Gamble, the American detergent and personal products company was one of the first companies to develop the use of marketing techniques in a practical business organisation.

Consumer durable manufacturers such as car makers were quick to adopt the marketing approach from the 1950s onwards. Service-sector organisations became very interested in the application of marketing techniques during the 1970s and 1980s.

Airlines and banks, for example, have been attracted to the marketing concept. The conversion of British Airways from a production-oriented company to a customer-led business by Lord King and Sir Colin Marshall which has led to huge financial success is one example of this.

Marketing for professional groups is also becoming popular. Professionals such as accountants, solicitors and lawyers are beginning to use marketing techniques.

Nonprofit making organisations such as educational institutions, charities and local authorities have been showing great interest in the use of the marketing concept for their types of organisations during the 1980s and 1990s. The use of marketing has enhanced consumer awareness. The use of marketing not only has improved profits for business organisations, but has also been used to promote governmental initiatives, and enhance the profile and increase the income of voluntary organisations.

Marketing is increasingly being adopted on an international scale in all sectors of the economy. International marketing is increasingly studied as a separate discipline. This book will suggest that organisations operating on a European or international basis should treat the multinational perspective as an inherent part of their marketing effort.

The application of the marketing concept to different kinds of organisations

The development of the application of marketing occurred in the (FMCG) industry. The previous section discussed this in more detail. Many other types of organisations are now trying to adopt the marketing concept within their own business context. It is important to remember, however, that the different types of organisations will have fundamentally different sets of objectives. The marketing objectives of different types of organisations are explored in Table 1.2.

Type of organisation	Marketing objectives
Profit making	To make profits at specified return
Nonprofit making and public sector	To maximise income and use it effectively and efficiently. To meet objectives laid down by government or funding bodies within specified budgets
Voluntary	To do most good for users of the services provided within the budget

Table 1.2 The marketing objectives of different types of organisations

The marketing programmes will be subtly different in these different types of organisations, so that the overall objectives of the organisation can be met. The underlying philosophy of putting the final customer at the centre of the business is applicable to all organisations.

Public-sector organisations can be defined as agencies operated and organised by Central and Local Government. This sector of industry has often been reluctant to incorporate the marketing philosophy into their business for a variety of reasons.

Marketing has often been considered by the officers of public bodies as being inappropriate because it has associations with competition and profits which does not fit in well with the aspects of social responsibility which these organisations are supposed to incorporate. There may even be issues regarding the ethics of collecting information during market research from the clients of public-sector organisations and issues around whether the data collected is used for political reasons rather than in the client's interest in providing better services.

Andraeson and Kotler (2003) described how their research carried out in the United States of America had indicated that many people within the nonprofit making sector have the view (often subconsciously) that marketing is basically bad due to aspects of wasting public money and the perceived qualities of 'hard sell' promotion. Many of these ideas have been challenged. Scholes (1991), for example, outlined the changes which had occurred in the UK public sector due to the creation of Compulsory Competitive Tendering and the creation of internal markets.

A change in management philosophy to a more market-oriented approach has been forced upon public-sector bodies faced with these legislative and administrative changes. The concept of 'best value' in the leisure sector today focuses on this type of approach.

Andraeson and Kotler (2003) outlined a series of reasons for public sector and non-profit making organisations which were suggested, to encourage the use of marketing techniques. These included:

- The organisation is often surrounded by a series of key public or stakeholders with whom it is important to maintain good working relations.
- Adverse publicity in the media may have far-reaching effects on the future operation of the organisation.
- Marketing will allow the organisation to offer very innovative products and services.
- Wider publicity regarding the public-sector organisation may open up opportunities to market segments which previously did not benefit from the product or service due to ignorance. Marketing in this way may even help the organisation build on factors associated with social responsibility.

Different approaches to the running of business organisations

Studies of organisations suggest that they fit roughly into three categories of organisation – the production-oriented organisation, the sales-oriented organisation and the marketing-oriented organisation. The historical development of many organisations often takes the organisations through these three stages sequentially, but this is not always the case.

The *production-oriented* organisation will concentrate all its efforts on producing the goods which the company knows it is good at producing, and then trying to sell these goods. The organisation should concentrate on producing products that are of the best quality and performance that customers will clamour to buy. Many old traditional industries have used this approach over long periods. This approach means that the managers put all their efforts into making the production processes better and more efficient. Little effort is spent considering the consumer. After all, they have always bought the products so why should things change now.

The *sales-oriented* organisation will produce products and then attempt to sell these products by the use of a variety of sales and promotion techniques. Profits will be obtained by sales volume. A good example of this type of approach is where a company is experiencing reducing sales levels and brings in a 'marketing officer' to try and address this problem. They spend time and money producing leaflets to promote the products without ever looking at the customer. Or a sales person is brought in to sell the product to potential customers, using 'hard sell' methods.

The *marketing-oriented* organisation considers the customer needs and wants before making any decisions about what to produce. Once production is started, the customer is constantly monitored for changing patterns of buyer behaviour and the products and services constantly altered to meet these changing demands. Profits are achieved through customer satisfaction.

The consequences of an organisation adopting a marketing approach

Interest in the application of marketing is intensifying in many organisations, including organisations from the nonprofit making and public sectors. This is happening because it has been recognised that marketing can contribute to an improved performance in the marketplace.

Piercy (2002) suggested that adoption of the market-led approach is essential for two reasons:

1. that ultimately all organisations are forced to follow the dictates of the market [i.e. the paying customer] or go out of business;
2. the organisation can pursue organisational effectiveness by being 'market led' and focusing on the customer needs, wants and demands.

The simplicity of the ideas of marketing as an underlying business philosophy seems obvious. The question which arises is why do organisations find it difficult to become market-led and actually fail in the implementation stage? Piercy (2002) suggested that there are three main reasons for organisations finding it difficult to adopt marketing. These can be summarised as follows:

- there are considerable barriers to the introduction of marketing such as ignorance of customer characteristics, lack of information, inflexible technology and competitive threats, which all come from the way in which an organisation is run;
- being 'market-led' may require substantial and painful upheaval in the way the organisation is structured, the way decisions are made, the key values which are communicated to employees and managers and how everybody in the organisation does their job;
- the introduction involves a programme of deep-seated fundamental strategic change in organisations, not just hiring a marketing executive, or doing more advertising, or any other short-term tactical ploy.

The introduction of a marketing philosophy into an organisation involves deep structural and cultural change which is often very hard to achieve in the short term.

The differences between strategic and tactical marketing

It is important that the differences between strategic and tactical marketing are understood. The real significance of a *strategic marketing plan* as opposed to a *tactical operational marketing plan* must be clearly defined if organisations are to operate effectively.

McDonald and Morris (2000) differentiated between the strategic marketing planning process and the tactical plan by defining the strategic marketing plan as:

> having a greater emphasis on scanning the external environment, the early identification of forces emanating from it, and developing appropriate strategic responses involving all levels of managers in the process.

They suggested that a strategic plan should cover a three- to five-year time period. The operational plan or tactical plan is a much more detailed programme of work, often on a smaller area of the business and covering a shorter timescale. The tactical marketing plan will include details of how the organisation is going to achieve their overall strategy.

The tactical marketing plan will include details of the appropriate annual *marketing mix* plans for each area of the business. The marketing mix is the term used to summarise the techniques which can be used by the organisation to influence demand. McCarthy (1960) developed this framework as the *4P's*. This is shown in more detail in Table 1.3.

P – Product	The good or service to be marketed
P – Price	The amount of money a customer has to pay to obtain the good or service
P – Promotion	All the methods of communicating the features of the good or service to the customer
P – Place	All the activities that enable the customer to obtain the product or service

Table 1.3 The marketing mix

Marketing and other business functions

It is vital that the marketing function fits into the whole business organisation in an effective manner. It could be argued that if everybody is considered to be marketer in an organisation then a separate marketing function within an organisation is not necessary. It is essential that everybody knows how they fit into the marketing activity which the organisation undertakes.

Organisations which have incorporated marketing into existing business disciplines have tended to have a separate marketing department. This can be seen at Marriott hotels that run their company in five main divisions:

1. People
2. Finance
3. Product and Service
4. Sales and Marketing
5. Development.

There is often confusion about the role of marketing within the other functions of the company. Kotler and Armstrong (2004) discussed the importance of marketing in relation to other business functions. In some firms, marketing is seen as just another function. In other firms it is given prime importance. The more enlightened firms put marketing at the centre of the business. The most enlightened, however, put the customer as the central focus of the business.

This chapter has tried to show the importance of marketing in bringing about success in organisations. Many strategic management academics have recognised the importance of marketing as a central business function.

Ohmae (1982), for example, expressed such views.

> In a free competitive economic world, there will be no stability in a corporation's performance if it allows its attention to be diverted from the basic mission of serving its customers. If it consistently succeeds in serving customers more effectively than its competitors, profit will follow.

Despite the obvious logic for using the marketing approach, there are still relatively few companies that practice it. Drucker (1985) expressed concern about this situation.

> Why, after forty years of preaching marketing, teaching marketing, professing marketing, so few suppliers are willing to follow. I cannot explain. The fact remains that so far, anyone who is willing to use marketing as the basis for strategy is likely to acquire leadership in an industry, or a market fast and almost without risk.

Most organisations even today, it seems, still have far to go to become customer satisfiers.

Is the marketing of services any different to the marketing of products?

It is widely accepted that the principles and practice of marketing techniques were developed by goods manufacturing industries. Literature which was published confined their examples to goods. There have been signs more recently of literature devoted entirely to the marketing of services. Books by Cowell (1984) and Bateson (1995) were early examples of textbooks which explored the application of marketing for service organisations. Palmer (2001) also investigated the application of marketing to service. The techniques of marketing have been embraced more recently by service organisations which for a variety of reasons, now try to make the marketing philosophy the central focus of the business. This has been particularly apparent when an organisation has moved from the public to the private sector of the economy, forcing the organisation to adopt a profit-oriented approach in the face of growing competition.

The developed countries of Europe have seen a gradual shift of emphasis in economic output from the product sector to the service sector. The development of services ranging from hotels to educational establishments, and from airlines to leisure parks has been both rapid and complex.

Many service organisations such as the banks and airlines have embraced the marketing philosophy. There are many service organisations, however, which have only just started to adopt the marketing philosophy. The marketing of higher education establishments, for example, has recently added a new perspective to service marketing.

The role of marketing in service industries and the management of intangibles

There has been considerable growth in the service sector in the world as higher living standards and technological developments stimulated the growth of many service industries. The use of new technologies has revolutionised and expanded customer service. The trend towards a growing service economy is predicted by economists, and the population of developed economies are to become richer and spend an increasing amount of their income on service.

Marketing theorists have attempted to define services in relation to their intangibility and the fact that a service never results in the ownership of anything; merely bringing the customer 'benefits' or 'satisfactions'.

Kotler and Armstrong (2004) define a service as:

> any activity or benefit that one party can offer to another that is essentially intangible and does not result in the ownership of anything. Its production may or may not be tied to a physical product.

Rushton and Carson (1985) stated that the fundamental differences between goods and service marketing are that goods are produced rather than services which are performed. Theorists have attempted to clarify the definitions by stating that services have characteristics which distinguish them from products.

The most commonly stated characteristics of services are:

1. Intangibility
2. Inseparability
3. Heterogeneity
4. Perishability
5. Lack of ownership.

Intangibility

Services have the characteristics of being intangible in that they cannot be seen, felt, heard, tasted or smelt before purchase.

Bateson (1977) refined intangibility further in that a service has not only a 'palpable' intangibility in that it cannot be touched by the consumer but also a 'mental' intangibility in that it can often be difficult for the consumer to grasp the idea of the service mentally.

Inseparability

Services have the characteristic of an overlap between the production and performance of the service, and the consumption of it. A service, in its purest form, has the provider and customer face to face. This should theoretically mean that the implementation of the marketing philosophy to the serviced industries should be an easier task, particularly in terms of being customer-centred. Service organisations have the benefit of having face-to-face contact with the final customer.

Heterogeneity

It is difficult for services to be provided to the same standard at every consumption occasion. This can be explained by reference to the example of a restaurant meal. Every time the same customer visits the same restaurant for the same meal, the experience will be different according to occasion, moods, staff performance, etc.

Perishability

Services have the characteristic of being perishable in that if the service is not sold, then the business can never be recovered. The empty hotel room or the seat on the train cannot be put into storage for later consumption. Empty rooms or seats mean lost business and therefore lost profitability.

Services marketing is also often faced with widely fluctuating demands at different times or periods in the year.

Lack of ownership

The customer has access to the activity or facility only when he or she buys a service. The customer never owns anything at the end of the transaction. Services often lead to feelings of satisfaction, rather than a tangible item which can be shown to other people.

Academic theorists have looked at the differences between product and service marketing. Judd (1968), for example, identified features which differentiate for services from manufactured goods. These included the fact that services cannot be stocked and that channels of distribution if they exist at all, are often short.

Service marketing

It has been suggested that the marketing theories which were developed for the fast moving consumer goods industries can be adapted for organisations which market services. Grönroos (1980), for example, conducted research on service organisations in Sweden and Finland and suggested that traditional marketing literature could offer little to service organisations. Other academics have argued that service marketing requires a different approach and different concept compared to product marketing (Shostack, 1977).

One of the problems associated with the concept of 'service marketing' is the fact that many organisations never market true products or true services. Shostack (1977) suggested that there is a goods service continuum dependant on the level of tangibility in the product or service offered for sale.

Marketing theorists have also tried to develop new marketing theories to apply to service marketing examples. Booms and Bitner (1981), for example, suggested an expanded marketing mix for services to try and recognise that people who perform or deliver the services are crucial and that setting atmosphere and layout may be important influences. The elements which need to be emphasised during the creation of marketing programmes for services are shown in Figure 1.3.

This expanded marketing mix stresses the importance of certain elements of the traditional marketing mix and suggests new categories for special attention: participants, physical evidence and process.

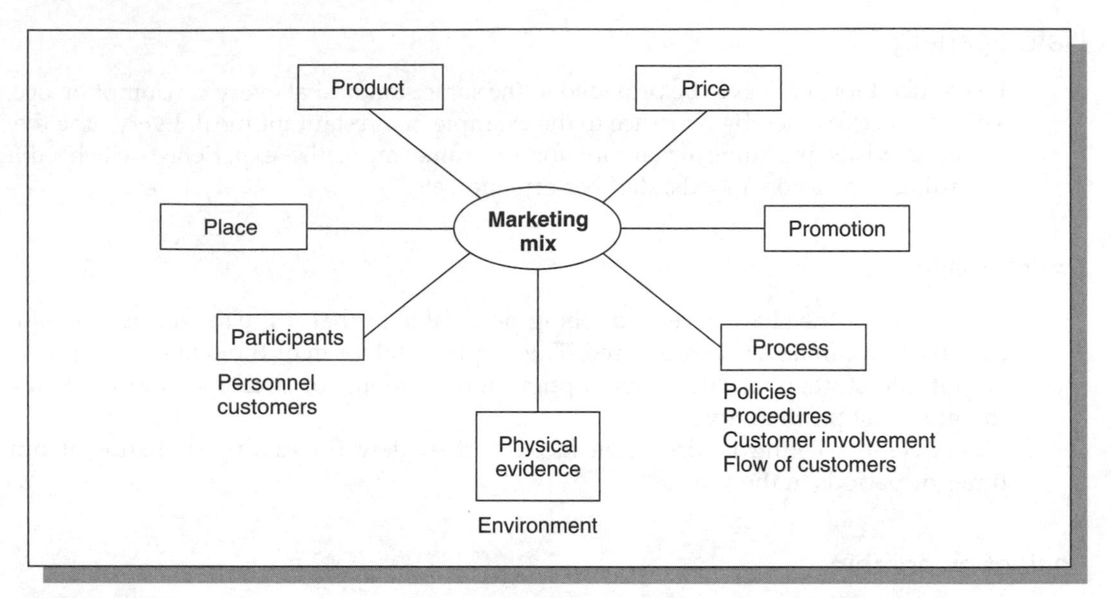

Figure 1.3 Elements to be emphasised during the creation of marketing programmes for services

Are products and services fundamentally different?

The philosophical question which must be asked is whether the marketing of services is substantially different from marketing products and whether the differences mean that fundamentally modified approaches are necessary when developing marketing programmes for services.

Levitt (1972) questioned the view that service marketing is any different to product marketing. Levitt argued that all companies sell intangibles in a market rather than simple products.

Industries which are generally associated with marketing services such as travel, repair, consulting, education and banking are not able to let the prospective customer try out or experience the product or service before purchase. The most basic of FMCG, such as shampoo and pizzas, have a strong element of intangibility, just like the services, because the consumer can rarely experience these products in advance. Branding of products, for example, adds intangible elements to a very tangible item. It denotes quality and can make the item desirable.

The conclusion which could be drawn from this analysis is that although services do have some special characteristics which require different approaches to marketing, they do have many characteristics which they share with products.

Contemporary marketing issues

There are a number of contemporary issues which have been growing in importance in the marketing field during the last part of the twentieth century. The first of these is the growing interest being shown by *nonprofit making organisations* in the philosophy and practice of marketing. Charities and local authorities, for example, have already begun to operate strong public relations campaigns and have seen the advantage of segmenting markets and using branding techniques. The use of marketing has been recognised by the Countryside Commission, for example, in the UK, in an area of activity where marketing would once have been criticised for being ideologically unsound.

The second contemporary issue for marketing is the link of marketing to *quality* and *total quality management* (TQM). Total quality management has become a management discipline in its own right. There is, of course, a great deal of similarity between the philosophy of TQM and the philosophy of marketing. Total quality management requires that the products and services produced by an organisation are right first time, and that employees are working for the good of the organisation and its customers. This is very close to an organisation introducing marketing-led philosophy. Both approaches usually involve a shift in the culture of the organisation.

The third contemporary issue for marketing is the growth in interest in *ethical issues and social responsibility*. It can be argued that a clever public relations campaign can allow an organisation to appear to be acting ethically and showing social responsibility without the underlying philosophy being present. It is clear that the addition of a 'green' product to a range of products which are questionable in terms of their formulation and positioning may not be enough in the future to satisfy the ever-growing number of critics.

It may become unacceptable to advertise to children and to other groups in the population. It may not be sufficient for large companies to donate small amounts of money to charities and other good causes in order to improve the reputation of the organisation in the eyes of the population, the customers and the shareholders. Acting ethically, and with social responsibility, in marketing is predicted to become a very important issue for all companies in the future.

The fourth contemporary marketing issue is the development of the concept of *relationship marketing* which encourages organisations to place as much emphasis on retaining existing customers rather than putting all their emphasis on attracting new customers.

Conclusion

This chapter has defined the marketing concept and considered various definitions of marketing. We have reviewed the history of marketing and the fact that marketing concepts were developed initially for production-oriented organisations. This chapter has reviewed the application of marketing to the service-sector, public-sector, voluntary-sector and charitable organisations. Contemporary issues in marketing are reviewed at the end of the chapter.

Discussion points and essay questions

1. Discuss the extent to which the idea of consumer-led or consumer-orientated marketing is feasible for existing organisations.
2. Examine the ways in which the marketing of services differs from the marketing of manufactured goods.
3. Evaluate the ways in which marketing objectives and approaches differ between organisations in the public, private and voluntary sectors.

Exercise

Students should interview those responsible for marketing within several different types of leisure organisations with the object of finding out their definitions of marketing and their views on the marketing concept.

The views of these managers should then be compared and contrasted with the definitions and ideas discussed in Chapter 1.

Finally, students should attempt to explain any differences which they identify between the views of practitioners and those of academics.

CHAPTER 2

What is leisure?

Key concepts

The main concepts covered in the chapter are:

- The nature of leisure
- Leisure time
- Leisure organisations in the public and private sector
- The management of leisure organisation.

Introduction

This chapter considers the concept of leisure in relation to individuals, organisations and society as a whole. It looks at:

- the nature of leisure in 2004 against the historical backdrop of leisure development;
- the concept of leisure time as a sociological phenomenon;
- different types of leisure activities, and the organisations that provide leisure products and services in the public and private sector;
- the importance of management theory in leisure organisations.

There has been a considerable degree of overlap and disagreement between the different aspects of leisure provision. Leisure organisations include these in tourism and hospitality sectors as well as the more traditional providers in the arts, sports and recreation sectors. Similarly, there is an increased level of blurring of what constitutes a leisure organisation through the eyes of the consumer. The retailer that provides shopping and eating experiences for the consumer, for example, can be just as important to them as the cinema, public house or football ground. It is true that leisure has become a much more holistic experience that incorporates a myriad of organisations providing a vast range of leisure experiences.

This chapter provides the reader with an introduction to the concept of leisure and is followed by three chapters that explore the international market, the international leisure consumer and the international business environment in some more depth. Before we do this, however, let us think of the concept of leisure and define what it means in the broadest sense.

The nature of leisure

Leisure is a term that has been used to encompass a whole series of experiences that people can undertake in their free time. To sociologists, however, leisure encompasses a state of mind that an individual finds herself or himself in at a particular time. We shall now explore these ideas in more depth with reference to key academic authors to illustrate the point made.

The concept of leisure permeates a wide range of responses and it could be argued that it is a sense of time, rather than a sector at all. The management and marketing of leisure experiences has had a profound effect on the lives of people in history and in the early stages of the new millennium. Leisure is also big business and has spawned economic growth in countries where societies had depended more on production industries rather than service industries.

But, before we consider the business of leisure we should consider the theoretical framework of leisure as it has been developed by commentators in the twentieth century on the basis of the long historical development of the concept from ancient times.

A useful framework is explored by Torkildsen (2001) in his wide-ranging book entitled *Leisure and Recreation Management*. He suggests that his analysis of the literature on leisure reveals five discernible but overlapping approaches which are useful to consider here. The five overlapping approaches to leisure are summarised in Figure 2.1. It can be seen from Figure 2.1 that leisure has been viewed very differently by different authors and that it can range from a sample activity to an all-encompassing state of mind

1. **Leisure as time**
   - Leisure is the time when someone is not working for money (Soule, 1957)
   - Leisure is residual time that an individual has after all other activities (Parker, 1971)
   - Leisure is the time an individual spends according to judgement and choice (Brightbill, 1964)
2. **Leisure as activity**
   - 'An opportunity to engage in some kind of activity, whether rigorous or relatively passive, which is not required by daily necessities' (Neumeyer and Neumeyer, 1958)
   - Activities on four levels – passive, emotional, active and creative involvement (Nash, 1960)
3. **Leisure as a state of being**
   - Leisure is a 'state of quiet contemplative dignity' (Brightbill, 1963)
   - Leisure is a 'mood of contemplation' (Larrabee and Meyersohn, 1958)
   - Leisure is a 'state of mind where an individual is free from thoughts of basic necessity' (Nakhhoda, 1961)
4. **Leisure as an all-pervading 'holistic' concept**
   - Leisure is all about relaxation, entertainment and personal development (Dumazedierl, 1967)
   - Leisure is a mental or spiritual attitude that links to culture (Pieper, 1952)
5. **Leisure as a way of life**
   - Leisure is about having ideas of freedom and a worthwhile life (Goodale and Godbey, 1988)

Figure 2.1 Five approaches to the concept of leisure (*Source*: After Torkildsen, 2001)

that brings relief from work and other unpleasant life experiences. The leisure sector, however, serves the needs of the consumer who wants to spend his time consuming leisure experiences, so it is worthwhile to spend a little more time considering leisure as a concept of time which we will do in the next section.

Leisure time

We have seen in Figure 2.1 that leisure can be seen as a concept of time. The idea that people have to spend time away from the time they spend providing themselves with the bare necessities of life and equipping themselves with the necessary resources for basic living is a powerful theme in the literature. Torkildsen (2001) also suggested that pleasure forms the central focus of the overlapping ideas of play, recreation and leisure.

We have an inbuilt desire to play. We seek recreational experiences, and we also have the need for leisure experiences that all give us feelings of pleasure. The question arises, however, how each individual decides to spend her or his leisure time given the huge range of opportunities that are on offer in the twenty-first century. We explore myriad opportunities that are open to an individual in their choice of leisure experience in Figure 2.2.

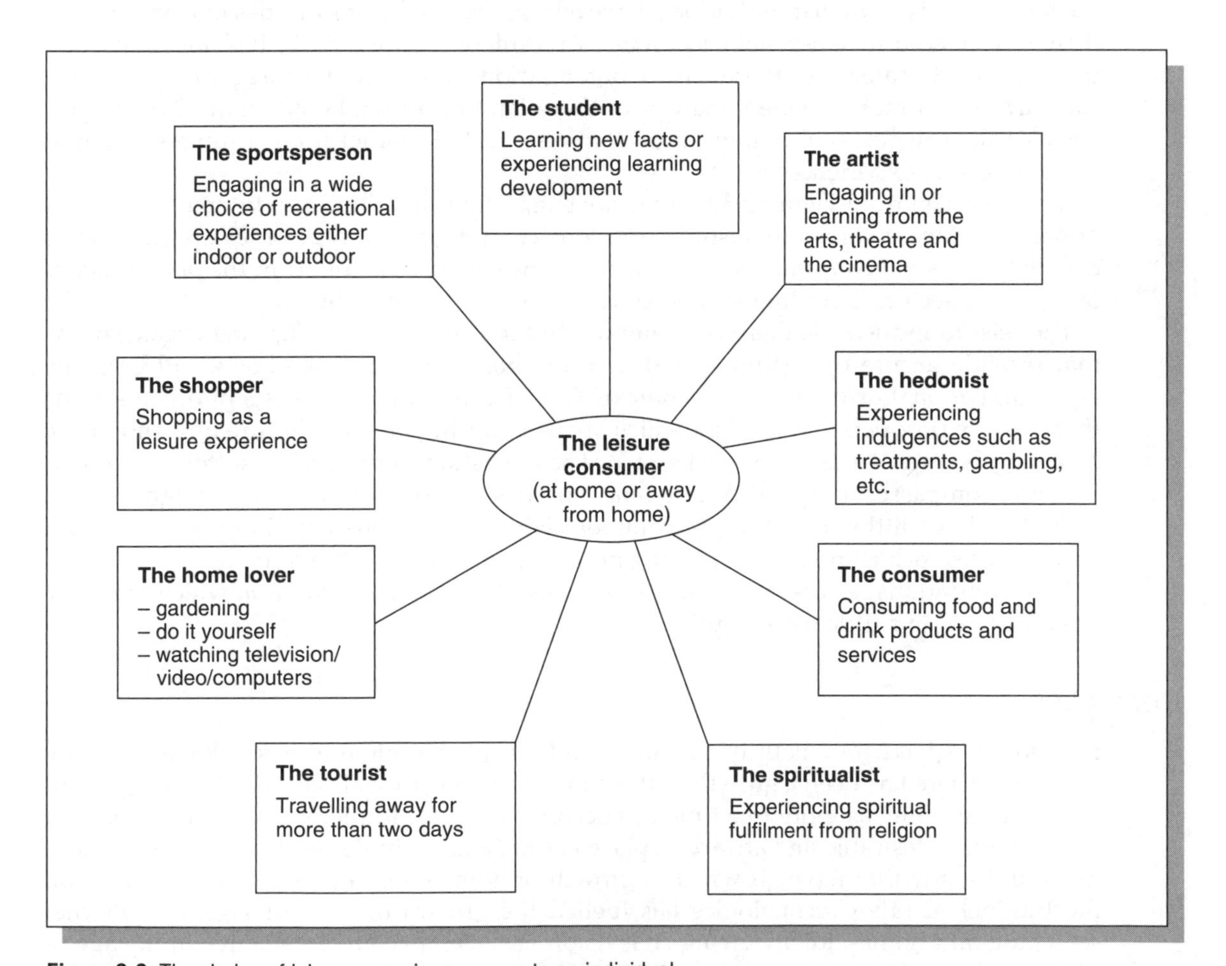

Figure 2.2 The choice of leisure experiences open to an individual

It can be seen from this figure that an individual can choose to spend their time engaging in a series of different experiences during their leisure time to gain different outcomes. Many of these states of mind do overlap – for example, it is possible for an individual to be a tourist, a hedonist and a consumer – during their holiday time spent in Las Vegas for example, when they will be away from home, staying and consuming in a hotel, and partaking of gambling opportunities while they are there. It can be seen from the analysis that leisure is not a simple concept and that an individual is often engaged in a series of leisure experiences to reach a particular psychological state.

The common theme in leisure seems to be that whatever the chosen activity the individual should derive a positive mental state as a result of leisure activities akin to the positive experiences gained by play in childhood.

It seems that leisure is a psychological state of mind derived from a range of different activities that are chosen by individuals from a vast array of opportunities. So, what are the different organisations that provide this vast array of leisure opportunities to us as consumers?

Leisure organisations in the public and private sector

We have already seen that individuals have a huge array of opportunities that are open to them to gain a positive psychological state as a result of leisure activity. It is now important that we start to categorise these leisure organisations into different categories so that we can carry out a more detailed analysis of these later on in the book. Figure 2.3 explores some of the categories of organisations that offer individual leisure consumers different types of leisure experiences.

It can be seen from Figure 2.3 that we are suggesting that there are different categories of organisations involved in leisure provision according to the type of leisure experience that they offer the consumer. These organisations can also be found in the *private*, *public* or *voluntary* sectors according to their constitution and membership.

The leisure industry is therefore composed of a number of overlapping organisations that provide leisure opportunities either in the home or out of the home, either in the regional, national or international context. The leisure industry consists of organisations that provide products and services which are used during people's leisure time (holidays, cinemas, theatres, amusement parks, etc.). The definition of the leisure sector is so broad that it encompasses a myriad of different activities and organisations that might, on the face of it, have little or nothing in common. For example, one could argue that leisure encompasses rock climbing and playing bridge, gambling and church-going.

Three important sectors of leisure are *recreation*, *hospitality* and *tourism*, which will now be considered in a little more depth.

Recreation

Individuals spend time both in the home and out of the home in recreational and play activities. There has been a growth in the number of recreational activities that people can engage in at home as more free time has become available to them, and the emphasis on the home as a desirable and attractive place has grown. Activities such as home entertainment and gardening have grown. The growth of home entertainment systems based on the Internet or other technologies has fuelled the growth of computer games, Internet searching and home-video viewing. Television has even become interactive in the age of digital technology.

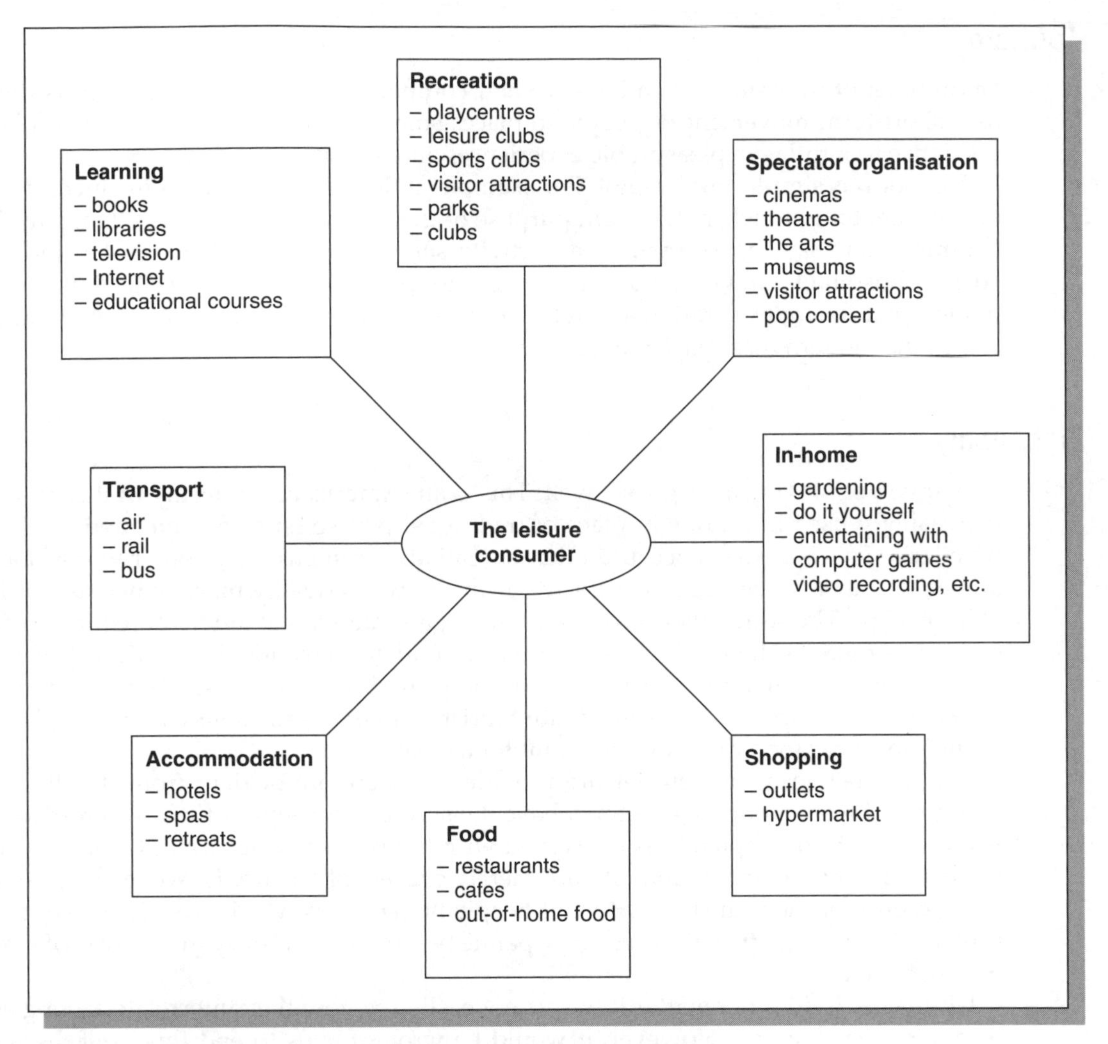

Figure 2.3 Different types of leisure organisations arranged by category

Individuals have also put an increasing emphasis on out-of-home recreation whether they are in the home or away from the home. There has been a growth of private leisure centres, for example, where people can engage in sports and beauty therapies. The growth in adventure tourism has fuelled the development of recreation and sport as being a central focus for a growing number of holiday experiences.

People do not simply sit around on the beach on holiday any more, but increasingly engage in a wide range of recreational and sporting activities. This interest in recreation and sport has also been fuelled by the increasing emphasis of individuals on their health, well being and weight control, a movement which continues to grow in the beginning of the twenty-first century.

The provision of out-of-home leisure relies heavily on two very important sectors of the total leisure sector, *tourism* and *hospitality*.

Tourism

Definitions of tourism tend to have several components. In general, tourism is defined as a short-term movement of people to places some distance from their normal place of residence to indulge in pleasurable experiences and activities.

This sounds simple, but it is not. For example, it does not encompass the lucrative field of business tourism where the main purpose of the trip is for work rather than play. Most commentators say that tourism is an activity serviced by a number of other industries such as hospitality and transport. If there is a tourism industry specifically, it is probably made up of the tour operation and retail travel sectors, which did not exist at all until the rise of the modern mass package tourism.

Hospitality

This involves looking after guests well. This is an 'Americanised' term but it is becoming increasingly used in Europe in place of traditional phrases such as hotel and catering or hôtellerie. This is perhaps because it has a qualitative dimension, in other words, looking after guests *well* which makes it attractive in an era when quality management is a fashionable concept. The sector also involves all the organisations that are involved in providing services for guests (hotels, inns, restaurants and other recreational activities). This means that hospitality is mainly concerned with the provision of places to sleep and food and drink. Not all hospitality consumers are tourists, therefore, as some will be people going to their local bar for a drink or restaurant for a meal.

The link between different leisure providers is therefore evident from the discussion about the three overlapping sectors above. Leisure is a concept of time, whereas tourism is an activity and hospitality is concerned with the provision of services. For some commentators, tourism and hospitality are merely subsets of leisure. However, this does not take account of the tourist activity and hospitality services which are related to business travel. Others argue that all three are separate, yet there are clearly great areas of overlap between them.

Ultimately it does not matter if we cannot easily see how they interrelate as long as we recognise that they do. However, it would be wrong for us to end this brief discussion without highlighting the problems which this ongoing debate causes for marketing in the field. These include:

- a lack of clarity and problem of duplication and gaps in marketing data;
- the absence in most countries of a single professional body with one voice in all areas of leisure which reduces the potential influence on decision-makers;
- ongoing debates in all three areas by education institutions that perhaps deflect some energy that might otherwise be spent on further improving the quality of education and training for marketing practitioners across the sector.

The blurring of the distinction between organisations in the leisure sector

It is now time to turn our attention to the second question, namely to what extent the overlap between leisure organisations is growing, and the distinctions between them becoming more blurred. Some have said this is a result of postmodernism, but whatever the reason it does appear to be a real phenomenon. Furthermore, it is a phenomenon which appears to be affecting both the demand side and the supply side in leisure.

A number of examples can be used to illustrate this point:

The resort complexes such as Club Méditerranée and Center Parcs offer both hospitality services and leisure facilities on the same site, under the ownership of one organisation. Furthermore, they offer this mixture to a market which largely consists of tourists, in other words, people who have travelled away from home and are spending at least one night away from their normal place of residence.

Theme parks are increasingly offering on-site accommodation units to encourage visitors to spend more time, and thus more money, on site. A good example of this is the Futuroscope theme park in Western France which now has several hotels, of different grades, within the boundaries of the park.

The trend amongst hotels in most European countries is to build in-house leisure facilities for their guests such as gymnasia and swimming pools. This is seen as necessary to attract two very different groups of clients, namely leisure visitors on weekends and business customers on weekdays.

- Leisure shopping is being developed as a tourist activity. Shopping is now used as a way of motivating trips to destinations as diverse as Liverpool in the UK, with its Albert Dock complex, the craft centres of rural Norway and the gold shops of Dubai.
- Sophisticated catering operations are being developed at visitor attractions to boost income. These can range from fast-food outlets to themed restaurants. Interestingly, many of these current developments in Europe are mirroring earlier ones in North America.

At the same time, we are also perhaps seeing a reduction in the gap that has traditionally been seen between the leisure and pleasure, and the business sectors of leisure. For example, theme parks like Chessington World of Adventures are increasingly offering their facilities for corporate hospitality. Likewise the existence of leisure facilities such as golf courses are being used more and more by destinations to attract business conferences, for instance. We are also seeing some changes within the industrial structure of tourism, leisure and hospitality that are blurring the distinctions between the three sectors. For example, some tour operators are buying shares in, or taking full control of, hotels and hotel groups. A good example of this is the partial ownership of the leading Greek hotel chain, Grecotel by the German tour operator TUI. Likewise, there are the hotel chains like Stakis in the UK which own and operate casinos, and tour operators and hotel chains offering holidays based on leisure pursuits such as white-water rafting, bicycling, painting and gastronomy.

However, it would be wrong to suggest that these examples of interrelationships between different leisure organisations are a recent phenomenon. For instance, in the early days of tourism, railway companies and airlines were major owners of hotels.

Nevertheless, the scale of the link within the sector is perhaps unprecedented and the sophistication of the links has not been seen before. This reflects the fact that leisure organisations are all relatively recent developments as 'major industries' and that they are still growing and developing at a very rapid rate. The blurring of the distinction between the three sectors is a truly global phenomenon, although there are national differences in its precise nature. Perhaps, the clearest and most highly developed form of integration between the three is, ironically, an American import, the resort complex concept.

The management of leisure organisations

We have already seen that leisure experiences are about participation in certain activities with the aim of bringing positive health and psychological benefits. Participation in leisure experience has grown over recent years but it has become important that these experiences are not just open to the most wealthy individuals in society, if positive benefits are to permeate the whole population.

The provision and management of leisure organisations is therefore crucial, so that correct choices of leisure organisations are made to match consumer demand in the first place. The effective and efficient management of the leisure organisation is also crucial so that both the consumer and the organisation can prosper in the long term to bring positive benefit to all. One of the key aspects of this management activity in the twenty-first century is the development of an effective marketing function so that the correct services can be provided and its benefits can be communicated to prospective consumers. This is vital in the private sector where profitability is a central force. It is equally important in the public sector where the organisation is trying to attract certain market segments to partake in their leisure activities. It is now important for us to focus on the international dimension of leisure in more depth before we consider the marketing function for leisure organisations.

Conclusion

We have seen in this chapter that there are varying views on what is leisure. At the simplest level, leisure refers to the way in which people spend their time when they are not at work.

Sociologists believe that leisure involves an individual reaching a particular psychological state, and it is much more about a holistic experience. Many different types of organisations are involved in the provision of leisure services and the management of these forms an important contribution for economic development.

Discussion points and essay questions

1. Critically evaluate the view that leisure is a concept of time.
2. Discuss the different ways that a person can gain the relaxation, entertainment and personal development that are all part of the leisure experience.
3. Evaluate the role that the public sector has in the provision of leisure services in a region or country of your choice.

Exercise

Choose one leisure organisation from the public, private or voluntary sector. Critically analyse the products and services that the organisation offers. Try to identify who you think the customers are, for the products and services on offer.

Discuss the benefits that you think these customers derive from the products and services provided by your chosen organisation.

Part Two

The international dimension

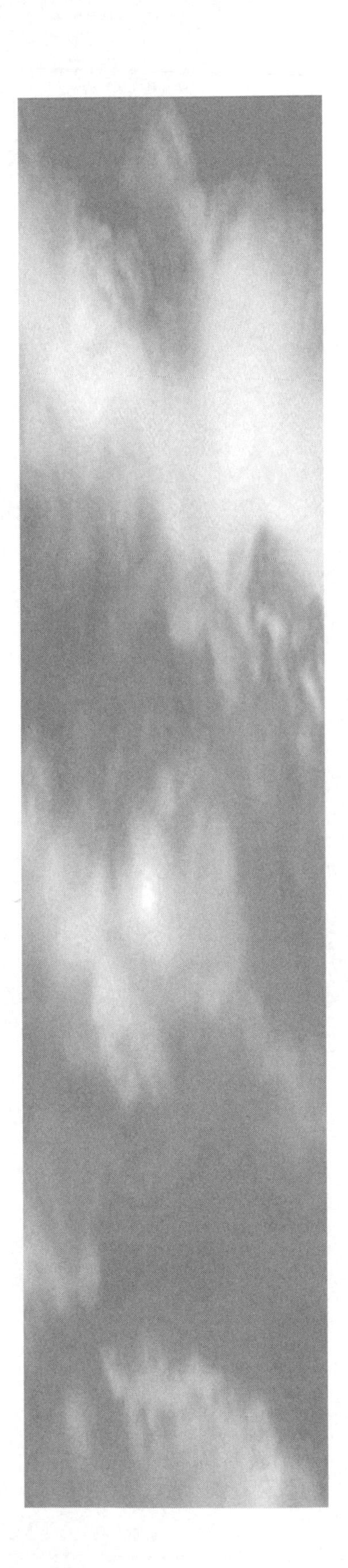

Introduction

Part Two focuses on the international context of leisure marketing worldwide.

Chapter 3 looks at the international market in all its aspects.
Chapter 4 concentrates on the supply side, in other words, the international leisure industry.
Finally, Chapter 5 covers, in some detail, the international business environment in which leisure organisations operate.

CHAPTER 3

The international market

Key concepts

The main concepts covered in the chapter are:

- Trends in consumer behaviour and purchase decision-making
- Factors influencing consumer demand – the concept of motivator and determinant
- Methods for grouping of consumers together by market segmentation techniques
- The concept of the 'global' consumer and the application of it to the leisure sector.

Introduction

It is important for you at this stage of the book to consider the leisure consumer in more depth. We have already discussed the different leisure activities that consumers engage in earlier on in the book. It is important for us to consider the influences on consumer behaviour so that we can design appropriate marketing mixes for leisure products and services. It is also important for us to consider the ways we can categorise consumers into groups by using different market segmentation techniques.

Trends in consumer behaviour and purchase decision-making

This is not a book on consumer behaviour, but it is important for us in this section to consider the concept and discuss different models that have been suggested to explore the various influences on consumers.

Clearly, if we are to optimise the effectiveness of our marketing activities, we need to understand how consumers make their decisions to buy, use or engage in leisure products and services. Then we know where and when we need to intervene in this process to achieve the desired results. The problem is that while many models have been advanced, relatively little empirical research has been conducted in order to test the models against actual behaviour. Nevertheless, it is still worth looking at some of these models.

We explored the various models of consumer behaviour in our book *Consumer Behaviour in Tourism* but we can consider some of the most important models here very briefly and leave you to go and read our other book if you require more detail.

The model recognises the importance of information in the consumer decision-making process. It also emphasises the importance of consumer attitudes although it tails to consider the attitudes of consumers in a repeat purchase situation.

The most frequently quoted consumer behaviour model is the Howard–Sheth model of buyer behaviour which was developed in 1969.

This model shows us the importance of inputs to the consumer buying process and suggests ways in which the consumer orders this input before making a final decision.

More recent models of consumer behaviour have tended to concentrate more on the exchange process and have attempted to assess the marketer's perspective on the process. One example of such a model is that developed by Solomon (1996).

He suggested that consumer behaviour involves many different actors and made us think that the purchase and use of a product or service may not be by the same person. This has fundamental effects on who we target in our marketing programmes. The family may be a key influence on the purchase behaviour patterns of individuals within the family, for example.

Foxall and Goldsmith (1994) suggested that it is vital that we understand how consumers act at different stages of their purchase decision-making processes. They divided the stages down as follows:

- the development and perception of a want or need;
- prepurchase planning and decision-making;
- the purchase act itself;
- postpurchase behaviour which may lead to repeat buying, repeat sales and disposition of the product after consumption.

The models that we have considered so far are general models of consumer behaviour that we can apply to the leisure sector. We have already considered the fact that leisure organisations are often service providers and also produce products. The leisure product or service is therefore intangible and often involves the consumer in a high spend of their discretionary income. We only need to think of the cost of a holiday, the cost of the ticket for the major music concert or the joining fee for the golf club to realise that the cost on leisure products and services is often substantial.

Some academics have tried to develop special models of consumer behaviour as a result of these differences. There have been a number of models suggested, for example, for the tourism sector and we can consider two of these briefly to consider their relevance for the whole of leisure.

The first of these models was devised by Victor Middleton in 1994.

It can be seen from the model that the process is 'based on four interactive components identified as stimulus inputs, communication channels, buyer characteristics and decision process and purchase outputs (response).

Gilbert (1991) suggested a model for consumer behaviour in tourism. This model suggested that there are two sets of factors that influence the consumer. The first level of influences are close to the person and include psychological factors such as perception and learning. The second level of influences include reference groups and family influences.

These two models that have been developed for tourism are relevant to all leisure organisations because of their similar characteristics. These characteristics are summarised in Figure 3.1.

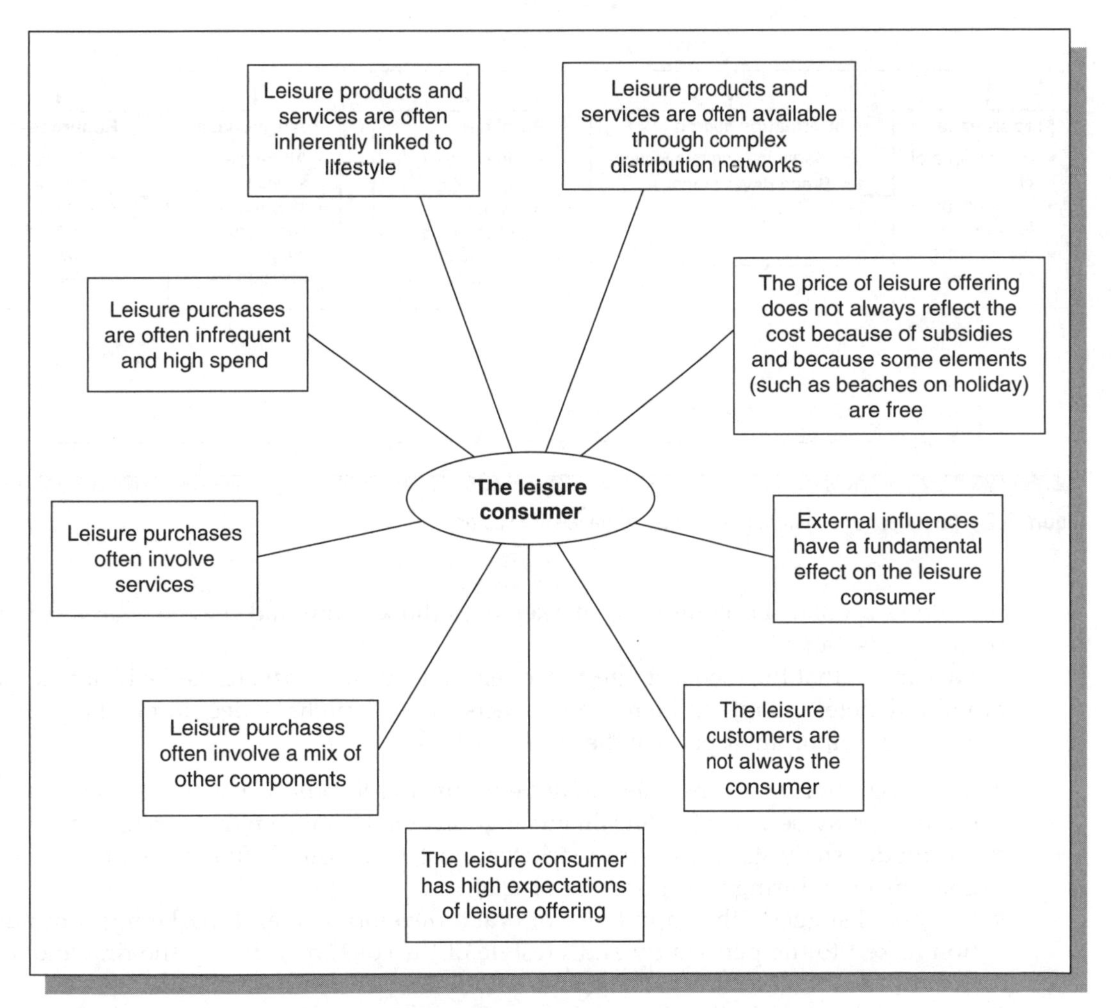

Figure 3.1 Characteristics of the leisure experience

On the basis of our analysis in Figure 3.1 of the special nature of the leisure sector and on the basis of all the models that we have discussed so far, we would like to suggest our own model for consumer behaviour in the leisure sector. This is shown in Figure 3.2. We must stress that the model has not been empirically tested as yet, but we feel that it

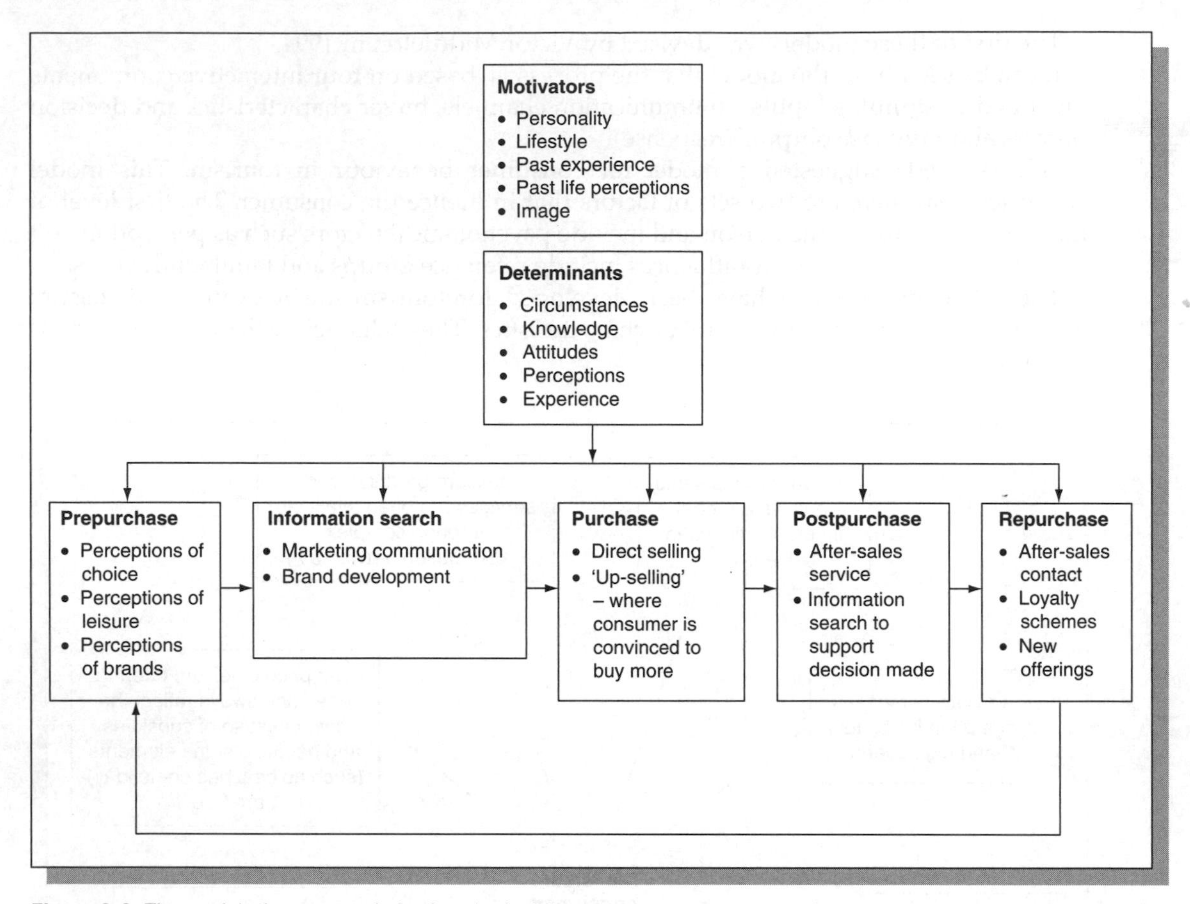

Figure 3.2 The model of consumer behaviour in the leisure sector

represents a good set of ideas for marketers to think about and maybe even test in their own organisations.

We can see that the model suggests the central focus for marketer is the idea that motivators and determinants influence all aspects of the purchase decision-making process. Some other important aspects of the model include:

- the recognition that consumers may be motivated to buy or use a product or service, but there may be a set of determinants that prevent them from the purchase or use;
- the model suggests the leisure marketer must focus on all five stages the consumer goes through during their purchase or use;
- the model suggests the importance of brand development and marketing communication linked to the personality and lifestyle of the consumer during the first and subsequent purchases of the consumer;
- the model suggests that the postpurchase and repurchase stages are just as critical as the first purchase;
- the model suggests that qualitative marketing research will be required with the target group to develop a deep understanding of consumer behaviour.

We now need to briefly consider the main factors that influence consumer demand in the leisure industry.

Factors influencing consumer demand – the concept of motivators and determinants

Motivators

Every leisure consumer is different and they are motivated by a different set of factors. The main factors that influence them however have been grouped together by Swarbrooke and Horner (1999) as:

1. *Personality* – in other words are they:
   - gregarious or a loner?
   - adventurous or cautious?
   - confident or timid?
2. *Lifestyle* provides the context for their purchase decision. The motivations are likely to be different for people who are very concerned with being fashionable or preoccupied with their health, live alone and want to make new friends or enjoy partying.
3. *Past experience* as a leisure consumer – for example, what types of products or services have they bought or used before and what are their perceptions of these?
4. *Past life* motivators, most notably nostalgia, are a direct result of people's life to date.
5. *Perception* of their own strengths and weaknesses, whether these relate to their wealth or their skills.
6. *Image* – how they wish to be viewed by other people.

It is also important to recognise that motivators will change over time for each individual according to changes in their personal circumstances. These could include:

- moving away from home;
- meeting a partner;
- having a child;
- improving or worsening health;
- increasing or decreasing income;
- experiencing new things in life.

It is important to note that leisure consumers will be motivated by more than one factor and the mix of motivations may well be different for different leisure products and services.

So, for example, the motivators for an individual to buy a holiday may be very different from the motivators to buy a leisure centre membership.

It is also important to mention that people from different cultures will also have very different sets of motivators which relate to their purchase decisions. This has an important consequence for leisure marketers who want to sell their products and services in more than one country.

Determinants influence whether the consumer will be able to purchase or use the leisure product or service even if they are motivated by a particular set of factors. The personal determinants of tourist behaviour (Swarbrooke and Horner, 1999) serve to illustrate the determinants in more detail and are shown in Figure 3.3.

Where some personal determinants are shared by large groups of the population, this often represents a major opportunity for the leisure industry.

The growth of the economy in the Pacific Rim coupled with the growth of European and American leisure companies, and the lack of leisure time available to many consumers has fuelled the growth of this intense short experience in the tourism, hospitality and recreation areas, for example.

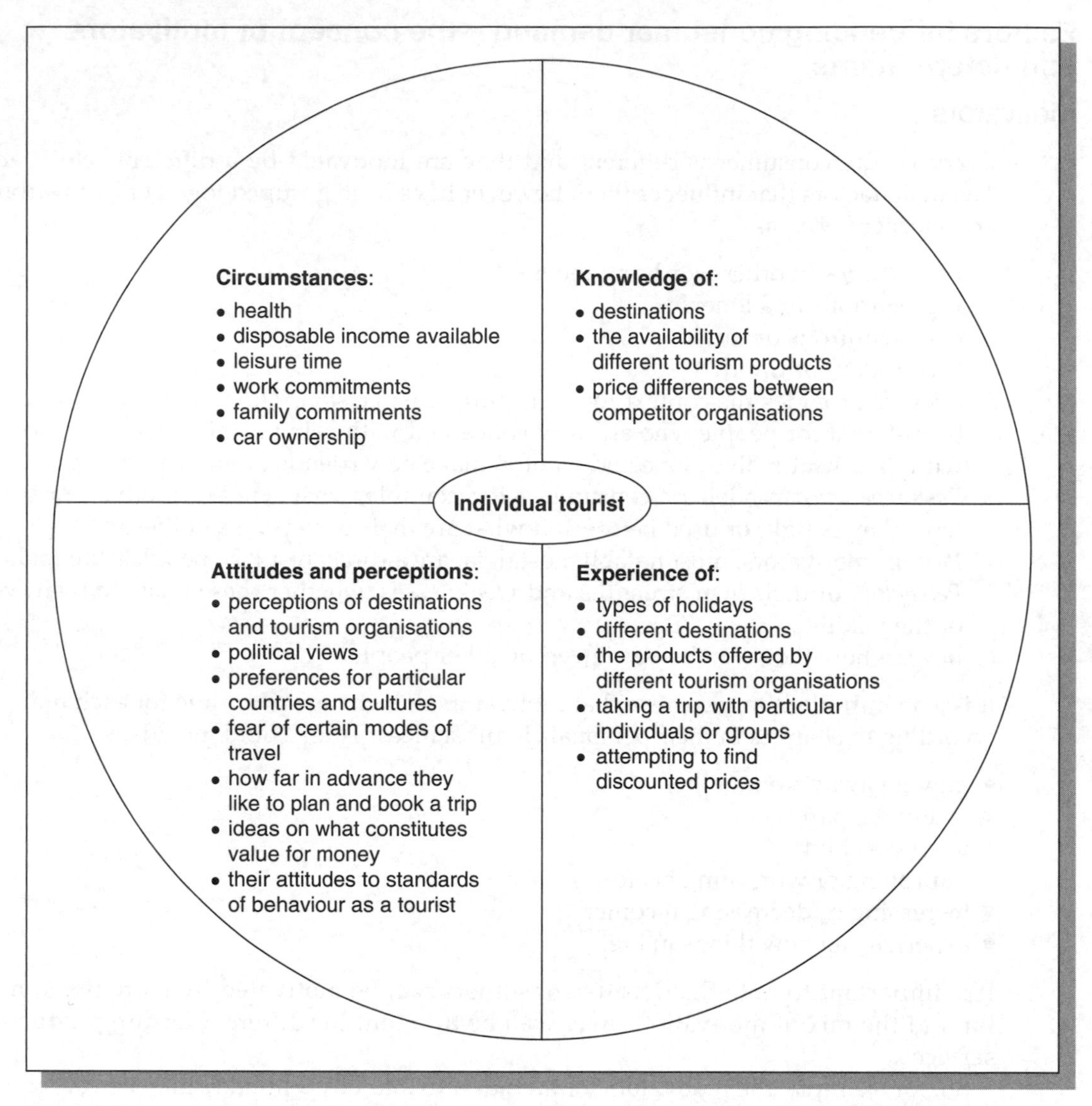

Figure 3.3 Personal determinants of tourist behaviour (*Source*: Swarbrooke and Horner, 1999)

Another example is the increase in the healthy older person in many developed economies, which has also fuelled the growth of leisure activities such as activity holidays and recreational facilities aimed at this burgeoning 'grey market'.

Other important aspects of determinants include:

- the role of unforeseen circumstances and opportunities may affect individuals;
- individuals may make purchase decisions on the basis of determinants or perceptions that are outdated;
- individuals may be strongly influenced in their future purchase decision-making as a result of a one-off bad experience.

So now that we have discussed consumer behaviour in some depth, it is important for us to consider the methods that organisations can use to group consumers together to enable them to target them more effectively.

Methods for grouping of consumers together by market segmentation techniques

One of the key techniques in marketing is the process of market segmentation which has been used by practitioners to effectively target groups of the population with specifically designed products and services.

Market segmentation has been defined by Dibb et al. (2001) as:

> The process of dividing a total market into groups of people with relatively similar product needs, for the purpose of designing a marketing mix that precisely matches the needs of individuals in a segment.

There are five classic ways of segmenting markets. This means that there are five different criteria that can be used to subdivide a total market into groups that share common characteristics. We will now consider these criteria in turn, in relation to their value for the leisure industry.

Geographical segmentation

This method categorises market group on the basis of where they live. Some examples illustrate this method:

1. The desire of urban city dwellers to visit rural locations for their leisure experiences as a contrast to their everyday environment.
2. The strong desire of people in a particular city or region to support their local football team.
3. The development of an airline business on the basis of geographical patterns in demand.
4. The development of theme parks on the basis of a local, regional, national or international focus.
5. Tour operators consider where their clients live when they decide which departure airport to offer flights from.

Socioeconomic segmentation

This method subdivides markets on the basis of socioeconomic variables. In the UK this approach is mainly based on the JICNARS classification which splits society into six groups – A, B, C1, C2, D, E. This is a relatively crude method of market segmentation but it is used extensively by leisure organisations which want to target particular groups. For example, the holiday company Center Parcs target the A, B and C1 socioeconomic group.

Demographic segmentation

This method of market segmentation is based on subdividing a population on the basis of demographic factors. This method has been used extensively by leisure organisations as the following examples illustrate:

1. *Sex* – The pay-to-view football customer who is usually a male and the stereotypical shopper who is a female.
2. *Age* – The specialist tour operators who have targeted older people (Saga) or younger people (Club 18–30).
3. *Religion* – This is at the heart of the pilgrimage product, for example.

Stage in family life cycle	Likely preferences and needs of consumers
Child	Stimulation. Other Children to play with. Parental guidance and support.
Teenagers	New experiences. Excitement. Status. More independence from parents. Opportunities for active participation. Social interaction with other teenagers.
Young adult	New experiences. Freedom of action. Opportunities for active participation. Social interaction with other young adults.
Young couple	New experiences. Romance.
Young couple with baby	Facilities for babies. Economy. Ease of access for pushchairs and prams.
Growing families	Economy, e.g. a family ticket. Something for all the family to do.
'Empty nesters'	Chance to learn something new. Passive rather than active participant most of the time.
Elderly	Watching rather than doing. Economy. Company of other older people. Easy accessibility for people with mobility problems.

Source: Adapted from Swarbrooke (1999)

Table 3.1 The family life cycle and visitor attractions

One demographic method of market segmentation that has particular relevance to the leisure sector is the *family life cycle* concept. The assumption here is that consumers' behaviour is influenced by where they are in relation to the family life cycle. Table 3.1 illustrates the family life cycle concept in relation to visitor attractions.

This approach is also used by other organisations from the leisure sector and is illustrated by the following examples:

- playcentres particularly aimed at younger children;
- theatrical performances particularly aimed at families with children;
- holidays, for teenagers holidaying separately from their parents;
- cruises particularly aimed at 'empty nesters' whose children have left home.

Two demographic criteria that are rarely used are race and nationality. Race is a very important criteria, however, in certain countries such as the USA. Leisure organisations that are increasingly marketing across national boundaries need to increasingly segment the market on the basis of race.

Psychographic segmentation

This method of market segmentation relies on the idea that lifestyle, attitudes, opinions and personality of people determine their behaviour as consumers. This is a very modern approach and is well suited to the leisure market as we can see from the following examples:

1. Health spas target consumers who are seeking a healthy lifestyle and beautiful body and mind.
2. People who are environmentally aware can be targeted with natural outdoor leisure experiences.
3. People who are thrill seekers can be targeted with the latest rides at visitor attractions.
4. People who are 'culture vultures' can be targeted with high profile ballet, opera and theatrical performances.
5. Popular music lovers can be targeted with high profile music events and festivals.

This method of segmentation is modern and the most talked about at the present time. It is also the most difficult to research in any systematic way.

Behaviouristic segmentation

This method of market segmentation relies on the consumer's relationship to the particular product or service. This was explored by Swarbrooke and Horner (1999) as follows in Figure 3.4:

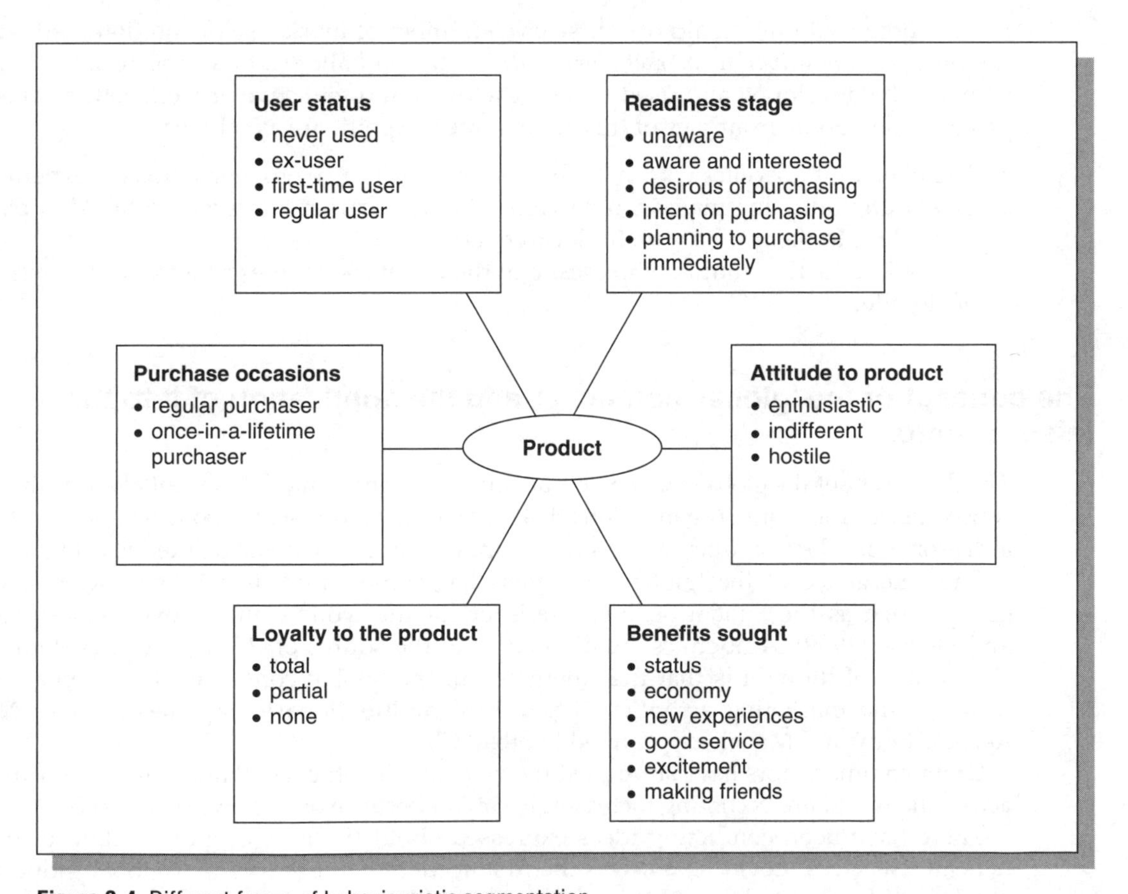

Figure 3.4 Different forms of behaviouristic segmentation

Behaviouristic segmentation is used extensively in the leisure sector as the following examples illustrate:

1. The purchase of the 'once in a lifetime' honeymoon package.
2. The regular purchase of a season ticket for a popular team by a loyal supporter.
3. The use of airline frequent flyer programmes (FFPs) to encourage loyal customers.
4. The development of budget hotels to satisfy the budget-conscious consumer.
5. The purchase of membership for a particular health or sporting club in order to get the status associated with membership.

There are three major criticisms that have been aimed at the different methods of market segmentation that are currently in use. A summary of these is as follows:

1. Some of the methods are dated and have not kept pace with developments in society. The traditional family life cycle model, for example, looks dated against the backdrop of fewer marriages, increasing divorce and a growth in single-parent families.
2. The traditional techniques often fail to recognise that the leisure consumers change over time and they may move between market segments as their income grows or their health deteriorates, for example.
3. The fact that market research is very limited in the leisure sector is a major stumbling block to the use of these different methods of market segmentation.

Leisure organisations should of course use a number of market segmentation methods in the process of *multivariate market segmentation*. This will allow a bigger picture of the consumer to be developed and used in the development of effective and efficient marketing programmes. Some examples of this to illustrate the point are as follows:

1. The female city dweller who is 'time poor' and visits a spa to gain a holistic experience.
2. The young outgoing male who downloads music from the Internet to his MP3 player and listens to the results with his local friends.
3. The old but active couple who escape to the countryside to escape from the pressures of city life.

The concept of the 'global' consumer and the application of it to the leisure sector

The debate about the global consumer is an interesting academic debate, but also one that has consequences for leisure organisations that have to make decisions about whether to standardise or adapt their products and services during their international marketing activities.

The emergence of the 'global consumer' has commenced, it has been argued, with groups such as the 'global business traveller' or the 'young music lover' (Swarbrooke and Horner, 1999). Academics are divided as to the source of this type of development. One school of thought is that the emergence of the 'global consumer' has been a direct result of the marketing activities of powerful multinational companies such as Nike, Reebok, Sony and Manchester United Football Club.

Other commentators have supported the view that it is the fact that groups of consumers across the world are becoming increasingly similar because of *customer convergence*.

There have been conflicting ideas expressed about the idea of globalisation of products and services. Levitt (1983) was the first academic to observe that globalisation was occurring at a rapid pace and this was supported later by other academic commentators (Ohmae, 1982; Guido, 1991).

Kotler and Armstrong in 2004 argued, however, that globalisation was only possible for large organisations such as McDonald's and Coca-Cola. Other smaller organisations would have to adapt their product and service offering on the basis of distinctly different cultural identities (Douglas and Wind, 1987; Kashani, 1989).

There is evidence, however, that an increasing number of global products and services are continuing to emerge. This is despite the fact that there has been a growing movement in the postmodern world to protect the consumer from globalisation on the basis of intellectual, ethical and practical reasons (Usinier, 1993).

Despite this, it is the very young that are the most likely to become the global consumers of the future for leisure organisations. The desire to be associated with global leisure products whether it is a McDonald's meal or a Disney film has never been better developed. Young children are now sensitive to global brands at a very early stage of their development. They are exposed to multinational satellite channels such as MTV, the satellite music channel. It will be interesting to observe whether these children will continue with their desires to be seen as a homogenous mass, or whether in time, they will seek to return to their local national cultural identity. The outcome of this development will determine whether leisure organisations will be able to increasingly standardise their products and services in the future, or whether they will have to adapt their offerings for local markets.

There are commentators who suggest that there will be an increasing number of individuals who express their personal identity by a return to an individualistic way of life. The following quote illustrates this point:

> People no longer identify themselves as part of a muse: they want to express their difference through identity with subsets of the once homogenous conception. Now there are plural, multiple, and niche-based sources of identity open to people, such as their sexuality, their culture, their ethnicity. Niche-based markets sustain these sources of identity.
>
> Clark and Clegg (1998)

This quote suggests that as people become more individualistic it will become more difficult to segment the market, and there will be more and more groups of individuals who demand very focused leisure products.

If this is true, then technology may allow us to produce very individually tailored products and services for these smaller and smaller groups.

Conclusions

We have considered the concept of consumer behaviour in this chapter with a particular emphasis on the motivators and determinants that affect individuals in their purchase decisions related to leisure products and services.

We have suggested that there are different ways to segment a market and that organisations should combine a number of methods together to give a clearer picture of the consumer.

The trend towards globalisation has been an important movement in some areas of the leisure industry. We only need to think of the fast-food operation, the music industry and the football teams to think of examples that illustrate this. Whether the trend towards globalisation will march on or whether we will see the emergence of increasing numbers of consumers who have an individualistic approach and demand niche leisure products remains to be seen.

Discussion points and essay questions

1. Critically evaluate the different methods of market segmentation and suggest reasons why leisure organisations should adopt multivariate market segmentation.
2. Discuss the opportunities and interests which the process of globalisation represent for leisure providers in your country of residence.
3. Examine the extent to which 'customer convergence' is happening in the international leisure market.

Exercise

Conduct a survey on a small number of individuals to explore the leisure interests they have and the reasons for their particular choices. Try and relate your results to the model of consumer behaviour.

The international leisure industry

Key concepts

The main concepts covered in the chapter are:

- The types of organisations that exist within the supply side of the leisure sector
- The role of transnational corporations in the leisure sector.

Introduction

The previous chapter looked at the nature of the international leisure market and the demand factors that need to be taken into consideration. This chapter will consider the supply side of the industry, the trends in the structure of the industry and the rise of transnational corporations.

It is important to reiterate that the leisure market is not served by one industry but by a combination of different types of organisations supplying very different products and services, including:

- transport organisations;
- tour operators and travel agents;
- visitor attractions;

- the hospitality industry including commercial accommodation suppliers and restaurants;
- recreation organisations.

These industrial sectors of leisure are shown in Figure 4.1. Destination markets include countries, regions and individual cities and towns. This type of marketing involves a complex of interactive products and services which the visitor 'buys' (Table 4.1).

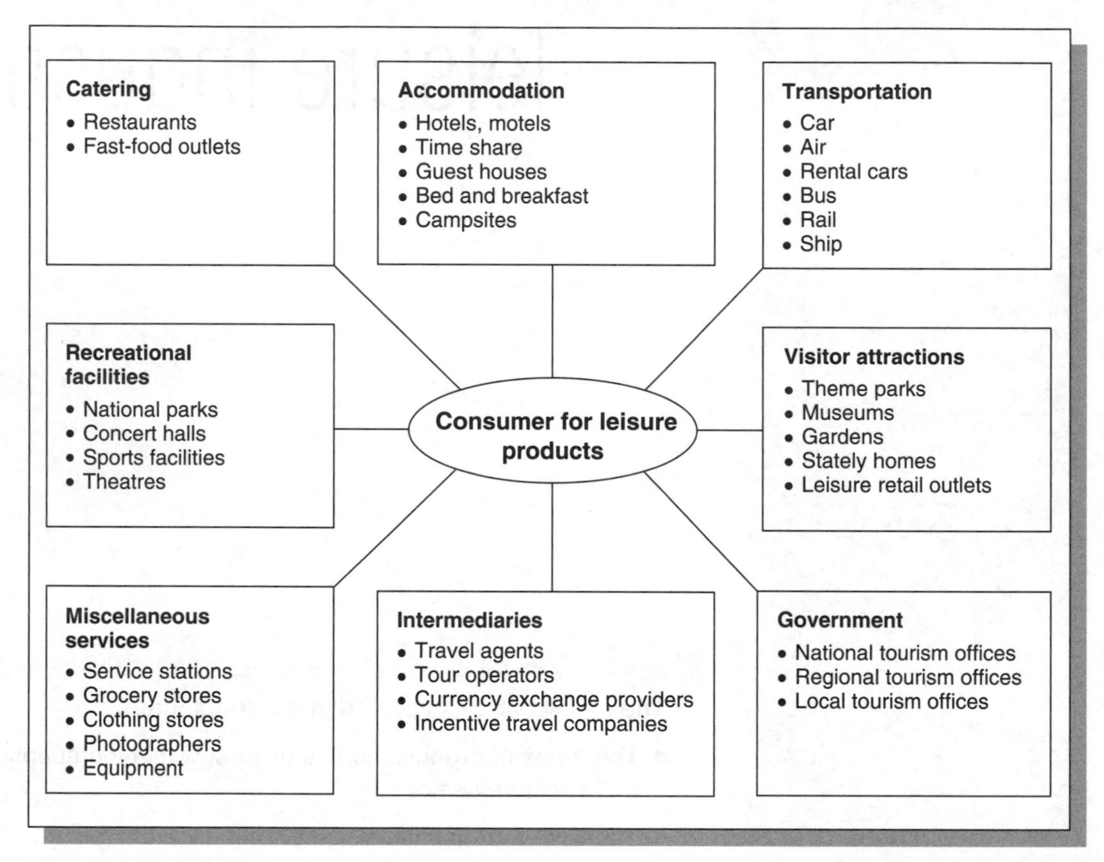

Figure 4.1 The industrial sectors of leisure

What the customer 'buys'

1. Beautiful location with clean beaches
2. Transport facilities within the town and links to surrounding areas
3. Accommodation
4. Catering products
5. Access to visitor attractions
6. Access to shopping for general and special purchases relating to the holiday
7. Access to recreational facilities such as leisure parks, bars, nightclubs, cinemas, water sports, etc.

Table 4.1 Destination market: large European seaside resort

Market structures

The international market for leisure products has been developed by organisations of different sizes. These range from local organisations in the voluntary and public sectors that have developed small organisations, to the global organisations in the commercial sector, which have developed businesses as part of their global strategy. The leisure market in general, however, is very fragmented in nature. Most of the major sections of the industry have a large multinational presence in the market. The multinationals, however, often only represent a small part of the total market size.

Most of the large operators have levels of business which only represent a small part of the total amount that is spent on leisure. Large companies, however, have already recognised that they can target customers who have things in common across national boundaries. We can now consider some of the major sectors of the leisure industry to explore these ideas in more depth.

Sectors of the leisure industry

Catering – fast food

The unification of Europe and the growing openness in Eastern Europe has opened up the European market to global fast-food chains. This development and growing openness developed in the areas of the world that had the most rapid growth in their economies in the late 1990s.

There was a tremendous opportunity for the rapid spread of the franchised fast-food chains. The younger generation were influenced by American culture and were keen to visit chains such as McDonald's, Pizza Hut and Burger King. The chains also encouraged the special occasion dining experience such as the child's birthday party across the world. The acceptance by governments and consumers alike to this type of catering outlet has fuelled the tremendous growth in franchise food outlets across the world, spearheaded by the chains. Dominance by the American chains in the development of this sector of the leisure industry could lead to the inevitable question of whether the development of markets in the future will be an 'Americanisation' process or whether people will return to an interest in their local cultures. What is clear is that the growth of the international restaurant franchise has been a major contribution to the globalisation strategies of leisure organisations.

Accommodation – hotels

The hotel industry is increasingly making a global push to attract the world's top business and leisure travellers. Hotel chains now operate on every continent of the world, except Antarctica. The market for international and national visitors and the total spend on hospitality products vary enormously between countries in the world. Despite this, there is a push for the major hotel groups to become global in nature. The global hospitality industry is dominated by the American corporations, but other chains such as the Europe-based company – Accor – are also becoming major international players.

The French-based Accor group has developed an increasing presence across the world from a strong French foundation. The company has developed their hotels from a strong portfolio of branches including Altea, Formule 1, Novotel and Sofitel. The company owns hotels in most European countries and is busy expanding across the world. It is typical of the type of global expansion that is characterised by larger hospitality providers.

The world's hotel stock still largely consists of unaffiliated and privately managed properties but the international chains (such as Cedant, Inter-Continental, Marriott, Accor, Choice Hotels International, Hilton Hotels Corporation, Starwood and Carlson Hospitality) still have distinct marketing advantages. Many hotel chains are beginning to increasingly target the leisure rather than the business traveller (for example, TUI Hotels and Resorts, and Sol Me La). There are also new trends beginning to emerge in the hospitality sector such as the budget hotel with little or no service and the boutique hotel targeting a very specific target group.

Transportation – airlines

The demand for airline travel via scheduled airlines is international in nature. This is due to sophisticated distribution and computer reservation systems, and the fact that the product is largely based on international travel.

Other forms of air travel are demanded on a national basis. The development of charter airlines, for example, has occurred to supply the needs of domestic tour operators. The airline industry has become global because the major airlines have grown by acquisition, merger and franchising agreements. The growth of the global route networks has been fuelled by an increasing trend to deregulation and privatisation. Airlines have had a period of extensive change and have increasingly used sophisticated market segmentation and branding policies.

The airline industry has therefore moved from a situation where there was a high degree of national protection encouraged by state ownership and government control of landing rights, to a highly competitive international industry. Major international airlines are American (for example American Airlines, United Airlines, Delta and Northwest), but other international airlines originate in other areas of the world (for example Air France Group (France), Lufthansa (Germany), British Airways (UK) and Japan Airlines (Japan)).

The growth of the international carriers and the major development of international airports, such as Schiphol (Amsterdam), Heathrow (London), Hong Kong (China) and O'Hare (Chicago, US), has meant that the market for airline tickets has become a global market. The ways in which the airline companies sell their seats to an increasingly international consumer using sophisticated distribution channels is the best example of a global business in the leisure sector.

Visitor attractions

Visitor attractions have been defined as:

> designated permanent resources that are controlled and managed for their own sake and for the enjoyment, amusement, entertainment and education of the visiting public.
>
> Middleton and Clarke (2001)

Middleton and Clarke (2001) expanded this definition by categorising visitor attractions into ten categories as follows:

- ancient monuments
- historic buildings
- designated areas, parks and gardens

- theme parks
- wildlife attractions
- museums
- art galleries
- industrial archaeology sites
- themed retail sites
- amusement and leisure parks.

Visitor attractions have been characterised by Swarbrooke (1999) into different groups according to their catchment area. These include attractions which are very local in appeal. The second group includes attractions that have a regional catchment area, such as smaller theme parks. Relatively few attractions have primarily national catchment areas and are usually market leaders in their field. Alton Towers in the UK is one example of an attraction with a national catchment area. Only a small number of attractions enjoy an international catchment area. These tend to be unique attractions which are world famous. Disney World is an example of such an international attraction.

Most attractions are therefore marketed on a local basis with small marketing budgets. It is the large international attractions which provide the opportunity for global marketing programmes. These larger operations need substantial operating and marketing skills. The attractions must be funded by the right financial package, must have an appealing theme so that large numbers of customers are drawn each year, and must have access to a large catchment area to encourage the large numbers of customers. To conclude, therefore, this sector is largely dominated by independently owned and marketed attractions. There are examples of larger operators that have specialised in the visitor attraction market. In the UK, Merlin Entertainment Limited is an example of a European attraction company that operates aquariums, bingo clubs, dungeons, and health and fitness operations across Europe.

The Tussaud's Group owns and manages a number of major visitor attractions including Alton Towers, Chessington World of Adventure, Madame Tussauds, The London Planetarium and Warwick Castle. It also manages the operation and marketing of the British Airways London Eye, London.

The National Trust is a registered charity that is responsible for more than 250 sites across the UK as well as the management of vast areas of countryside and coastline. It can be seen that a wide diversity of organisations in the public, private and voluntary sector own and manage visitor attractions.

Recreational facilities

Recreational products and services can be provided both inside and outside the home. They consist of a vast array of products in the home (reading, home entertainment, house and garden, and hobbies and pastimes) and out of home (gambling, sports and activities, and hobbies and pastimes). Some of these recreational products have been provided by local suppliers who have concentrated very much on local customers. Examples of these are local authority leisure centres, garden centres and local sporting clubs. There are signs, however, in certain areas of recreational provision of the growth of global players who are beginning to dominate the market.

Examples of these include the in-home gaming machines sector dominated by Sony and Nintendo; the CD, record and tape industry dominated by Universal, EMI, BMG, Warner and Sony and television dominated by international television and film production companies such as Warner Brothers, Sky, Columbia, Tristar, CIC and Fox and Warner. The growth of the use of the Internet as a source of recreational entertainment has been the ultimate in the development of a global business.

Intermediaries – tour operators

The demand for holidays, particularly package holidays, has grown in many markets during the last fifty years. This has resulted in a growth in the number of tour operators in particular regions of the world where demand is more well developed.

In Europe, for example, there has been an explosion in the number of package holiday companies that have established a substantial market in recent times. These include companies which operate on a European-wide basis such as TUI (Germany), Kuoni (Switzerland), Club Méditterranée (France) and Grupo Viajes (Spain).

The expansion of tour operators into other markets is one means by which tour operators have sought to improve their market position. There has been a particular growth in recent times of global companies who have realised that travel products and services can be sold very well through online distribution systems. This is a substantial threat to the tour operators and high street travel agents.

International companies have expanded rapidly in recent years and the amount of travel business that is booked online is growing year by year. International players in this market who are all predicted to take the travel market in the future from more traditional intermediaries include:

Expedia (US)
Priceline (US)
Ebooking (UK)
Travelocity (US)
Hotels.com (US)
Lastminute.com (UK).

Conclusion

This chapter has looked at the structure of the leisure industry. It has been seen that although there are signs that global organisations have emerged in each of the major sectors of the industry, the industry is still dominated by smaller nationally based organisations. The targeting of international market segments such as the international business traveller or the global teenager has allowed certain organisations to develop an international business. We predict that these organisations will continue to grow and emerge as new opportunities in the leisure sector emerge. It is important to recognise, however, that the market is still dominated by many millions of small suppliers in the public, private and voluntary sectors. This means that there are many opportunities still for the small entrepreneurial leisure providers to establish a worthwhile business.

Discussion points and essay questions

1. Discuss the patterns of ownership found in the airline tour operation and hotel sectors.
2. Choose a major European tourism, leisure or hospitality company. Describe how the organisation has grown over time and explain why it has developed in this way.
3. Analyse the effect the Internet is having on organisations in one chosen sector of the leisure industry.

Exercise

For the country in which you live, select *one* of the following sectors:

- visitor attraction;
- accommodation;
- arts and entertainment;
- catering;
- sports centres.

For your chosen sector you should:

(a) outline the balance between small businesses and large corporations within the sector;
(b) identify the respective roles of the public-, private- and voluntary-sector organisation;
(c) discuss the involvement, if any, of major organisations in your chosen sector and in other leisure businesses.

CHAPTER 5

The international business environment

Key concepts

The main concepts covered in the chapter are:

- The macroenvironment including political, economic, social and technological factors
- The microenvironment including the nature and structure of the organisation itself, suppliers, marketing intermediaries, existing customers and competitors
- Factors that may potentially make the international business environment more homogeneous.

Introduction

This chapter looks at the business environment in which leisure and organisations operate today. It examines the forces and factors that are in action within this environment, currently, and assesses their likely impact on these sectors.

Where appropriate, the authors will highlight those areas where there are differences between these sectors and between different countries, in relation to the business environment.

For the purposes of this chapter, the business environment will be split into two parts as follows:

1. The *macroenvironment* which is made up of societal forces that cannot be controlled by organisations. They can only try to anticipate them and respond to them as effectively as possible. We will consider these factors under four headings, namely political, economic, social and technological.
2. The *microenvironment* consists of those factors that are within the immediate business environment of the organisation. As such, they are capable of being either controlled or influenced by the organisation. We will consider these factors under five headings. In other words, the organisation itself, suppliers, marketing intermediaries, existing customers and competitors. The organisation must seek to manage those factors in line with its objectives.

However, it is important to note that the two are interrelated. For example, the relationship between an organisation and its suppliers and marketing intermediaries is partly influenced by a political factor, namely government legislation on contract law, to give just one instance.

The macroenvironment

The macroenvironment has an impact on the three elements of the marketing system: the product, the market and the ways in which the product is marketed to the consumer.

Furthermore, in the context of this chapter, it is important to recognise that macroenvironmental factors operate at three geographical levels, at least, namely:

1. The *national level* where the factor is purely significant for organisations operating within the domestic market of that one country. Nevertheless, this could also mean foreign companies who sell their product in that country. For example, a change in German tax law would have an impact on a French hotel chain that operates units within Germany.
2. The *European level* where the factor is significant within Europe specifically. Given that Europe does not exist as a single political or economic entity at the moment, any such factors are likely to be confined to the member states of the European Union only. An example of this is the Package Travel Directive.
3. Those issues which exist on a *global scale* and have an influence which is on a scale greater than that in Europe. An example of this is the computer reservation systems (CRS) which are becoming increasingly global in nature.

Clearly there are two sides to this set of factors. In other words, there are those which originate in Europe and go on to influence countries outside Europe, and there are those which, though non-European in origin, have an impact on the European business environment.

Many argue that, currently, leisure organisations are living through a period when their business environment is particularly volatile. This perceived volatility has underpinned many developments in management thinking, such as the concept of 'Thriving on Chaos' championed by Tom Peters.

We will now begin to look at the current macroenvironment to attempt to see how volatile it is in reality. Certainly, it is a truism that the macroenvironment is always undergoing some change. It is therefore obvious that any discussion of it in this book can only ever be a snapshot taken at a specific time.

Political factors

Europe is clearly in a period of rapid political change, which is of great significance for the European leisure sector.

On the *national level* there are a number of political factors that influence the product, market and marketing activity within these sectors. A few examples will illustrate this point.

- *Government policies* on topics as diverse as the following:
  - governmental financial assistance for the leisure sector;
  - the funding levels enjoyed by local government;
  - individual and corporate taxation;
  - state ownership within the economy, including the privatisation of state-controlled industries;
  - social security policies;
  - the quantity and dates of public holidays;
  - the curriculum in schools;
  - the conservation of historic buildings;
  - border controls and the freedom of movement granted to the citizens of a country;
  - relations with particular foreign countries.
- *Government legislation* on a range of issues including:
  - health and safety at work;
  - consumer protection;
  - advertising;
  - holiday entitlement;
  - transport operations.

  These lists, in relation to government policies and legislation, are both short and selective but they do give an impression of the breadth of influence governments may have over these sectors.

  Government policies and legislation are notoriously unpredictable as they usually reflect short-term domestic political factors, such as election campaigns.
- *Political stability* is crucial, given that leisure activity only tends to flourish when the political situation is stable. Instability can take a number of forms, including:
  - Politically motivated strikes and demonstrations which can disrupt tourism sectors, by closing down airports and rail networks, for example. Given the importance of the leisure industry to many national economies, as well as the importance which citizens attach to their holidays, trade unions realise that disrupting tourism can give them a powerful weapon. Air traffic controllers, for example, have used this tactic successfully in recent years.
  - Terrorism, where in some countries, tourists have become deliberate targets. Terrorist groups, who wish to undermine governments, seek to harm the national economy which may well mean attacking tourism, given that in many countries, tourism is a crucially important sector of the economy. In other cases, tourists may be attacked because of their perceived lack of moral values, by terrorists whose motivation is both religious and political.
  - It is often the perception of terrorism rather than the reality that has the greatest impact on tourism sectors. For example, although tourists were never deliberately targeted during the years of conflict in Northern Ireland, the perception of the situation undoubtedly harmed the development of tourism in the region.
  - The terrorist attacks in 2002 in Bali and Kenya have demonstrated the catastrophic effect that terrorist attacks can have on the leisure and tourism market in destinations.

- The events of September 11, 2001 in the USA also showed the disastrous impact terrorism could have on people's general willingness to travel worldwide.
- Wars which make leisure activities impossible for the local population and make it unattractive or impossible for outsiders to take trips to the war zone. A sad example of this is the former state of Yugoslavia, where civil wars seriously damaged the once booming tourism and hospitality sectors. Only when war ceases can such places begin to rebuild their tourism and hospitality sectors as we have seen recently in Croatia, for instance.
- The extent to which governments are seen to be in control of the country, so that law and order can be maintained, rather than day-to-day life being largely determined by groups who are not part of the state. This is clearly a problem in Russia, with the rise of powerful organised crime syndicates.

A few examples will demonstrate that while the impact of national political factors is predominantly domestic, they do have an influence on people and organisations beyond the national boundaries. These examples include:

- the civil war in the former Yugoslavia which forced foreign tourists and tour operators to seek alternative destinations, both within and outside Europe;
- the package of financial and nonfinancial assistance offered by the French government which helped persuade the Disney organisation to site Disneyland Paris in France;
- the growing freedom of movement of citizens of the former communist countries of Eastern Europe which is leading, slowly, to more of their population taking holidays in Western Europe and beyond.

If we turn our attention now to political factors which exist at a *European level*, the most important one clearly relates to the European Union.

The European Commission affects tourism, leisure and hospitality, within member states, in a wide variety of ways, including:

- Legislation such as the Package Travel Directive which sought to improve consumer protection, in the field of package holidays, across all member states.
- The activities of its directorate, DG XXIII, which is charged with developing tourism within the European Union.
- The funding of tourism projects through a range of schemes, including the European Regional Development Fund, for example. It is probably not an exaggeration to say that in some countries, such as the UK, more public funding for tourism has come from the European Commission than from national governments in recent years.
- European Union-wide tourism marketing campaigns on themes such as cultural tourism, involving organisations such as the European Travel Commission.

The current area of enlargement of the European Union means that these influences are encompassing more and more countries.

At a pan-European level, the Council of Europe continues to play a role in leisure through its work in the field of conservation.

If we look at political factors on the *global scale*, we can see that they operate in two directions as we noted earlier. First, there are those factors which originate outside Europe, but which influence European consumers and organisations.

For example, there are the policies and legislation of non-European governments. This includes the attitudes towards tourism of the governments of the main destination countries for European tourists such as the USA, Egypt, Israel, Kenya and Thailand for example, together with that of other generating countries such as the USA and Japan.

Conversely there are those European factors that influence consumers and organisations outside Europe, such as the European Commission's campaign to attract non-European tourists to visit Europe to arrest the decline seen in recent years in Europe's position in the global tourism market.

The only agency operating on a global scale in leisure is the World Tourism Organisation (WTO) based in Madrid. It brings together governments from around the world and is particularly active in the areas of global policy, data collection and training.

However, today, the major political factor in the global business environment for leisure is terrorism which is a truly global phenomenon. The activities of the terrorist groups together with the so-called 'war on terrorism' are felt worldwide.

Economic factors

Mirroring the structure of the last section, we will begin by looking at economic factors at the *national level*. These include the following:

- Interest rates which affect both market demand and investment in new physical products such as hotels, theme parks and leisure-shopping complexes.
- Inflation figures, given the higher level of inflation, the more difficult it is to engage in long-term financial planning.
- Levels of unemployment, as these affect overall demand.
- Social security benefits which, if they are low, may mean that many people who are jobless, elderly or sick may be unable to afford the products of the leisure sector.
- The distribution of wealth in society, in other words, is a small group rich while the majority are relatively poor, or is wealth more evenly distributed? This has an impact on the value and nature of demand and is largely influenced by taxation policies.
- Salary levels, which if high may encourage companies to try to find ways of reducing the labour needs of their operations.
- Currency-exchange rates which affect outbound tourists and those organisations which service their needs.
- Countries with balance of payment deficits in general, or specifically in relation to tourism, may be motivated to bring in policies designed to boost tourism and leisure spend.

Clearly, these factors have implications beyond the national frontiers. For example, if a country has relatively high wage rates, hotel chains may seek to recruit staff from countries where pay rates are lower. Thus, German hotel companies recruit Turkish workers, while many London hotels recruit staff from the Philippines, for example. Likewise, low interest rates and a buoyant economy in a country may encourage investment from foreign companies.

At the *European level*, the key economic factors are increasingly those which are being influenced by the actions of the European Commission. As these are politically motivated, they were outlined in the section on political factors. They include:

- the abolition of duty-free sales between member states;
- the idea of harmonising sales taxes, both in terms of the rate and the goods and services on which they are levied;
- deregulation and liberalisation of markets that have been largely regulated by individual national governments, such as air travel.

Perhaps most significantly, there is the Euro Zone within the European Union. While fraught with difficulties, this project has already had a marked effect on the leisure market in the 12 countries currently using the Euro.

The tourist flows between member states which have always been influenced by currency exchange rates, have been encouraged by the removal of uncertainties in exchange rates. It has also made forward planning by the tourism industry a much more practical activity. It will also increasingly take away the income as many travel agencies and some hotels and airports earn from currency exchange transactions.

At the supranational but sub-European level, Eastern Europe again stands out as a distinctly different region. Its relatively low level of economic development makes it attractively inexpensive for Western Europeans; hence the popularity of skiing holidays in Bulgaria and Romania. On the other hand, the lack of economic stability and high inflation rates put off potential foreign investors.

Within the overall pan-European context, differential levels of economic development and wealth between countries are still a motivator for flows between certain countries. It is one of the reasons, along with others, why more Swedes visit Greece than vice versa.

On the *global scale*, the only real truly global economic factors are, perhaps, the trade treaties like the GATT agreement and the continuing moves that are increasing the power of transnational, vertically and horizontally integrated corporations. Europe is playing a leading role in this trend through hotel chains such as Accor with its ownership of the Motel 6 chain in the USA. However, Europe is also affected by this trend in reverse; hence the growing presence in Europe of McDonald's over the years.

Finally, on the global scale, differences in levels of economic development are still a motivator for trips to certain regions. This is particularly true of tourist flows from Europe, where places such as Thailand, Goa Beach, Dominican Republic and Cuba are becoming particularly popular for sun and sand holidays, because they are inexpensive for most Europeans, due to their relatively low level of economic development.

Social factors

These can, somewhat subjectively, be divided into several categories, namely:

- demographic factors, in other words, those concerned with population structure in terms of characteristics such as age, sex, religion, race, education, and birth, death and fertility rates.
- social concerns like crime, health and environmental issues.
- the emergence of distinctive subcultures within societies that share certain values, and perhaps, characteristics as consumers. It could be argued that these are the core of the 'lifestyle marketing' which we have increasingly seen since the late 1990s.

At the *national level* the most important *demographic characteristics* include:

- The age structure of the population which is important both in terms of the target markets for an organisation's marketing, and its recruitment policies.
- The role and influence of women in society and their participation in leisure activities, tourism for pleasure and business travel. In some countries, including most of those in Western Europe, women are already important markets in leisure.
- The existence of ethnic minority communities within individual countries who may well differ from the majority of the population in terms of race, language and religion. These groups may provide well-recognised valuable niche markets for airlines, who can sell tickets between the country where the person lives and the country where their

families originally lived, or still live. This is seen in relation to Turkish people living in Germany, for example.

The other side of the coin is where attempts are made to encourage people from ethnic minorities to take part in leisure activities in their country of residence. For example, great efforts have been made in the UK to encourage people from the Asian and Afro-Caribbean communities to experience countryside recreation.

If we look at these same three factors at the *European level*, we will see there are large differences between individual countries.

People in Western Europe have been told they are living through an explosion of the so-called 'demographic time bomb' where populations will become increasingly aged. This growth in older people reflects improved health care, for example, and is clearly being seen in countries like Germany and the UK.

However, in other parts of Europe, the main characteristics of the population in terms of age is that of a youthful population. This is true not only in terms of numbers, but also spending power. Spain provides a good illustration of this point.

While the role of women in societies in Europe is, apparently, slowly becoming increasingly similar between different countries, there are still differences between some countries of Europe such as Norway and Greece, for example.

Finally, some European countries have large ethnic minority communities, largely as a result of immigration, while others have relatively small such population. Generally, those countries with strong colonial traditions, such as Britain and France, and those where the demand for labour has outgrown indigenous supply, such as Germany, tend to have the largest such communities. Conversely, smaller countries with no such colonial tradition such as Ireland tend to have small ethnic communities.

However, in some countries, there are minority groups which are long established and are not a result of immigration, yet they remain culturally distinct from the rest of the population. This is true of the Walloons in Belgium, the Basques of Spain and the Corsicans in France.

In terms of the *global level* in relation to demographic factors, the main link between Europe and the rest of the world is principally a matter of demographic change in countries outside Europe where European transnational corporations sell their product.

Let us now turn our attention to *social concerns*, beginning with the *national level*. We will focus on the following concerns, which all have an influence on leisure.

- Crime discourages people from visiting places which develop a particularly bad reputation in terms of crime generally, and crime against tourists more specifically. On the other hand, if the appeal of the place is strong enough, it may simply result in tourists exercising more caution. Some Italian cities, have suffered in this respect, for instance.
- Health issues, which can be both a threat and an opportunity, for tourism sectors. The threat is posed if countries, or parts of them, are perceived to represent risks to visitors' health in some way. For example, many beaches in the UK are perceived to be a health threat because of pollution. Other health threats present in some European countries include rabies, a water-borne virus in St Petersburg and a relatively high risk of food poisoning in some of the hotter countries. In early 2003 we also saw how the SARS virus decimated the inbound tourism market and the domestic leisure market in China and Singapore. In every country, skin cancer and AIDS are now widely recognised to be tourism-related diseases.

  However, health concerns are also an opportunity for tourism sectors as is evidenced by the growth of leisure facilities within hotels, the resurgence of many spa resorts and the opening of numerous health farms. They have also provided new opportunities for caterers to develop new menus and themed restaurants.

- Lastly environmental issues, which again represent both threats and opportunities for tourism sectors. The threats relate to the concerns with what tourism can do to the physical environment in particular, such as high-rise development in coastal resorts and the waste in hotels in terms of everything from water to packaging material. These concerns might theoretically result in consumers rejecting organisations that they believe are involved in harming the environment. There is also a danger that governments will legislate if public concern reaches a serious level. Much of the industry is therefore currently engaged in attempting to regulate its own behaviour to prevent both threats becoming reality.

The opportunity is the fact that many consumers, in some countries, will pay a premium price for a more environmentally friendly product or will show brand loyalty to a company which they believe shows a responsible attitude towards the environment. A frequently quoted single example from the hospitality sector is the Hotel Ariston in Milan.

Again, if we consider these three issues on a *European level* we can see that there are substantial differences between individual European countries.

Crime, for example, is not perceived to be on any significant scale in Scandinavia, even in the capital cities. Conversely, in Russia, for example, crime against tourists is almost an accepted part of life.

There are also situations in Europe where certain nationalities develop a reputation for criminal activities they perpetrate on tourists, rather than they themselves suffering from criminal activities. An example of this is the reputation which – rightly or wrongly – British 'lager louts' have in the islands of Greece.

Across Europe there are also large variations in what is considered criminal activity that needs to be suppressed by the authorities. In cities like Amsterdam, for instance, organised prostitution is not only tolerated, but it has almost become an accepted part of the tourism product, just another aspect of the city's heritage. Meanwhile, in other European countries, prostitution is perceived as a serious problem, to be actively discouraged.

When we move on to look at health issues, there are also large national variations. Again, Scandinavia is seen to be a place with few of the health risks outlined earlier, while countries like Russia are seen to be relatively much less healthy.

Finally, concern over environmental issues is far more highly developed in the countries of Northern and Central Europe, than those in Southern and Eastern Europe, generally. Maybe this reflects the fact that the former were industrialised and urbanised relatively early and so have had to face the resulting problems, for longer.

There are also variations between countries in terms of what are considered to be the most important environmental issues. In some it is industrial pollution, while in others it is waste and recycling. Wildlife protection is a major political issue in some countries and of little significance in others.

Interestingly, in the three issues we have focused on here, there appears to be something of a division in Europe, between North and South, and East and West.

If we look at these issues on a *global scale* what is instantly clear is that the differences within Europe appear minor compared to those between Europe and the rest of the world.

Europe, for instance, has no country where street crime and random killings reach the level found in many cities in the USA, while levels of assault and robbery in the street come nowhere near those found in many cities in Africa and South America. On the other hand, there are regions of the world where the level of casual street crime in Europe might appear high, such as much of the Middle East.

In terms of health, the differences are even more dramatic, with large areas of Africa and Asia subject to the risk of Malaria, Yellow Fever, Hepatitis, Typhoid and Cholera. However, again, there are also countries as healthy or even healthier than Europe as a whole, for example, Canada.

In relation to environmental issues, there are also some variations. In some countries, rampant development is the order of the day with little concern for the environment. Examples of this include the Amazonian rain forest in South America, and some of the newly industrialised countries of Southeast Asia. However, there are also many examples of countries with a strong environmental ethos outside Europe, like Canada again.

Lastly, there are the *subcultures*. These are interesting because many of them appear to cross national boundaries. It is therefore largely irrelevant to seek to divide them into *national level*, *European level* or *global level* factors, as we have done elsewhere in this section. These subcultures include:

'Euro-students' who go to other countries to study
animal rights campaigners
teenage consumers
Internet users
participants in fashionable sports such as snow-boarding.

Three points can be made about these subcultures in relation to marketing as follows:

(i) Each subculture is reflected in lifestyles, so that when targeting these market segments, marketers need to adopt a lifestyle-based approach to their marketing.
(ii) Most of these subcultures are dominated by younger people.
(iii) They are found in all or most countries of Europe to a greater or lesser extent. Perhaps these subcultures are the forerunners of the much-vaunted 'Pan-European Consumer'.

The four groups outlined earlier all have a relevance to marketing in tourism sectors. 'Euro-students' are major customers for packages such as the 'Inter-Rail' scheme, while animal rights campaigners are a threat to some types of visitor attraction like zoos or bullfights. Teenage consumers are increasingly being offered the chance to take holidays separately from their parents, usually based on activities or special interests.

Internet users may be the first to start using home-based new technology to access tourism products, thus bypassing the travel agent. The final group are niche markets for the growing range of activities and special interest holidays. However, it is also interesting to note that most of these subcultures probably originated outside Europe, particularly in the USA.

Perhaps they are thus not a result of the development of a 'Euro-youth' subculture, but rather are evidence of the growing power of American global power in the media and consumerism.

This global marketing power of brands has been seen particularly strongly in the leisure industry through brands as diverse as Reebok, Nike and Manchester United Football Club.

Technological factors

The last of the four macroenvironmental factors that influence the business environment of leisure is also the one for which national boundaries are the least relevant. It could be argued that new technology is the key to the growth of the 'global village', which is making national boundaries appear less and less important for industries. This is clearly the case in leisure where technology is a catalyst for globalisation. This is partly because the cost of developing these technologies is so great that cooperation between major national corporations in different countries is required, while the developments in communication technology are making communication on a global scale easier all the time.

We will, therefore, simply discuss each of the most significant technological developments and their implications for leisure marketing. They can be divided into several categories, namely:

- operational technologies
- communication technologies
- transport technologies
- product technologies.

Let us begin with the *operational technologies*. These include:

- Computer reservation systems which are becoming ever more sophisticated. At one time, most related just to the product of one company such as an airline or a hotel chain. Now there are, increasingly, Global Distribution Systems (GDS) which are worldwide in coverage and link together the products of a large variety of suppliers. This makes it possible to put together ever more complex packages, but it also offers potential for travellers or travel agents to put together tailor-made individual itineraries.
- Smart Cards, which can store a multitude of information and can be used for a range of purposes already, even at their current relatively low level of sophistication. They can function as keys to help guests gain access to hotels, individual bedrooms and health clubs. In addition, airlines are experimenting with their use instead of tickets.
- Computer databases which can increasingly handle more and more data, so that marketing messages can be targeted more precisely to various target markets.
- Computer-based management information systems which provide managers with up-to-date information on matters as diverse as stock levels, visitor numbers, financial performance and information on guests' tastes and preferences.
- Food production and service technologies which are being utilised to reduce labour input and thus hold down costs.

Then there are the *communication technologies*, which leisure in particular is beginning to exploit, including the following:

(i) Multimedia systems such as CD-ROM which can give consumers direct access to three dimensional images – and sounds – in relation to leisure products. In theory therefore, a guest might call up an image of a resort that a tour operator is featuring, and then go on to study an image of the beach. They would then look at images of the hotel facilities such as the restaurant and swimming pool. Finally, they would look at the interior of the specific room they would be allocated, and the view from the window.

This way the visitor would have realistic expectations and this should lead to less complaints from those consumers who believe that they have been misled by the traditional brochure.

Some operators are beginning to install multimedia kiosks in some branches, but multimedia systems are also increasingly being bought by people for installation in their own homes.

(ii) Interactive television, which allows people to not only receive information via their television, but gives them an opportunity to take action in response to this information.

In other words, a consumer is able to call up information on their television screen and then make a booking via the television.

(iii) Internet and other data services provided through computers, which give consumers access to information on a worldwide scale. The Internet has become a major factor in both distribution and promotion in leisure, and has brought new organisations into the leisure industry such as Microsoft with its Expedia online travel organisations.

(iv) The well-established Mintel system in France which is an interactive system linked to the telephone. People in France, who have this system in their home, call up information on rail services and holidays, for example, and then make direct bookings via the small computer which is linked to their telephone.

All four of these developments in communication technologies have had, and will continue to have dramatic effect on the distribution chain in the leisure sector. They give the consumer the potential ability to access information and book directly without the need for a marketing intermediary.

Amongst the areas where the Internet has become important in leisure marketing are:

- reserving theatre tickets
- booking airline tickets
- booking a package holiday
- purchasing tickets for sporting events.

The relevant intermediaries, including theatre booking agencies and travel agents, could thus be eliminated from the transactions. This has attractions for the theatres, hotels and tour operators, who would no longer have to pay commission, usually around 10 per cent, to these intermediaries. Thus they could either reduce their prices and/or increase their profit margins.

However, this scenario could fail to develop further for a number of reasons, including:

- intermediaries responding by emphasising personal service and reducing commission rates;
- consumers' resistance to using the new technologies;
- those who control the technologies deciding not to feature their competitors' information to prevent potential competition.

It is interesting to note that both the operational and communication technologies we have discussed could have another dramatic impact on the distribution of products in leisure specifically. Many of them, such as smart cards, will also increasingly be introduced by companies in other industries, food and clothes retailers and banks, for example. It is possible that these latter types of enterprise will increasingly use these technologies to begin to act as travel agents, selling package holidays. Thus, in the future, the premises of such businesses may offer the ultimate package holiday, and the consumers may not only book the holiday there using the smart card and a multimedia system, for example, but may also purchase their clothes, suntan creams and insurance, as part of the package using credit offered by the store or bank.

The last type of communication technologies, we will consider, relate specifically to the business travel sector. It is argued that a number of ongoing technological innovations will reduce the need for business travel. These include:

- E-mail
- Video conferencing
- Computer conferencing.

However, while these will undoubtedly have an influence on business travel, they are unlikely to reduce it dramatically, given that business travel is thought important for two main reasons, namely:

- it is seen as a 'reward' by staff or as a 'perk of the job';
- it is often essential for sales people to meet their customers face to face and socialise, before the latter will agree to purchase.

Transport technologies have always been important, particularly to leisure, and at present, the following seem to be the main relevant areas of innovation:

- Fast trains, particularly the French TGV, with the introduction of a train capable of covering 500 kilometres in an hour. This will lead to increased competition on short-haul routes in Europe for airlines and could also stimulate the weekend break market, where speed is of the essence, as time is limited. This fast train network will spread across Europe over time, until we have a pan-European fast rail service network.
- The development of larger aeroplanes and faster aircraft. These could reduce per capita costs and thus prices, while also making longer-haul destinations more accessible for short break holidays.
- In-car navigation systems that can provide tourists travelling in a foreign land with a print out of a route to their chosen destination. They will also help motorists avoid traffic jams.
- Faster ferries, both conventional and those based on newer methods of propulsion and innovative design. These may speed up loading times which should make them more competitive.

In terms of *product technologies* the most important current development must be the field of virtual reality. Some people are claiming that virtual reality could destroy leisure by taking away people's motivation to travel for pleasure.

The argument is that virtual reality will offer people such incredible simulated experiences in their own homes or in high street arcades and centres that they will have no desire to travel to undergo the authentic experience.

Virtual reality uses sensations that are transmitted through gloves, helmets and complete suits to give the consumer a multimedia sensual experience that mimics reality.

Thus, in the future, the consumer may be able to enjoy a range of virtual reality experiences, including:

- 'attending' a Pavarotti concert any night you want rather than having to wait until a concert is scheduled near your home town;
- feeling the sun on your face, and hearing the waves lapping the shore as you lounge on a beach on a deserted Pacific Island;
- enjoying a meal in a three-star Michelin restaurant in your own home.

The list of potential virtual reality experiences is almost endless.

But virtual reality is not only striving to be as good as reality, it aims to be even better than the real thing.

For example, its interactive nature means you can do things you would never be allowed to do in real life, such as pilot a jet fighter or shoot someone in a gunfight in a Western saloon. It also allows you to be good at activities that in the real world are beyond your abilities, such as playing football for your national side or windsurfing when you cannot swim, or are frightened of water.

Some have even suggested that virtual reality could be a valuable tool in the development of sustainable tourism. Even if people can be given a good simulated experience at home, they may choose not to seek the equivalent authentic experience. In other words, a virtual reality trip around Venice may deter someone from making the trip to the real place. This could be a good way of reducing numbers of visitors to sites and cities that are already receiving too many visitors.

However, this ignores the factors that motivate trips, which would not be met by virtual reality substitutes, namely:

- social contact with local people and other tourists;
- the status value attached to visiting the authentic place.

It is also true to say that virtual reality is currently only at a very early stage in its development, such that it is still dominated perhaps by products aimed at younger males. While visual images are often good, the other senses are not well catered for, particularly smell and touch. It is largely too, more of an individual than a group activity. Nevertheless, virtual reality will be both a serious threat and a huge opportunity for leisure sectors in the years to come.

In addition to virtual reality, there are other product technologies which are influencing leisure, including:

- improved in-flight entertainment systems in airlines;
- increase in our ability to create 'artificial environments' such as the domes at Center Parcs, which may one day lead to underwater holiday centres, for example;
- new sports based on technological innovations.

The macroenvironment and leisure

There is no doubt that the key factors in the macroenvironment for different types of organisations within the leisure sector are different. This is illustrated in Table 5.1 which outlines what the authors consider to be key issues in the macroenvironment threats and opportunities for six types of organisations. Only one threat and opportunity are listed for each organisation, although in reality there are clearly a number for each organisation. While this is a highly simplistic and generalised picture, a number of points do emerge, including the following:

- Some factors are highly relevant to more than one sector, for example – virtual reality.
- A factor which is an opportunity for one type of organisation (recession for a mass market, low price tour operator) can be a threat for others (such as international hotel chains). Likewise, new communication technologies allows tour operators to bypass travel agents so that they represent opportunities for the former, but threats for the latter.
- Some factors can be both potential threats and opportunities for an organisation. Virtual reality could thus be a threat for a theme park, if it were introduced by competitors, but an opportunity if the theme park was first to introduce virtual reality. Whether a factor is an opportunity or a threat, therefore, is often a function of how the organisation responds.

Clearly the table is highly subjective, but hopefully it does give an impression of the diversity of the business environment and the different ways in which the environment might affect different types of leisure organisations.

Perhaps we should conclude the section by trying to make some general comments about the macroenvironment in relation to leisure organisations.

Area of the business environment sector	Political		Economic		Social		Technology	
	Opportunities	Threats	Opportunities	Threats	Opportunities	Threats	Opportunities	Threats
Local authority sports centre	Government policies to encourage people to exercise for the sake of their health	Government control on local authority expenditure	Economic recession	Growth of private sports centres and health farms	Growing concern over health	If medical opinion changes on the health benefits of exercise	New types of exercise equipment	Virtual reality
Private-sector theme park	Reduction in corporate taxation	Stronger health and safety at work legislation	Growth in disposable income	Rise in interest rates	An increase in young people as a proportion of the population in some countries	A reduction in young people as a proportion of the population in some countries	Virtual reality	Virtual reality
International hotel chain	Political change in eastern Europe, the Middle East and southern Africa	Strong labour protection laws in the countries in which they hope to expand	Low interest rates	Recession	Environmental concerns about design, waste disposal, pollution and energy	Environmental concerns about design, waste disposal, pollution and energy	New food production service systems	New communication technologies such as e-mail and computer- and video-conferencing
Major European airline	Deregulation and liberalisation of the skies	Increased competition due to deregulation and liberalisation of the skies	Reductions in fuel prices	Recession	Growing number of women business travellers	Environmental concerns over noise and pollution	New operational technologies such as smart cards	New communication technologies such as e-mail and computer- and video-conferencing

Table 5.1 Key issues in the macroenvironment by different sectors

Continued

Area of the business environment sector	Political		Economic		Social		Technology	
	Opportunities	Threats	Opportunities	Threats	Opportunities	Threats	Opportunities	Threats
Major mass volume, low price tour operators	Single European currency	Further European Commission consumer legislation	Recession	Major fluctuations in currency exchange rates	A growth in the number of students and families who are likely to be major customers for their products	Fear of skin cancer and AIDS in mass-tourism destinations	Interactive television which will allow them to sell directly to consumers	Virtual reality
Small independent travel agencies	Reductions in corporate taxation	Single European currency which will reduce currency transac-tions on which commission is earned	Rise in disposable income	Recession	Growing number of older people who may want to buy high value holidays such as cruises	Any trend towards more independent travel	New GDS installed in agencies	New GDS accessible directly to consumers in their own home

Table 5.1 Key issues in the macroenvironment by different sectors (*Continued*)

First, it appears there may well be a difference between organisations in leisure and those in tourism or hospitality. Many leisure organisations are affected mainly by factors that are mostly domestic in nature, rather than is the case for most tourism and hospitality factors, where international factors are often very significant. For example, in terms of political factors, the most important one for leisure organisations is probably domestic government policy on health and local government spending, for example. The most important factors for most tourism and hospitality organisations, on the other hand, will probably be international, such as the price of raw materials, such as food and fuel which are sourced from abroad, global distribution systems and the impact of political change in other countries on market demand. Secondly, there are differences between the three sectors in terms of which category of factor is of most significance. For leisure organisations, social and economic factors such as health concerns and recession are very important, while for tourism and hospitality, political factors and technological factors are of crucial significance.

There are clearly also differences in the macroenvironment based on other criteria, such as whether organisations are in the public, private or voluntary sector, and their size.

Meanwhile, it is time to switch our attention to the microenvironment.

The microenvironment

We will consider the microenvironment under five headings as follows:

1. the nature and structure of the organisation
2. suppliers
3. marketing intermediaries
4. existing customers
5. competitors.

These are the elements which are important in the microenvironment of organisations in leisure, and over which the organisation in question either controls or influences.

Each of the five elements will be considered in relation to the following questions:

- How do they vary between organisations in the leisure sector?
- How, if at all, do they differ between different European countries?

The nature and structure of the organisation

There are a number of aspects of the nature and structure of the organisation which have a direct bearing on its marketing function. These include:

(i) The range of products the organisation offers, the market segments at which they are targeted and the way in which the marketing function is organised to communicate with these markets.

(ii) Whether the organisation is in the public, private or voluntary sector. Stereotypically, public-sector organisations have a complex set of objectives, rather than simply commercial success. Local authorities, for example, often use tourism as a tool for urban regeneration or development, and as a way of improving infrastructure and amenities which are also of benefit to residents. They are controlled by politicians rather than by managers and boards of directors so that their decisions are often made for political reasons.

Private-sector companies tend to have a more straightforward set of objectives, namely profit maximisation and increasing market share. Decisions are usually taken on the basis of financial considerations, such as the reduction of costs and increasing income.

For voluntary-sector bodies, tourism is often a means to an end. In the case of the National Trust in the UK, for instance, the money generated from tourism is used to further the conservation work which is carried out by the National Trust. It is therefore often a matter of these bodies encouraging tourism, but not when it may conflict with the organisation's main interest, which in this case is conservation.

This issue of the sector in which an organisation exists is an influencable and controllable matter, so that it is appropriate to include it in a section on the microenvironment. For example, some local authorities in the UK, while being in the public sector, have transferred their museums to voluntary-sector trusts. A number have also placed the promotion of their area as a destination in the hands of private-sector companies, which they have set up with commercial partners. In both cases, the main reason for this was to remove them from the bureaucratic restrictions that public ownership can entail.

(iii) The structure of the organisation, in other words, whether it is monolithic or is subdivided into smaller units. If the latter, these units might be based on functional factors, as is the case with strategic business units (SBUs) for example, or geographical factors, such as regions or countries. The choice of structure has implications for the nature of the product and the marketing function, as well as the market.

Also important, in relation to this subject, is the power of different departments within the organisation, and whether or not it is a marketing-centred organisation or one where the finance department is all-powerful and marketing is merely a small separate department.

(iv) The decision-making structure of the organisation is also highly significant from a marketing point of view. Sometimes, decision-making is highly centralised, with all major decisions being taken by a head office that could be thousands of kilometres away from the place where the impact of the decision will be felt. Such geographical isolation of decision-making can lead to problems where centralised decisions do not make sufficient allowance for cultural differences between places.

There is undoubtedly a trend towards decentralised decision-making where decisions are taken locally by people who live in the area. While this can be very good, from a local morale point of view, it can also lead to fragmentation.

(v) Corporate culture is an important factor and has been receiving increasing attention from management theorists in recent years. Cultures can vary in a range of ways, including the following characteristics:

- entrepreneurial or bureaucratic
- aggressive or defensive
- dynamic or inert
- risk-taking or cautious
- outward-focused or inward-focused
- backward-looking or forward-looking.

Most corporate cultures, of course, fall somewhere between these extremes.

(vi) Linked to corporate cultures is the issue of management styles, which do vary. These are often characterised by the terms 'old' manager and 'new' manager. The main differences between both types of managers that are relevant to the marketing function are outlined in Table 5.2.

This is clearly an oversimplistic view and most managers fall between these two extreme positions. It is also possible for someone to be an 'old' manager on one issue and a 'new' manager on another.

The old manager	The new manager
Believes in ad hoc tactical marketing	Believes in strategic marketing planning
Practises crisis management	Practises forward planning
Makes decisions based on judgement, experience and intuition	Makes decisions based on marketing research and factual information
Does not delegate very much to subordinates	Constantly delegates appropriate work to colleagues, wherever possible
Sees himself as a leader making all the key decisions and issuing orders	Sees himself as a team manager, working with the rest of the team and managing through consensus
Believes in experience rather than educational qualifications and training	Believes in experience, educational qualifications and training
Responds to functional problems by cutting costs	Responds to financial pressures by trying to boost income

Table 5.2 The old manager and the new manager

The nature and structure of organisations does vary between tourism, leisure and hospitality, and between countries. However, great differences are also seen between organisations in one sector within a single individual country.

Nevertheless, there are a few generalisations we can make, which although oversimplistic, do contain an element of truth. First, the organisations in the private sector – hotels, tour operators and privately owned airlines – do tend to be more entrepreneurial and dynamic than those in the public sector, including municipal tourist offices, state airlines and sports centres.

Secondly, management decision-making strategies and styles are, perhaps, more centralised and formal in Southern Europe than in Northern Europe, although this situation is slowly changing.

The suppliers

The relationship between a producer and its suppliers is crucial to the quality of the final product. This is true whether the suppliers provide goods or services to the organisation. The supply function also influences the organisation in terms of its costs, and thus its pricing policies, and ultimately, its profit margins.

In leisure, links with suppliers are becoming ever closer, due to two main factors, namely:

1. The growing emphasis on quality, where the quality of the final product is largely dependent on the quality of goods and services provided by suppliers. For example, tour operators are reliant on the quality of rooms allocated to their clients by hotels while restaurant meal quality is partly dictated by the quality of the ingredients chefs receive from their suppliers.
2. Product liability legislation which makes producers responsible for the product they sell, including any defect in it that may be the responsibility of the organisation's suppliers. Under the EC Package Travel Directive, UK tour operators are held legally responsible for the death of a client in a fire in a Spanish hotel, if this were due to negligence on the part of an hotelier.

For these reasons, more and more organisations are seeking to develop closer and closer links with suppliers, to enhance product quality and reduce the risk of legal action.

At one end of the scale this can mean tight controls and occasional inspections by the staff of the organisation. However, in extreme cases, it may mean organisations take over their suppliers through vertical integration, or simply set up operations so that they can supply themselves. Hence, some hotel groups have food production facilities to produce ingredients and meals for its hotel restaurants.

In some cases, vertical integration can be a defensive tactic in a field where particular suppliers are essential. For example, tour operators often buy up or establish their own charter airlines, so they are not dependent, for flight seats, on other carriers which may be owned by their competitor. For, if a tour operator cannot obtain seats on flights, there will be no product for them to sell.

However, we must recognise that the supplier network in many leisure organisations is incredibly complex as can be seen from Table 5.3. These networks can incorporate dozens or even hundreds of suppliers, large and small, at home and abroad.

A private hotel	**A local authority museum**
Food and drink supplies, both raw ingredients and preprepared meals and drinks	Other departments of the local authority who supply financial, personnel and building services to the museums
Launderers	Consultants who advise the museum on specialist matters
Uniform suppliers	Food or drink for sale in catering outlets
Builders	Souvenirs for sale in retail outlets
Landscape contractors and gardeners	Dealers from where they buy artefacts
Professional advisers such as accountants	Members of the public who donate artefacts to the museum free of charge
The schools, colleges and professional bodies that train their personnel	The schools, colleges and professional bodies that train their personnel
Equipment suppliers in relation to kitchens, for instance	Contractors who make exhibition cases
Furnishers, in terms of chairs and beds, for example	Equipment suppliers who provide tills for the catering or retail outlets, for example
Interior decorators	Furnishers in relation to the museum displays and its offices, for instance
Printers who produce their promotional literature	Printers who provide their guides and catalogues and promotional literature
Computer and telecommunications companies that install and maintain computers	Stationers
Stationers	
Investors who supply capital	

Table 5.3 A private hotel and a local authority museum

There can be differences in supplier–producer relations between countries, based either on law or custom and practice. For example, in some countries, bills are expected to be settled immediately while in other countries, payment is often made some time after the goods and services have been provided.

The supply chain in leisure can be very complex and individual organisations can function both as producers and suppliers, simultaneously. For example, a resort hotel is a producer in relation to some customers, while for a tour operator, putting together a package, it is just another supplier.

Marketing intermediaries

The same complexity is true also for marketing intermediaries, namely those organisations which provide the interface between the producer and its customers.

Interest in marketing intermediaries has also been growing in recent years in leisure for the same reasons as was the case with supplier relationships, namely:

- quality, given that the messages given to potential customers by marketing intermediaries about the organisation's products will affect the market image of the product;
- product liability legislation by which the producers may be held accountable in law for misleading representations of their product, through the EC Package Travel Directive, for example, in the case of tour operators.

Many leisure organisations use an enormous range of marketing intermediaries, through both formal and informal relationships. Figure 5.1 illustrates the range of marketing intermediaries that may be used by a large hotel chain.

As shown in the figure, most of the links with marketing intermediaries are two-way, or at least they should be, for they should also provide information on consumer feedback for the hotel.

This diagram leaves out one vitally important set of marketing intermediaries, namely past customers. There is much research to show that in leisure, many people make purchase decisions based on word-of-mouth recommendations from other people, or their own past experience.

The marketing intermediaries will vary depending on the type of customer being considered. Most business travellers are reached through their employers and specialist business travel agents, for example, while package tourists are communicated with through travel agents. Independent travellers, on the other hand, may rely heavily on tourist information centres and the media.

There are some differences between the intermediaries used by leisure organisations and by those in hospitality and tourism. The main one appears to be that the ones used by leisure organisations tend to be much more local than those used by tourism and hospitality organisations. This may reflect the fact that leisure products often have a much more local market than their hospitality and tourism counterparts. Therefore, while leisure products such as local authority sports centres use local newspapers, their neighbourhood hotel may be using nationally distributed directories and airlines will be making use of national newspapers in other countries.

There are also some national differences in relation to the use of certain types of marketing intermediaries. For example, in France, travel agents are not as important as intermediaries for tourism products, as they are in the UK.

As we noted at the beginning of this section, organisations can both be marketing intermediaries and use marketing intermediaries themselves at one and the same time. For

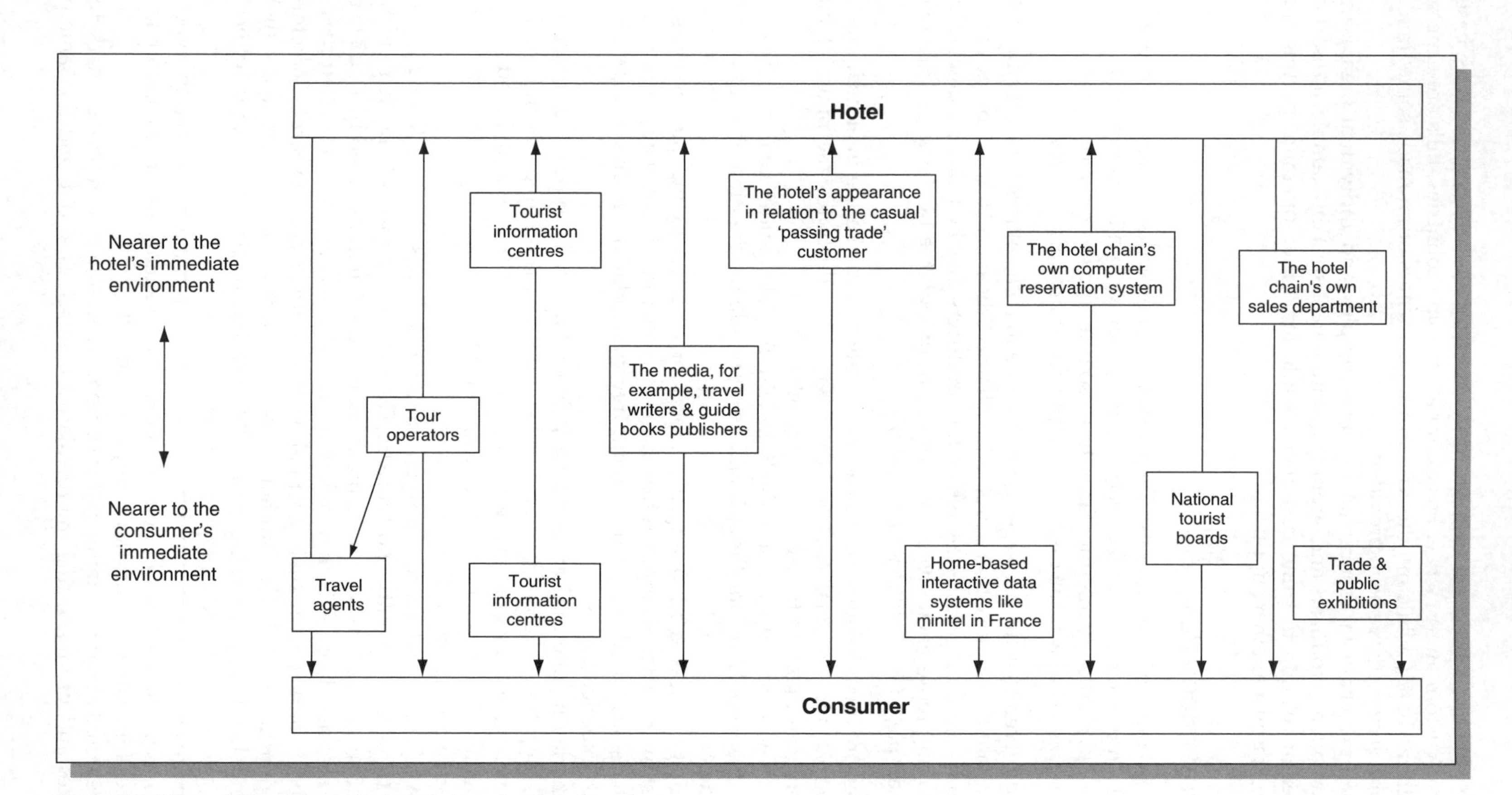

Figure 5.1 The marketing intermediaries of a large hotel chain

example, a tour operator can be an intermediary for a hotel, but also needs intermediaries himself. This also illustrates that there can be more than one layer of intermediaries, in other words, the hotels' message may well reach consumers via both tour operators and then the travel agents which are used by the operator.

Finally, the degree of control and influence an organisation can exercise over its intermediaries does vary dramatically. For example, a hotel has far more influence over the way it is promoted by the company's own sales people than it does over guide books where everything is based on objective inspections.

Existing customers

Existing customers are an important element in the microenvironment of organisations in leisure, because the organisation can influence them in ways which can enhance the effectiveness of its marketing activity.

These ways include:

- Impressing first-time visitors to a theme park, for example, by the quality of product and service offered so that they wish to visit again in the future.
- Encouraging satisfied customers to persuade their friends and relatives to visit a particular hotel or resort, for instance.
- Using incentive schemes to encourage increased use of the organisation's products by existing customers. This is the rationale behind the 'Frequent Flyer Programmes' of airlines and the season tickets offered by some attractions.
- Obtaining valuable data on the nature of the current market for the organisation, from existing customers, which can be used to improve either the product or the way it is marketed, or both.

As these examples illustrate, the relationship between the organisation and its customers is two-way where both influence each other.

Failure to successfully 'manage' existing customers can cause problems for organisations, particularly those which rely on repeat visits. There are times when the wishes of the existing customers can come into conflict with an organisation's desire to attract new customer. For example, removing underoccupied first-class carriages on a train and replacing them with second-class ones because the existing second-class accommodation is not adequate, may upset the loyal first-class passengers who are regular users. This could lead them to changing their mode of travel to the airlines, with a loss of that premium price business for the railway.

The importance of keeping existing customers happy is summed up by the oft-quoted phrase that while a satisfied customer might tell five people about a product, those who are not satisfied will probably tell twenty-five people about their dissatisfaction!

In recent years, the concept of relationship marketing has grown up in leisure as in other industries, in recognition of the importance of managing existing customers effectively.

Competitors

There is a complex interrelationship between an organisation and its competitors. They influence each other in a number of ways including:

- price levels
- product development
- distribution systems

- promotional techniques
- operational practices
- corporate structure and culture.

Strategies in relation to competitors vary between organisations. Some aim for market leadership through innovation while others are content to follow where others lead and learn from their mistakes. Some decide to compete on price while others focus on product differentiation.

While some organisations seem obsessed by their competitors, others seem unaware that they have any competition!

However, for this to be relevant, there has to be competition in the market and that is not true in some sectors of leisure.

Examples of this include:

- The European scheduled airline market where, in spite of the European Commission's 'liberalisation' of the market, there is still no true and full competition. This is partly because many airlines are still in the ownership of the state and receive large public subsidies.
- Local authority leisure provision which is limited by local government boundaries so that one authority will not offer a product in the area of a neighbouring authority. However, there can be limited competition from commercial-sector operators.
- There can also be informal price-fixing in sectors such as hotels in some resorts and urban centres, for instance.

Finally, even if a market is competitive, it is not always easy to identify precisely who its competitors are.

A theme park, let us say Parc Asterix in France could be said to have a myriad of potential competitors, including:

- All other theme parks in the country (Disneyland Paris and Futuroscope, for example), and even theme parks in adjacent countries such as De Efteling in the Netherlands.
- Other attractions in the Ile-de France which are aimed at a similar market, namely families. These might include special events like travelling fairs and circuses or permanent attractions such as La Villette.
- Activities which appeal to families, although they are not formal attractions, and provide opportunities for them to spend their leisure time and disposable income. Such activities might include eating out, strolling in the park or even playing in the garden or on computer games at home.

Furthermore, an organisation might have different competitors for different market segments. For instance, Eurotunnel is probably competing against the cross-channel ferries in the leisure market and the airlines in the business market. The same may well be true in the case of Eurostar.

The microenvironment and national differences

There are some striking national differences in relation to microenvironmental factors. Where they do exist, they are often seen in the following fields:

- Management styles and decision-making structures which are more formal in some countries like Spain, perhaps, than in Scandinavian countries like Sweden, for example. However, this difference is perhaps lessening as modern theories on management style gain broad acceptance across Europe.

- Some elements of the supply chain where differences may reflect differences in contract law and business practice.
- The issue of competition, between countries with different levels of state intervention in the market. The UK for example has consistently, over recent years, reduced its role in the ownership and control of rail travel while in other countries rail operators are still totally state-controlled.

We need to recognise that the microenvironment of organisations has been influenced in recent years by thinking from different parts of the world, including:

- the writings of American management theorist researchers, such as Tom Peters, on corporate culture and structure;
- Japanese theories on supply chain management;
- developments elsewhere in the world, such as the deregulation of the US airline industry in the 1980s which has provided some lessons for the liberalisation of the European air-travel market.

The link between the macro and the microenvironment

There are clear links between the macro and the microenvironment. A few examples will illustrate this point adequately as follows:

- Corporate culture, ideas on management styles and organisational structures are often influenced by social and cultural change such as the growing role of women in business and demographic change.
- Technological developments are often a means by which some organisations can seek to gain an advantage over their competitors.
- Problems with the relationship between suppliers and producers and the need to protect existing customers can lead to political action in the form of legislation, hence the EC Package Travel Directive which was designed to protect consumers and make both suppliers and producers liable for the product they sell.
- Economic recessions can change the basis of competition in a market, where price becomes more important, and can also make organisations more concerned about building brand loyalty amongst their existing customers. It is often more cost-effective to do this than to try tempting people to become new customers in a very competitive market.

Conclusion

The business environment is so complex and diverse that the drawing of all-encompassing conclusions is neither desirable nor possible. The authors will therefore limit themselves to some observations.

- Any picture of the business environment is, like the one presented in this chapter, by definition, dated even on the day when the book is published. The macroenvironment, in particular, is changing dramatically at present, particularly in relation to political change and technological innovation. We may simply be living through an era of rapid change and soon the pace of change may slacken or maybe the business environment of today is the shape of things to come and rapid change is going to be the order of the day in the future.
- At the moment, business environments, particularly the macroenvironment, also vary in many ways between different countries. However, within the European Union, there

are forces at work which are bringing them closer together. Nevertheless, as far as leisure is concerned it is probably still a case of the business environments of Europe rather than the European business environment.
- There are subtle differences between the business environment of tourism and hospitality organisations on the one hand, and leisure organisations on the other. However, overall there are probably more differences between organisations based on their size and type of ownership rather than to which of these three sectors they belong.
- There are many factors at play in the European business environment which have their origin outside Europe. The actions of European leisure organisations are also affecting the business environment in non-European countries.
- Many of the factors in the business environment of leisure organisations are also influencing other sectors of the economy. They are particularly relevant to industries like food manufacturing and retailing, for example, or even education.

These last two points are particularly important, for we should never forget that leisure is a global activity and is part of the broader consumer society as a whole.

Discussion points and essay questions

1. Discuss the current impact of European Commission policies and directives on leisure in Europe, and examine whether or not its influence is likely to grow in the future.
2. Evaluate the factors in the macro or microenvironment which have encouraged some leisure organisations to adopt strategies involving vertical integration.
3. Discuss what you consider will be the three most important factors in the macroenvironment, over the next five years, for *one* of the following organisations:
   (i) Center Parcs, UK
   (ii) TUI, Germany
   (iii) Accor, France
   (iv) Real Madrid, Spain
   (v) Disney World, USA
   (vi) McDonald's, USA.

Exercise

Choose a specific organisation within *one* of the following sectors:

- tour operation
- airline
- accommodation
- arts
- fast food
- sport.

For your chosen organisation, produce a model of its current business environment, including both its macro and the microenvironment.

Bearing in mind its current policies together with trends in the sector, and the world as a whole, produce another model of what you believe its business environment may be in ten years time.

Finally, on one sheet of A4 paper, you should outline the assumptions and evidence on which you have produced this second model.

Part Three

The marketing mix and leisure

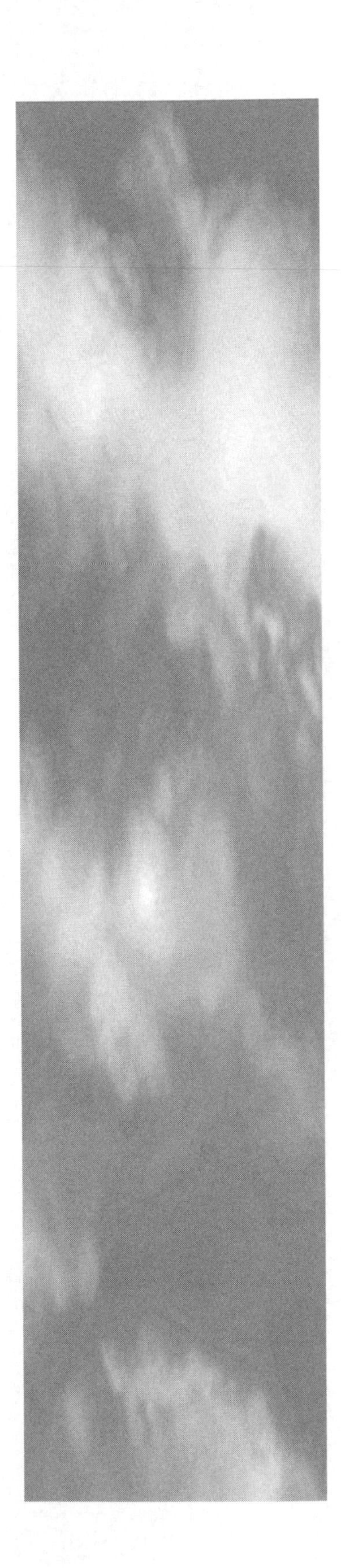

Introduction

This section of the book examines the application of the marketing mix in leisure. In other words, the 4 Ps of product, price, place and promotion.

The chapter will seek to identify similarities and differences in the 4 Ps between leisure industries.

Consideration will be given to how the concept of the marketing mix is changing within leisure, in response to a range of factors, including technological developments.

Where appropriate, the chapter will also endeavour to highlight where there are differences in the application of the 4 Ps between different countries.

Four chapters address the following topics:

CHAPTER 6

Product

Key concepts

The main concepts covered in the chapter are:

- The concept of a product
- Core, augmented and ancillary products
- The benefits customers seek from products
- Branding
- Product and market positioning
- Product life cycle
- New product development.

Introduction

Clearly, the product is at the heart of all marketing in leisure. It is what gives consumers the benefits they are seeking and its production and delivery is the core activity of all leisure organisations.

The aim of this chapter is to examine the nature and scope of the product in leisure. It will therefore cover the following topics on the supply side:

- the types of products offered in terms of their designed characteristics, both tangible and intangible;
- the service element of the product;
- branding and package positioning.

We will also look at products from the demand point of view, for example, in terms of the benefits consumers expect when they purchase a product.

Later, the chapter will go on to look at the concept of the product life cycle, in terms of its application to leisure products. This will include a discussion of relaunches, together with a number of recent examples.

What is a product?

The term 'product' is commonly used and often defined. Many definitions of the word exist, none of which are universally accepted. A large number of them are derived from manufacturing industries:

> A product is anything that can be offered to a market for attention, acquisition, use or consumption that might satisfy a want or need. It includes physical objects, services, persons, places, organisations and ideas.
>
> Kotler and Armstrong (2004)

In recent years, the growth of service industries has led to new concepts of product, linked to the fact that in most services, the product is a mixture of tangible goods and intangible services. This concept has come to be known as the 'product/service mix' from which other definitions have flowed.

> The product/service mix is the combination of products and services aimed at satisfying the needs of the target market.
>
> Renaghan (1981)

Dibb, Simkin, Pride and Ferrell defined a product as:

> Everything, both favourable and unfavourable that is received in an exchange. It is a complexity of tangible and intangible attributes, including functional, social and psychological utilities or benefits. A product can be of an idea, a service, a good or any combination of these three.
>
> Dibb et al. (2001)

This definition again stresses the tangible and intangible elements of the product/service mix.

Services are, of course, intangible and are the result of the application of human and mechanical efforts to people or objects. Services are often bought on the basis of promises of satisfaction. The holiday brochure, for example, offers you the promise of exotic locations and luxurious hotels. These promises are often strengthened with symbols.

There are a number of special characteristics that make services different from products. Most of them relate to the idea that 'services are consumed in the process of their production' (Sasser et al., 1978). A number of factors make the problems of service marketing very different from that of product marketing. The concepts of *intangibility, inseparability, perishability* and *heterogeneity* have already been explored in Chapter 1.

These factors mean that the staff involved in producing and delivering the product are part of the product itself. The customer is also an inherent part of the production process.

It also means that service products cannot be standardised. This is very important when it comes to the development of quality management systems. The fact that a service is perishable and cannot be stored means that it is often difficult for the provider to manage the balance between supply and demand. Capacity planning and utilisation are therefore vital management tasks.

The intangibility of the service means that the customer cannot inspect the item before purchase. Customers only have a 'feeling' left after consumption of the service. Coupled with this, the service will never be the same for the customer twice. The visitor experience of a restaurant, for example, may differ according to the conditions at different eating occasions.

Service providers do have the advantage of being face to face with the customer. This factor can alleviate some of the added complexities of services marketing if used correctly by the providers.

Work was carried out in the late 1970s and 1980s trying to develop a terminology for service products and there were different views put forward (see Sasser et al., 1978; Grönroos, 1980; Eiglier and Langeard, 1981).

These academics agreed that all services have different elements, which make up the total item which the customer purchases.

Sasser et al. (1978) explained the concept further by reference to the example of an expensive restaurant. In this case there are goods and services on offer which they defined as:

1. The physical items (e.g. food, drink)
2. The sensual benefits or explicit services (e.g. taste, aroma, service)
3. The psychological benefits or implicit services (e.g. comfort, status).

Leisure products and services have a varying degree of tangible and intangible elements in their 'product–service mix'. Shostack (1977), for example, argued that a fast-food outlet has an equal mix of tangible and intangible elements, whereas an airline has a dominance of intangible elements.

The three levels of product

Kotler and Armstrong (2004) expanded their original definition of products to include the service elements. They termed this concept as the three levels of the product. The three levels of the product include the core product, the actual product that includes important features such as the brand name, quality, styling and features, and the augmented product which includes delivery and credit, installation, warrant and after-sales service (Kotler and Armstrong, 2004).

This three-level concept tries to explain the fact that the consumers do not just purchase a product, they purchase benefits such as brand names, service elements and after-sales service.

The core product is what the customer is really buying. It consists of the main benefit or benefits the purchaser identifies as a personal need that will be met by the product.

Marketers need to turn the core product into an *actual product*. The *actual product* will include features, brand name, quality, styling and packaging.

Finally, there is the *augmented product* which includes all the additional services and benefits the customer receives. The augmented product is the total product bundle that should solve all the customers' problems, and even some they have not thought of yet (Lewis and Chambers, 2000).

This model was developed with the manufacturing company in mind. However, it has been adopted, with modifications, to services such as visitor attractions by Swarbrooke as is illustrated in Figure 6.1.

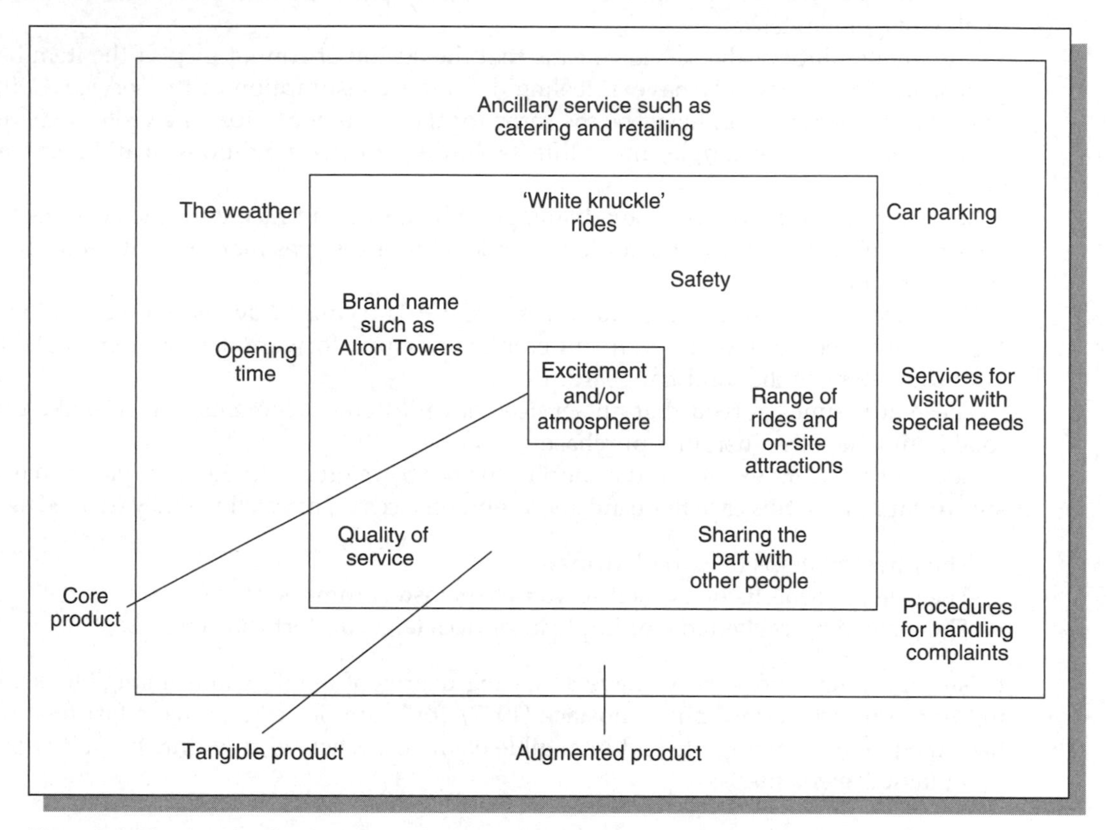

Figure 6.1 The three levels of product – the example of a theme park (*Source*: Swarbrooke, 1999)

Kotler and Armstrong (2004) envisaged that all the elements of the augmented product are under the control of the producer. Swarbrooke (1999) pointed out that for service products such as attractions, some of the elements are outside the control of the service deliverer. The weather, for example, is outside the control of a visitor attraction provider, but may have potential positive or negative effects on sales.

The concept of the augmented product has also been developed for leisure organisations. According to Buttle (1986), every hotel offers the same core product but this is modified and enhanced to make it more attractive to the target market. Competition, he says, takes place largely at the augmented level. This includes added services such as customer recognition and information services in accomodation and customer advice and overall quality of services in the food and beverage area of the business.

Lewis and Chambers (2000) stressed the three levels of product for hospitality products. They talk about formal, core and augmented product. They define the formal product as the thing that the customer thinks they are buying – it is in fact what the customer can easily articulate.

In truth, however, it may not be the real underlying reason why the customer is buying the product. They may be covering up their real needs which are deep-seated ones.

The consumer benefit concept

Customers who are buying leisure products are buying benefits not products.

Bateson (1977) argued that it is only from the idea of a consumer benefit that the service concept can be defined. As Bateson said:

> For any firm the 'consumer benefit concept' will be a bundle of functional, effectual and psychological attributes. It is important to separate this consumer benefit concept from the product itself.

The task of the marketer of leisure products and services is to try and understand the benefits which customers seek. This is a complex issue, because different customer groups who purchase the same service may be seeking different benefits.

As an example, some of the main benefits sought by groups of customers with different characteristics for a fast-food chain are shown in Table 6.1.

Customer characteristics	Main benefits sought
Young, adventurous personalities	Excitement New experience
Fashion-conscious	Status Being seen taking part in a fashionable activity
Families with young children	Entertainment for children Special events for children Economy Reliability
Health-conscious	Healthy, nutritional food Clean environment
Elderly people	Reliability Safety Economy

Table 6.1 Customers for a fast-food chain and the benefits sought

Clearly this diagram is based on stereotyping. Nevertheless, the idea of using customer characteristics to speculate on the types of benefits particular groups of customers will seek is a useful tool for the development of products and services.

Customer characteristics are only half the story. The second factor which influences the benefits sought is the nature of the product itself. This was developed by Swarbrooke (1999) when he looked at certain types of attractions and the main benefits sought as shown below in Table 6.2.

The key to the success in the development of leisure products depends on the ability to match the product which is offered with the benefits sought by the customers. The matching of the two is a challenging process.

Types of attraction	Main benefits sought
Theme park	Excitement Variety of on-site attractions Atmosphere The company of other users Value for money Light-hearted fun
Beach	Suntan Sea bathing Economy Company of others *or* solitude
Cathedral	History Aesthetic pleasure derived from architecture Atmosphere – sense of peace and spirituality
Museum	Learning something new Nostalgia Purchasing souvenirs
Theatre	Entertainment Atmosphere Status
Leisure centre	Exercise Physical challenges and competing against others Status

Table 6.2 Types of attraction and benefits sought (*Source*: Swarbrooke, 1999)

Branding and packaging

Branding and packaging are part of the product's tangible features that help customers decide which products to buy.

Branding

Kotler and Armstrong (2004) define a brand as:

> a name, term, symbol or design or combination of them, intended to identify goods or services of one seller or group of sellers and to differentiate them from those of 'competitors'.

Brand names, logos or trademarks encourage people to buy particular products because they give the customers the benefits they are seeking. These benefits may range from familiarity and safety to status and self esteem. Branding offers particular advantages to organisations that are marketing services.

Given the intangible nature of services and the potential difficulty of differentiating one service from another, branding provides a significant method for achieving a degree of product differentiation.

Some leisure organisations have developed a long-term branding strategy. Disney, for example, has developed a brand which offers customers a reliable product linking their film, video and leisure products.

There has also been a flurry of service organisations in the leisure industries, which have been implementing branding strategies in the last decade. Forte, for example, has developed a strong branding strategy. The company has been transformed from the old Trusthouse Forte name into Forte on the back of a well-developed branding strategy. This is allowing the company to develop internationally, which was a key objective of the branding strategy.

Organisations have also tried to use brands to give themselves a perceived improved image with customers. Large football clubs such as Manchester United FC and Barcelona FC use branding to develop a clear positioning statement and brand image.

The value of established brand names such as Holiday Inn and McDonald's is closely related to the perceptions of consistency and quality which they represent internationally. The disadvantages of branding are that it requires large amounts of expensive advertising. This means that brands tend to be developed by large organisations because they have the necessary money.

Branding in Europe

Research has shown that consumers in Europe express a growing desire for brands which are well known. The Frontiers Research (1991/92) which was an international survey in Europe showed that consumers in European countries thought that 'buying branded articles is best as you can trust the quality'.

There are questions now being asked about the future of brands in the postmodern era. This is a theme that will be covered later in the book.

Branding does, at the moment, however, seem to offer an organisation one way of developing a European or international marketing strategy. A multinational company can sell an identical product in the form of a global brand throughout the sales area. Alternatively, it can make modifications which will take account of local differences in taste. Local brands, although different in name, may also be endowed with corporate values (Wolfe, 1991).

The central question, therefore, is whether an organisation marketing across national boundaries should *standardise* their product offering and branding or *customise* it to meet a local set of conditions. This will be dependent on the type of product which is marketed and the local conditions in the individual countries in which the product is sold.

The *standardised* approach has been characterised by the Holiday Inn company. The company recognised early on that the Holiday Inn concept and brand could be standardised and offer customers high levels of service on an international basis.

The *customised approach* has been characterised by the Hilton International hotel company. Hilton have developed a Japanese service brand 'Wa No Kutsurogi' meaning 'comfort and service' to appeal to Japanese business and leisure travellers (Bould et al., 1992). This has been adopted both in Japan and internationally. It consists of distinctive service features and special amenities appealing to both Japanese business and leisure travellers.

The company has customers that approach their products and services within brand identities. The customised approach is also used by exclusive service organisations such as luxury hotels.

New approaches in branding

There are indications that other sectors of the leisure market are beginning to recognise the value of branding. Some recent examples of the use of branding are shown in Table 6.3. Branding is being used as a marketing technique by an increasing number of leisure organisations.

Sector	Examples	Comments
1. Destination sector	Spain – España Passion for Life	Tried to improve image of Spain
	The 'English Riviera' Torquay, Brixham and Paignton	Local authority created 'brand'. Intended to revitalise the market
2. Accommodation sector	Formule 1	Development of the budget sector – Accor
3. Attractions sector	Alton Towers Air Oblivion Tussauds Group	The use of the rides as brands in their own right
	Port Aventura	Development of a new attraction in Spain
4. Transport sector	Eurostar, Eurotunnel	Development of the cross-channel tunnel project
5. Tour operators sector	TUI – Thomson	Rebranding of the package holiday company due to change of ownership

Table 6.3 Use of branding techniques in leisure organisations – some recent examples

Packaging

Packaging is very easy to understand in the case of manufactured goods, but what does it mean in the context of services? The answer will depend on what we mean by packaging. Packaging could be defined as the thing which makes it easier for customers to pick up, transport and use the goods.

Packaging in the context of services could therefore include:

- the use of brand names and logos;
- attractive entrances;
- attractive merchandising materials;
- the use of other organisations such as tour operators or ticket companies to sell the product as part of a package.

Product positioning

One of the key objectives of an organisation's marketing strategy must be to create a favourable impression of the organisation's products amongst their target customers. This is achieved by creating a favourable *product position*. It is also often referred to as *market positioning*. Kotler and Armstrong (2004) defined *product positioning* as:

> The way the product is defined by consumers on important attributes – the place the product occupies in the consumers' minds relative to competing products.

Market positioning

It is defined as:

> arranging for a product to occupy a clear, distinctive, and desirable place relative to competing products in the minds of target consumers. Formulating competitive positioning for a product and a detailed marketing mix.

The logic is that if a product is perceived to be exactly the same as the competitors' product, then the customer will have no reason to buy or use it. The positioning of a product means that the organisation must identify how it is going to offer greater value to chosen segments. This may be by charging lower prices than the competition or, alternatively, it may offer greater values associated with the product.

Effective positioning therefore, involves the organisation *differentiating* its products and services in the eyes of the target customers. Dibb et al. (2001) suggested that there is a step-by-step approach which can be used to develop a positioning plan. This approach involves seven key steps as follows:

1. Define the segments in a particular market.
2. Decide which segment(s) to target.
3. Understand what the target consumers expect and believe to be the most important when deciding to purchase.
4. Develop product(s) which cater specifically for these needs and expectations.
5. Evaluate the positioning and images, as perceived by target customers, of competing products in the selected market segment(s).
6. Select an image which sets the product(s) apart from the competing products, thus ensuring that the chosen image matches the aspirations of the target customers.
7. Tell target customers about the product (promotion) as well as making it readily available at the right price. This is the development of the marketing mix.

A good example of a positioning strategy in the hospitality industry has been the development of the *budget hotel chains*.

In the last decade, the budget market has become the fastest growing hotel sector in the UK and much of Europe. The opportunity for budget hotels was first recognised by companies such as Forte and Whitbread. The opportunity could be shown on a positioning map which showed consumer preferences in the UK hospitality market and made predictions about the way these would move (Figure 6.2).

Research had shown that customer preferences in certain market segments were moving towards a hotel offering a lower service element, but offering accommodation of a reasonable standard and lower price. This was clearly a marketing opportunity.

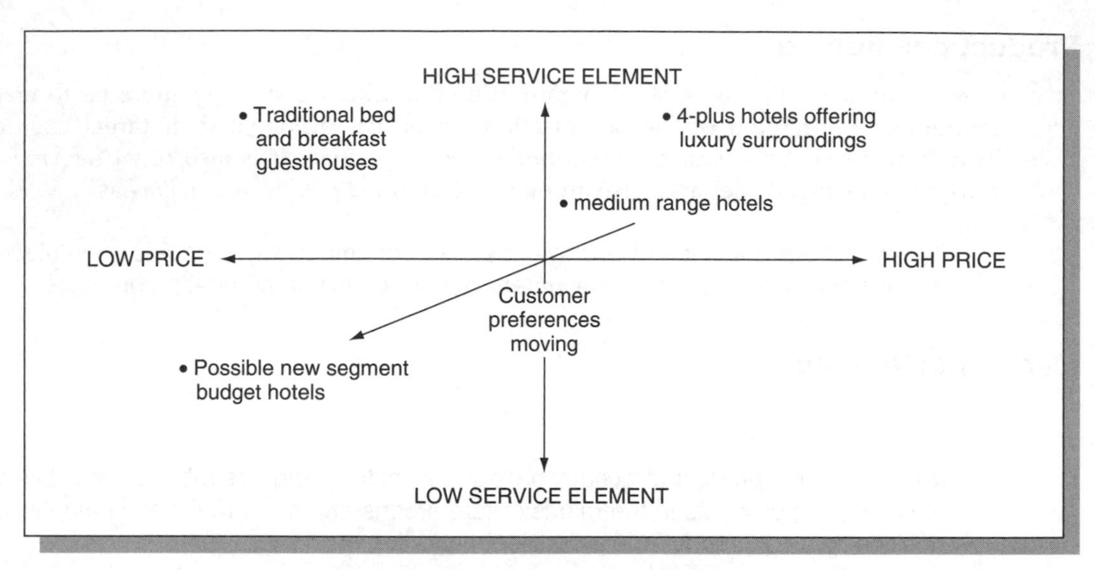

Figure 6.2 The position map of the UK hospitality industry prior to the development of the budget market

As a result of this, many hotel companies have now entered the budget sector in Europe and the major players are shown in Table 6.4.

Ten top budget-hotel brands in Europe by room capacity

Rank brand	Owner	Number of hotels (Europe only)	Number of rooms (Europe only)
1. Ibis	Accor	528	51,731
2. Formule 1	Accor	325	23,538
3. Campanile	Group Envergure	369	22,582
4. Etap	Accor	229	16,489
5. Comfort Inn	Choice	236	14,417
6. Travel Inn	Whitbread	266	14,000
7. Premiere Classe	Group Envergure	176	12,337
8. Travelodge	Compass	208	10,825
9. Kyriad	Group Envergure	170	9,090
10. Express by Holiday Inn	Six Continents	91	8,374
Total		2,598	183,383

Source: Mintel (2002a,b)

Table 6.4 Key players in the European budget market

The companies involved in the budget sector are now having to differentiate their products by developing their brands. This is particularly important because Holiday Inn Worldwide entered the UK market, in the early 1990s, with its own budget brand, Holiday Inn Express.

This budget market trend has been seen even more strongly in the airline sector, with companies like Southwest in the USA and Ryanair in Europe.

The product life-cycle concept

There is a view that products pass through stages during their lifetime like people. This is the basic premise of the product life-cycle concept, which was originally developed by marketing academics for manufactured goods.

Figure 6.3 shows the traditional model for the product life cycle. Table 6.5 illustrates the suggested characteristics and strategic responses at each stage of the life cycle.

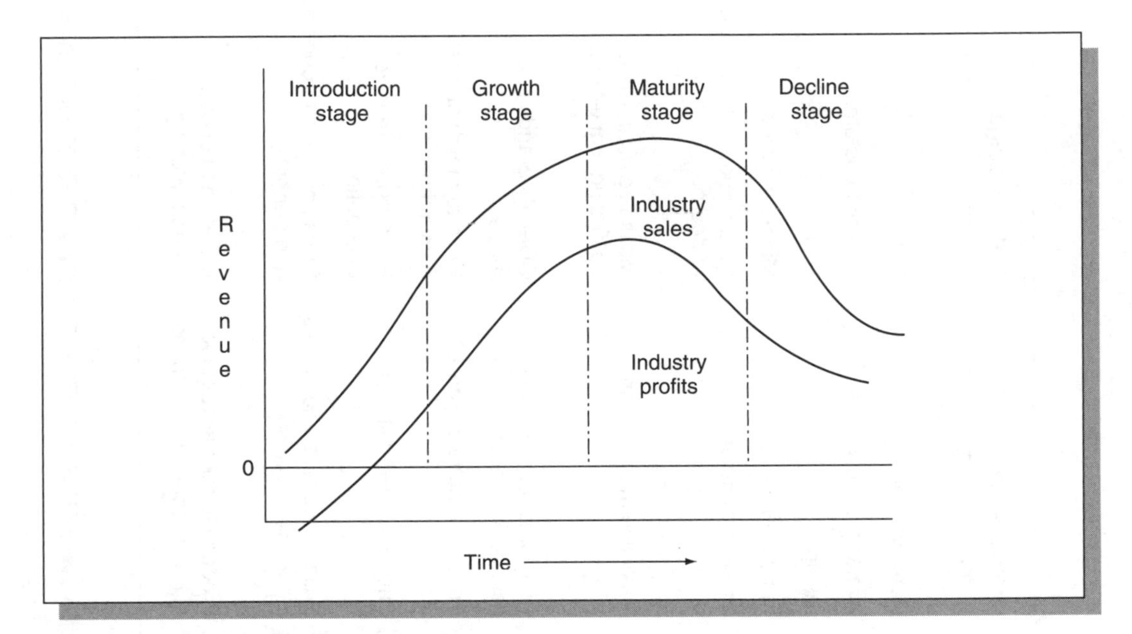

Figure 6.3 The four stages of the product life cycle

There are a number of general points which can be made about the product life-cycle concept:

1. It is suggested that the product life-cycle curve will be 'S'-shaped.
2. The product life-cycle curve will comprise four stages which have been termed – *introduction, growth, maturity* and *decline.*
3. Product life cycles are used to describe the sales behaviour of items, brands, types, lines or classes of products.
4. The characteristic of each of the four stages are shown in Table 6.5. The cycle begins with *product innovation* and *development* when an organisation finds an acceptable new product idea. The *introduction* stage is characterised by slow growth and low profits. If the new product is successful it then enters the *growth stage* which is characterised by rapid sales growth and increasing profits. The product then enters the *maturity stage* in which sales growth peaks and profits stabilise. The company seeks here to renew sales growth typically relaunching the product. Finally the product enters a *decline stage* in which sales and profits decrease. The organisation then has to decide whether to get rid of the product, maintain it or harvest it.

	Introduction	Growth stage	Maturity stage	Decline stage
Characteristics				
Sales	Low	Rapidly rising	Peak	Declining
Costs	High per customer	Average per customer	Low per customer	Low per customer
Profits	Negative	Rising	High	Declining
Customers	Innovative	Early adopters	Middle majority	Laggards
Competitors	Few	Growing number	Stable number beginning to decline	Declining
Marketing objectives				
	Create product awareness and trial	Maximize market share	Maximize profit while defending market share	Reduce expenditure and milk the brand
Strategies				
Product	Offer a basic product	Offer product extensions, service, warranty	Diversify brands and models	Phase out weak items
Price	Use cost-plus	Price to penetrate market	Price to match or best competitors	Cut price
Distribution	Build selective distribution	Build intensive distribution	Build more intensive distribution	Go selective: phase out unprofitable outlets
Advertising	Build product awareness among early adopters and dealers	Build awareness and interest in the mass market	Stress brand differences and benefits	Reduce to level needed to retain hard-core loyals
Sales promotion	Use heavy sales promotion to entice trial	Produce to take advantage of heavy consumer demand	Increase to encourage brand switching	Reduce to minimal level

Source: Horner and Swarbrooke (1996)

Table 6.5 Summary of product life-cycle characteristics, objectives and strategies

Problems with the product life-cycle (PLC) concept

The PLC concept has been criticised by various individuals and groups. The most notable critics were Dhalla and Yuspeh (1976) who argued that

> The PLC is a dependent variable, which is determined by marketing actions; it is not an independent variable to which companies should adapt their marketing programmes.

A further problem is the fact that a temporary plateau in sales can be interpreted as the onset of maturity, which may be an incorrect assumption. Some attractions, for example, have a bimodal profile because they achieve an initial spectacular success which is temporary and are relaunched based on a change of core attraction or massive new product developments (Swarbrooke, 1999). The use of the PLC curve as a predictive tool for this type of organisation would be very dangerous indeed.

The shape of the PLC curve may not always follow the 'S'-shape model; it may be bimodal with two peaks or skewed, perhaps with the growth not occurring until the last quarter of the timescale. Researchers have found that there are at least seventeen variants on the shape of the PLC curve (Tellis and Crawford, 1981).

A fad product will show a shape which represents a period of rapid growth followed by an equally rapid collapse.

Product life cycles can vary dramatically in their time span. Products which are sold in a traditional market may have life cycles measured in decades, whereas fashion-conscious products may last only a few weeks. Studies have also shown that products do not necessarily pass through all the four stages (Rink and Swan, 1979).

Many products sold by organisations seem to have been in the mature stage of their life cycle for decades and show no signs of entering the decline stage. Old traditional hotels such as Claridges and The Savoy are examples of these types of organisation. Many products may also never enter the growth stage because they are refused in the marketplace, and fail.

Decline of products is not inevitable. Most products in their mature stage are subject to intense marketing activity to delay any possible loss in sales. It is possible to recycle the PLC curve through further growth stages by increasing promotional spend, relaunching the product or introducing the product to new markets and users.

The relaunch of major attractions is an example of this type of activity. Most attractions introduce new rides, use new technology or improve support services to effectively relaunch the product. The introduction of a new 'white knuckle' ride at a major attraction is often enough to revitalise the market. One such recent example of this is the introduction of the 'Oblivion' and 'Air' rides at the Alton Towers theme park in the UK.

Hotel chains have also shown evidence of relaunching their products. The introduction of leisure and health facilities within hotels has been a good example of this type of activity.

Organisations can therefore change the course of the life cycle if they adopt a proactive approach to marketing activity.

There is also some dispute about the level to which the PLC concept applies. It seems to have validity at the product level, rather than the brand level (Dhalla and Yuspeh, 1976). This means that it could be applied to the beer market in general, for example, but it would be less appropriate to apply it to an individual brand such as Guinness.

The PLC cannot be used to predict when a product will move from stage to stage. This means that it only has limited value to product planners. Product life cycle is therefore a generally accepted, if rather simplified, model which can form the basis for discussion when formulating marketing strategies for individual products.

Product life cycle in use

The PLC concept cannot be applied to all products and its value to managers is highly questionable. However, it may allow an organisation to focus attention on some of the key characteristics related to their products and markets. Let us consider an example of how a tour operator could use the PLC concept in setting their marketing strategy. This example is shown in Table 6.6.

Product	PLC stage	Marketing strategy
1. Summer sun holidays or fully inclusive tours (FITs)	Maturity	Relaunch with new destinations Heavy promotion
2. Long-haul holidays or FITs	Introduction stage	Heavy promotion to build awareness Sales promotions with distributors
3. Fly-drive holidays to the USA	Growth stage	Use promotion to build brand preference Work on improving distribution

Table 6.6 Example 1 – The tour operator product-portfolio

Product development

Product innovation and product development are key activities in which any organisation in the leisure industry should be involved. The PLC concept has shown that products at some time enter maturity and decline. It is very important that an organisation replaces these outdated products with new innovative ideas.

Sources of new ideas

New product ideas may arise from sources both inside and outside the organisation. The sources of new product ideas for a hotel are shown in Figure 6.4.

Inside the organisation

New product ideas can come from a number of sources inside the organisation. It will be one of the key functions of the *marketing department* to think about the future and the sort of products and services to be introduced. They should also be thinking about how to continually upgrade their current products and services to meet new customer demands.

The marketing department may look to ideas which originate from other sources in the company. If the hotel is part of a chain, new ideas may be generated at the *head office* level. They will supply new ideas and may even help the hotel staff with their introduction.

Figure 6.4 Sources of new product ideas for a hotel

If the hotel is strongly branded or franchised, it is likely that new product development will be controlled by the head office of the company, so that quality standards can be maintained throughout the group.

This is common in other organisations. The introduction of new products at the McDonald's chain, for example, is managed by the head office of the organisation. If the hotel is part of a large group, ideas may come from other parts of the organisation. The ideas which are generated from other companies in the group can be particularly different and innovative if they originate from another country.

Other *staff members* can also have ideas for new products. These ideas should be encouraged at all levels in the organisation and discussed openly and fairly. The senior managers of the company are also likely to be travelling abroad, both for work and in their leisure time. They should be encouraged to look around at other leisure organisations and consider any new ideas which arise.

Outside the organisation

Many new ideas originate from outside the organisation. The marketers in the organisation must make sure that they have the system in place to make themselves aware of these potential sources.

Customers can provide a vital source for new product ideas, particularly if the organisation carries out regular quantitative and qualitative market research surveys with them. A customer, if questioned, can often talk about the area in the hotel where improvements could be made, and offer very good suggestions for possible additional products and services which would make the hotel more appealing. Corporate customers can also give some vital clues to the ways in which the hotel could improve and offer new products and services. Corporate customers can represent a substantial part of the hotel's sales, and so it is particularly important that their ideas are considered.

Suppliers can offer new product ideas. This may be in the form of new recipe ideas, or new equipment which will offer competitive advantages.

It is important to consider that the supplier may not necessarily come from the traditional sources of food materials or equipment. The suppliers of compact business equipment, for example, have allowed hotels to develop sophisticated 'business' rooms where customers can use computers, faxes, etc. This has offered the leading hotels, in this market, significant competitive advantage.

Marketing intermediaries can offer new product ideas. The travel agent, for example, can suggest new ideas for destinations to the tour operators as a result of customer feedback.

Competitors can also give the hotel ideas for the future. These may range from the marketers at the hotel noticing the new products that the competitor is developing, and copying these, to working in a joint venture to produce new products. Joint ventures can be particularly attractive if the development costs are very large.

Management consultants can be used as a source of new ideas. Consultants are often used if the organisation is planning major investment in new products. If the hotel is planning to build a major extension to the hotel, or build a new hotel, it will often employ a management consultant to provide ideas and carry out feasibility studies.

Advertising agencies can also help with the development of new markets and products. They can be employed to look at one particular market area and make suggestions for future developments. Using an agency, such as a management consultant, has the advantage of a 'fresh pair of eyes'. This may give the organisation very innovative and novel ideas which they had not previously thought of.

Private research organisations are a source of ideas for new products. They produce commercial reports which the hotel can buy and use. The hotel can also commission a specially designed piece of research on a particular market and use a private research organisation to carry out the work.

Phases of new product development

Once the new product idea has been generated, the organisation must then develop the idea so that it can be commercially sold. This involves a series of steps which the organisation must carry out. These steps are summarised by Dibb et al. (2001) as being:

1. Idea generation
2. Screening
3. Business analysis
4. Product development
5. Test marketing
6. Commercialisation.

Idea generation

The organisation must seek to generate new ideas. The sources of ideas have already been discussed. There will be more ideas generated than it is possible for the organisation to develop, so there must be a screening process carried out to select possible developments.

Screening

All the new product ideas should be screened to see which are acceptable for the organisation. This may involve talking to experts or market research with potential customers. This stage should prove that the ideas are suitable for the market.

Business analysis

Once the ideas have been selected, the organisation should carry out a business analysis to see whether it is possible commercially to develop the idea. There should be estimates of predicted cost involved in the development. This should be balanced against the likely pay-back period. It is only then that the organisation can assess whether it can afford to carry on with the development process.

Product development

Work will now be carried out to produce a prototype product. For manufactured goods this involves the production of a mock-up product which can then be researched. In service organisations, the prototype ideas may be in the form of an illustration. Some of the elements of the new service may be produced. If the new service involves a new uniform for example, this can be made.

Test marketing

This is a very important step in the development process. The product or idea is test marketed before it is introduced commercially. In a hotel chain this could involve testing the new product or service idea in one hotel to see whether it is well accepted. This will prevent the organisation from spending the large amounts of money involved in the final commercialisation process, if the product or service idea is generally rejected.

Commercialisation

This is the final stage when the new product idea is introduced to the market. This will usually involve a large marketing budget to promote the product or service, and build customer awareness and preference.

New product development in the leisure industries

New product development in the leisure industries often involves investment in new facilities which involve a high capital.

The 'feasibility study' is carried out to test the potential viability of the proposed project as accurately as possible before a decision is made to go ahead. This is particularly important if the project involves a large financial risk for the organisation, in the case of attractions, for example. The stages of the feasibility study have been discussed by Swarbrooke (1999). These stages are summarised below in Figure 6.5, in relation to a visitor attraction.

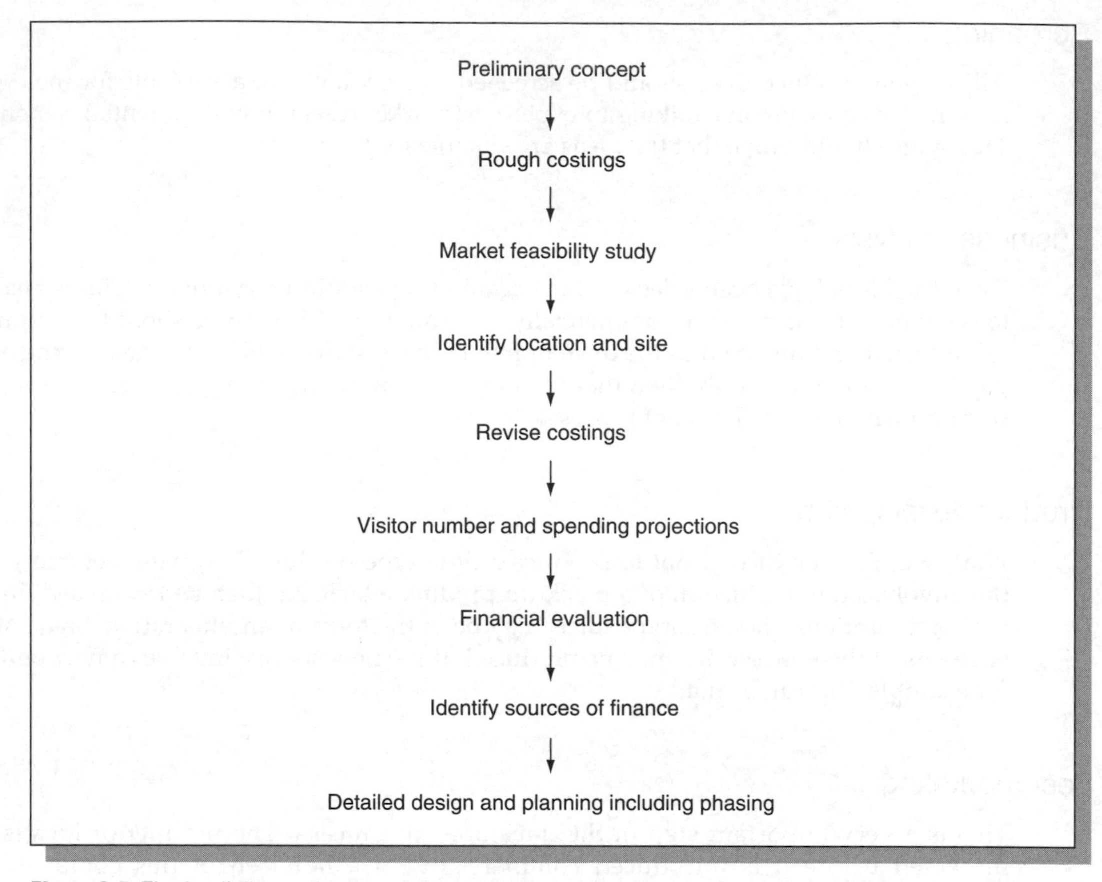

Figure 6.5 The feasibility study process for a visitor attraction (*Source*: Swarbrooke, 1999)

Key points of the feasibility study include:

- The penetration factor – predictions for actual numbers of people in each market segment.
- Analysis of where the visitors will come from and when they will come.
- Analysis of capital costs and estimated likely income. Breakeven analysis may be used here.

However, where relatively little capital or financial risk is involved the 'feasibility study' process may be shorter, quicker and far less structured. An example of this might be the decision to offer a new destination within a tour operator's summer sun programme.

Recent trends

One of the recent trends in the leisure markets has been the move of the large service organisations to European and international trade.

International trade in services is becoming more and more important because of several important market developments (Segal-Horn, 1989). There is an increasing importance in the use of information technology in services which leads to important economies of scale in service delivery. This is most notable in the airline reservation systems.

A second development that Segal-Horn (1989) identified, which encourages the internationalisation of services is the emergence of the 'global consumer'. This was looked at earlier in the book. A third factor is the internationalisation of business itself, which leads to the internationalisation of services that are provided to the business traveller. The international hotel chains such as Hilton, Marriott and Intercontinental are examples of this development.

Segal-Horn (1989) also argued that the internationalisation of services is just as important as the internationalisation of manufacturing firms. It is however, different, she says. In services the internationalisation process tends to involve the replication of the 'service delivery outlet' such as with a McDonald's hamburger outlet or a Hilton International hotel. This internationalisation is often accompanied with a global marketing campaign.

International services also offer a uniform quality of service delivery no matter where they are delivered.

If it is in fact possible to internationalise services, on the supply side, then will the demand for these products be there? European market segments were identified many years ago by the Italian research company Eurisko (reported by Martin, 1988) as being:

- Young people who have unified tastes across Europe in music, sports and cultural activities.
- The trendsetters and social climbers are wealthier and more educated Europeans who tend to value independence, refuse consumer stereotypes and appreciate exclusive products. Europe's business people are a rich target audience of approximately six million people. They are about 40 years old, regularly travel abroad and have a taste for luxury goods.

The targeting of these market segments will involve a special approach in marketing strategy. It has been recognised that it is easier to standardise products and brand names, for example, than it is to standardise pricing and distribution (Porter, 1986). This is shown in Table 6.7.

Easy to standardise	Difficult to standardise
Brand name	Distribution
Product positioning	Personal selling
Service standards	Training sales personnel
Warranties	Pricing
Advertising theme-packages	Media selection

Table 6.7 Marketing activities according to ease or difficulty of standardisation

Many organisations in the leisure industries own the outlet, and this theoretically makes the introduction of European and global products an easier task. Once the target market segment has been identified, the organisation can develop its product strategy to meet their needs (Guido, 1991). These developments should focus on gaining production and marketing efficiencies. As more uniform standards are introduced, the organisations are more and more likely to target pan-European consumer segments. The ownership or acquisition of strong national brand names will allow the organisation to develop these throughout Europe with common positioning strategies.

It is more important to carry out detailed market research to assess the potential response of customers to new products in all the countries in which the organisation intends to market the product or service.

Patenting and branding of products is also a significant step in the product development phase.

It is easy to be carried away with these new developments, and assume that the market will be dominated by large companies targeting the new Euro-consumers with specifically designed products. It is important to remember, however, that although this is an important recent trend, the industry is still fragmented and dominated by small operators. These two areas of business must continue to develop products hand in hand.

Conclusion

This chapter has explored the issues in relation to the product element of the marketing mix. It has looked at the augmentation of products and their positioning. The final part of the chapter has looked at the recent trends in products for leisure organisations.

Discussion points and essay questions

1. Discuss the main characteristics and components of *either* the tour operation product *or* an arts product, *or* a sport product.
2. Examine the 'consumer benefit' concept in relation to *either* a visit to a theme park *or* the purchase of a fast-food meal.
3. Critically evaluate the current role of branding in the leisure industries.
4. Discuss the value of the PLC concept for marketers in the leisure sector.

Exercise

Choose one of the following products:

- an airline flight
- a theatre performance
- a package holiday or FIT
- a restaurant meal.

For your chosen product you should identify the core, actual and augmented elements of the product.

You should present your ideas in diagram form, together with a brief explanation of the content of your diagram.

CHAPTER 7

Price

Key concepts

The main concepts covered in the chapter are:

- Traditional methods of calculating price
- Strategic and tactical pricing policies
- State intervention in the setting of prices
- Differences in pricing issues.

Introduction

Pricing is clearly crucial to the successful marketing of any product or service. The prices that the organisation charges for its products and services must strike a balance between gaining acceptance with the target customers and making a profit for the organisation. Even for organisations that do not seek to make a profit, the pricing of products and services is the key to ensure uptake.

The decision to offer a product free to encourage uptake should however also be a conscious decision which is made by the management of the organisation in question.

Price is a key element in the marketing mix because for a profit-motivated organisation, the prices which are set relate directly to the total revenue and ultimately the profit made by the organisation.

Many features of leisure markets mean that pricing of their products and services is an extremely complex procedure.

This chapter will concentrate on the following issues:

- general pricing theory and the methods used for calculating prices;
- the use of pricing as a tactical and strategic weapon in the marketing process;

- the special nature of leisure organisations and the effect that this has on pricing policies;
- the international dimension to pricing policy.

General pricing theory and the methods used for calculating prices

The setting of prices for products and services will be influenced by the objectives of the organisation which is marketing them. The organisation may have the objective of gaining maximum turnover and profits which will result in a satisfactory return on investment for the shareholders. The organisation may be trying to build market share which will have an effect on the pricing levels. Some organisations, particularly in the public sector, are simply trying to encourage usage of their products and services by customers. This may result in the product or service being offered free of charge or at reduced rates. Whatever the strategy of the organisation is, clear pricing objectives should be established before price levels are set.

The key factors which determine pricing decisions have been summarised by Dibb et al. (2001). These factors have been summarised as:

- Pricing objectives
- Organisational and marketing objectives
- Channel member expectations
- Costs
- Legal and regulatory issues
- Competition.

Organisations should relate the prices set to the organisational land marketing objectives. The Formule 1 chain which is the budget chain of the French company Accor, for example, is priced so that it is seen to be of outstanding value for money. The prices are set at a reasonable level in relation to product quality. This will allow the company to develop this brand at the budget end of the market in line with their other brands.

Other organisational goals may include the desire to be the brand leader in the marketplace. This will usually be reflected in higher prices in the long term. An organisation may sustain a decrease in prices in the short term to try and gain market share in the long term. This strategy can be particularly relevant when an organisation is launching a new product or entering a new geographic market area.

Pricing objectives

The organisation should also have clear objectives in relation to their setting of prices. Organisations may have different objectives when prices are set. The organisation may have a requirement for a certain target return on investment. There may also be a requirement to achieve a certain sales volume and a particular market share. The organisation may also be looking for a period of rapid and sustained cash flow which can only be achieved by a temporary boost in sales.

For nonprofit making organisations, the objectives may be to encourage new users. This is often achieved by *differential pricing strategies* where different prices are charged for different market segments. Museums, for example, often charge a lower admission fee for students, senior citizens and the unemployed to try and encourage people from these market segments to visit the museum.

Costs

The setting of prices should incorporate a calculation of how much it takes the organisation to produce the product or service. If the company is profit-oriented, a margin will be added to the cost price to derive the selling price. An organisation can decide, however, to sell below cost price for a period of time. This is often referred to as a *tactical price reduction*. Tactical price reductions can be made, so that the competitor's prices are temporarily matched or undercut with the aim of increasing sales, generating cash flow and gaining market share.

Other marketing mix variables

Pricing decisions always have an interaction with the other elements of the marketing mix, namely promotion, distribution and product design. Consider the example of the luxury hotel room for which the organisation charges the customer a high price. This high price has to be reflected in other elements of the marketing mix. It is vital that the quality of the hotel service meets the expectations that the high price has generated in the minds of the customers. Price usually gives the customer the first indication of perceived product quality.

Distribution of the hotel room is likely to be via an exclusive distribution channel to reflect the high quality image and resulting high price. This may involve the use of a high quality marketing consortium, for example, where luxury hotels are grouped together for distribution and selling purposes.

The promotion of the hotel will have to reflect the quality and prices. The messages which are given in the promotion will have to be of an appropriate standard. A high level of personal service will probably be included as part of the promotional package. This example has shown that pricing of the product or service is inextricably linked to all the other marketing mix variables.

Channel member expectations

A marketer must consider the intermediaries in the distribution channel when pricing a product or service. The sale of luxury hotel rooms by a particular organisation, for example, may be carried out by an exclusive travel agency chain. This intermediary in the distribution channel will expect certain things from the hotel in relation to price.

The travel agency will have to make a profit in the form of a commission when the hotel rooms are sold. It will probably also require discount from the hotel, particularly if it sells a large number of rooms and obtains rapid payment from the customers. The agency will also require service support in the form of promotional materials and training. All of these items will cost the hotel money and they will have to be incorporated in the setting of the room rate and prices for other ancillary services.

Buyers' perceptions

The prices which are set for products and services must reflect the customers' perceptions in the target market.

It is important that the customer sees the link between the price charged and the product quality. In the tourism sector, for example, customers expect a high level of service and special features if a high price is being charged. This can be seen in the airline sector, where airlines charge high prices for first-class services.

In return, the customer expects excellent check-in and waiting facilities, extra comfort and room on the plane, and extra personal service and benefits such as free drinks. A speciality holiday company can also charge high prices if they are offering a higher level of service and individually tailored products.

The most important issue is whether the customer perceives that the price which they have paid represents good value for money and matches their quality perceptions.

Competition

Organisations which sell products and services in competitive markets try to win customers from rival competitive organisations. This can be achieved in one of two ways:

1. *Price competition* is the first method that can be used. It involves offering the product or service at a lower price than the price charged by the competition.
2. *Nonprice competition* involves the organisation trying to increase market share or sales by leaving the price of the product or service unchanged but persuading the target customers that their offering is superior and has advantages compared to the competition.

Whether an organisation uses price competition or nonprice competition depends on the state of the market. In a very competitive marketplace, the organisation is more likely to resort to intense price competition to sell their products and services.

In an oligopolistic market where there are few competitors, there is little to be gained from price competition and organisations tend to concentrate more on nonprice competition.

The UK package tour operators are a good example of a sector which has competed largely on the basis of price, to date. The focus in the past few years has been on price cutting to gain market share and the customer, for package holidays in the UK has come to expect substantial discounts. In an industry where operating margins can be as low as two per cent, spiralling discounts can be very damaging. The latest idea in this market is to try and compete more by nonprice methods rather than the damaging discounting methods. TUI, for example, is adopting a strategy of nonprice competition. This has involved the company in differentiation of identifiable products and the development of a clearer branding strategy which is reflected in the advertising campaigns.

Organisations can use a mix of price competition and nonprice competition for different market areas. *Selective discounting* can be a method which is used in service marketing to overcome the particular problems of perishability of services coupled with the burden of large fixed overheads. These ideas are explored in Figure 7.1.

A *seasonal discount* is often used by organisations marketing leisure products, to try and even out demand across the year. Hotels and airlines, for example, offer seasonal discounts in their slacker periods. Package holiday companies offer discounts in the form of free child places to encourage sales at quieter periods of the year.

Legal and regulatory issues

There may be legal and regulatory restrictions which control the ways in which an organisation fixes prices. An organisation such as a gallery or museum, for example, which is heavily subsidised by the government, may be pressurised to keep prices low to encourage visitors to come and visit. The state may also regulate prices which are charged by commercial organisations.

A 300-bedroom hotel

Target: 90% occupancy on weekdays (Monday–Friday)
: 20% occupancy on weekends

Current Sales: 70% occupancy on weekdays
: 10% occupancy on weekends

Hotel has large fixed overheads

Marketing solution

Week (Monday–Friday) sales	**Weekend sales**
• Nonprice competition	• Price competition
• Price competition e.g. conference discounts	• Selective discounting – weekend breaks – discount breaks for business travellers
• Intensive promotion	
• New distribution channels – central reservation system	• New distribution channels

The hotel uses a mix of price and nonprice competition to reach target. Selective discounting addresses problem of perishability.

Figure 7.1 Examples of pricing for a hotel

On a more general level, legal restrictions are often placed on the practice of price-fixing and collusion. The Monopolies and Mergers Commission in the UK, for example, looks at the likely effect on price and the possibility of price collusion when a merger or takeover is proposed. If this results in a significant reduction in competitiveness in the marketplace, then they may take action to prevent the merger or takeover occurring.

Different approaches to pricing

Organisations involved in the marketing of leisure products use different methods of calculation to set prices. Pricing methods fall into three main categories:

- Cost-oriented pricing;
- Demand-oriented pricing;
- Competition-oriented pricing.

Cost-oriented pricing

This is where the price of a product or service is calculated and a margin applied to derive a selling price. This is the simplest method of pricing and is often used by companies for calculating prices. It has the disadvantage of not taking into account the economic aspects of supply and demand and often does not relate to pricing objectives. The concepts of mark-up and gross profit margin are not used extensively in the leisure industries.

In *cost plus pricing* the seller's costs are calculated and the price is set by adding a specific amount which is often referred to as a margin.

Mark-up pricing is a commonly used method of pricing in retailing. The product's price is determined by adding a predetermined percentage of the cost of the item. Mark-ups obviously have to reflect the strategic vision regarding costs, risks and stock turnovers.

Demand-oriented pricing

This method allows for high prices when the demand is high and lower prices when the demand is low, regardless of the cost of the product or services. One example of this is London hotel accommodation which is much more expensive in the summer than in winter due to demand. Price for seats in football grounds are more expensive when a major game is played. Demand-oriented pricing allows an organisation to charge higher prices and therefore make higher profits as long as the buyers value the products above the cost price.

Competition-oriented pricing

The firm fixes the prices of the products and services in relation to the competitor's prices. This has the advantage of giving the organisation the opportunity to increase sales or market share.

In practice all three influences are often taken into account when settling prices. In the long term, organisations need to more than cover their costs if they are going to prosper. In doing this they can only go so far as competition and the prevailing strength of the market will allow.

Skimming and penetration pricing

Organisations use different methods of pricing when they are launching new products. If the organisation is launching a product which is fairly unique and therefore offers the customer a new experience, it can afford to operate a *skimming pricing policy*. This is where a high initial price is charged in the hope of gaining maximum profit at the early stages of the product's life.

A specialist tour operator can afford to charge higher prices for the unique service which it offers to the customer, particularly when new product development results in a holiday with unique features.

If the organisation, on the other hand, is trying to get maximum distribution for the product or service in the initial stages, it will probably price at a lower level to get maximum sales and market share. This method is commonly used in the marketing of FMCGs where rapid distribution stocking is essential for the success of the product. This is referred to as *penetration pricing*. The fierce price competition which the UK tour operators have operated over the past years is an example of this.

Discriminatory pricing

Organisations can often alter their prices charged to suit different customers, products, locations and times. Discriminatory pricing means that the organisation is selling a product or service at two or more prices, despite the fact that the product costs are the same. Discriminatory pricing is often used by organisations that are involved in the marketing of leisure products for a variety of reasons. Consider the examples which are shown in Table 7.1. Each of the organisations shown is using discriminatory pricing for different reasons.

Example	Pricing method	Reasons
Leisure centre	Customer segment-based	To encourage groups to take part in sporting activities To increase revenue in quiet periods
Theatre	Location-based	To encourage different customer groups into the theatre To get maximum revenue at each performance
Hotel	Time-based	To encourage 'off peak' visitors To cover high fixed overhead costs

Table 7.1 Discriminatory pricing examples

The leisure centre is trying to encourage groups in the community to take part in sports activities at the leisure centre. This may be profit motivated, in that the centre can at least recoup some of the costs of opening the centre during quiet periods. The managers of the leisure centre may also have a social aim of trying to encourage particular groups of people who do not currently engage in recreational activities to use the centre with the aim of increasing general health in the population as a whole.

The theatre will charge different prices for seats according to their particular location. This will enable the theatre to get maximum sales at any one performance and target different market segments.

Hotels also use discriminatory pricing, based on particular times. This will encourage off-peak visitors and help to contribute to the high fixed overheads costs.

The market must be segmentable if discriminatory pricing is going to be an effective strategy. Care should also be taken that discriminatory pricing does not lead to customer resentment. It should also be legal. The deregulation of the airline industry in most European countries has meant that discriminatory pricing has been used much more in this market.

Strategic and tactical pricing

Organisations in the leisure industry operate pricing policies at the strategic and tactical level. This is very much because the nature of the business means that prices have to be set a long way in advance so that brochures and guides can be published. This means that prices are determined early on in the planning of the marketing strategy. These pricing decisions will be based on the long-term view of corporate strategy, product positioning and value for money in the marketplace.

The fact that organisations, however, cannot stock services means that if the planned supply exceeds demand in the marketplace for whatever reason, the organisation must try to sell excess capacity. This means that the organisation has to resort to tactical pricing strategies often in the form of discriminatory pricing or discounting.

One of the best examples of tactical pricing techniques are the moves the UK-based package tour operator makes in response to a lack of demand. Last-minute highly discounted selling of package holidays in the UK to generate extra bookings has almost become the norm in the market. This has led analysts to worry that the long-term profitability of these package holiday companies will decline, because the customer has come to expect last-minute bargains and has therefore changed their purchasing habits. The only way out of the aggressive price discounting strategy it seems is to increasingly differentiate the product in the marketplace. The question is whether customers who are used to aggressive price discounting will accept this type of strategy.

The dumping of airline seats at heavily discounted prices is another good example of tactical pricing. The purchase of airline seats from newspapers, teletext services or bucket shops means that the customer can often get a substantial last-minute price reduction. This ensures that the airline fills the empty seats, which would otherwise represent lost revenue.

Hotels have also become skilled at operating last-minute tactical pricing methods to fill unoccupied rooms. The customer can often negotiate a substantial reduction on the rate if they ring the hotel during the evening that they want to stay.

This use of tactical pricing techniques means that pricing of leisure products is an extremely complex and difficult task, which requires a great deal of knowledge of the market, ongoing customer demand and trading conditions.

The special nature of leisure organisations and the effect it has on the pricing policy

We have already seen in this chapter that the fixing of prices for leisure organisations is a difficult task which involves strategic and tactical measures. This section will now consider the special nature of the organisations involved in the sector and the effect that this has on their pricing policies.

It was recognised by Cowell (1984) that the special characteristics of services means that prices are influenced. He grouped the impacts of these service characteristics into five categories which are summarised as follows:

1. Service perishability means that prices have to be adapted to meet fluctuating demands.
2. Customers can delay or postpone the use of services and may choose to perform them for themselves. This leads to keen competition between service providers.
3. Service intangibility has many price implications. The higher the material content of the service, the greater the tendency will be to standardise prices. Prices are often negotiated between buyer and seller.
4. Where services are homogenous, price will be highly competitive. The more unique a service is, the greater will be the discretion in pricing. Price will be an indicator of quality and reputation of the organisation.
5. The inseparability of the service from the person providing it places limits on the market that can be served. The degree of competition operating within these limits will influence the prices charged.

Adapted from Cowell (1984)

The characteristics of services, outlined by Cowell, indicate the importance of differentiating the service offered to gain competitive advantage and therefore give the organisation more discretion in pricing. This is particularly important in service markets where perishability is common. The special nature of travel and tourism products, in particular, has been considered by Middleton and Clarke (2001) and these characteristics are shown in Figure 7.2.

- High price elasticity in the discretionary segments of leisure, recreation and vacation travel markets.
- Long lead times between price decisions and product sales. Twelve months or more are not uncommon lead times when prices must be printed in brochures to be distributed months before customer purchases are made, as is typically the case for tour operators.
- No possibility of stockholding for service products, so that retailers do not share with producers the burden and risk of unsold stocks and tactical pricing decisions.
- High probability of unpredictable but major short-run fluctuations in cost elements such as oil prices and currency-exchange rates.
- Near certainty of tactical price-cutting by major competitors if supply exceeds demand.
- High possibility of provoking price wars in sectors such as transport, accommodation, tour operation and travel agencies, in which short-run profitability may disappear.
- Extensive official regulation in sectors such as transport, which often includes elements of price control.
- Necessity for seasonal pricing to cope with short-run fixed capacity.
- High level of customers' psychological involvement, especially with vacation products, in which price may be a symbol of status as well as value.
- The high fixed costs of operation, which encourage and justify massive short-run price cuts in service operations with unsold capacity of perishable products.
- High level of vulnerability to demand changes reflecting unforeseen economic and political events.

Figure 7.2 The characteristics of travel and tourism services that influence pricing (*Source*: Middleton and Clarke, 2001)

Figure 7.3 shows some of the difficulties in the fixing of prices for leisure products in general. Swarbrooke (1999) illustrated the difficulty of setting prices for a visitor attraction product with reference to six main features. These are summarised in Figure 7.3.

These features illustrate the complexities which are involved in the setting of prices for an attraction product, which relate both to the supply side and the demand side of the market. On the demand side, the customer often expects entrance to an attraction to be free. If the customer expects to pay, their total price for their time spent at the attraction may include a sum of nondiscretionary and discretionary spending. On the supply side, the attraction which is in the public sector may never have had to set market prices. This will often lead to an awareness of competition by the manager of the attraction. It may also lead to general complacency in the management team and an almost total ignorance of customer needs.

The main complication in leisure pricing is the role of *state ownership and regulation*. Some examples will illustrate this point as follows:

- The public sector owns, and subsidises, elements of the leisure product, namely museums, galleries, leisure centre and theatres, for example. Due to these *subsidies* and the social objectives of many of these public-sector bodies, a market price is not charged for the use of these products.

  These subsidies will usually hold down the price for all customers. In addition, concessions may also be made to allow people from disadvantaged sectors of society to pay an even lower price than other users for using these products, in the belief that they may otherwise not be able to use them. Such groups might include students, the elderly, disabled people and those who are unemployed. Concessions are offered either because it is thought morally wrong that such people should be deprived of the opportunity to use these products because they cannot afford the normal price, or

1. Many of the organisations that operate attractions in the public sector are subsidised and do not look for an economic rate of return.
2. The 'price' of buying the attraction product usually has three components, namely:
   - the direct cost of using the attraction, for example, the entrance charge at museums
   - the cost of extra discretionary purchases made by visitors such as meals and souvenirs
   - the cost of travelling to and from the attraction which can often be far greater than the direct cost of using the attraction.

   The many possible permutations of these three costs makes the pricing issue a very complex one.
3. Some attractions operate an all-inclusive price covering all on-site activities, facilities and services, while others charge on an item-by-item basis.
4. A number of attractions have no entrance or usage charge at all. For example, most natural attractions, some man-made attractions like churches and country parks, and many events are to all intents and purposes, free except for the cost of travelling to and from them.
5. The lack of perceived competition in some sectors of the attractions business and confusion over what exactly constitutes competition in other sectors makes it difficult to operate pricing based on what competitors are charging.
6. The prices charged for direct use of the product tend to vary depending on who the customer is, with discounts being offered to groups, and concessions being offered for families, the elderly, students, and those who are unemployed.

Figure 7.3 The features which explain the difficulty in fixing the price of the attraction product (*Source*: Swarbrooke, 1999)

because the product is thought to be so beneficial that everyone ought to be encouraged to use it. This is true of leisure centres, because of the health benefits they can bring, or the cultural enrichment that is thought to be gained from visiting an art gallery, for example.

- These state subsidies are often seen as unfair by private-sector providers, offering similar products, who have to make a profit to survive and who do not receive any state subsidies.

The decision on what should be subsidised and what should not be subsidised is a political choice, and is often based on historical factors and tradition. In the UK, for instance, opera is heavily subsidised while cinema receives much less subsidy. Swimming pools often receive large subsidies but local bingo clubs do not. Subsidy is often used to maintain the viability of operations. If consumers were asked to pay the true cost of providing the product, it would not be a viable activity.

Subsidies take a number of forms in leisure. This may be direct like those outlined above or indirect where, for example, the infrastructure in a tourist resort is paid for by local taxpayers. Visitors who use infrastructure such as roads and sewers pay nothing directly towards the cost of providing it; thus they receive an indirect subsidy from the local taxpayers.

The international dimension to pricing policy

Research by Porter (1986) showed that the pricing policy is one of the most difficult aspects of the marketing mix to standardise across national boundaries.

The different currencies and differences in the cost of living in different countries means that it is very difficult to standardise the price for leisure products across the world. Customers in different countries of Europe also have different perceptions of price levels linked to value for money. One example of this is the price which customers are prepared to pay for entrance to premier football matches. Prices in Spain and Italy for entrance to premier football grounds are relatively higher than the prices charged for first division grounds in the UK. This can be explained only by the fact that customer perception of price for football entrance is different in different countries.

The fanatical football supporter will pay any price to see their team. The idea that entrance charges to football grounds should be kept down, as a social service, is also a belief which has had an influence on the development of the market. State regulation can affect the price consumers pay in a number of ways, as follows:

- The levying of *tourist taxes* by which tourists can be asked to make a contribution towards the cost of providing some of the services they require. An example of such a tax is the Taxe de Séjour in France, which tends to be low at a few Euros per person per night.
- State controls on prices, for example in Greece where hotel prices are controlled by the State.
- The traditional regulations of air fares in many countries, through cooperation between the relevant national governments. This often has the effect of making prices higher than they would be if free competition was allowed on the routes. Governments have often used this as a way of protecting national 'flag carrier' airlines, which have usually been state owned. However, this artificial price-fixing is now being tackled, at least within the European Union, through the 'liberalisation' of air travel, which has been part of the creation of a single European market.

In addition, there are often factors that influence price differences between countries in leisure, notably:

- The widely *differing levels of economic development* found in countries affects both the cost of producing leisure products and the ability of people in different countries to be able to afford these products. For example, the lower level of economic development in Bulgaria, compared to Switzerland, is reflected in lower labour costs and hence lower prices for skiing holidays. At the same time, these same low levels of economic developments in Bulgaria, compared to the UK and Germany, make Bulgaria a cheap holiday destination for British and German tourists. However, in time, tourism may help to reduce these differential levels of economic development between these countries. Ironically this could lead to them becoming less attractive destinations for British and German tourists with a resultant loss of revenue.
- *Policies on taxation* and the differentials in those between governments. An example of this are sales taxes (VAT in the UK, TVA in France and so on). These vary dramatically around the world, both in terms of the rate at which they are levied and the range of goods on which they are levied. Some governments have seen such taxes as such a disincentive for tourism that they have cut them on tourist-related services such as hotels, as happened in recent years in Ireland. Within the European Union, there is a move towards harmonising sales taxes across the market states as part of the move towards a single European market.
- Given that leisure is a truly transnational industry, *currency-exchange rates* have an impact on prices. Fluctuations in exchange rates between generating countries and destination countries affect the price of hotel rooms, travel, meals and excursions. Currency fluctuations make financial planning by tour operators difficult and can lead

Pricing issue / Type of product and organisation	Market (M) or Subsidised (S) or Regulated (R) price	Method of pricing	Degree of tactical pricing to stimulate demand at less busy times (high, medium, low)	The emphasis is on discounting (D) for commercial reasons or the granting of concessions (C) for social reasons	Principal external bodies which are beneficiaries of a proportion of the income generated by the sale of the organisation's products in addition to suppliers	Opportunities for adding value	How similar are the pricing issues within the sector across Europe Very similar (V) Quite similar (Q)
State owned scheduled airline seat	M/R/S	Competitive cost plus	Medium	D	Taxes paid to government bodies. Commission paid to marketing intermediaries	Offering FITs	V
Hotel chain bedrooms	M (R in some countries)	Competitive cost plus	High	D	Taxes paid to government bodies. Commission paid to marketing intermediaries. Shareholders' dividends where appropriate	Restaurant meals and mini-bars	V
Tour operators FITs	M	Competitive cost plus	High	D	Taxes paid to government bodies. Commission paid to marketing intermediaries. Shareholders' dividends where appropriate. Financial bonds	Excursion programme	V

Theme parks	M	Competitive cost plus	Low	D	Taxes paid to government bodies. Shareholders' dividends where appropriate	Corporate hospitality catering	V
Private taxis	R (in most places in Europe)	Fixed price set by licensing authority – operator has no freedom to fix prices	Not applicable	Not applicable	Fees paid to licensing authority. Taxes paid to government bodies	Not applicable	V
Local municipality museum	S (for there may be no charge made)	Where there is a charge fixed, the price is to allow the organisation to operate within its budget	Low	C	Contribution to the overall costs of the municipality	Guided visits	Q
Public-sector theatre	S	The price is fixed to allow the organisation to operate within its budget	Medium	C	Fees paid in return for the right to use copyrighted material such as plays and music	Pre- and post-performance suppers	Q
National park	No direct charge is made for using a national park	Not applicable	Not applicable	Not applicable	Not applicable	Charges may be levied for the use of car parks, the sale of publications and guided tours	V

Table 7.2 Pricing of leisure products in Europe

to supplements being charged to customers if the fluctuations are substantial and to the detriment of the tour operators. Within the European Union, therefore the introduction of the Euro has had significant implications for the leisure industry in the twelve countries in which it currently operates.

One other interesting aspect of pricing seen in some poorer countries in Europe is *differential pricing*. In other words, situations where an identical product is sold at one price to local people and at another, usually higher price, to nonlocals. This system reflects a belief that these 'foreigners' are more affluent than the locals and can therefore afford the higher price. It may also, however, be a function of growing impatience with tourists on the part of local people, and a desire to make them pay higher prices, almost as a form of punishment.

Finally, we must note that in some cases, the direct price is charged for using a product in leisure, although indirect costs will be incurred by the user, for example, travel costs. Such products include entrance to a tourist destination such as a seaside resort, and some attractions such as public-sector museums, traditional facilities which take place in the street and natural phenomena like beaches.

Conclusion

Organisations involved in the marketing of leisure products find that pricing is a difficult and complex strategic task. Pricing is used both as a strategic and tactical weapon in the marketing process. Standardisation of prices across the world is very difficult due to differences both in the supply and demand side of the market. Different countries have different economic conditions and the level of competition in any particular market will vary from country to country.

The levels of state intervention in pricing policies varies in different countries. All of these supply side factors will influence the prices which organisations can charge for products. On the demand side, the presence of the Euro-consumer or global consumer has already been evaluated. Despite the growth of this target group, there are still marked differences in consumer perceptions in different countries to prices and perceived value for money. This is particularly noticeable in certain markets, for example, leisure products.

A summary of the pricing for different categories of product in the leisure industry in Europe is shown in Table 7.2. This shows the complexity of pricing for different kinds of organisation and the impacts the European dimension has on these processes.

Discussion points and essay questions

1. Critically evaluate the different methods of calculating prices. Outline what you believe would be the most appropriate method or methods for calculating the price of *one* of the following products.

   (i) A restaurant meal;
   (ii) An airline seat;
   (iii) A theatre ticket.

2. Discuss the ways in which the public-sector intervenes in the pricing process of the leisure sector in different countries.
3. Explain the differences between strategic pricing and tactical pricing in the leisure industry.

Exercise

You should select both a public- and a private-sector organisation within leisure.

For your chosen organisations, you should discover the method, or methods, of pricing they use and the factors they take into account when fixing their prices.

Finally, you should attempt to identify, and explain, differences in approaches adopted by your two chosen organisations.

CHAPTER 8

Place

Key concepts

The main concepts covered in the chapter are:

- The main distribution channels in leisure
- The impact of technology on distribution systems
- The growth of direct marketing
- Factors which influence the type of distribution system in different sectors and different countries.

Introduction

Place is clearly a crucial aspect of marketing, for consumers may like a product and be willing to pay its price, but if they cannot gain access to it no sale will result.

In this chapter, we will explore the nature of place, or distribution, in leisure. In particular, consideration will be given to three aspects of distribution, namely:

(i) the distribution channels which operate in the leisure sector and the role of marketing intermediaries, such as travel agents;
(ii) the growth of direct marketing, where producers communicate directly with potential consumers, without the involvement of intermediaries;
(iii) the development of distribution channels in leisure.

One clear theme that will be developed during the chapter is the increasing influence of technological developments on the distribution system in leisure. These include computer reservation systems and multimedia systems, for example.

The distribution of leisure products can take two forms, like that of other products, namely:

- directly from the producer to the consumer;
- indirectly from the producer to the consumer via one or more intermediaries.

The distribution channels which operate in the leisure sector and the role of marketing intermediaries, such as travel agents

The distribution of leisure products takes place using distribution channels. Distribution channels can take two forms, namely:

- directly from the producer to the consumer;
- indirectly from the producer to the consumer. When the product is distributed indirectly, there are one or more intermediaries that are involved in the distribution channel.

An organisation may use one or a combination of direct and indirect distribution channels. The choice of these will depend on the costs involved, the predicted levels of success, the degree of control and the level of service required. The market characteristics will also determine the type of distribution channel which is used. In the tourism industry, for example, many domestic producers, such as small hotels, bed and breakfasts, travel companies and holiday centre companies, sell their products and services directly to the customer.

Direct sale has been helped with the growth of sophisticated targeting techniques for direct mail and the use of advanced distribution technology. The products which constitute the outbound tourism market, however, are almost exclusively distributed directly via a series of travel agents. The travel agent acts as a retailer for the tour operator who negotiates the package from different suppliers and presents the finished result in a brochure.

A simple distribution channel consists of a producer who sells directly to the final consumer or uses intermediaries. This is shown diagrammatically in Figure 8.1.

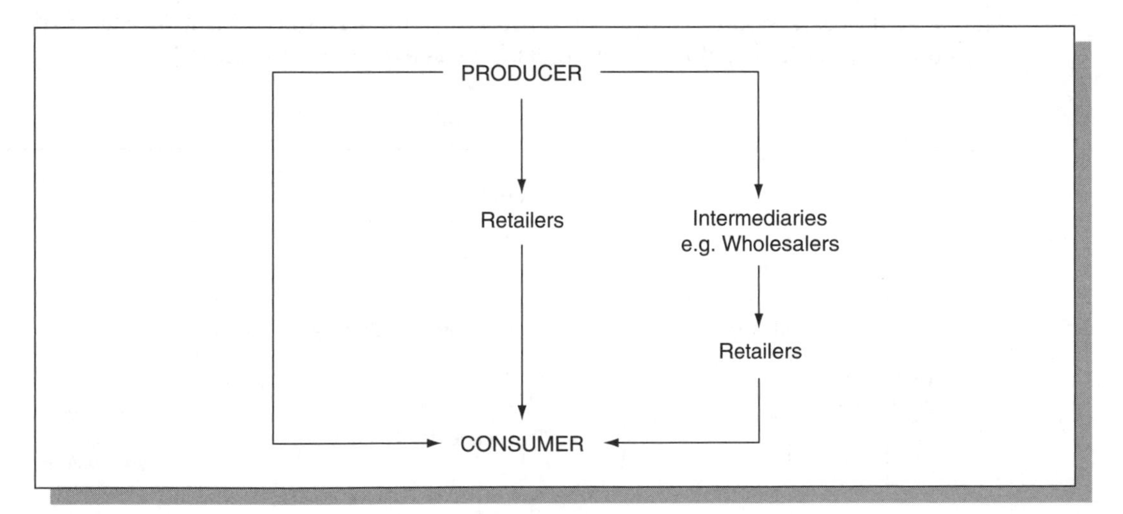

Figure 8.1 An example of different distribution channels

A wholesaler is a trader who buys a product or service in bulk from the producer and then sells them in smaller quantities, especially to retailers. A retailer is a person or business company that sells products or services to the general public. The retail outlet may be in the form of a shop, a multiplex, a supermarket, a restaurant, a public house, etc. The retailer is usually the last link in the distribution channel before the customer. The retailer will carry out a number of functions on behalf of the producer. Figure 8.2 shows the functions which a retail travel agent carries out on behalf of the holiday and travel companies.

- Stocks brochures and information databases
- Provides advice for customers
- Sorts the products ready for display
- Merchandises the products in attractive displays
- Handles promotions on behalf of the companies represented
- Negotiates terms of sale with the customer
- Uses computer reservation systems to expedite customer bookings
- Receives payment from the customer
- Transmits tickets to the customer
- Analyses sales data and provides companies with marketing information
- Offers ancillary products such as insurance and currency exchange
- Handles customer complaints.

Figure 8.2 The functions of the retail travel agent

One of the key activities of the retail travel agent is to merchandise effectively so that consumers are attracted to the shop to purchase. The retail travel agency should also offer a reliable and efficient service which encourages sales. A simplified model of distribution shows that the producer can use a number of intermediaries ranging from a wholesaler to a retailer. This general model can be applied to the leisure industries. Airline seats are a good example of a product which is sold in a number of different ways using specific distribution channels. This is explored in Figure 8.3.

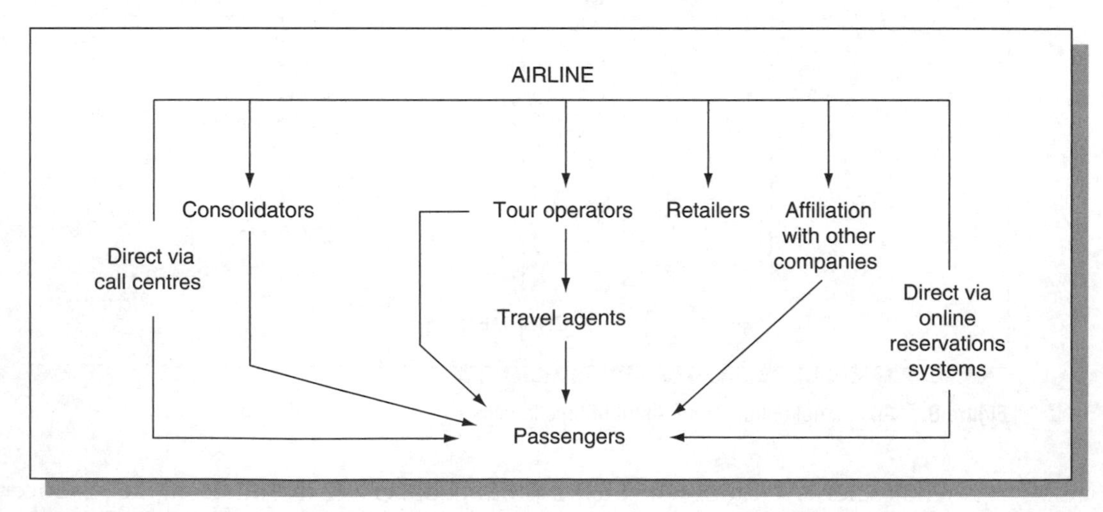

Figure 8.3 The distribution channel for airline seats

The model shows that airline companies use a variety of distribution channels to sell airline seats to the final customer. They sell direct to the passengers using telephone or interactive systems like Minitel in France, for instance. They can also sell tickets in their own retail outlets. Most of the major national airlines have their out shops in major cities of the world. Airlines also sell seats by using the tour operator and travel agents as intermediaries in the distribution channel.

The airline can negotiate directly with the tour operator, which then presents a package that is either directly sold to the passenger, or sold in a travel agency which serves as a retail outlet. Consolidators also act as intermediaries in the distribution channel, and may sell either direct to the passenger or may use other intermediaries. Airlines often form loose affiliations with other organisations in order to sell airline tickets to the final customer.

Increasingly, however, airlines also sell directly to consumers through online reservation systems and call centres.

The distribution of airline tickets also relies heavily on the use of Computer Reservation Systems (CRS). The use of technology in the distribution process is discussed in more detail later in this chapter.

Organisations that are marketing leisure products have developed special systems for distribution. This is probably partly explained by the intangible and perishable nature of services in general.

In some cases the organisations use marketing channels which are similar to those used by more traditional manufacturers. Examples of intermediaries in these types of distribution channels include company owned, managed or franchised networks. In other cases, the organisations rely on unique distribution methods. Examples of intermediaries in these unique systems include consortia, central reservation systems, affiliations and specialist organisations such as tour operators and travel agents.

Organisations must also decide whether they own, manage or franchise the intermediaries in the distribution channel. A major hotel chain which is trying to expand internationally, for example, must decide on whether to own the new outlets itself. There are advantages and disadvantages of ownership which are summarised in Table 8.1.

Advantages	Disadvantages
Owning provides the best chance of controlling the product quality	Capital monies are spread thin. The company may not have sufficient resource to fund rapid expansion plans
Owning gives the company reassurance about consistent quality, internationally	It may be a very slow process to own new hotels, particularly in areas where they have to be built from scratch

Table 8.1 The advantages and disadvantages of expanding a hotel chain by ownership

Organisations can also manage the property owned by others (Table 8.2).

The final method of expansion for the hotel chain is to enter into franchising agreements.

Franchising is an agreement in which a retailer is granted the exclusive rights to retail certain products or services in a specified area in return for a payment. The franchiser grants the franchisee the use of its trademark promotional facilities and merchandising

Advantages	Disadvantages
The next best thing to owning, for quality standards and consistency	Can be difficult financially and can encourage over supply
Much quicker than owning – managing usually involves existing properties	Owners may refuse to refurbish when the managing company considers it is essential
Little capital investment	

Table 8.2 The advantages and disadvantages of expanding a hotel chain by management

expertise. Franchising has been used extensively by hospitality providers as a way of achieving an effective distribution channel in a short space of time. Hotel companies such as Holiday Inn and Accor, and fast-food operators such as McDonald's and Burger King have all used franchising as a way of developing distribution channels in extensive geographic areas. The development of a franchised network will allow the organisation to spread the distribution of the product or service at a rapid rate. It also allows the organisation to use the business experience of others which can be particularly important if the market is one in which the organisation is not totally familiar. The control of quality and consistency may be difficult and will require very carefully designed management systems to cope with this. Organisations often choose to use a mix of ownership, management and franchising agreements to develop an effective distribution system.

Other intermediaries in the distribution channels of leisure organisations include:

Consortia

A Consortium is a loosely linked group of independently owned and managed organisations which join up to operate a joint marketing distribution process. An example of a consortium of hotels is the French Logis de France which represents almost 5000 family-run hotels of varying sizes and quality. The properties are tied together by a logo and the consortium carries out marketing activities aimed at target markets. There is some measure of control placed on membership which differentiates them from reservation networks. Membership of a consortium offers an organisation the advantages of access to improved marketing channels and exposure to more target customers. The organisation can also use a brand identity which will often open up the possibility of distributing on an international basis. The fact that the organisation needs to meet certain standards means that there may be some initial investment requirement.

There is also the danger that the member of the consortium is seen as a chain operation with little individual identity. The way that the Logis consortium in France has tried to overcome the potential problem is by the requirement that each Logis must have a local menu which reflects the local traditional cuisine. This ensures that each Logis has an individual and unique identity. Examples of hotel consortia are shown below in Figure 8.4.

Best Western Hotels
Exec Hotels
Leading Hotels of the World
Quality International Hotels
Relais du Silence Hotels
Relais et Chateaux Hotels
Logis de France
Auberges de France

Figure 8.4 Examples of hotel consortia

Reservation networks

Central reservation systems have become a key factor in the market activity of hotels. Buttle (1986) has identified three forms of organisation for these types of systems:

1. A corporate group
2. A voluntary association or consortium
3. A franchise group.

The large hotel chains rely heavily on computerised reservation systems and the information which these systems generate can provide vital marketing information.

Marriott Hotels, for example, has a CRS which provides the company with a massive database of marketing information which the company uses in a number of ways including accurate targeting of customers and potential customers.

Smaller groups and consortia of hotels have also joined together to establish reservation systems. Leading Hotels of the World, for example, represent a group of luxury hotels which have joined together for reservation and marketing reasons. Hotel reservation systems offer the hotel operator a number of advantages including:

- a convenient method of booking for the customer;
- automatic invoicing systems;
- marketing information opportunity;
- manipulation of room rates to improve profitability.

There are also a number of independent organisations which are using CRS as a central focus for this business. Companies have developed systems that can handle all the bookings on behalf of corporate clients.

The company then has direct links with hotel central reservation systems to arrange the booking. Because of bulk purchasing power, individual corporate clients can be offered more attractive rates than they can achieve for themselves. The reservation system intermediary also benefits through commission on its bookings. Hotels have to decide whether the increased business which they can obtain compensates for the pressure on rates achieved.

Travel agents

A travel agent is an intermediary in a channel of distribution who makes reservations on behalf of companies. The travel agent is compensated in the form of a commission. Travel agencies are nearly always equipped with computer systems to handle the complex set of variables involved in booking individuals, business travellers and group booking. There has been a rapid growth in recent years of call centres and the development of global online retail agencies which sell a mix of products, such as hotel rooms, holidays and airline seats, over the Internet.

Tour operators

Tour operators are also intermediaries in channels of distribution. Hospitality companies often rely heavily on tour operators to distribute their services. Tour operators may provide valuable customers and can generate substantial demand. This can be particularly valuable to hospitality companies at off-peak times although some businesses are permanently positioned towards the tour market. Disadvantages of being dependent upon this market are that numbers arriving can fall short of that anticipated when room allocations are made. Also tour operators often demand extremely competitive rates. A further disadvantage is that tour customers may not 'fit' with other market segments being targeted by the company.

The distribution and selling of leisure products has already been revolutionised by the rapid development of new electronic databases which can be incorporated in telecommunication systems. The future of distribution in these markets will depend on the development of electronic channels of distribution via a multimedia marketing.

Advances in indirect marketing channels in the last few years include CRS and GDS.

Computer Reservation Systems and Global Distribution Systems

These were developed initially by American airlines companies in the 1970s. The CRS was developed to form a link between the airline and travel agency. The first CRS system to be developed was SABRE which was developed by American Airlines in the USA. This was followed by the development of a similar system by British Airways in 1977 called TRAVICOM (now called GALILEO). The European market was developed by a consortia of companies during the 1980s.

These included the consortia of Air France, Iberia, Lufthansa, Finnair, SAS, JAT, Braattens, Icelandair and Linjeflyge forming AMADEUS on the UNISYS system, and the consortia of Swissair, Alitalia, KLM, Sabena, Olympic, Austrian, Aer Lingus, Air Portugal and BA in GALILEO on the IBM system.

The development of GDS came out of the initial development of CRS. Global distribution systems can now provide travel agents with access to the world's most comprehensive range of travel products and services. The top four distribution systems are SABRE, WORLDSPAN, GALILEO and AMADEUS.

These GDS provide the opportunity for the buyers and sellers of travel products to be directly connected together. The systems also allow massive amounts of information to be ordered which can then ease the purchase of the product on a worldwide basis. The information superhighway is therefore going to continue to have a significant effect on the distribution of leisure products. It will also mean that the distribution of many products and services in the industry will be controlled by the owners of the GDS, rather than the owners of the outlets.

Viewdata is information which is transmitted by telephone line on VDI or TV. It excludes teletext (Ceefax and Oracle) which are communicated via TV transmitter. The first system to be introduced in the UK was PRESTEL which was developed by the Post Office.

Thomson, the tour operator, developed its own system and installed direct access reservation systems in a wide network of travel agents in the 1980s. The trend is to link CRS and Viewdata systems together. ISTEL is connected to GALILEO and WORLDSPAN, for example.

Electronic distribution systems will provide an increasingly important role in the distribution of leisure products.

Many organisations in the industry see the development of effective global sales and distribution as being a key strategic objective. Forte, the UK-based hospitality company, for example, began the development of a global sales and reservation network within the hospitality industry back in 1994. Fortress II was developed with a £20 m budget to link all Forte's sales offices and hotels throughout the world. The system interfaces with 400,000 travel agents and all the major airline systems. The company developed a Freephone system which can answer calls in twelve languages. Hospitality reservation systems have become even more far-reaching in recent years.

The growth of direct marketing

The developments in multimedia systems mean that there are many opportunities to develop direct marketing channels. This will effectively remove the necessity for the marketing intermediaries such as travel agents in the longer term.

The opportunities for increased use of direct marketing systems means that it is easier for producers to distribute products and services on an international or European basis.

Point of Information (POI) systems are multimedia computers which stand alone. They can provide the customer with interactive services. Point of Information systems have already appeared in travel agencies in Holland and are being investigated by other tour operators in other European countries.

Point of Sale (POS) systems are systems which are already operating in airports and stations. They allow the customer to buy their ticket directly and can be linked to Electronic Fund Transfer at Point of Sale (EFTPOS) systems for direct payment. These systems can be linked to POI systems so that the customer can buy direct in shops, departure points, or even from home.

The growth of direct marketing via the Internet for all manner of leisure products and services has grown rapidly over recent years and is beginning to be a serious threat to the high street retailers. The Internet allows instant booking and encourages consumers to put together their own leisure products.

The issue of prebooking

Distribution networks tend to exist where prebooking is the norm, which means airline seats, package holidays and hotel rooms for example, in the context of leisure. Where prebooking is rare or there is no provision for prebooking, it is difficult to identify anything that might be termed a distribution network. In this situation a distribution network is unnecessary or impractical. Examples of this in leisure include most visitor attractions and countryside recreation such as walking along footpaths.

Location and 'passing trade'

P for Place in the marketing mix, as we know, means distribution channels. However, in some sectors of leisure, it can literally mean place or location. In sectors such as hotels and attractions, where so-called 'passing trade' is an important element of the market, this is the case. For example, someone walking around Bruges or Barcelona in the evening looking for a hotel room will select a hotel by walking up and down the street until they find a hotel they like the look of and which has vacancies. Here it is the hotel's location which has given the customer access to the product.

The development of distribution channels in leisure

It is well recognised that distribution is one of the most difficult parts of the marketing mix to standardise (Porter, 1986). Distribution channels in different countries of Europe, for example, show very different patterns of development. Retailing has also been developed on an individual country-by-country basis.

The opportunity to standardise the distribution channels for leisure products across Europe depends on a series of factors. These factors are explained below.

The market characteristics

The type of market will determine whether it is possible to standardise the distribution channels. The international airline business, for example, is showing increasing signs of standardisation of distribution with the use of CRS and GDS. Standardisation will become particularly well developed if the channels of distribution become shorter and direct selling becomes the norm. International airlines, however, still use a network of nationally based retailers in individual countries to distribute their product.

The hospitality industry is also beginning to show signs of a standardised approach to distribution. International hotel chains are beginning to develop distribution channels which use CRS and GDS systems, although nationally based retailers are also used to distribute their products and services. Fast-food chains such as Burger King and McDonald's have used a standardised approach to distribution in different countries. The fact that consumers in the market are expected to go to a similar outlet in a major strategic location and buy a similar fast-food product has allowed the fast-food retailers to develop in a standardised way using a variety of techniques, such as ownership and franchising.

The size of the supplier

The size of the supplier of the leisure product will determine the approach to distribution. A small hospitality outlet such as a hotel or restaurant will have a small geographic market area. For this type of operation, distribution or 'place' will literally mean the location of the operation rather than a channel of distribution. The question of whether to standardise or not, will not be an issue for a small business such as this.

The leisure industry has also been characterised by small organisations which are often in the public sector. The small size of these operations such as leisure centres or theatres will also mean that distribution or 'place' refers to the location of the operation.

It is the large organisations in the industry that have the ability to market in different countries which have the most opportunity to standardise their distribution channels. This includes international airlines, international hotel chains and multinational fast-food chains. The use of CRS and GDS will help in this standardisation process.

The availability of standardised distribution channels

If an organisation has the desire to develop a standardised approach to distribution it must have the availability of standardised channels which the customer readily accepts.

Many large organisations in the leisure industry have a mixed approach to distribution because of their portfolio of products and services. In some market areas they may be operating a locally developed distribution system to meet local trading conditions. In other market areas, they may be trying to standardise their distribution channels so that they can compete more effectively.

Bass, for example, the UK-based brewing and leisure group has operated different strategies in different areas of the business. The development of this mixed strategy was discussed way back in 1994.

> The competitive benefits of scale arising from size and brand leadership operate at different levels in different markets. Our strategy is, therefore, to focus our efforts sharply on the level that will yield most benefits locally for pubs and leisure retailing, nationally for brewing and soft drinks and internationally for hotel franchising.
>
> Ian Prosser, Chairman of Bass

In other words, the company's focus was on a local, national and international basis according to the particular market. This is explored in more detail in Figure 8.5.

1. *Local focus*
   Bass Taverns – public houses
   Bass Leisure – bingo, betting, bowling and electronic leisure
2. *National focus*
   Bass Brewers
   Britvic soft drinks
3. *International focus*
   Holiday Inn Worldwide
   International expansion by franchising

Figure 8.5 The strategy of Bass plc for different products and services

Distribution and promotion

It could be argued that the trends we have just been discussing are blurring the distinction between distribution and promotion.

Consumers will increasingly be able to access promotional material, directly, without the need for marketing intermediaries. They will then be able to book or buy the product at the same time through interactive television, for instance.

The choice of focus whether it is local, national or international has been determined by the market characteristics and consumer buying behaviour.

In general there has been a growth in the number of indirect channels of sales in the leisure industry. The closer that these intermediaries are to the consumer, the more local they have tended to become. Travel agents, for example, have developed at a local and national level in individual countries of Europe.

The distribution networks are likely to change in the next few years from the current structure of networks of travel agencies, tour operation, corporate travel offices, hotel chains and government tourism promotion bodies. The role of these members of the distribution channel will change as the communications technology move forward.

Third parties with highly developed software and infrastructure will increasingly control the capacity. The revolution in the distribution of leisure products across increasingly larger geographic areas has only just begun.

Conclusion

This chapter has explored the importance of place in the marketing of leisure products. It has looked at the direct and indirect methods of distribution which exist in the industry. Important issues such as the growth of direct marketing are discussed. The chapter concludes by looking at the development of distribution channels in leisure and the use of information technology to help with this process.

Discussion points and essay questions

1. Discuss the different types of distribution channels which exist within the leisure sector.
2. Critically evaluate the ways in which technological developments are likely to affect the future distribution of leisure products.
3. Examine the factors that will stimulate and obstruct the growth of direct marketing in the leisure sector.

Exercise

Choose *either* of the following pairs of organisations:

- a mass market tour operator and a niche market specialist tour operator;
- a major international hotel chain and a small local private hotel;
- an international sports team and a small community-based sports team.

You should produce, for each organisation, a model of their distribution network. You should then identify the similarities and differences between the distribution networks of the two organisations and account for the differences.

CHAPTER 9

Promotion

Key concepts

The main concepts covered in the chapter are:

- The role of promotion within marketing
- The different forms of promotional technique or marketing communication
- 'Push and Pull' strategies
- The stages involved in the creation of a promotional campaign
- The growth of the international media scene
- The legal framework for promotional activities.

Introduction

The previous three chapters have looked at the development of well-designed products and services which are distributed effectively. The effective marketer must also communicate these product and service ideas to the target customers.

Effective communication with target customers is carried out by a variety of methods which in total is referred to as *marketing communication*. This chapter will look at the different methods of promotional techniques which are used by leisure providers.

For many people, marketing *is* promotion, for promotion is the highly visible, public face of marketing. However, this chapter is based on the view that promotion is only one of the four Ps, and is only part of marketing. It is the tip of the iceberg, the part which can be seen by passersby, while only a few scientists have an opportunity, as head of office, to see the whole iceberg.

We will look at the role of promotion in the leisure sector. In doing so, consideration will be given to a number of promotional techniques, including:

- advertising
- brochures
- press and public relations
- sales promotions
- personal selling
- direct mail
- sponsorship
- point of sale material.

The chapter will go onto look at how organisations decide which promotional techniques to utilise and how to combine them in a promotional plan for a particular product.

Towards the end of the chapter, there will be a discussion of the ways in which technological developments are changing the nature of the promotional mix in the leisure sector.

The role of promotion

The role of promotion is to convince potential customers of the benefits of purchasing or using the products and services of a particular organisation. Promotion is defined as:

> The role of promotion is to communicate with individuals, groups, or organisations so as to directly and indirectly facilitate exchanges by informing and persuading one or more of the audience to accept an organisation's products.
>
> Coulson-Thomas (1986)

The organisation will use marketing communication methods to take potential customers through a series of steps before they adopt a product or service. These steps can be illustrated below:

Awareness	The potential customer becomes aware of the new product or service. This is often activated by mass communication methods.
Interest	The next stage is to get the potential customer interested in the new product or service. This is often achieved by linking the product or service to a well-known brand name or company name. Mass communication methods are also used at this stage.
Evaluation	The potential customer will then evaluate the product or service offered. This will often involve them referring to reports about the product or service and talking to friends and relatives about its potential benefits.
Trial	The potential customer must then be encouraged to try the product or services. This is the stage in which personal selling and sales promotions are often used to encourage trial.
Adoption	The potential customer is finally convinced that adoption of the product or service is appropriate. This will be achieved by the perceived quality of the product or service. The customer will also talk to friends and relatives to reassure themselves that they have made the right decision. Mass communication techniques will also reinforce their decision to adopt the product or service.

Organisations use marketing communications for many reasons other than simply launching new products. The main uses of advertising, for example, have been explored by Dibb et al. (2001). Clearly the organisation which is using marketing communication will be using a variety of techniques to achieve these particular objectives.

An organisation may, for example, be trying to encourage potential customers to try their product or service at the same time as encouraging their existing customers to purchase or use the product and service again.

The main uses of advertising:

- Promote product organisations and causes;
- Stimulate primary and selective demand;
- Offset competitors advertising;
- Aid sales personnel;
- Increase use of a product;
- Remind and reinforce;
- Reduce sales fluctuation.

Source: Dibb et al., 2001

Different methods of marketing communication

Organisations use different methods of marketing communication to achieve their aims. It is important that they choose the correct mix of the different methods to achieve an effective *promotional campaign*. The different methods of marketing communication are shown in Figure 9.1.

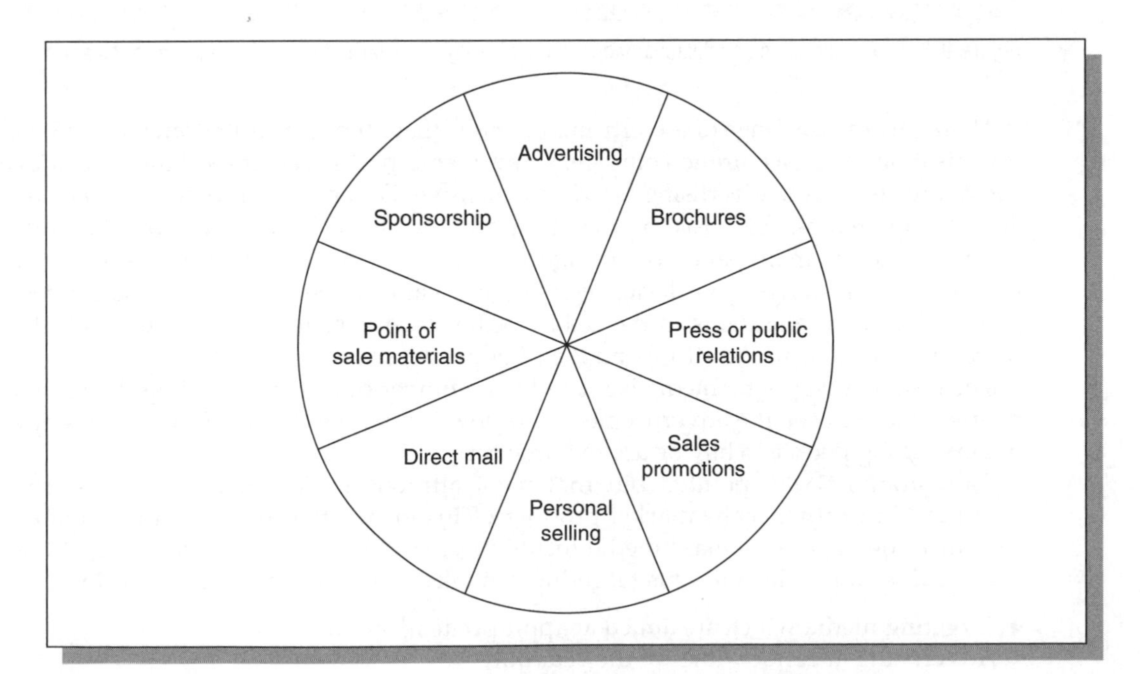

Figure 9.1 The different methods of marketing communication used by organisations

Advertising

Advertising is a paid form of non-personal communication about an organisation's products or services which is transmitted via the media of television, radio, newspapers, magazines, public transport, outside displays and catalogues. Advertising has been defined by Kotler and Armstrong (2004) as:

> Any paid form of non-personal communication and promotion of ideas, about goods, or services by an identified sponsor.

The choice of media to be used will depend on the objective of the campaign and the budget to be spent. Organisations often use a variety of methods and techniques at the same time to meet their marketing objectives. There are both advantages and disadvantages of using advertising as a method of marketing communication. These are summarised in Figure 9.2.

Advertising has the advantage of targeting large audiences via different methods, but it is expensive to design and implement and it is often difficult to monitor its effectiveness.

Advantages

- It is very flexible and can target large audiences or more precise market niches.
- Can be cost efficient as the aim is to reach a large number of people at a low cost per person.
- The message can be repeated regularly and via different medias, e.g. TV, magazines, outdoor displays, etc.

Disadvantages

- Expensive to design and carry out, particularly on primetime television.
- Relatively difficult to monitor its effectiveness. This is because the aims of advertising are often long term in nature.

Figure 9.2 The advantages and disadvantages of advertising as a method of marketing communication

There are a wide range of advertising methods that an organisation can use. Some large organisations such as airline companies and theme parks, and important special events can afford television advertising which is expensive. Other smaller organisations may use advertising on a one-off basis to promote special events such as open days. The press is a major part of the main paid advertising medium which many organisations in this sector use. These may range from local, regional and national newspapers to magazines and guides. Many organisations in the public sector have very low advertising budgets and therefore have to learn how to spend their budget wisely.

The cost of advertising media is related to a number of factors including the number of people who will see the advertisement and how influential the medium is thought to be in persuading people to buy or use the product.

Swarbrooke (1999) pointed out that most attractions do not market mass market products, but rather niche market products. This means that they usually do not need to utilise the expensive mass media techniques. Highly targeted advertising strategies are usually more relevant. This targeting can take a number of forms including:

- Targeting media which are aimed at appropriate niche markets;
- Advertising at certain times of the year only;
- Targeting potential customers in a particular geographical area.

The types of advertising that can be used by an organisation are shown in Table 9.1:

Types of Advertising	Comments
Television	Visual and moving Reaches wide audience Expensive
Radio	Relatively low impact Inexpensive
Newspapers	Visual image Can be stored Modest production costs Often tied to particular times
Periodicals	Visual image Good for reaching target audience Often infrequent production
Annual guides and yearbooks	Often consulted by groups of people who are interested Often high cover price
Posters and visual displays	Visual image Colourful Stationary image May be expensive for prime sites

Table 9.1 The types of advertising that can be used by organisations

Brochures

The brochure is one of the main forms of marketing communication in the leisure industry. The services which are on offer by the organisation are often depicted in a brochure to enable the potential customer to choose the right product. Boyer and Viallon (1994) recognised that the brochure is of particular use in the communication of tourism products.

Brochures are increasingly being accompanied by video cassettes. These help the organisation to show real images of the holiday, destination or hotel. In the future, the use of virtual reality images will allow the potential customer to view the actual location and even to 'try out' the potential purchase. In the meantime, the brochure production exercise forms a major part of the promotional activity budget of many major leisure companies.

Marketers, clearly, also need to consider the importance of brochure distribution as a superb brochure is ineffective if it does not get into the hands of the right people at the right time.

Press and public relations

Publicity refers to non-personal communication in news story form about an organisation on its products, transmitted through the media for no charge. Kotler defines publicity as:

> Non-personal stimulation of demand for a product, service, or business unit by planting commercially significant news about it in a published medium or obtaining

favourable presentation of it on radio, television or stage, that is not paid for by the sponsor.

Kotler and Armstrong (2004)

The public relations mechanism should be well established by an organisation and it should control and manage the use of effective publicity. Many large organisations are now employing *public relations agencies* to help them manage their publicity effectively. An organisation should also develop an effective method of generating press releases and develop suitable relationships with the editors involved in the media with their coverage. Public relations are therefore an important part of the communications process. Buttle (1986) defined this role as follows:

> Improving awareness, projecting credibility, combating competition, evaluating new markets, creating direct sales leads, reinforcing the effectiveness of sales promotional and advertising, motivating the sales force, introducing new products, building brand loyalty, dealing with consumer issues and in many other ways.

Press and public relations activity is important in both the public and private sectors of leisure. The opening of a new hotel, for example, would involve an extensive press and public relations campaign. Some of the activities which would be involved in the launch of the new hotel are shown in Figure 9.3. It can be seen in this example that the activity involves both paid and non-paid communication methods.

- Arranging of news releases to all regional, national and international media at the appropriate time.
- Arranging a 'pre-opening' campaign by inviting press, local dignitaries, etc. to look around the new facility.
- Arranging an opening reception for the facility with a major personality to carry out the official opening and having an impressive guest list for this event.
- Making sure that well known and liked dignitaries who make news are invited as the first guests to get maximum media attention.
- Making sure that the new facility is well covered in all the major trade press in the country in which it is operating.
- Making sure that the new facility is well publicised in other facilities and advertising material within the group.

Figure 9.3 The press and public relations activities involved in the launch of a new hotel

For organisations that are operating in the public sector, the correct handling of press and public relations is very important. It is important for a museum, for example, which is funded by government or local authority sources of money to develop a very favourable impression with the local, regional and national media. This will encourage the media to cover the stories about the museum which shows it in a good light. Unfortunately, the development of a high profile image will also encourage the media to cover any issues which show the organisation in a bad light.

If an organisation which has been developing a reputation for 'green' products and services, for example, is suddenly shown to have carried out an activity which is damaging to the environment, then it is almost guaranteed that the media will cover the story. The amount of coverage will depend on the interest of the story and the handling of the press and media by the press offices of the organisation.

Organisations should also develop a well thought out press and public relations strategy to cope with incidents which could damage the long-term reputation of the business. Many large organisations have now established various forms of 'emergency committees' which are composed of a number of key individuals who assemble to deal with a major disaster. This could range from the death of a customer to a major pollution incident. The emergency committee will then deal with the incident and talk to the press and media in a well thought out and planned approach to try and minimise the damage caused by the incident.

It is when these major incidents happen that it is vital that a good relationship with the media has been developed over a number of years. This will help the organisation to deal honestly and effectively with the media with the objective of minimising the long-term negative effects of bad publicity.

Press and public relations activity is therefore vital for any type of organisation involved in the leisure industry. It will help to show the organisation in a good light and enable the organisation to cope with major incidents which could damage the organisation's long-term image.

Sales promotion

Sales promotion is an activity or material that acts as an inducement to sale for potential or existing customers. It includes the use of coupons, bonuses and contests which are all examples of techniques which an organisation can use to boost sales. Sales promotion has been defined by Kotler as:

> Short term incentives to encourage purchase or sales of a product or service.
>
> Kotler and Armstrong (2004)

The emphasis here is on the short term, rather than the longer-term objectives of advertising. Sales promotion is often used by companies at irregular intervals, particularly if the market is seasonal. The package holiday companies, for example, boost initial sales or their summer sun holidays by sales promotion techniques such as free holidays for children. Sales promotions can offer *discounts*. An example of this would be 'money off' promotions which are offered to stimulate demand. Sales promotions can also *add value* to the product or service offered. This means keeping the standard price, but offering the customer more for their money.

Hotel companies have become very skilled at using added-value sales promotion techniques. The bottle of champagne which is provided in the guests' room on arrival is an example of the use of sales promotion techniques.

Personal selling

Personal selling techniques are of key importance to organisations which are marketing service products because of the inseparable nature of the offering. Personal selling involves persuading customers to purchase products and services in a personal face-to-face situation. The nature of leisure products means that there should be a heavy emphasis on personal selling effort as part of the marketing communications process.

Personal selling has been defined by Kotler as:

> Oral presentation in a conversation with one or more prospective purchases for the purpose of making sales.
>
> Kotler and Armstrong (2004)

The oral presentation can be made to the final customer and also to intermediaries in the distribution channel.

Personal selling has both advantages and disadvantages. It is directed at smaller groups of people or individuals compared to advertising, but has the advantage of achieving greater impact and immediate feedback.

When a sales person and customer meet face to face in a personal selling situation, it is important that the sales person give the right signals to the customer and recognise their needs.

It is important to remember that all 'front of house' personnel in leisure organisations are sales personnel. The person who serves you in a restaurant, a sports centre or a travel agency, for example, all carry out selling activities. It is important that all sales personnel give the customer the right signals. Consider the example of the food server in a restaurant shown in Figure 9.4. This example shows that the customer is looking to the food server as an important sales person and can have many expectations which will affect their overall experience in the restaurant.

The customer of the restaurant will look for one or more of the following features:

- The way the food server dresses should befit the customers' expectations.
- The language which is used. This will be both spoken and unspoken. Body language such as how the food server moves his head, eyes, arms and hands is just as important as what he says. Hand gestures and head nodding are often important.
- The way in which the menu is presented to the customer and what, if anything, is recommended.
- The way in which the food server gets the balance right between ignoring the customer and visibly hovering over them. The customer requirements will depend on who they are with and their particular mood.
- The way in which the food server deals with children as customers.

It is important to remember that each customer will be looking for a different set of features.

Figure 9.4 The food server as a sales person

This example shows that personal selling is very much an 'art' and is very complex in nature. There is a great difference between a 'soft' sell and a 'hard' sell approach. The 'soft' sell seeks to point out opportunities which the customer may wish to take advantage of. The 'hard' sell puts customers under pressure to purchase.

Restaurant companies often try to increase their spend per head by encouraging service staff to 'upsell'. This means that customers are encouraged to buy drinks or extra menu items which they had not otherwise considered purchasing.

The sale of excursions by package holiday representatives at the resort or the selling of themed merchandising at major music concerts or football matches, are other examples of upselling. It is important, however, that customers are not pushed into spending levels that they are uncomfortable with. This may increase their spend in the short term, but significantly reduce their repeat-customer level.

Personal selling to the final customer or to intermediaries in the distribution channels is a key part of the marketing communications mix for leisure organisations. It is vital that the methods are well developed and the front-line personnel are well chosen and trained to deal with their important selling function.

Direct mail

Direct mail and telephone selling are used to contact prospective customers to initiate sales. They are also used to contact existing and past customers to initiate repeat purchases. The use of these techniques has been developed over several decades and targeting of customers is becoming more sophisticated particularly with the use of computers.

Many service organisations involved in the marketing of leisure products have access to sophisticated customer databases. This makes the use of direct mail selling a particularly attractive proposition as a promotional technique. The use of direct mail as a promotional technique is not just confined to customers. It can also be used to target customers in the distribution channels which are often referred to as business-to-business marketing.

It is essential that direct mail is correctly targeted, and that the material which is sent is designed so that it encourages the receiver to open it. To achieve effective targeting, organisations must develop *mailing lists*. These can either be generated internally from previous sales data, which is very attractive for service organisations which deal directly with customers. Alternatively, the mailing list can be purchased from mailing houses or list brokers. Many of the geodemographic techniques of segmentation produce databases which are used for direct mail purposes.

Direct mail can be customised to the individual which makes it an attractive method of marketing communication. The disadvantages include the fact that people often consider direct mail as junk and never open it. There are critics who also hate the idea that organisations can 'buy' their name and address to send them targeted mail. These criticisms are likely to grow as organisations have more and more information concerning individuals and their associated lifestyles.

The development of long-term contact with customers has become a topical issue over the last few years and academics have published books and journal articles about *relationship marketing*. It will be interesting to see how this develops in the future.

Point of sale materials

For many organisations marketing leisure products, the POS material is often a very important promotional opportunity. Point of sale material is any material which is used to promote the products and services on offer, and is usually displayed close to retail units.

Point of sale material has been defined by Dibb, Simkin, Pride and Ferrell as:

> A sales promotion method that uses items as outside signs, window displays, and display rails to attract attention, to inform customers and to encourage retailers to carry particular products.
>
> Dibb et al. (2001)

Customers often enter into a leisure business knowing that they are going to purchase something but not quite sure what. It is more likely that the customer has been attracted to the range and type of food on offer at a restaurant, for example, rather than a specific list. In a hotel setting, the customer knows they are staying there, but perhaps is unaware of the extra services which they will use. A customer entering a travel agent is often keen to buy a holiday, but is unsure of the various products on offer.

Here there is a promotional opportunity. The organisation can use POS promotional material to influence the customer and steer them towards a particular choice. The restaurant, for example, may want to steer the customer to try a new dish on their menu, with the intention of broadening appeal and increasing the frequency of the visit. Alternatively, it may want to steer the customer towards selecting a dish which produces more profit. It may also wish to increase customer spend by encouraging the customer to purchase a starter, dessert, side dish or bottle of wine. Care needs to be taken when designing POS material.

It is not in the long-term interest of the organisation to 'push' people into purchase decisions that they later regret. If a customer goes out for an everyday meal but ends up spending more than anticipated, then they may not select the venue for another meal occasion.

Use of selective POS material which is sensitively designed has a very important role to play in communicating products and services to customers. In the restaurant setting, counter displays and posters are all forms of POS material. In hotels, for example, hotel service brochures play a vital role in promoting services of which the customer may otherwise be unaware. Reception staff can also use the check-in period as an important opportunity to promote other hotel services. Point of sale material is also very important at major events such as music concerts or sporting events.

Point of sale material may also have a role to play in achieving objectives which are not financially related. An employee restaurant, for example, may want to encourage its staff to eat more healthily. A public house or bar may want to encourage its customers to drive responsibly by not drinking and driving, and selecting low alcohol alternatives.

For these reasons, POS promotion is used extensively in leisure organisations and is an important component in the overall promotional mix.

Sponsorship

Sponsorship has been defined by Dibb, Simkin, Pride and Ferrell as:

> the financial or material support of an event, activity, person, organisation, or product, by an unrelated organisation or donor. Generally funds will be made available to the recipient of the sponsorship deal in return for the prominent exposure of the sponsor's name or brands.
>
> Dibb et al. (2001)

Sponsorship has become very popular in the arts. Some theatrical companies, museums, and galleries rely more and more on sponsorship, as government subsidies of the arts decreases. The Victoria and Albert Museum, for example, covered in the case study, relies heavily on major sponsorship deals to finance many of the large-scale exhibitions.

Another area in leisure which relies on sponsorship are organisations involved in sport. Football teams, for example, found that gate receipts were insufficient to cope with rising bills and operating costs. The way round this financial dilemma was to encourage sponsorship deals. Sponsors were encouraged to appear on players' shirts and new spectator stands, for example.

Sponsorship has also been a major part of promotional activity for major sporting events. The Olympics, for example, are always accompanied with an array of official sponsors, ranging from drinks to sportswear manufacturers. If the company feels that company image or brand awareness will be helped by sponsoring an organisation or event, then it will go ahead with this type of promotion.

For the recipient organisation, this is often an important part of their revenue.

Push and pull strategies

Organisations use different promotional strategies as part of their overall marketing communications mix. These have been referred to by Kotler and Armstrong (2004) as *push strategy* and *pull strategy*. These two different forms of promotional strategy are shown in Figure 9.5.

Push strategy refers to a method by which the organisation promotes directly to the intermediaries in the distribution chain, thereby hoping that these organisations promote the items to the final customer. For a package holiday company, this would involve the organisation promoting their holidays to travel agents who will then sell them directly to the final customer.

Pull strategy relies on the idea that if an organisation communicates to their final customer, then the customer will demand the item from the intermediaries. The package holiday companies, for example, advertise directly to the customer via television, magazines and press advertising. It is hoped that the customer will then demand the holidays from the travel agent. The package holiday companies can also use data on their advertising programmes to convince the intermediaries, in this case the travel agent, to stock their brochures.

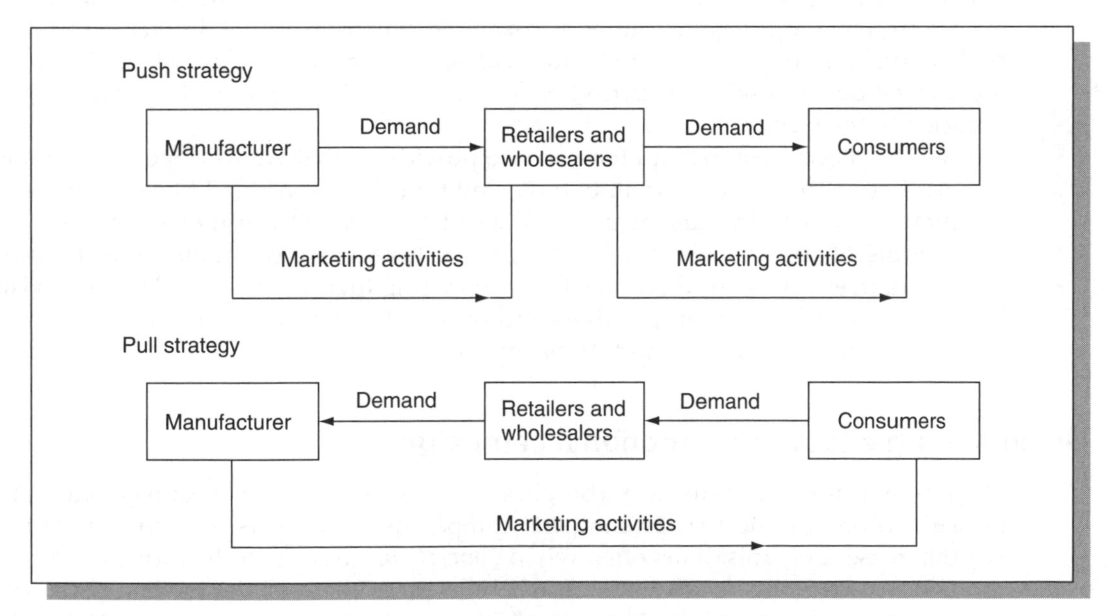

Figure 9.5 Push versus pull strategy (*Source*: Horner and Swarbrooke, 1996)

In reality, organisations use both *push strategies* and *pull strategies* in their total marketing communications strategies.

The special nature of marketing communication in services marketing

The *intangibility* of services means that they require special treatment when the marketer is planning the promotional campaign. It is difficult to know what to feature in advertising because of this intangibility. Service providers often use *symbols* to stress the nature of the service on offer. German operator TUI uses a symbolic smiling face to suggest the psychological effects that a customer will derive from one of their holidays.

It has also become important in service organisations to differentiate effectively between competitors. Many service organisations have used *branding* as a very effective method of differentiation and a platform for their promotional activity. Accor, for example, the French hospitality group has used a portfolio of brands including Novotel, Formule 1 and Thalassa International to differentiate their service offerings in a crowded market. It is also important that the advertising for services emphasises the special nature of what is on offer. This is often achieved by using a slogan or a phrase.

The *inseparability* of service means that the role of personnel selling by front-line employees of the organisation is paramount. Training of these staff in selling techniques should be an important part of the promotional activity. It is important that the customer quickly recognise and associate with the front-line employees.

This is often achieved by the use of a well-designed and attractive uniform. The development of sophisticated leisure centres such as Greens or Esporta has incorporated the development of staff uniforms that pick up on the brand identity.

The *perishability* of services means that organisations often have to try and smooth out demand by using sales promotions techniques. These are often combined with some form of discounting. Large leisure centres, for example, will try to target different groups in the population at quiet periods of operation with special packages. This will avoid closure of the facility during this quiet period as long as enough people in the target group are attracted to the facility.

The final special requirement for a service provider is that word-of-mouth communication has been shown to be very important, and for this reason should be encouraged. The restaurant who asks the customer to tell their friends about it if they enjoy their visit is an example of this. Hotels can encourage word-of-mouth communication by offering customers free services or discounts for encouraging their friends or relatives to visit the hotel. Theatres often rely on positive word-of-mouth communication to encourage more people to attend productions and special events.

Designing an effective promotional campaign

Marketing communication is a complicated concept and organisations often find it difficult to design effective promotional campaigns which persuade customers to buy. For this reason, organisations often rely on *advertising agencies* to help them design their promotional campaigns, advise them where to place them in the media, and finally to help them buy the space in the appropriate media whether it be for print, or television or radio schedules. The organisation should provide the advertising agency with an *advertising brief* which is a statement of the aims of the advertising campaign. This should be agreed between the client and the advertising agency before work begins on the promotional campaign.

A creative brief to an advertising agency should contain the items shown in Figure 9.6.

- What is the advertising trying to do? e.g. address falling sales, increase sale levels in the next period
- The size of budget
- What is expected exactly from the promotional mix?
- Who is being addressed? This should include a statement about the target customer
- What is the single most important point that the target customer should take from the promotion?
- Is there evidence of emotional support by the customer for the product/service? For example, a well-recognised brand name
- Any other information which is relevant.

Figure 9.6 The components of a creative brief for an advertising agency

Advertising agencies are very creative but will produce effective campaigns only if they are briefed correctly.

The organisation should consider the objectives of the campaign and should decide on an appropriate budget. The types of messages which will be used in the total campaign will be formulated and decisions made as to where the promotional campaign will be placed in the appropriate media. Finally, the organisation will have to decide on how a campaign is to be evaluated. This process, described above, is shown diagramatically in Figure 9.7.

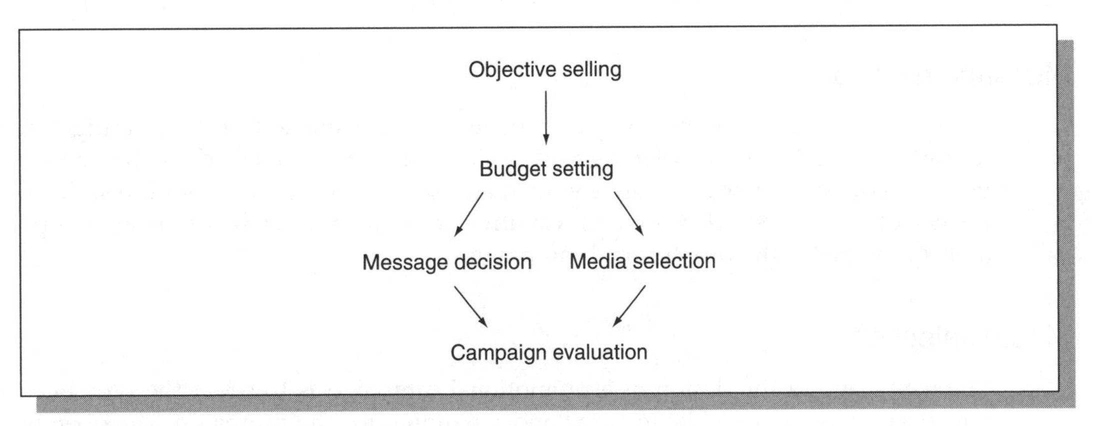

Figure 9.7 The main stages involved in creating a promotional campaign

To illustrate these various stages in the creation and evaluation of a promotional campaign, an example of an organisation opening a new hotel will be considered.

Objective setting

The organisation should consider the overall objectives of the promotional campaign. There will be a mixed set of objectives for a campaign for the opening of a new hotel, including:

- Raising awareness amongst target customers;
- Raising positive 'word of mouth' response from the general public, press and potential customers;
- Encouraging trial of the hotel by target users;

- Raising the profile of the hotel amongst many important distribution intermediaries, e.g. travel agents, tourist offices;
- Achieving a set sales level and occupancy level in a set period of time.

The organisation will have to prioritise the objectives which have been identified.

Budget setting

The next stage in the design of the promotional campaign is to set a budget. This can sometimes be difficult for a new operation, since there is no established level of sales and profitability. The organisation should however, in the planning process, establish an estimate of expected levels of turnover for the new business.

The budget for the promotional campaign could be based on one or more of the following items:

- A percentage of predicted annual sales;
- The levels of promotional spend which competitive organisations are spending;
- Past budgets which have been used by the organisation;
- The amount that the organisation can afford;
- The level of budget which the objective of the campaign dictates. A huge capital investment in a new hotel, for example, will dictate the level of promotion necessary to recoup the money invested over a set period of time.

Message decision

Once the objectives of the campaign have been established and the budget set, it is important that the types of messages which are to be portrayed in the campaign are established. The advertising agency often advises organisations about the style, tone and format of the proposed campaign. Creative copy is produced to portray the proposed sorts of image for the promotional campaign.

Media selection

The next stage in the design of a promotional campaign is to select the type of media in which the campaign will be featured and the timing for the campaign. The opening of the new hotel will probably use different types of promotion. These will probably include:

- Media advertising
- Publicity launch
- Sales promotion.

The campaign will be featured in a number of media types including:

- Local and/or National Press;
- Speciality magazines and Trade Press;
- Direct mail to existing customers of the group.

There will be a series of timings which will be crucial for the successful launch of the new hotel. These will include:

- A press campaign leading up to the launch;
- Major press activity at the time of the launch;

- Direct mail prior to the launch and on an ongoing basis;
- A continuing campaign after the launch to sustain market growth.

The selection of the media used for a promotional campaign will vary for every organisation, depending on the objectives of the campaign and the available budget.

Campaign evaluation

It is important that the results of the campaign are monitored by the organisation on an ongoing basis to see if the original objectives are being met. There are a variety of ways in which the effectiveness of a campaign can be measured. Some of these methods include:

Sales

The build-up and continuing sales revenue from the hotel can be measured at regular intervals. This could be broken down into separate profit centres, e.g. restaurant, rooms, conference facilities, health clubs, etc.

Customer reaction

The reaction of final customers and the distribution intermediaries to the promotional material for the hotel can be monitored.

Audience achievement

The target audience for the promotional material can be monitored to see if they actually saw the promotion.

It is vital for the organisation to establish whether the original objectives of the promotional campaign are being met on an ongoing basis. If this is not the case, then corrective action will have to be taken.

International marketing communication

We have already seen that many leisure organisations are becoming international players. The question arises in marketing communications as to whether these organisations can adopt standardised marketing communication strategies or whether they have to adapt these to the local setting. There has been a long debate in the academic literature about this topic. Levitt (1983) proposed that organisations should treat the world as a single marketplace but should 'think global, act local'.

Research carried out by Porter (1986) found that it was easier to standardise certain elements of the marketing communications mix such as brand names and advertising themes, but more difficult to standardise other elements such as personal selling and media selection. This research was supported by Moriarty and Duncan (1990) who found that it was easier to develop a standardised creative concept theme and that media buying was much harder to standardise. We can think of some of the international brands that have been developed in the leisure sector such as Nike, who have adopted this approach.

Research has also suggested that consumers actually like advertising styles that are sensitive to different national cultures and that different nationalities like different styles of advertising. Different European countries, for example, have adopted very different approaches in advertising styles (Munzinger, 1988; Lannon, 1992).

There is also the requirement to produce advertisements in the language of the consumer, although this can be overcome by either producing advertisements that can be dubbed over with another language or producing them in English with the assumption that English is becoming more universally spoken. Care must be taken, however, in simple translation because of the inextricable link between advertising and culture. This was explored by Anholt (1993) as follows:

> Advertising is so intrinsically linked with the popular culture, the social fabric, the laws, the conventions, the buying habits, the aspirations, the style, the humour, and the mentality of the people that messages just cannot be communicated in precisely the same way in different countries.
>
> Anholt (1993)

This suggests that the copy for advertising has to be written in a different way, rather than just written as a straight translation. He illustrated the point with reference to the Nike commercials that had the same appearance but different copy for the English, French, Italian and Flemish regions.

It is easier to run standardised sales promotions across boundaries because of the emergence of common international interests. These were explored by Toop (1992) and have developed further since the early 1990s. Common interests include sports such as football, the Olympic Games, tennis, motor racing; music such as that of international pop stars; travel items such as destinations and luxury cars; television programmes such as *Friends*; children's interests such as Lego and Disney; international fashion item such as Levis and Benetton, and social concern issues such as Oxfam and the World Wide Fund for Nature.

It is interesting to note that many of these common interests are leisure pursuits. The interest in Lego and Disney, for example, provides us with a common international theme that companies such as McDonald's have used as the basis for sales promotions to target children on an international basis.

The evidence suggests that although there are substantial differences in the expectations of people from different cultures in relation to the style of advertising, there is an opportunity to build on common international themes in certain forms of advertising and promotion.

The growing availability of *international media sources and international advertising agencies*, and growing *harmonisation of legal frameworks* have also fuelled the development of standardised marketing communications strategies.

Access to cable and satellite television channels across the world is growing and there has been a growth in the number of printed newspapers and magazines that appear internationally. Women's magazines such as *Cosmopolitan*, *Marie-Claire* and *Elle*, and men's magazines such as *Penthouse* and *Playboy* have a strong international presence. Publications aimed at international business people such as *Reader's Digest*, *The Economist*, *Inflight* magazine and the *Financial Times* also have wide international circulation.

There has also been a growth in the number of international advertising agencies to help organisations deliver international campaigns. Organisations that do want to promote across national boundaries have to recognise the different legal frameworks for every country in which they operate. Different European countries, for example, do have different legislative requirements but there are signs that Europe is increasingly trying to harmonise the legislation related to marketing communication. The control of sponsorship in the leisure industry by companies who were previously banned from advertising by other means is a particular issue for the leisure sector. Restrictions on companies such as tobacco companies and alcohol producers in sponsorship will mean that many leisure companies and events organisers will have to look for alternative sources of funding.

Discussion points and essay questions

1. Outline the role of promotion within marketing, particularly in relation to the other elements of the marketing mix.
2. Compare and contrast the promotional techniques used by a major hotel chain with those adopted by a small public sector museum.
3. Discuss the obstacles that are restricting the growth of common international approaches to advertising.

Exercise

Choose *one* of the following hypothetical new products:

(i) A new long-haul holiday destination in a tour operator's programme, which is aimed at an up-market clientele who seek exclusivity. You must base your project on a real destination.
(ii) A newly built theme park aimed at a family market. You should specify where your hypothetical theme park is located.
(iii) The launch of a new service between two cities by a scheduled airline.

For your chosen product, you should:

(a) Design a brochure that will appeal to the target market.
(b) Prepare an advertising campaign to promote this new product, including your choice of media that would be used and the design of proposed advertisements.

Part Four

Marketing planning in leisure

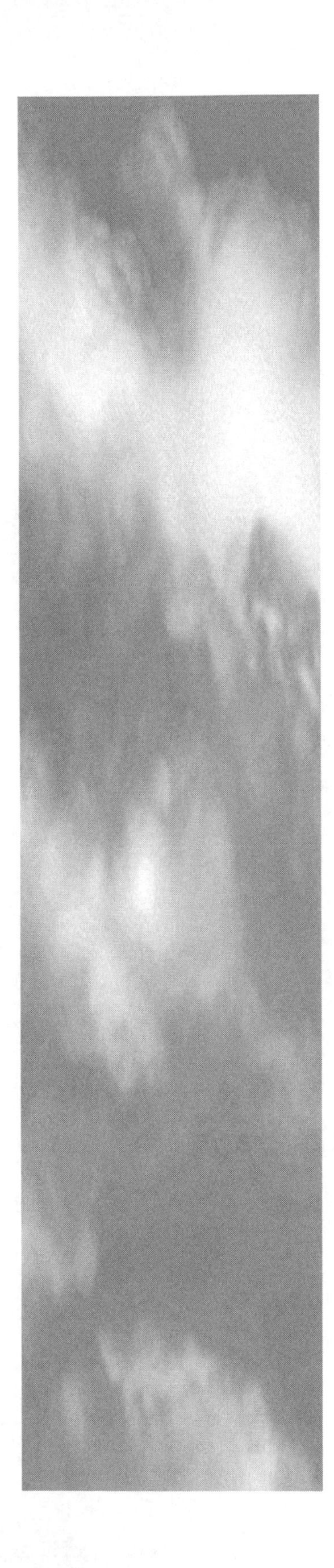

Introduction

In this part of the book we examine the application of the principles and techniques of marketing planning to leisure.

Each of the four chapters in this section addresses one of the classic four questions, which comprises the process of marketing planning as follows:

Chapter 10: Where are we now? This chapter looks at how organisations can analyse their current marketing situation as the context for a marketing planning exercise.

Chapter 11: Where do we want to go? – the setting of goals and objectives. In this chapter, we explore the setting of goals and objectives and the generation of mission statements.

Chapter 12: How will we get there? – developing the strategy. This chapter looks at the evaluation of strategic options and the creation of marketing strategies. It then goes on to look at the role of marketing plans in implementing these strategies.

Chapter 13: How will we know when we get there? – monitoring, review and evaluation. This chapter covers monitoring, review and evaluation – the techniques by which the implementation of the strategy is kept on the right track.

CHAPTER 10

Where are we now? Current situation analysis

Key concepts

The main concepts covered in the chapter are:

- Current situation analysis at different levels including whole organisations, complete product portfolios, strategic business units or SBUs and individual product
- SWOT analysis
- Boston Consultancy Group Matrix
- Marketing audits.

Introduction

Strategic marketing planning always begins with an objective analysis of the organisation's current marketing situation. This analysis needs to take place at a number of levels, including:

- the organisation as a whole;
- its product portfolios;
- individual strategic business units or SBUs;
- individual products.

A number of techniques exist to help with the analysis of the current situation, in terms of these respective levels, as follows:

- SWOT (Strengths, Weaknesses, Opportunities, Threats) analysis is a good technique for considering the organisation as a whole.
- The Boston Consultancy Group (BCG) Matrix can be a useful framework for analysing the current performance of the organisation's overall product portfolio or even its SBUs.
- Product positioning and the product life cycle are particularly relevant at the level of individual products.

Clearly, this is just a selection of relevant techniques, there are a number of others. Furthermore, many of these techniques not only relate to the current situation, they also can be used to see how a product or SBU or a whole portfolio are behaving over time.

In this chapter, we will look at how leisure organisations can analyse their current marketing situation and how these techniques, outlined above, contribute to this process.

However, one has to bear in mind that a current situation analysis rarely begins with a clean sheet. It is undertaken in the context of existing strategies, the organisation's history and culture and involvement in physical planning, for example.

The book, up to now, has defined and explained the marketing concept and identified the ways in which it can be practically implemented. Marketing has become very fashionable in the leisure industry.

However, while this growing recognition of the importance of marketing is welcome, many organisations are becoming involved in marketing without a clear understanding of what it is, and the implications of introducing a marketing approach.

Marketing should be planned in a systematic and rigorous way if it is to be implemented effectively. To help with this process the discipline of *marketing planning* has been developed. This marketing strategy will be developed for the organisation in the marketing planning process.

A marketing plan was defined, way back in 1988, as:

> A written statement of the marketing aims of a company, including a statement of the products, targets for sales, market shares and profits, promotional and advertising strategies, pricing policies, distribution channels etc. with precise specification of time scales, individual responsibilities etc.
>
> Manser (1988)

To achieve this marketing plan, the organisation will have to go through a number of stages which take the form of questions as follows:

(i) *Where are we now?*
The analysis of the current marketing situation.
(ii) *Where do we want to be in the future?*
Setting the objectives.
(iii) *How are we going to get there?*
Creating the strategy.
(iv) *How will we know when we get there?*
Monitoring and evaluation.

The next four chapters will mirror this situation. Each chapter will give an overview of this four-stage process. If you require further in-depth analysis of the marketing planning process, you should refer to the work of Ansoff (1988); Day (1990); Ohmae (1982); Porter (1983); and Kotler and Armstrong (2004).

An overview of the marketing planning process

The marketing planning process was developed as a systematic way of incorporating marketing into an organisation. One of the leading academics and writers on the subject in the United Kingdom is Malcolm McDonald. The marketing planning process includes:

1. Corporate objectives
2. Marketing audit
3. SWOT analysis
4. Assumptions
5. Marketing objectives and strategies
6. Estimated expected results
7. Identify alternative plans and mixes
8. Programme
9. Measurement and review.

This model incorporates the stages which have to be completed in order to arrive at a finished marketing plan.

The plan should contain:

- A summary of all the principal external factors which affect the organisation's marketing performance during the previous year, together with a statement of the organisation's strengths and weaknesses.
- The competition and how the organisation is performing in the marketplace (SWOT analysis can help with this).
- Assumptions about the key determinants of marketing success and failure.
- Setting of overall marketing objectives and strategies.
- Programmes containing detailed timings, responsibilities, costs, budgets and sales forecasts.
- Methods for measuring and reviewing progress made.

The feedback lines in the model indicate that in a real planning situation, the steps will have to be completed more than once before the final plan can be written.

There are different models and concepts which can be used as the organisation progresses through the model to the finished marketing plan. These will be covered in more detail in this chapter and the following three chapters.

The style of the finished marketing plan will differ, according to the type of organisation. One suggestion for a marketing plan is shown in Figure 10.1.

If the organisation is planning to market the product in more than one country, then the plan will have to include important issues such as consumer views, legal position and distribution plans. The process of marketing planning in international marketing is however, in essence, an identical process to that carried out in national markets.

- Management summary
- Current position of the product in the market
- Future prospects for the market
- Market research requirement
- Product strategy
- Promotion plan
- Sales plan
- Distribution plan
- Pricing policy
- Performance measures and controls.

Figure 10.1 A suggested model marketing plan for an organisation

Where are we now?

The analysis of the current marketing situation can be divided into three stages as follows:

1. An evaluation of the organisation itself in terms of its products, its markets, its customers, its structure and culture, and how it organises its marketing.
2. An appraisal of the external business environment and how it affects the organisation including political, economic, demographic, socio-cultural, natural and technological forces.
3. An examination of the organisation's main competition.

The marketing audit is composed of a number of sections, which has been produced as a result of a detailed review of internal and external factors. The parts of the audit are shown in Figure 10.2.

The marketing audit for a UK tour operator

To show the marketing audit in more detail and to consider its application to the industry, this section will look at the procedure which a UK tour operator would go through to complete a marketing audit.

Step 1: Who would carry out the audit?

The tour operator could use one of their existing staff to carry out the audit. It is often better, however, if the company can afford it, for an impartial consultant to carry out the audit. This has the advantage of a person who is not involved in the day-to-day marketing activity giving a fresh view of the particular sets of circumstances.

Step 2: How should they start?

The audit should look at the overall Corporate Mission of the organisation.
In the case of the tour operator, this could be:

> We seek to maintain our number one position in the package tour business in the United Kingdom.

The Corporate Mission of the organisation will give an overall view of where the organisation sees itself going in the future.

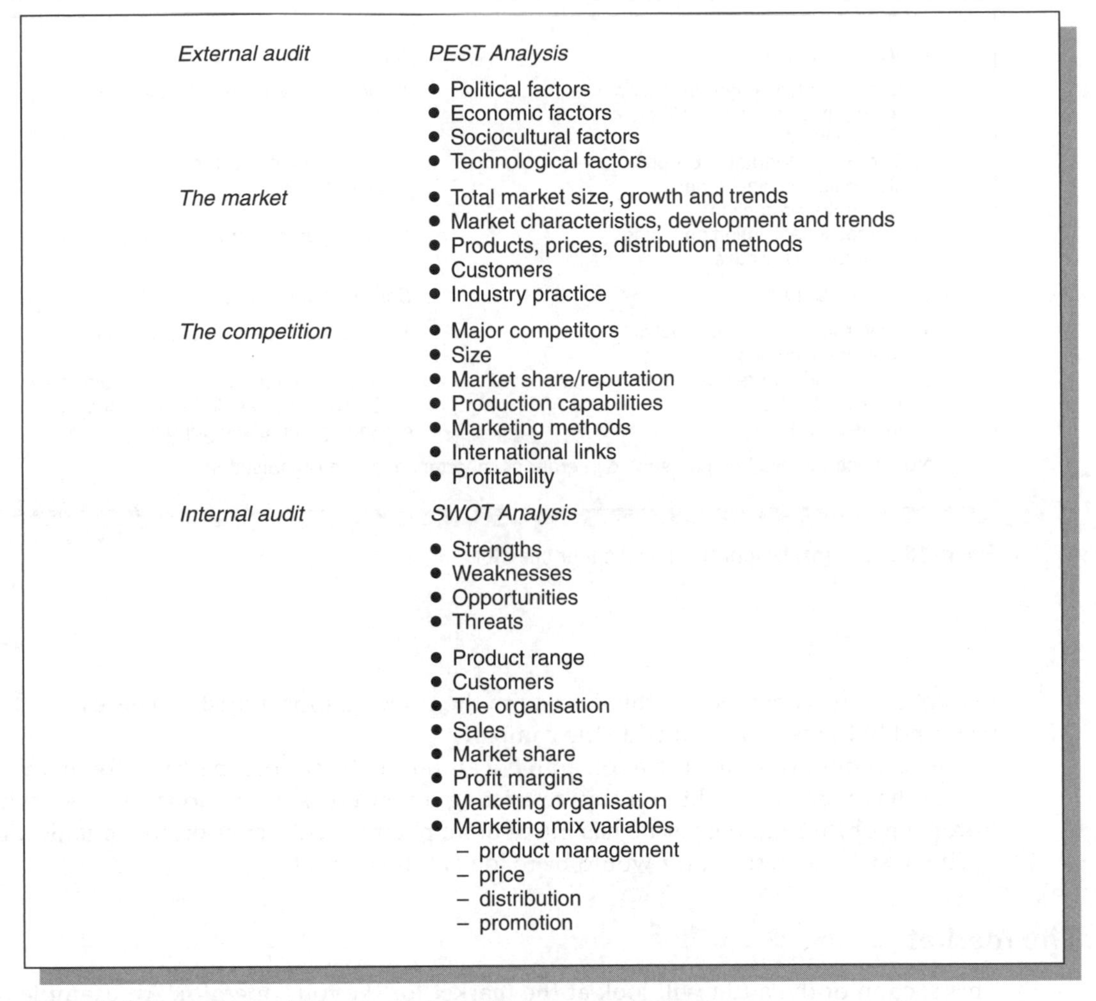

Figure 10.2 An outline model for a marketing audit for an organisation

Step 3: External environment

The next stage of the audit procedure will be for the tour operator to consider the external environment. This refers to the general forces which may affect the organisation but which are outside its control, although it may of course influence some of them through lobbying. They include political, economic, sociocultural and technological forces. This analysis is sometimes referred to as PEST analysis or STEP analysis and is covered in further detail in Chapter 7.

The most successful are those that accurately anticipate changes in these forces, and respond quickly and in the most effective manner. An example of an outline external audit for the tour operators is shown in Figure 10.3. Factors have been identified in each category, and then considered in relation to this particular organisation, so that they can be presented in rank order. By doing this, the organisation will know which of the identified factors they should concentrate on.

The consultant or individual who is carrying out the audit will find it very usual to use the *Delphi technique* to create this external audit. This involves speaking to industry and

Political factors	*Technological factors*
1. European Union legislation. For example, European Package Travel Directive	1. Developments in CRS systems
2. The Single Market in Europe	2. Virtual reality systems
3. Domestic legislation on consumer protection	3. Smart cards
4. Domestic legislation on timing of statutory holidays	4. Management information systems
Economic factors	*Sociocultural factors*
1. Government economic policy affecting incomes	1. Growing interest in green issues
2. Recession and recovery from recession	2. Growing interest in independent travel
3. Availability of credit	3. Growing interest in health issues
4. Interest rates	4. Ageing and static population

NB Factors have been presented in order of importance for the organisation

Figure 10.3 External factors affecting the tour operator

market experts concerned in this case, with the package tour industry. These experts may be found both inside and outside the company.

It is also important for the audit to have an international perspective. Too many companies have been caught out by restricting themselves to national issues, when a European or international issue has much more potential influence on the organisation.

The next stage in the audit would be to look at the market.

The market

This section of the audit will look at the market for the tour operator. An example of the content of this audit for a UK operator is shown in Figure 10.4. It is very useful for the individual or consultant completing the audit to seek expert advice to complete this section of the audit. The market characteristics are a very important part of the audit because it will provide general information about this particular market area. This will prove invaluable to the organisation when it starts to set the marketing objectives later on in the marketing planning process.

Competition

The next part of the audit would be an analysis of the competition in this market. For the tour operator, this will involve looking at other tour operators in the national market and also considering potential new competition from European or international markets. The organisation needs to recognise that they operate in a highly competitive environment and they should analyse their main competitors in terms of their particular strengths and weaknesses. This will hopefully allow the organisation to gain a competitive advantage over them.

In some parts of the industry, particularly in the public-sector, organisations and managers find it difficult to identify their main competitors. This is particularly so if there are many fundamentally different products and markets.

Total market
- Estimated at £X m in the UK;
- The number of major players;
- Growth in package holiday market;
- Growth of large European players;
- Seasonality of the market.

Customers
- Are customers price sensitive and loyal to the company or not, for example?

Products
- Issues such as whether branding is important to customers
  A review of the image and reputation of the company products and how they are perceived by the customer.

Price
- The features of the pricing strategies in the market. For example, are 'discounting' and 'inclusive' pricing common features?

Distribution
- The special features of distribution such as the use of dedicated travel agencies and direct sales.

Communication
- The type of promotion which is currently used such as the importance of brochures, television advertising at specific periods and sales promotions.

Industry practice
- Special industry practice such as ABTA bonding.

Figure 10.4 The market for tour operation

Competitors could be organisations offering similar products, targeting the same market segments, charging a similar price or operating in the same geographical area. Competition might also include any activity that offers a similar benefit to the customer.

The identification of competitors in the leisure industry, for example, is further complicated by the fact that in some instances such as local authority museums services, the main competitor in the geographical area may be a facility owned by the same organisation.

Organisations in national market also tend to view other national organisations in the same market sector as their competition. This may be so in the short term, but in the long term there may be the unannounced arrival of a multinational competitor who views the national market as a window of opportunity.

An example of a model for a competitor audit for the tour operator is shown in Figure 10.5. It can be seen that this audit has looked at both existing national competitors and potential international players.

Step 4: Internal business environment

By this stage, the organisation will have a good knowledge of the external environment, their major competition and an overall view of the market. The next stage is to look internally at all the features which make up their particular organisation. This will involve four stages:

- A SWOT analysis to look at overall features
- A review of the current customers
- A review of the organisation's product ranges
- The organisation.

Competitive company	Market share	Turnover	Profitability	Geographical coverage	Major brands	International links	Marketing methods	Key strengths and weaknesses
Potential competitive company								

Figure 10.5 The competitor audit for the tour operator

The SWOT Analysis

This technique of audit is often referred to as a SWOT analysis, shown below:

S	*Strengths* e.g. brand leader	Internal to the organisation
W	*Weaknesses* e.g. poor staff training	
O	*Opportunities* e.g. growing market	External to the organisation
T	*Threats* e.g. new legislation	

Some of the factors which appeared in the PEST analysis will reappear in the SWOT analysis. The analysis should also help the organisation to rank the individual items in the categories in order of importance. An example of a SWOT analysis for our hypothetical UK tour operator is shown in Figure 10.6.

One of the important aspects of the SWOT analysis is that the links can be seen between the different categories. The best organisation will be one which can turn threats into opportunities by the effective use of resources. For example, the tour operator may be threatened by the consumer who is worried about environmental issues and tourism. It may turn this threat into an opportunity by using its strength at branding to create a new 'green' holiday brand. This is an example of an organisation linking the items in the audit together in a creative manner.

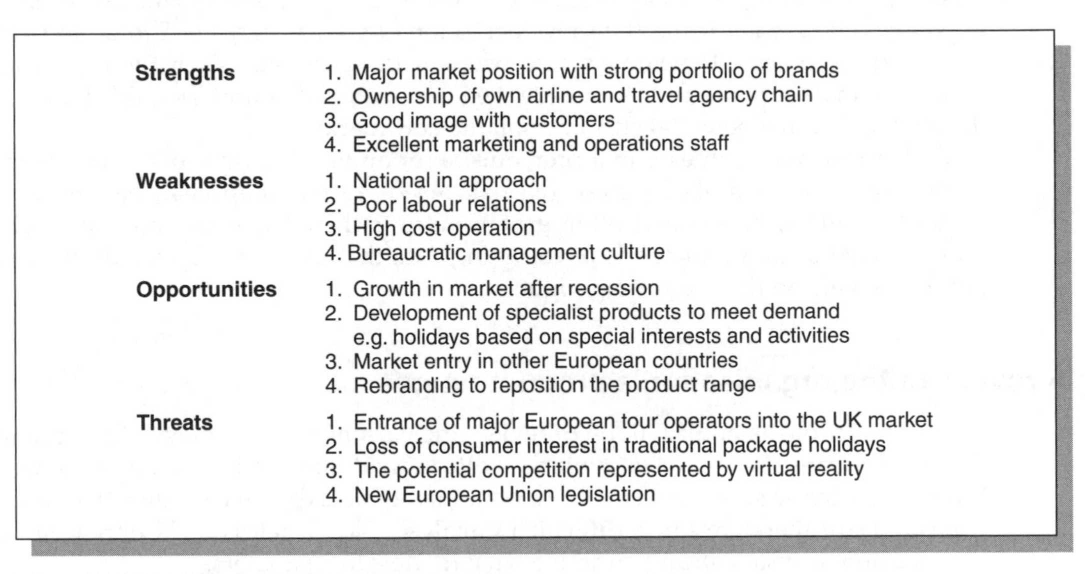

Strengths	1. Major market position with strong portfolio of brands 2. Ownership of own airline and travel agency chain 3. Good image with customers 4. Excellent marketing and operations staff
Weaknesses	1. National in approach 2. Poor labour relations 3. High cost operation 4. Bureaucratic management culture
Opportunities	1. Growth in market after recession 2. Development of specialist products to meet demand e.g. holidays based on special interests and activities 3. Market entry in other European countries 4. Rebranding to reposition the product range
Threats	1. Entrance of major European tour operators into the UK market 2. Loss of consumer interest in traditional package holidays 3. The potential competition represented by virtual reality 4. New European Union legislation

Figure 10.6 The SWOT analysis for the tour operator

A review of the current customers

The next stage of the audit procedure is to establish who the customers are for the organisation's products and services and find out more about them and their attitudes to its products. This analysis should include:

(i) The place of residence of customers;

(ii) Demographic characteristics about the customers such as age, sex and stage in the family life cycle;

(iii) Whether customers are using the product in their leisure time or when on business;
(iv) If the customers use the products as individuals or as part of groups;
(v) Socioeconomic data including education and income;
(vi) Lifestyles of the consumers;
(vii) The benefits sought from the product including status, value for money and service;
(viii) Whether customers are frequent users, occasional users or first-time users;
(ix) Customers' opinions of the product and the organisation in terms of strengths and weaknesses.

This exercise will demonstrate the different market segments which will have different motivations, different characteristics and display differences in behaviour. Each segment can then be targeted with a different set of messages about the product which can then be communicated through different marketing medias. This concept of 'segmentation' is the key to successful marketing.

It is important to remember that the organisation may also have intermediary 'customers'. For the tour operator, for example, this will be the retail travel agents. The customer analysis must reflect the importance of these 'customers' as well as the final 'customers'.

As well as finding out about existing customers, the organisation will also need to look at people who are not using their product to identify what they need to do in the future to turn these potential customers into users of the product. When the organisation is looking to market their product outside their own national boundaries, this will involve a detailed look at the potential customers in the new markets.

Market research is an essential prerequisite for an organisation to analyse its markets in the ways outlined above. Research data needs to be comprehensive, accurate and up-to-date which means it is often expensive to gather. There are, however, relatively inexpensive but useful methods of collecting data that can be used including surveys of holidaymakers on their returning flights.

A review of the organisation's product ranges

The next part of the audit will be to review the current product range. The organisation should evaluate the products it offers, both individually and as a range or portfolio. Products in the leisure market are often an intangible experience rather than a tangible good and are therefore often difficult to analyse. Nevertheless, it is important for the organisation to systematically examine what it offers to customers.

It is important to remember here that the customer is buying *the benefits* of the product, rather than just the product itself. The examination of the products offered by the organisation should look at the factors shown in Figure 10.7.

The level of branding of the product will be a particularly important aspect of this analysis, since it is the branding which will give the product the 'added value' appeal to the customer. A leading brand will communicate an aura of quality and reliability which will provide competitive advantage over lesser-known brands.

The position in the *product life cycle* is also of concern for all the organisation's products. Products which have just been launched will be costing the organisation money, with the hope of financial rewards later on. Products which are in maturity, on the other hand, will be hopefully bringing the company substantial cash turnover.

Product	Core attractions	Service component	Image and reputation	Branding
Holidays for the elderly	Ready-made package holiday	Care and attention of all staff	Leading prestigious and reliable company	Strong brand name – X

Guarantees and warranties	Main competitive products	Pricing policy	Distributor	Promotion
After-sales help (money back offers)	Other major tour operator	Value for money (all inclusive)	Via retail travel agents and direct sell	Company advertising (high quality brochure)

Position in the product life cycle	Profitability	Other factors
Recently launched (still in growth stage)	Will break even this year	Recognised as 'premier' product in this market (first to be launched)

Figure 10.7 Analysis of the product range of the tour operator

Strategic Business Unit

The concept of strategic business unit is important in the marketing planning process. The SBU is a division of product line, or other profit centre within an organisation that sells a distinct set of products and/or services to an identifiable group of customers. This set of products will compete against a well-defined set of competitive products. Costs and revenue are directly attributable to the SBU, and should be monitored and evaluated in an effective controlling system. The SBU should also be regularly researched through marketing information systems.

The concept of SBU can be applied to any type of organisation. Later on in this chapter, the model will be developed for the tour operator. Before this, the concept of the SBU will be applied to hospitality organisations.

The concept of the SBU was adapted for the hospitality organisation by Teare et al. (1994). They suggested that a typical hotel could develop a leisure-based business portfolio, for example. This idea has been developed into a model shown in Figure 10.8.

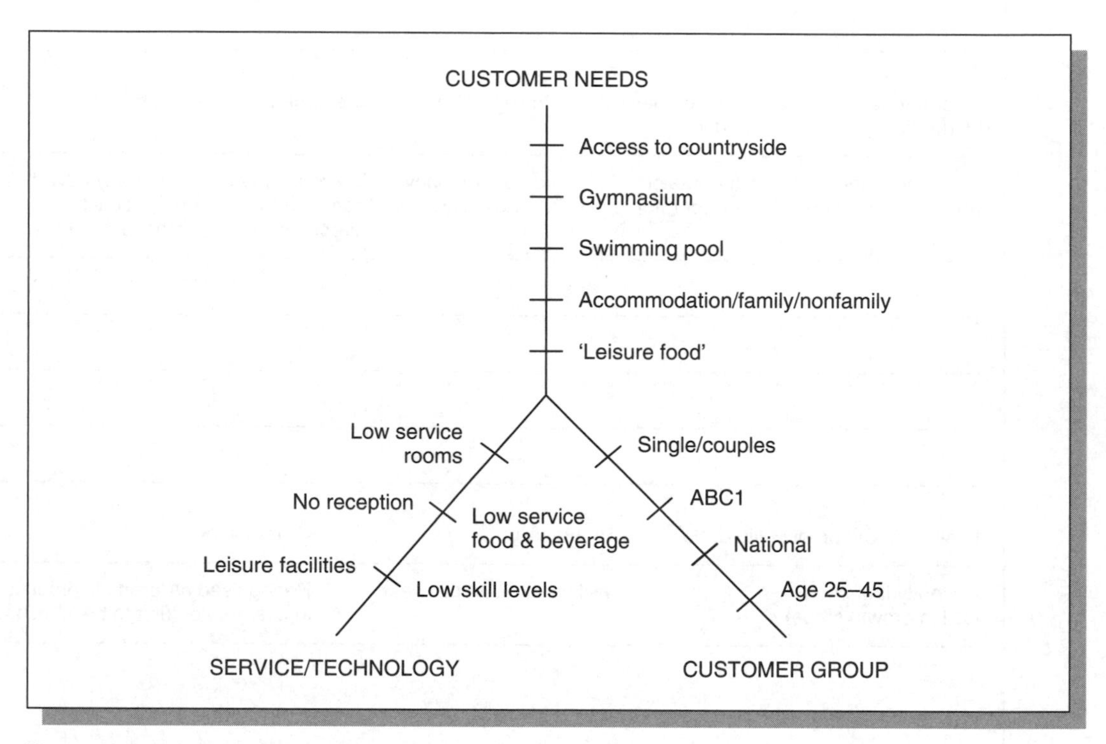

Figure 10.8 Definition of a leisure-based hotel business portfolio

Product portfolio

One method of analysis which is used to help with the marketing planning process is the idea of product portfolios. This is based on the idea that products which are sold by organisations cannot be treated in isolation, but must be looked at as being parts of SBUs, or within product portfolios. An example of product portfolio, for a tour operator, is shown in Figure 10.9. It can be seen that this tour operator has divided his business down into four SBUs. Within each SBU, there are a series of brands which make up the business unit. The idea of a product portfolio is that the organisation should meet its objectives by balancing sales growth, cash flow and risk. It is essential that the whole portfolio is assessed regularly and that the organisation has an active policy of getting rid of old products and developing new products.

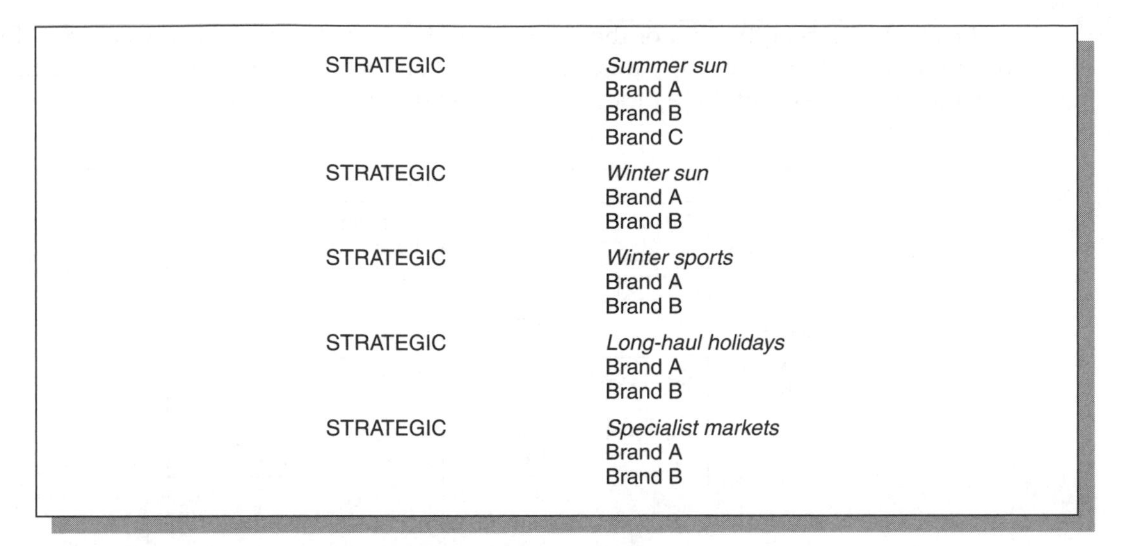

Figure 10.9 An example of a product portfolio for a tour operator

Various models have been suggested which aim to help the marketing planner with their analysis of the product portfolio of an organisation. One of the most famous of these is the *Boston Consulting Group (BCG) product portfolio analysis.*

The BCG approach is based on the philosophy that *relative market share* and *market growth rate* are important considerations in determining marketing strategy. All the organisation's products are integrated into a single overall matrix.

The overall matrix can then be evaluated to determine the appropriate strategies for individual products or SBUs. The measure of market share used in the BCG Matrix is the product's share *relative* to the organisation's largest competitor. This is important because it reflects the dominance enjoyed by the product in the market.

The BCG Matrix suggests that products can be categorised into four main groups:

1. The *star* is probably a new product which has achieved a high market share in a growing market.
2. The *cash cow* is a leader in a market where there is little additional growth. These are excellent generators of cash.
3. The *dog* has little future and can be a cash drain on the organisation. The organisation should be thinking of divesting this product unless there is good reason to keep it.
4. The *problem child* (sometimes referred to as a question mark) is a product which has not yet achieved a dominant market position or perhaps it has slipped back from a better position. The organisation will seek to move the question mark product into the star category.

The BCG Matrix can be used to show market position of products. This is shown by the area of each circle which is plotted on the matrix. The bigger the area of the circle, the better the product's contribution to the total organisation's sales volume. An example of the BCG growth share matrix applied to the tour operator's product portfolio is shown in Figure 10.10.

It can be seen that the area of the circle for each product represents the contribution of the product to the overall organisation's sales volume. The company can start to plan what to do with each of these products, armed with this information.

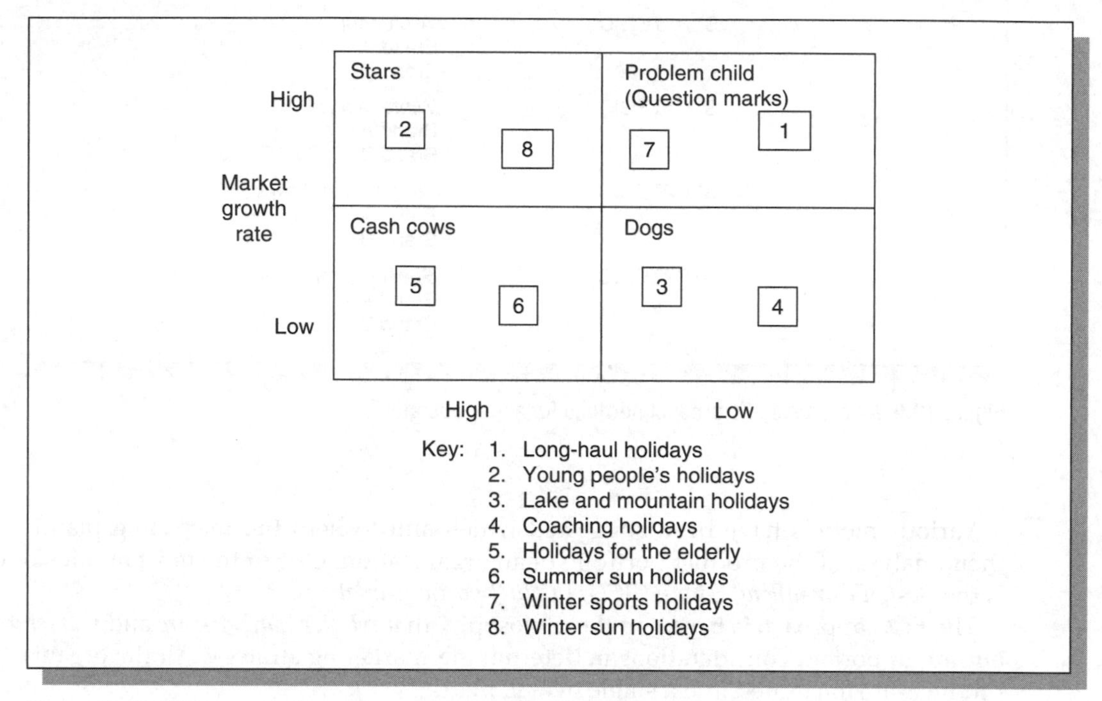

Figure 10.10 BCG growth-share matrix applied to a tour operator

To summarise, therefore, the audit of the organisation's product range should include a product life cycle for each major product. It should also contain a product portfolio matrix showing the present position of the products.

The organisation

A number of characteristics and features of the organisation are relevant to the marketing of its products and should be included in the current marketing situation analysis, including the following:

(i) The influence of marketing within the corporate decision-making structure relative to other functions such as finance and operations and the attitude of the organisation as a whole towards marketing.
(ii) The culture of the organisation – is it innovative, adventurous, dynamic and risk-taking or traditional, cautious, bureaucratic and stagnant?
(iii) The financial performance and resources of the organisation and the degree of control it exercises over its budgeting and financial management.
(iv) What are the strengths and weaknesses of the staff and how willing is the organisation to invest in training and staff development?
(v) To what extent do managers and staff have the power to make decisions and show initiative?

(vi) The mission statement, objectives and corporate strategies of the organisation.
(vii) The organisation's suppliers and its relationship with them.
(viii) The organisation's approach to quality and its quality control system.

This section should establish how the organisation as a whole obstructs or facilitates the marketing function.

Conclusion

By this stage of the marketing planning process, the organisation should have a clear view of its current marketing situation and direction. The next stage of the process is for the organisation to decide its future direction and where it wants to be at some future date. This involves the setting of objectives and the basis for the creation of a marketing strategy to guide the organisation towards its desired future destination.

Discussion points and essay questions

1. Outline a model for a marketing audit and explain the main reasons why it may be difficult for organisations to follow this model in reality.
2. Explain the ways in which an organisation might seek to establish its current market position.
3. Critically evaluate the contribution which the BCG Matrix can make to an organisation's analysis of its current situation.

Exercise

Select *one* of the following organisations:

- Cathay Pacific Airlines, Hong Kong
- Ryanair, Ireland
- Sun City, South Africa
- Legoland, Denmark
- Hermitage Museum, St Petersburg, Russia
- The Mardi Gras Gay Festival, Sydney, Australia.

Or a similar organisation.
For your chosen organisation, you should carry out a detailed SWOT analysis.

CHAPTER 11

Where do we want to go? The setting of goals and objectives

Key concepts

The main concepts covered in the chapter are:

- The setting of goals and objectives
- Mission statement
- Generating and evaluating strategic options
- Ansoff's matrix
- The concept of the 'business mix'
- Corporate and product positioning.

Introduction

This stage in the marketing planning process tends to consist of three main elements as follows:

1. setting goals and objectives that will guide the organisation's marketing over a particular period of time, based on the outcome of the current situation analysis and a consideration of the organisation's resources, history and culture;

2. the development of an appropriate mission statement that reflects the goals and objectives;
3. the establishment of a framework, within which possible strategic options will be evaluated.

This stage in the process is not about technique, rather it is about judgement, and a clear sense of direction on the part of those making these judgements.

In this chapter we will consider the ways in which tourism, leisure and hospitality organisations may go about setting goals and objectives, and developing mission statements.

However, to begin with, the authors need to define what they mean by goals and objectives. The difference between them is a blurred one, but in this context, goals are defined as broad aims while objectives are the more specific aims, which contribute towards the achievement of the goals.

In the previous chapter we looked at how an organisation can assess where it is at one particular time. The organisation will now know what its strengths and weaknesses are, and what the opportunities are for the future. It will have a clear view of its financial position and what it can afford to do next.

The next question in the marketing planning process is to set marketing strategies for the future. Where the organisation will want to go depends on the corporate strategy of the organisation and where the various stakeholders would like to see the organisation going in the future.

> 'Would you please tell me which way I ought to go from here?' said Alice to the Cheshire Cat. 'That depends a good deal on where you want to go' said the Cat.
>
> Lewis Carroll

One of the skills in marketing is deciding where you want the organisation to go.

In the marketing planning model (McDonald's) shown in the previous chapter, this stage in the process involves both Step 5 – Setting marketing objectives and strategies and Step 6 – Estimate expected results.

An *objective* is what you want to achieve. A *strategy* is how you plan to achieve your objectives. Marketing objectives are about *products* and *markets*.

Strategic options

Organisations can take a number of stances in relation to a particular market. The *market leader* is the organisation which has the largest part of the market. The market leader will set the trends in the marketplace.

The *market challengers* are not market leaders themselves, but will attack the market leader at all times. These organisations are usually number two, three or four in the market.

The *market followers* are low share competitors who copy the main innovation in the market.

Markets also usually have *market nichers*. These are companies which focus on a very small part of the market and offer speciality products. Speciality holiday companies and restaurants are examples of market nichers.

Michael Porter has described three generic strategies which he maintained could help organisations to achieve competitive advantage.

These three routes to competitive advantage were summarised by Porter (1980) as being: cost leadership, differentiation and focus.

The *cost leadership* approach involves the organisation in achieving a low cost structure which allows high returns even when the competition is tough.

Differentiation, the second generic strategy, involves an organisation developing product or service which is clearly superior in the customer's eyes, to its rivals.

Products and services which are developed by organisations which pursue a differentiation strategy are often superior in image or design which is usually reflected in their higher price.

Branding of products and services is often a method which is pursued by an organisation which operates a differentiation strategy.

Focus is the third generic strategy outlined by Porter. This is where an organisation concentrates on one particular segment of the market. Products and services are usually specialised and attract a specific customer group. Porter warns that organisations should not get 'stuck in the middle'; in other words, they should decide very firmly to pursue one of the three generic strategies. There has been some debate about this theory since it was published, because it has been suggested that it may be possible for organisations to offer a brand portfolio that incorporates more than one route to competitive advantage under the same company umbrella.

Mission statement

Once the organisation has decided on the broad strategic direction in which to go, it is usual to write a *mission statement*.

The style and content of the mission statement of an organisation will differ. Consider the examples of mission statements or business visions of organisations from the leisure industry as shown in Figure 11.1.

1. Whitbread
   Our business is focused on growth sectors of the UK leisure market – lodging, eating out and active leisure.

   By focusing management effort and future investment we can achieve higher earnings growth and improved return on investment.
2. Rocco Forte Hotels
   As Europe's premier luxury hotel operator, Rocco Forte Hotels has established an unrivalled reputation for the elegant style and individuality of its properties. With hotels in key locations from Edinburgh to Rome and St Petersburg to Brussels, Rocco Forte Hotels is focused on delivering the highest standards of service in stylish accommodation, sophisticated restaurants and rejuvenating spas.
3. Esporta Clubs
   Two key principles of Esporta are to offer superior facilities and a level of service that is second to none.

   With over 207,000 members, the company is now established as one of the country's fastest growing and most successful health club chains.

   The luxurious clubs and high quality facilities, place us firmly at the premium end of the market.

   Esporta's biggest asset is our positive, friendly and enthusiastic team. Always on hand to offer support and advice, members are made to feel at ease from the moment they enter the club.

Figure 11.1 Mission statements or business visions of organisations in the leisure industries (*Source*: Company Reports)

The mission statements or business visions try to focus on the strategic direction in which the organisation wishes to go. This vision should then be reflected in the marketing strategies and marketing objectives.

Corporate objectives

The mission statement defines the organisation and the boundaries of the business. Corporate objectives must now be set for the organisation as a whole. These may concentrate on one or more of the following items:

- Return on investment
- Profitability
- Image with the stock market, public, customers and employers
- Social responsibility
- Environmental policy.

Corporate objectives will set the framework for the *marketing objectives* for each *strategic business unit* to be set.

Marketing objectives

Once the corporate objectives have been set and the marketing audit completed, the organisation can then move to setting the marketing objectives. The setting of marketing objectives is one of the key activities in marketing because it seeks to match the organisation's resources with the external environment.

The marketing model which has been used extensively in the marketing literature to describe the various options open to an organisation when it is setting its marketing objectives is the product–market matrix developed by Ansoff, which is illustrated in Figure 11.2.

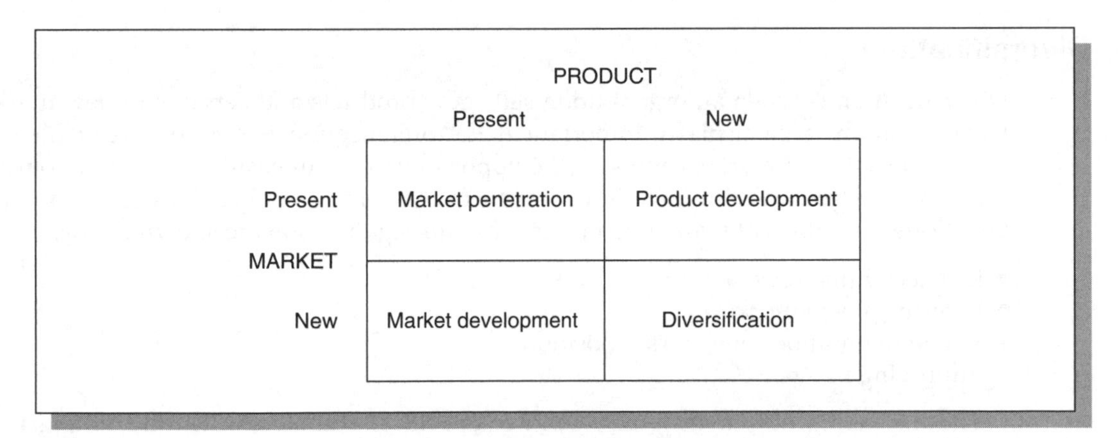

Figure 11.2 Ansoff's product–market matrix (*Source*: Ansoff, 1988)

Market penetration

Market penetration involves an organisation trying to sell more of its products and services in an existing market.

Burger King, the fast-food chain, was founded with one restaurant in Miami in 1954. The chain has grown to 11,450 restaurants in 58 countries as a result of an aggressive franchising policy.

Market development

Market development involves an organisation trying to sell its current products in new markets. Organisations often do this by selling their products and services in new geographic areas. The introduction by the French hotel chain Accor of its brands such as Novotel into the UK is an example of market development. The group has developed an international market by the use of their portfolio of brands in the hotels and service-related areas.

Product development

Product development is a strategy of developing new products for the existing market. The move of the Victoria and Albert Museum into the corporate hospitality market with specially designed services is an example of imaginative product development.

It is very important for holiday centres and visitor attractions to always have significant product development plans so that facilities are upgraded and new attractions are added. Center Parcs has carried out extensive product development and refurbishment programmes in their holiday complexes. The introduction of their new Spa and Aqua Sauna complexes at the Center Parc complexes in the UK has provided a distinct competitive advantage.

Whitbread, the UK-based brewing and leisure group, have also carried out substantial product development programmes in a number of their businesses. They have developed their restaurant business to include a portfolio of brands which include Beefeater, Brewers' Fayre, Brewsters, Costa, TGI Friday's and Pizza Hut.

Diversification

Diversification is when an organisation sells new products and services in new markets. Diversification is particularly important if the organisation wants to spread their risk across a number of markets and sees the opportunity of purchasing a brand or company.

Marketing objectives also have to be linked to the corporate objectives of the organisation. Some examples of marketing objectives of an organisation are shown below:

- Increasing market share
- Entering a new market
- Achieving number one market position
- Improving image.

The marketing objectives which will be set will of course result from the marketing audit which has already been completed.

The life cycle and portfolio analysis will allow the organisation to come to some logical decisions. For example:

- It is important to maintain the position of a 'cash cow' product or a product in maturity.
- It is important to improve the sales of a 'star' product or a product in the growth phase.

- It is important to decide what to do with a 'dog' product or a product in decline. The organisation may decide to keep the product and 'harvest' the last remaining benefits or it may decide to exit from the market.
- It is important to decide when to enter a new business with products and services. The development of new products and services will involve a market research programme so that expected results can be estimated.

The marketing objectives will also specify what the organisation wants to achieve in terms of market shares and volumes.

The business mix

Organisations in the leisure industries have a particular set of issues which must be considered when they are setting their objectives. Their demand is often highly seasonal and uneven in character which means they must try and balance demand at different times by attracting different market segments and altering their market mix.

To illustrate this point, we can consider the case of a visitor attraction and hotel. Both of these organisations have peaks and troughs in demand. It is important for each type of organisation that the business mix maximises profitability. This will mean that particular market segments are targeted in the quieter periods. It is important that during periods of high demand, the maximum revenue possible is collected. The organisation must not rely heavily on one market segment. For example, if a visitor attraction tries to fill quiet periods by targeting educational groups only, problems may occur when educational budgets are cut. The development of the most appropriate and balanced business mix is an important part of the marketing planning process. Table 11.1 illustrates issues in relation to the business mix of attractions and hotels.

Organisation	Nature of demand	Marketing strategies to overcome the problem
Attraction	Very seasonal Peak times at weekends and holidays	Offer different products at quiet periods to attract other market segments – educational trips/corporate hospitality Alter marketing mix accordingly
Hotel	Seasonal peak times Business clientele on weekdays	Offer different products – business – leisure – weekend – health – special events Alter marketing mix accordingly

Table 11.1 Getting the right business mix

Marketing strategies

Marketing strategies set the direction for the organisation. Marketing strategies define how the organisation is going to get there. Strategy is the overall route to be followed to achieve the specific objectives. The strategy will describe the following things:

- the means to achieve the objectives;
- the time programme;
- the resources required to achieve the objectives.

The differences between the strategy and the detailed implementation plan are clear. Marketing strategy reflects the broad marketing aim of the organisation. The plan which comes from the strategy will detail specifications and timing and will identify key responsibilities for people in the organisation.

Marketing strategies are therefore designed to meet the requirements of the marketing objectives. They give a broad direction. Table 11.2 demonstrates the move from marketing objectives to the marketing strategies.

Marketing objectives	Marketing strategies
Increase market share	Range extension and/or price competition and/or high advertising spend
Enter new markets	Develop new products and/or acquire a product, brand or company
Achieve number one market position	Exclusive distribution and/or high quality promotion and/or high price
Improve image	High profile public relations campaign and/or major relaunches of product range

Table 11.2 Marketing objectives and marketing strategies

Corporate and product positioning

The concept of product positioning was introduced in Chapter 6. It is important that the organisation also positions itself in a favourable light. This can be referred to as corporate positioning. When an organisation is seeking to spread its marketing activity across national boundaries, it is particularly important to have an excellent corporate positioning strategy.

One of the best examples in leisure markets has been the conversion of the British Airways company into a serious global airline. This included the 'putting people first' campaign which tried to change the staff's perception of the company and the long-term ongoing public relations campaign. Recent downturns in demand for airline seats as a result of terrorist attacks have put this strategy into question. The company has decided to offer lower prices in the short-haul market to address this issue.

There is also a link between corporate positioning and brand positioning. The French hotel chain Accor, for example, have tried to position their product range on an international basis, using a number of well-developed brands – Novotel, Sofitel, Thalassa, etc.

Beefeater, the Whitbread-owned dining chain successfully repositioned itself in 1993/94. It achieved this by designing the interior to appeal to a broad range of ages and tastes. This redesign gave the pub restaurant a pleasant, informal and contemporary ambience.

The repositioning strategy in combination with new menus helped Beefeater broaden its customer base and increase the number of visits from existing users. Whitbread has continued to reposition all their brands in a positive way, strongly linked to their market segmentation strategy.

Summary

The organisation has now set the overall marketing objectives and decided on an appropriate strategy to meet these objectives.

We considered the tour operator in Chapter 10 and looked at the process which the organisation would go through to gather together the information contained in the marketing audit. We can now look at the next stage (see Figure 11.3).

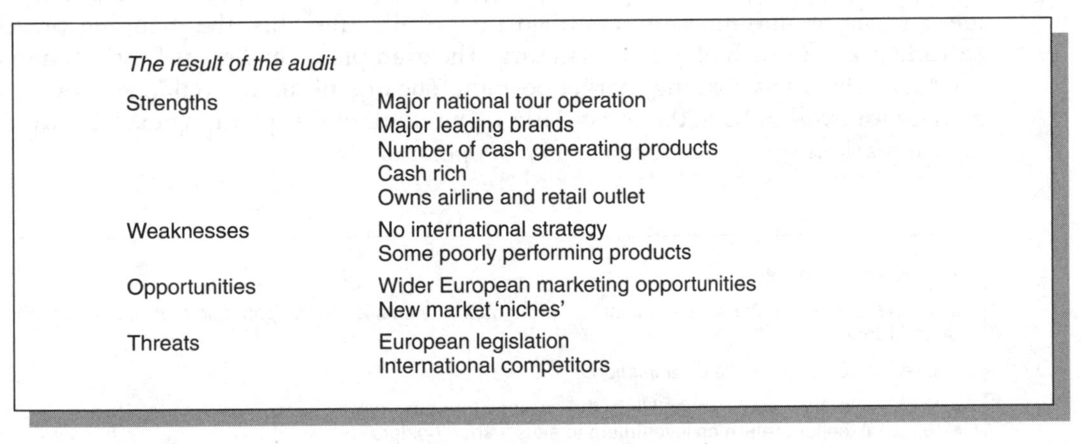

The result of the audit

Strengths	Major national tour operation Major leading brands Number of cash generating products Cash rich Owns airline and retail outlet
Weaknesses	No international strategy Some poorly performing products
Opportunities	Wider European marketing opportunities New market 'niches'
Threats	European legislation International competitors

Figure 11.3 The tour operator – setting marketing objectives and strategies

Competitive position

Organisation is in number one market position but the market is very competitive with some other strong players. There are signs that European companies are planning market entry.

Customers

Customers in the UK are not brand loyal and they look for sales promotions and discounted products.

Market

The market is strong and profitable while there is a trend by operators towards vertical integration through the ownership of airlines, retail travel agents and hotels. There are also signs that the market is fragmenting into smaller 'niches', e.g. holidays on cruise ships, 'green' holidays and 'weddings in tropical places'.

Portfolio analysis

This would give the organisation some clues as to what to plan for each of the products within their range.

The organisation could carry out a portfolio analysis based on the BCG Matrix discussed in Chapter 10. The results of this analysis could be as follows:

Cash cows	Summer sun Holidays for the elderly
Stars	Winter sun Young people's holidays
Question marks	Winter sports Long haul
Dogs	Coaching holidays

An outline of the development of the marketing objectives and strategies resulting from the marketing audit is shown in Figure 11.4. The overall objectives and the strategies for the organisation are identified first of all. After this, the planning process can cascade down to each of the SBUs in turn. The example given here is for the Summer sun product, which has a strong market position. The organisation would carry out a similar activity for every SBU in the organisation. The result of this planning exercise would be a logical marketing strategy for each area of operation.

The planning process

Mission statement – We seek to maintain our number one position in the package tour business in the United Kingdom.

Marketing objectives – the organisation

- to be the market leader in the UK in the package tour business
- to give excellent return on investment to satisfy shareholders
- to maintain our excellent image by strong differentiation
- to act in a socially responsible manner
- to look to develop in other European markets

Marketing strategies – the organisation

- to intensify our marketing programmes
- to implement a high profile public relations campaign
- to investigate the purchase of other European travel companies
- to implement an environmental policy

Marketing objectives – example one: strategic business unit summer sun

Marketing objectives

- Keep our number one market position
- Take market share from our UK competitors
- Enter new market segments in the UK and overseas

Marketing strategies

- Relaunch the product. Build brand awareness
- Introduce new destinations
- Aggressive preseason advertising campaign and sales promotions
- Investigate opportunities which arise from planned company purchase

Figure 11.4 The tour operator – setting market objectives and strategies

Conclusion

At the end of this stage of the marketing planning process, the organisation should have a clear view of what the objectives and strategies will be for the next period. The next stage will be to set detailed implementation plans so that the objectives will be met within the broad strategies which have been set.

Discussion points and essay questions

1. Briefly discuss the role of 'mission statements' and suggest a hypothetical mission statement for an organisation of your choice, explaining the reasoning behind the statement you have devised.
2. Critically evaluate the concept of 'business mix' and outline how you would go about developing an appropriate business mix for a hotel, *or* a visitor attraction, *or* an airline *or* a leisure centre.
3. Discuss the factors you might take into account when selecting a strategy from a range of options.

Exercise

For a leisure organisation of your choice, you should:

(i) carry out a brief SWOT analysis;
(ii) develop a set of marketing objectives and marketing strategies, for both the organisation as a whole and one of its SBUs, based on the model found in Figure 11.3.

You should present your ideas in the form of a written report together with a verbal presentation.

CHAPTER 12

How will we get there? Developing the strategy

Key concepts

The main concepts covered in this chapter are:

- Long-term strategies and short-term tactical plans
- Sales forecasting
- Marketing plans.

Introduction

This stage in the marketing planning process is about turning goals, objectives and mission statements into clearly expressed policies and programmes of action.

The final strategy will have two elements usually, namely:

1. A strategy covering the whole planning period, which will normally be measured in a number of years.
2. Tactical plans that detail the action which will be undertaken to ensure that the strategy is implemented. These are often produced annually so that there will be a number of them during the life of a single strategy. These plans are based on manipulating the four 'Ps' of the marketing mix, to implement the strategy. This difference is what distinguishes a marketing strategy from a marketing plan.

In this chapter we will look at the process of generating marketing strategies and plans within leisure organisations.

We will begin by looking at how strategy options are evaluated and the final one is selected. This will be followed by a detailed examination of the content of marketing plans and the issues which affect this content. Consideration will be given to the organisation of marketing activities at this stage too.

The organisation has now progressed through the marketing planning to the stage where the broad marketing objectives and strategies have been set. The next stage of the process is to estimate the expected results for each strategic business in the organisation and to plan the marketing mix which will achieve these objectives.

Setting the budget

The marketing budget must be estimated. This will be determined once the marketing objectives have been set. The budget will represent an estimate of the costs required for each planned activity on the different elements of the marketing mix usually for the next year. This will be worked out by the relevant marketing manager. The budget will determine the type of activity that can be planned. If the resource is inadequate then the plans will have to be amended. The setting of the budget and the agreement by the organisation to the proposal will be dependant on the *sales forecast* which the marketing manager will also be required to produce.

The marketing budget is very often linked to the past sales and profitability of the individual product line.

Sales forecasting

A sales forecast is the amount of a product that the company actually expects to sell during a specific period with a specified level of marketing activity. The sales forecast will be an essential piece of information which will be required so that the organisation can set their marketing budget.

Sales forecasts help the organisation to measure marketing attractiveness, monitor performances and plan production levels.

There are various techniques which can be used by a marketer to produce sales forecasts. The methods which are used depend very much on the company history and culture, the levels of risk involved and the resources available. When the organisation is taking a major financial risk, such as entering a new geographic market, the level of detail of the sales forecast should try to minimise the risks involved.

Marketers tend to use a series of methods to develop sales forecasts. These methods include:

- *Executive judgement* – This is where the past experience and intuition of the key executives in the organisation is used to develop the sales forecast.
- *Surveys* – This is where the organisation carries out surveys with customers, sales personnel or experts, to determine future trends. The *Delphi technique* is a very popular method of survey which is often used by organisations when they are preparing sales forecasts. This is where a series of experts are asked about their view of the market.
- *Time series analysis* – This technique is where a forecaster uses the historical sales data to discover patterns in the organisation's sales over time. Computer programmes can be used to help in this forecasting method. Time series analysis is very useful for organisations where the sales of the product or service is very stable. It is much less likely to be successful for organisations which sell products and services which have erratic patterns of demand.

- *Correlation methods* – This technique involves the use of historical sales data. The forecaster tries to find a correlation between past sales and one or more variables such as per capita income.
- *Market tests* – This technique involves the organisation testing out the acceptability of a product or service with customers or distributors. This method is used extensively during new product development when there may be little or no historical data to help with the setting of the sales forecast.

The sales forecast should give a clear estimate of the expected results for a period of time. This is usually for a financial year. The sales forecast should include:

- Predicted sales volume
- Predicted sales revenues
- Predicted profitability
- Predicted market shares.

The organisation will then be able to assess the suitability of the budget proposal and allocate resources effectively. This stage can involve the organisation going round this process on a number of occasions before the final decisions are made. This can be represented diagramatically in Figure 12.1.

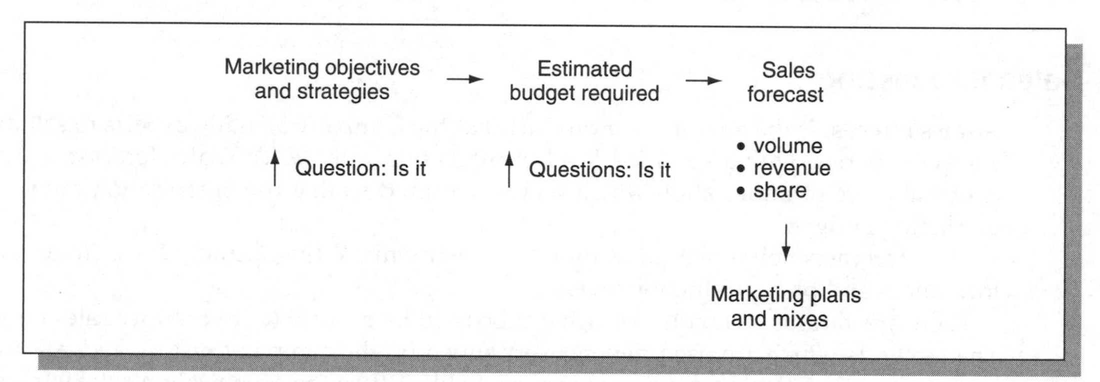

Figure 12.1 The coordination of marketing objectives, budgets and programmes

Identify alternative plans and mixes

Once the budgets and sales forecasts have been agreed, the organisation can then set the action programmes for the individual products and segments. This is usually presented in the form of a *tactical one-year marketing plan*.

The organisation may of course produce alternative plans and mixes which are assessed before a final decision is made.

Once the final decision is made, the tactical marketing plan will be written and circulated to key personnel in the organisation. It will include the major steps which are required in the implementation phase of the plan, and who will be responsible for implementing the steps, and how resources and time will be allocated.

An outline model for a one-year marketing plan is shown in Figure 12.2. An important part of this suggested plan is the inclusion of operational considerations.

The marketing plan will have to include tactical activities which will help the organisation to meet its marketing objectives. These could include items related to any part of the marketing mix, including:

Product	product development relaunch introduction of a new product
Pricing	discounting commission to retailers
Promotion	sales promotions merchandising material advertising campaigns brochure production public relations
Place	increase the number of marketing intermediaries, distribution and sales staff support

1. **Management or executive summary**
2. **Marketing objectives**
   (a) Company mission statement
   (b) Detailed company objectives
   (c) Product group goals
3. **Product/market background**
   (a) Product range and explanation
   (b) Market overview and sales summary
   (c) ABC sales: contribution financial performance assessment
   (d) Directional policy matrix evaluation of the product portfolio
4. **Marketing analyses**
   (a) Marketing environment and trends
   (b) Customers' needs and segments
   (c) Competition and competitors' strategies
   (d) Strengths, Weaknesses, Opportunities, Threats (SWOT) analysis
5. **Marketing strategies**
   (a) Core target markets (segments)
   (b) Basis for competing/differential advantage
   (c) Desired product/brand positioning
6. **Statement of expected sales forecasts and results**
7. **Marketing programmes for implementation**
   (a) Marketing mixes
   (b) Tasks and responsibilities
8. **Controls and evaluation: monitoring of performance**
9. **Financial implications/required budgets**
   (a) Delineation of costs
   (b) Expected returns on investment for implementing the marketing plan
10. **Operational considerations**
    (a) Personal and internal marketing relationships and communications
    (b) Research and development/production needs
    (c) Marketing information system
11. **Appendices**
    (a) SWOT analysis
    (b) Background data and information
    (c) Marketing research findings

Figure 12.2 Suggested format for one-year marketing plan

The organisation must check that all the planned activities fit in with the overall marketing strategies and can be funded within the planned marketing budget. It is also important that the organisation checks whether the existing personnel are capable of achieving the plan. It is sometimes important that outside agencies, such as advertising agencies, for example, are considered early in the planning stage and become actively involved if required.

Summary

When the programmes are set, the organisation will know where it is going and how it will get there. It will also have a clear view of how this is going to affect the organisation and its employees in the long and the short term.

We can now return to the tour operator which we looked at in Chapter 11. At this stage the organisation had considered the overall marketing objectives and strategies.

Summer sun

1. **Overall objectives**
   - Keep our number one market position
   - Take market share from our competitors
   - Enter new market segments in the UK and overseas
2. **Overall strategies**
   - Relaunch the product
   - Build brand awareness
   - Introduce new destinations
   - Investigate the purchase of European travel company to extend geographical market
3. **Financial objectives**

	Current year	*Next year*
Holidays sold	2 million	2.24 million
Turnover	£700 m	£784 m

4. **Marketing objectives**

	Current year	*Next year*
Market share	25%	28%

NB Assumes market remains static

NB The organisation may also produce detailed weekly or monthly sales estimates to help with the monitoring and evaluation process

5. **Detailed actions/tactics and estimated costs/responsibilities**

Total marketing budget £6.75 m

NB The organisation should also prepare detailed planning documents for major activities such as a rebranding exercise.

6. **Contingency plan**
   - This one-year marketing plan is based on the assumption that the total market for package holidays in the UK remains static next year.
   - Problems will arise if overall market demand drops in the year. Monitoring will have to take place once a week to check weekly sales levels. Tactical measures will have to be taken if market demand drops.

Figure 12.3 One-year marketing plan – The tour operator's Strategic Business Unit

Strategic Business Unit

Summer sun

We will now consider the writing and preparation of the detailed tactical marketing plan for the next year for this SBU.

The finished draft of the marketing plan is shown in Figure 12.3 and Table 12.1. The plan gives the overall objectives and strategies for the current year. A financial objective is also given to show the targets for this particular SBU.

Activity	Timing	Budget	Responsibility
1. *Product range*			
(a) Negotiate two new destinations for next season	Ongoing	£100,000	AB
(b) Handle relaunch of summer sun brand	Ongoing – to be completed for next season	£500,000	TC
2. *Promotion*			
(a) Handle ongoing PR campaign	Ongoing	Central budget	Publicity manager
(b) Prepare next year's summer sun brochure	Ongoing	£500,000	TC
(c) Sales promotion with trade	January	£100,000	AC
(d) Plan and execute TV/Press advertising campaign	Ongoing	£5 m	Liaise with advertising agency AB
(e) Start work on rebranding exercise	Ongoing – initial ideas by May	£500,000	Liaise with advertising agency and design studio AC
3. *Distribution*			
(a) Work on distribution direct sales idea	Initial ideas by May	£50,000	BD
4. *Prices*			
(a) Set prices for next year	Initial ideas by May	–	Liaise with finance department
Other activities			
Investigate possible purchase of European travel company	Report on feasibility in June	–	'Purchase Team' AB – from marketing
Ongoing market research with customer	Final report available in November	Central budget	Marketing research company controlled by AB

Table 12.1 Detailed marketing activities

This would in practice be expanded to a monthly or weekly sales estimate which would be used to evaluate performance on an ongoing basis. The plan also includes detailed plans, budgets and responsibilities for the various activities which will be required to meet the objectives of the plan.

This marketing plan would then have to be looked at in combination with all the other proposed marketing plans from other SBUs in the organisation to see if they were congruent. Once the marketing plan is agreed, it can be used as a way of communicating to all staff within the company and particularly those in the marketing and sales departments.

Conclusion

The organisation has now drawn up a detailed marketing plan for all of the SBUs' brands and product lines. These can now be agreed and implemented for the next period. The organisation must now move to the final part of the marketing planning process – the monitoring and evaluation stage or 'How will we know when we get there'.

Discussion points and essay questions

1. Outline a hypothetical marketing plan for an organisation of your choice based on the model of Dibb et al. (2001).
2. Critically evaluate the one-year marketing plan for a tour operator's SBU, which is outlined in Figure 12.3.
3. Discuss the main techniques involved in sales forecasts and examine the problems involved in sales forecasts.

Exercise

You should choose a leisure organisation. For the organisation selected you should:

(i) ascertain the organisation's current marketing objectives;
(ii) taking the organisation's current marketing situation into account develop a one-year marketing plan for the organisation, based on the model set out within Figure 12.2.

You should arrange to present your marketing plan to the organisation and its managers, asking them to comment on its strengths and weaknesses.

CHAPTER 13

How will we know when we get there? Monitoring, review and evaluation

Key concepts

The main concepts covered in the chapter are:

- Performance evaluation techniques
- Marketing information systems
- Marketing control mechanisms.

Introduction

Last, but crucially important, in the marketing planning process is the issue of monitoring, evaluation and review. This is the control mechanism in the process which ensures that the outcomes are meeting expectations.

It follows a number of stages:

- monitoring the organisation's performance against the target set in the marketing strategy/plan;
- identifying variances and seeking to explain them;
- institution action, wherever possible, to put the organisation 'back on track' to ensure that the strategy/plan, as originally conceived, is implemented in full;

- where the pattern cannot be put right in this way, because the original strategy was over-ambitious or circumstances have changed since it was adopted, then the strategy/plan has to be modified;
- the product of the monitoring, review and evaluation phase of the process becomes the starting point for the current situation analysis stage of the next cycle of marketing planning.

In this chapter we will look at how monitoring, review and evaluation can be undertaken in leisure.

We will also consider the prerequisites for successful monitoring, review and evaluation.

The final stage of the marketing planning process is the monitoring and evaluation process. This will allow the organisation to regularly review whether their plans are being adhered to and whether the targets which were set are being met.

Controlling marketing activities

To achieve the marketing objectives, the organisation must control the marketing efforts. This control will consist of setting performance standards and establishing how the organisation is achieving these standards on a regular basis. This is a fundamental activity in marketing, but evidence shows that organisations often fail at the final stage. The methods of control which are used will depend on the type of organisation, the business in which it operates, and the culture and management styles.

Performance standards must be set for all areas of the business. These will be a mix of financial goals and other standards which should also be met. Some examples of performance standards will appear in the detailed one-year marketing plan for an individual product.

Examples of performance standards might be planned in relation to weekly or monthly sales targets, successful completion of activities such as production of brochures, or rebranding exercises or increases in the total customer base. Performance standards can also relate to product quality.

The controlling process will involve looking at actual performance in relation to the performance standards and taking corrective action if necessary (Figure 13.1).

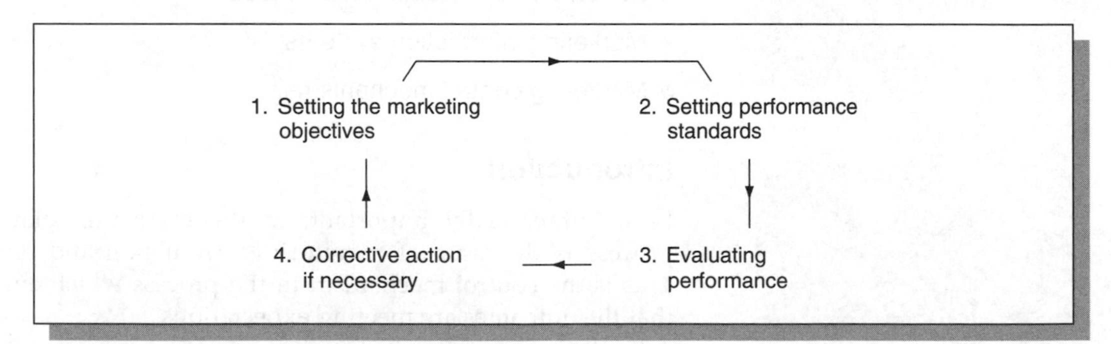

Figure 13.1 Summary of the marketing control process

Methods of evaluating performance

There are various methods which can be used to evaluate the organisation's performance in relation to set standards. The most commonly used method of evaluating performance is the use of sales data.

Sales analysis

Sales figures are used to evaluate the organisation's performance. Sales data is usually available and it is the most direct method of analysing the customer reaction to changes in the marketing mix. The customer response to a new destination or a new brochure, for example, will be reflected in the level of sales which results from these developments.

The danger with sales data is that it is presented in a form which cannot be used by the marketing manager. Sales data should be summarised before presentation if at all possible. The data should be presented in a form which relates to the sales estimate. For example, if there is a target for £500,000 of sales in one month of trading, the manager can look at the resulting sales figure and judge exactly how close the sales of the product are to this estimate.

Sales data can be presented in the form of sales volume, sale value or market share. Sales volume for a product will tell the marketer how the particular product sales are progressing. Market share data will tell the marketer how the product is performing in relation to the competition.

It will be particularly serious, for example, if both the sales volume and the market share for a product are declining. The sooner the manager knows, the sooner that corrective action can be taken to improve performance. Total sales figures should be broken down by individual products. They can also be broken down by geographic area and customers. It will be particularly important for a tour operator, for example, to know sales performance in different retail travel agents.

Marketing cost analysis involves a careful look at the costs involved in the marketing activity.

It has been suggested by Teare et al. (1994) that a marketing information system for hospitality organisations is composed of

- Accounting systems
- Data collection and market analysis
- Administration and control
- Market research.

The marketing information system for a large hospitality organisation has been evaluated by Teare et al. (1994). The model which was developed shows the components of the marketing information system and the interrelationships between them. This shows the dynamic nature of the marketing information system in a hospitality organisation which is typical for all business organisations.

One of the problems with this type of analysis is that it is often difficult to apportion central costs to specific product groups or individual products. The organisation should have a way, however, of analysing the functional costs of specific product groups, geographic areas or customer groups.

Problems with marketing control

Organisations often have fundamental problems with their marketing control processes. These problems can be summarised under three main headings:

- *Environmental changes* – Organisations often introduce changes in marketing mix programmes at the same time as something happens in the business environment. Customer demand or economic conditions may change, for example. These will both have an effect on sales.

- *Time lags* – There is nearly always a time lag between carrying out marketing activities and their effects. The marketer must allow sufficient time before sales data is analysed. The definition of 'sufficient time' will largely be a matter of judgement by the marketer based on previous experience. In a completely new market, where experience is limited, the judgement will have to be developed.
- *Difficulties in determining costs* – It is often difficult for an organisation to determine the full cost of a marketing activity for a particular product.

Despite these potential problems, the monitoring and evaluation of marketing activity detailed in a marketing plan is a very important activity. Marketing information systems should be developed which help the marketer to carry these out in a simple and effective manner.

What to do if things go wrong

The advantages of a well-developed monitoring and evaluation system is that the organisation will know at an early stage when things are going wrong.

If sales and/or market shares begin to fall, the organisation can take corrective action immediately. There may be a variety of tactical measures which an organisation can use to help in these types of situation. For example, the organisation may:

- introduce a sales promotion;
- temporarily reduce price;
- increase advertising spend;
- reduce capacity.

The organisation may also have to adjust the original marketing plan to reduce the over-ambitious sales estimates.

It is just as critical to the organisation if the indications are that the sales estimates were too low. This may mean that the company cannot meet demand and therefore will lose revenue. It may also mean that customers become unhappy and begin to look at competitor's products. This will be particularly damaging if customers are not 'brand loyal' because they will quickly change their allegiance to the competitor's products.

Summary

The final stage of the marketing planning process is very important to ensure an organisation's success. The marketer must review how the products are performing in relation to previously agreed performance standards.

We can now return to the tour operator which we looked at in Chapter 12. At this stage the organisation had completed the one-year marketing plan for the Summer Sun SBU. It is important now that the marketing manager plans a method of review and evaluation for this area of the business, so that ongoing progress can be evaluated.

Setting of performance standards

The one-year marketing plan had proposed a series of performance standards. These are summarised in Figure 13.2.

Source		Format
1. Financial performance data	(a)	Yearly sales estimates
	(b)	Sales estimates broken down into (i) weekly volume targets (ii) destination volume targets (iii) customer type targets
	(c)	Marketing budget allocated to different activities e.g. advertising budget
	(d)	Market share data
2. Key activities for the year	(a)	Overall plan with critical data and budgets
	(b)	Individual plan for specific projects, e.g. production of brochures
3. Market research of customer response		Overall targets

Figure 13.2 The tour operator – Summer Sun Strategic Business Unit. Summary of performance standards

The marketing manager for the Summer Sun product should therefore make sure that the marketing information system which has been outlined by Piercy (2002) is in place.

Piercy describes the characteristics of a marketing information system as:

- it stores and integrates information on marketing issues from many sources;
- it provides for the dissemination of such information to users;
- it supports marketing management decision-making in both planning and control;
- it is likely to be computerised;
- it is not simply a new name for market research.

In the case of the tour operator, the marketing information is coming from a number of sources.

The key activities which the manager should put in place are as follows:

- Make sure that there is a weekly summary produced of financial data, including weekly sales figures, market share and budget spend.
- Make sure that he/she has a regular review of marketing data, e.g. Mintel, Press reports, etc. Ideally once a week or minimum of once a month.
- Regular weekly/monthly meetings with key organisation staff to monitor process on individual projects.
- Regular weekly/monthly meetings with key agency staff, e.g. market research agencies, advertising agencies, etc. to monitor progress.
- Monthly review of plans for individual high profile projects, e.g. creation of the Summer Sun brochure.
- Early feedback on key market research programmes. The research of customer attitudes is very important here.
- Regular review with destination managers – how is business going? Are there any problems, etc.?

The marketer should then act on the information received and take corrective action, if necessary. It is important that both quantitative and qualitative data is received, evaluated and responded to.

Conclusion

The marketing planning process is not finished until the plan is put into action and it is continually reviewed and evaluated. It is also important that any lessons which are learned from the previous year's planning process are incorporated into subsequent years.

Discussion points and essay questions

1. Discuss the main methods of evaluating marketing performance, highlighting the difficulties involved in implementing these methods.
2. Evaluate the most important marketing control mechanisms and outline the problems associated with each of them.
3. Using examples, examine the role of performance standards in ensuring the effective implementation of marketing plans.

Exercise

Choose *one* of the following SBUs:

- the business class service offered by a privately owned scheduled airline;
- the ski-holiday product of a tour operator;
- the food and beverage operation of a major hotel.

For the SBU you have selected, you should:

(i) Suggest a range of performance indicators that would help an organisation monitor the marketing performance of its SBU.
(ii) Outline the action that might be taken if an SBU failed to meet targets set for it in relation to these performance indicators.

Part Five

Marketing in the different sectors of the leisure industry

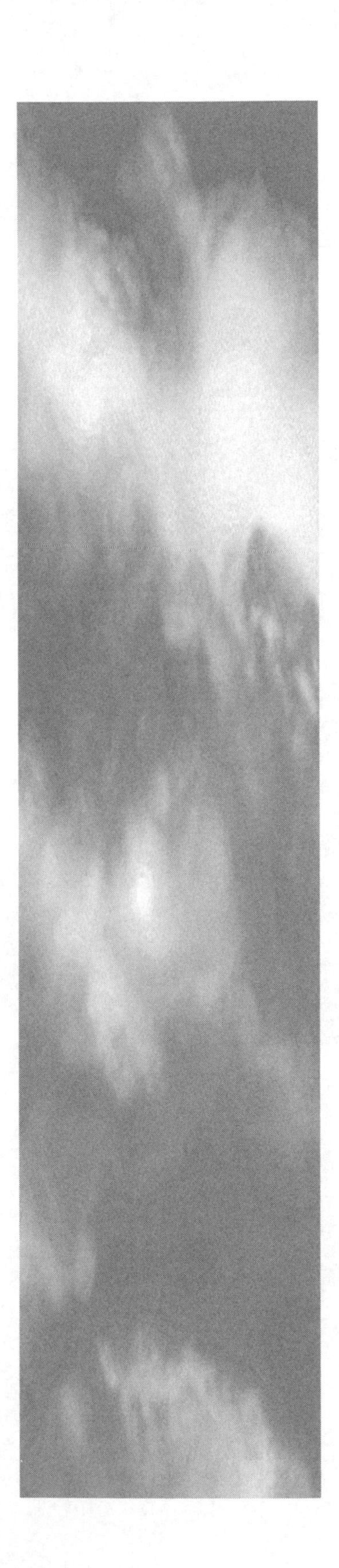

Introduction

In Part Five, the authors explore the role of marketing in eleven different sectors of leisure as follows:

Chapter 14 Visitor attractions
Chapter 15 Accommodation
Chapter 16 Tourist destinations
Chapter 17 Tour operation
Chapter 18 Transport
Chapter 19 Resorts
Chapter 20 Retail travel
Chapter 21 Arts and entertainment
Chapter 22 Recreation and sport
Chapter 23 Leisure shopping
Chapter 24 Restaurants and catering

The aim will be to identify the key factors which influence the practice of marketing in these sectors, and compare contrasting approaches to marketing between these sectors.

The main issues which will be covered to achieve these aims include:

- the marketing objectives of organisations within each sector;
- the marketing mix;
- the business environment;
- the nature of competition.

The sectors we will be considering do not represent every sector of leisure. However, they are the major ones and they do clearly illustrate the diversity of approaches to marketing that are found in leisure.

CHAPTER 14

Visitor attractions

Key concepts

The main concepts covered in the chapter are:

- Types of attractions
- Differences between the marketing of attractions in the public, private and voluntary sectors
- The role of marketing consortia
- The marketing of attractions by other organisations.

Introduction

It is very difficult to generalise about the marketing of visitor attractions as it is such a heterogeneous field. This heterogeneity results from two main factors, namely the fact that there are four different types of attraction and the fact that attractions are owned and managed by three different sorts of organisation.

Types of attraction

The *four main types of attraction* are as follows:

(i) Natural features in the landscape, such as beaches, caves, woodlands and rivers.

(ii) Man-made phenomena which, while not designed to be visitor attractions, now function, at least in part, as attractions, including cathedrals and castles.

(iii) Man-made phenomena that have been designed specifically to attract visitors and for whom the attraction of visitors is their sole function. This category includes theme parks, for example.

(iv) Special events and festivals, which are neither physical or permanent but which attract visitors to a particular location at a specific time. These may be traditional such as the Passion Plays of Oberammagau or more modern creations designed to encourage tourists to visit places they might not otherwise visit.

In the case of the first two types of attraction, the usual marketing objective is not to increase the number of visitors, but rather to manage demand, so that the attraction is not damaged by overuse. On the other hand, with attractions in the third category, the main aim of marketing is to increase visitor numbers and revenue. As far as the last category of attractions are concerned, the aim can be either managing demand to prevent the event being ruined by too many visitors, or increasing attendance to maximise the economic benefit of tourism for the local economy. In this chapter we will focus on those two types of attraction, which seek to attract more customers.

However, as we noted earlier in the book, there is an increasingly 'grey area' in terms of the distinction between attractions and destinations. Some man-made attractions, such as Disneyland Paris and Futuroscope in France, while technically attractions, appear to have more in common with destinations than with most other attractions. In terms of the area they cover and their visitor numbers, and the fact that they have on-site accommodation, for example, they appear to be more like destinations. However, the fact that they are usually in single ownership, rather than multiple ownership, confirms that they are not like other destinations, as does the fact that they usually have a single core product or theme, unlike most destinations.

Ownership and marketing objectives

The three types of organisation which own and manage attractions, and have different motives and objectives, are as follows:

Public-sector bodies which tend to be particularly dominant in certain sectors of the attraction business, including museums, historic sites, galleries, theatres and leisure centres, for example. The marketing of public-sector attractions is unusual in that the aim is rarely to make a profit, but rather to break even or operate within a given deficit budget.

We can split public-sector bodies into two types, namely central government and national agencies on the one hand, and regional and local government on the other.

For national governments and agencies, their ownership of attractions often has the following two major objectives:

1. protecting the nation's heritage in terms of historic buildings and archaeological sites, for example;
2. using them to attract foreign tourists with the result that the national balance of payments is improved.

In the case of regional and local government, its objectives for operating attractions can often include:

- increasing the range of leisure facilities which are available to the local community;
- using museums to teach children about the history of their area;
- utilising them as a way of improving the image of the area with external audiences;
- using attractions as a catalyst for the further development of the local tourism industry.

Perhaps most significantly in recent years, there has been a growing trend towards the use of attractions to stimulate economic development and regeneration.

Private-sector companies are particularly important players in certain sectors of the attraction business such as theme parks and industrial tourism. Usually, their main aim is to generate a certain level of profit or achieve a given rate of return on investment. Some of these companies, such as the Tussauds Group in the UK, are transnational operators, owning and managing attractions in a number of countries. Tussauds not only owns a number of leading attractions in the UK, such as Warwick Castle, Alton Towers and The London Eye, but also owns Heide Park in Germany. Likewise, the Lego Corporation of Denmark has developed new Legoland attractions at Windsor in the UK and in California, to add to its existing site in Denmark.

Many of these larger private attraction corporations have substantial financial resources for both product development and promotion. At the same time, the majority of private attraction operators are small- and medium-sized enterprises with much more limited budgets.

Voluntary-sector organisations play an important role in the attraction sector in some parts of Europe, such as the UK and France. Tourism is often not their core business or their main interest, rather it is used as a means to an end where the end can be conservation and community development, for example. Income generated from tourism is used by voluntary bodies to further their main work. Two examples of such bodies will illustrate their role in the attractions field:

1. The National Trust has more members than any other organisation in the UK, and celebrated its 100th year in 1995. Its main concern is with the conservation of Britain's built and natural environment. It uses its income from tourism to further this, and buying and maintaining buildings and landscapes. Its tourism-related revenue comes from entrance charges to the properties it owns, income from self-catering cottages which it lets to tourists, together with money from its catering and retailing operations.
2. The Ecomusées in France are usually run by voluntary-sector bodies set up under the Association of Law of 1901. One of the most impressive of these is that based at Puy-du-Fou in the Vendée region. However, Puy-du-Fou is not just an Ecomusée. It is also the site of, perhaps, Europe's largest theatrical spectacle.

   Each summer, over a thousand local people, all volunteers, dress up to help re-enact scenes from local history for visitors, in a show called the Cinéscénie. These performances now attract hundreds of thousands of spectators. However, all the income from the event is used for the benefit of the local community. In the past this money has been used to provide grants for local students going to study elsewhere in France and to fund a local radio station, for example.

   At the same time, the Cinéscénie has stimulated the local tourism industry and increased custom for local businesses. It has also funded the development of a heritage-based 'theme park' on the site.

There are a number of other interesting characteristics of the marketing of attractions which we will now consider.

The *attraction market* is interesting in a number of ways, notably:

- The distance people are prepared to travel to visit attractions. In some cases, attractions are the main motivation for people to travel thousands of kilometres away from their home, for example Disneyworld in Florida or Disneyland Paris in Europe. At the same time, some types of attractions such as local authority museums and most theatres appeal largely to a local audience.
- The frequency with which people visit attractions. Some people visit attractions regularly while others may rarely or never visit any attractions. Others may only visit one type of attraction.
- The motivation for visiting attractions can vary dramatically from the desire for excitement in the case of a 'white knuckle' theme park ride, to education in the case of museums, and to aesthetic pleasure at an opera performance – to give just three examples.

- The most relevant ways of segmenting the attraction market include education groups, coach parties, families and corporate users.
- The geography of demand is changing with a rapid growth in the markets in China, for example.

While little hard data exists, it also seems that there may be significant national differences in attraction-visiting behaviour in Europe.

Pricing is a very complex issue in the attraction field because of the following issues:

- Some attractions which are publicly owned make no charge for using them, even though they may be world famous and of the highest quality. Others will be subsidised so that they do not need to charge a true market price.
- Discounts are used in a variety of ways for marketing purposes, either to attract market segments which are thought to be especially desirable such as families, which tend to be relatively high spenders, and groups, because of their size. Likewise, discounts can be used to attract visitors at quiet times of the year. Attraction discounts can take two forms, namely 'added value' such as 'two admissions for the price of one' offers, or reduced price discounts such as 'fifty pence off', for example.
- Concessions, which are particularly offered by public- or voluntary-sector-owned attractions, for social reasons. The idea behind them is that they can allow 'disadvantaged' people to be able to afford to visit an attraction who might not be able to afford to visit if they had to pay the full price. These concessions are often targeted at unemployed people, the elderly, the disabled and students.
- The concept of value-for-money can be more important than the price which is charged. Consumers are often happy to pay a relatively high price if they feel they are getting good value in return, rather than paying a low price for a less impressive product. Hence the fact that, in Europe, the most expensive theme parks are also the ones which receive the most visitors such as Disneyland Paris.

Value for money in relation to attractions often seems to be based on the length of stay, the uniqueness of the attraction's product and the quality of on-site services and facilities. Some customers also believe that value for money means that the attraction charges an 'all-inclusive price' covering everything rather than those attractions where one pays on an item-by-item basis.

Distribution, in the formal sense of the term, is little developed in the attractions sector as many purchases are made, spontaneously, when people pass an attraction they think looks interesting. Indeed, as there is relatively little advance booking of attractions – except for theatres and sports events, for instance – there is little need for distribution channels. However, there are a few specialist agencies which specialise in attraction bookings. Probably the largest in Europe is that operated by the Keith Prowse organisation which offers tickets for a range of attractions in the USA as well as in the UK, France, Germany, the Netherlands and Scandinavia. Most of the attractions it deals with are theme parks with relatively high prices, so that the agency can generate a reasonable commission on selling their tickets.

Most attractions in Europe have limited budgets for *promotion*, so that for most of them television advertising is not a viable option. Most of their advertising tends to be in the printed media such as newspapers and magazines. Perhaps the most important promotional device for most attractions is their general brochure which is designed to encourage people to visit the attraction and to provide practical information to help them when they do visit. Relatively little use is made by most attractions of other types of promotions such as direct face-to-face selling or sponsorship, for example. However, press and public relations are used by many attractions to gain free media coverage.

The degree of *competition* varies between different sectors of the attractions field in Europe. The theme park business, for example, is highly competitive, while in the case of local council-owned museums and leisure centres the council only operates these attractions in its own area. There is no overlap with other areas, so that one council does not operate in such attractions in areas covered by other councils.

In these cases, the only competition tends to be internal competition where the only museums in an area will belong to one council and the only real competition will therefore be between these museums which are owned by the one organisation. The competition for attractions is, however, not limited to other attractions. It can include any other use of leisure time or form of leisure spending, such as gardening or home entertainment systems.

Competition is also complicated in the attractions sector by the pricing issues we discussed earlier; in other words, state subsidies mean that the prices paid do not always reflect the value of the product. This could be seen as a form of unfair competition by commercially managed attractions.

Attractions are often *marketed by other organisations*, as well as themselves, where they are used as part of other people's products. Examples of this phenomenon include:

- Tour operators, for whom attractions represent excursion opportunities for their clients, which may be a reason why some people choose to take a particular package holiday. For instance, some tourists may be encouraged to take a holiday in Crete because they can visit the temple site at Knossos. Likewise, tour operators selling Denmark promote Legoland in their brochures, and tour operators with programmes featuring Russia do the same for the Hermitage Museum in St Petersburg and the 'White Night Festival' which takes place in June.
- Destination-marketing agencies at the national, regional and local levels. They use attractions to persuade visitors to make trips to their particular destination, rather than to another place. Thus, in its promotional campaigns in the UK market, Maison de la France, the French government national tourist office, uses Futuroscope and the many arts festivals in France, for instance. At the same time the promotional activity of many municipalities seem to be strongly based on major attractions which they have in their area, including the following, for example, Bilbao in Northern Spain with its Guggenheim Museum.

Marketing consortia are also important in some regions, with attractions joining together to promote each other on a cooperative basis. These consortia tend to be of two types, namely:

1. those made up of similar types of attractions such as stately homes or museums;
2. those which bring together attractions in a certain geographical area.

These consortia can vary considerably in terms of their activities. In some cases, attractions simply agree to display each other's brochures, while in others cases joint brochures are produced and joint advertising campaigns and sales promotions are organised.

Conclusion

As we have seen, attraction marketing is a complex, heterogeneous activity due to the nature of the attraction product and market and the ownership structure of attractions.

Attraction marketing is particularly important for tourism and hospitality marketing in general because it could be argued that attractions are the reason why most people travel for pleasure with their resulting need for all the other tourism and hospitality services.

Discussion points and essay questions

1. Discuss the different marketing objectives that are found in the attractions sector between the public, private and voluntary sectors.
2. Examine some of the most important characteristics of pricing, distribution and promotion in the attractions sector.
3. Select one attraction which you believe has been particularly successful at marketing itself and explain the reasons why you believe it has been so successful.

Exercise

From your local area choose an attraction from each of *two* of the following types of visitor attraction:

- museum
- theatre
- shopping centre
- theme park
- leisure complex.

CHAPTER 15

Accommodation

Key concepts

The main concepts covered in the chapter are:

- Types of accommodation
- The influence of different forms of ownership on marketing objectives
- The service element of the accommodation product
- Different forms of competition in the accommodation business.

Introduction

The idea of providing somewhere for tourists to sleep is simple, but the ways in which the industry provides for this need are myriad. There are many different types of accommodation which are usually categorised on the basis of whether they are fully serviced, partly serviced or nonserviced. The following short, selective list of different types of accommodation will illustrate the diversity of accommodation types that exist:

- resort complexes
- hotels
- motels
- 'bed and breakfast' establishments
- state-owned historic hotels such as the Paradores of Spain and the Poussadas of Portugal
- youth hostels
- holiday centres and villages

- clubs and institutions
- inns, auberges and tavernas
- farmhouses
- cruise liners and ferries
- narrow boats and canal boats
- buses and coaches which can be converted for sleeping
- sleeper trains
- horse-drawn carriages
- schools with residential facilities that are available during school vacations such as the Edda Hotels of Iceland
- university and college halls of residence that are available during vacations
- timeshare developments
- campsites
- caravans both touring and static
- self-catering cottages, villas, apartments or gîtes
- privately owned second homes which are available for rent for part of the year
- homes that were used by workers but are now available for use by tourists such as the former fishermen's shelters on Rorbus of the Lofoten Islands in Norway
- mountain huts and refuges.

Even within some of these categories there are some major differences. In the private hotel sector, for example, there is a world of difference between a château hotel in the French countryside, a family-owned hotel in the suburbs of an industrial city and a high-rise hotel chain next to a beach.

Let us begin by looking at the question of *ownership* which is a complex matter in the accommodation sector, yet it is important for it influences the marketing objectives which are set for the relevant accommodation unit. A few examples will illustrate this point as follows:

- The major privately owned hotel chains set out to maximise the profits of their individual properties.
- The state-owned hotels such as the Poussadas and Paradores of Portugal and Spain respectively are designed to help conserve historic buildings while encouraging tourism to the regions in which they are located.
- Farm-based accommodation may be used as a way of supplementing the farmer's income so that the farm can remain financially viable.
- Voluntary-sector-owned accommodation, such as many youth hostels have social objectives such as making it possible for people on limited incomes to visit the countryside and encouraging youth tourism.

A vital issue in accommodation marketing is the *location* of the accommodation establishment which determines the likely level of business a unit will receive and which target market it will serve. Accommodation locations include:

- city and town centres
- suburbs of towns and cities
- major road junctions and roadside sites
- villages
- open countryside
- mountains
- coastal areas.

A unique, scenically attractive location can justify the charging of a premium price.

Location will also dictate the pattern of demand an accommodation unit will experience over a week and over a year. For example, a city-centre hotel will probably be busier on weekdays than at the weekend due to its reliance on business travellers. Likewise, coastal hotels are likely to enjoy higher occupancy rates in the summer than in the winter. In the first case, the main aim of marketing activity may well be to create more weekend business, while the latter establishments may well wish to attract more business in the off-peak season.

The *service element* of the accommodation product is important in the accommodation sector in two contrasting ways as follows:

1. In those properties where a very high level of personal service is used to differentiate it from its competitors and to justify a higher price. This is particularly true of grand old hotels such as the Dorchester and Claridges in London and the George V and Crillon in Paris, for instance.
2. In those units where little or no service is offered which is reflected in lower prices as their operation requires less labour. This is part of the thinking behind self-catering accommodation and the rise of budget motels like the French 'Formule 1' brand.

While service is usually provided by paid and trained staff, in some forms of accommodation much of the attraction to the tourist is that the service is not 'professional' as such. Hence the 'bed and breakfasts' of Britain are popular, because the 'hosts' deliver personalised attention rather than a professional standardised type of service.

The *pricing* of accommodation is influenced by a number of factors including:

- location
- facilities in the unit and in the bedroom
- level of service offered
- time of the year and day of the week.

Discounting may be used to achieve many marketing objectives, with discounts being given for a number of different reasons such as:

- to attract volume business such as conferences and coach groups;
- to reward regular customers;
- to encourage people to use the hotel at quieter times.

Last-minute discounting is a common phenomenon because once the night comes, the room no longer has any value. Therefore, hoteliers reduce prices dramatically once the evening arrives because they would rather receive some income for the room which they can set against their costs rather than nothing. They always hope that a guest may then spend elsewhere in the hotel, such as the bar and the restaurant.

Accommodation prices vary dramatically across Europe. Sometimes, a similar type of hotel might cost four, five or six times more in one European city than another. The factors that influence these price differentials include:

- the level of economic development in the country, which is usually reflected in land prices and labour costs, for example;
- the level of demand, both domestic and international, that is present in the area, region or country;
- state price controls in some countries such as Greece;
- differences between countries in terms of corporate taxation policies.

The main *distribution channels* for most accommodation establishments is still the travel agent. However, for large hotel chains, their own computer reservations systems are usually their main distribution mode. On the other hand, many small units often rely on local tourist offices in their home area. Accommodation is often also distributed via tour operators who function as wholesalers. Finally, in some cases, where accommodation units rely on 'passing trade' – people see the unit, like it, and make a spontaneous decision to purchase its product.

Most accommodation establishments have limited budgets for *promotion*, with the majority of it being spent on simple promotional brochures. Their advertising is also usually limited to the brochures produced by local destination-marketing agencies or national accommodation guides. It is the larger accommodation providers, such as the transnational hotel chains, that do spend considerable sums of money on advertising.

Because of the diversity of accommodation types, it is difficult to make generalisations about the *accommodation market*. However, we will endeavour to offer some comments which are relevant particularly in relation to hotels.

- The different target markets serviced by a unit have different needs which determine the types of facilities the unit must offer. For example, business travellers usually require single rooms, increasingly with features such as desks, fax machines and facilities for the use of portable computers. On the other hand, families look for rooms with two double beds and plenty of space, together with the availability of children's menus and baby-minding facilities.
- To be successful, hotels need to develop a mix of customers that allows them to maintain their occupancy at all times of the week and year. Conferences and individual business people are the preferred weekday market while families and coach groups are looked to at the weekends.
- The nature of a unit's market can vary from the summer to the winter. An Austrian mountain resort hotel, for instance, will be used primarily by walkers on individually planned holidays and coach parties in the summer, and by skiers in the winter.
- As it is heavily dependent on business tourism as well as leisure tourism, the hotel market is greatly influenced by the economic state of particular countries. Thus, given the dramatic differences in national economies, it is not surprising that there are great variations in national hotel markets across the world at any one time.

Competition is generally very strong in the accommodation sector. There are two main types of competition, namely:

1. that between different types of accommodation such as hotel versus villas in Mediterranean resorts like Benidorm and Albufeira;
2. that between different units which are all of a particular type of accommodation, such as major hotel chains within a city centre.

Price has traditionally been the way in which accommodation operators have sought to achieve competitive advantage. Other methods can include the following:

- offering facilities for particular types of customer such as families and women business travellers;
- the development of in-house leisure facilities;
- in-bedroom services such as satellite television;
- the growth of niche services such as the recent development of the stylish boutique hotels that target a particular market.

There are two particularly interesting forms of competition faced by some commercial accommodation establishments as follows:

1. Those people who offer accommodation, wholly or partly as a 'hobby' rather than a commercial business. This is true of many people living in large houses who rent out one or two rooms. They often deliver an excellent service and provide large bedrooms at a low price, with which larger commercial hotels cannot easily compete.
2. The phenomenon of 'visiting friends and relatives' (VFR) where people stay away from home as tourists at the homes of friends or relatives, free of charge. However, this is not really competition as most of these people would not travel in the first place to the location in question if they did not have friends or relatives there.

Accommodation units are often *marketed by other organisations* apart from themselves because they are part of the product offered by other organisations. This usually relates to one of two different types of organisation, namely:

1. Destination-marketing agencies for whom the stock of accommodation available in their area is a crucial part of their offering as a destination. Accommodation is usually promoted through the brochures produced by the destination-marketing agency.
2. Tour operators who feature and promote accommodation units in their brochures to encourage their prospective clients to purchase the holiday based in the accommodation unit which is being offered by the tour operator.

Consortia play a growing role in accommodation marketing. Three types of consortia that are particularly relevant to accommodation marketing are as follows:

1. marketing consortia which provide marketing expertise for their members such as Relais et Châteaux;
2. reservation systems which provide a central reservations service for their members, which was the origin of the UTELL organisation;
3. so-called 'referral consortia' which are often links between hotels and airlines where one would recommend the other to its customers – Golden Tulip Worldwide Hotels was an early example of such a consortium.

In some countries there are state-backed or state-controlled consortia designed to function as marketing consortia for particular types of accommodation. Gîtes de France in France is an example of such an organisation.

Accommodation corporations, particularly the major hotel chains, have in recent years started increasingly to use three modern types of *growth strategy* as a way of expanding at a relatively low capital cost.

1. *Franchising* is where the organisation or franchiser generally owns the brand name and sets a range of specifications which franchisees must follow. The franchiser usually offers the franchisee a range of support services such as IT systems and marketing advice, together with training and purchasing. The franchisee can be an individual or a company, and they pay the franchiser fees based on room turnover, as well as providing all or part of the capital required to buy or build the unit.
2. *Management contracts* involve accommodation corporations taking contracts to manage, rather than own, particular accommodation units. Their fee tends to have two components, a basic fee and a share of operating profits. Sometimes the contractor will take a minority equity stake in the unit in question. In Europe, a number of hotel chains are involved in management contracting such as Bass plc in the UK.

3. *Leasing* is where an accommodation corporation pays rent to the unit's owners and then keeps the rest of the hotel's profit for itself. This system has proved particularly popular with UK-based companies, including Stakis and Ladbroke, in the past.

Conclusion

We can see from the above discussion that accommodation marketing is a diverse field due to the many very different types of accommodation that exist, and the different types of individuals and organisations that offer accommodation.

Discussion points and essay questions

1. Discuss the main issues involved in pricing within the accommodation sector.
2. Evaluate the concept of competition within the accommodation sector and outline the different forms of competition that exist.
3. Explain the role of consortia within the field of accommodation marketing.

Exercise

Choose an accommodation establishment which you are able to visit. For your chosen establishment you should produce a report evaluating the quality of product it offers in relation to the following criteria:

- location
- facilities
- service
- value for money.

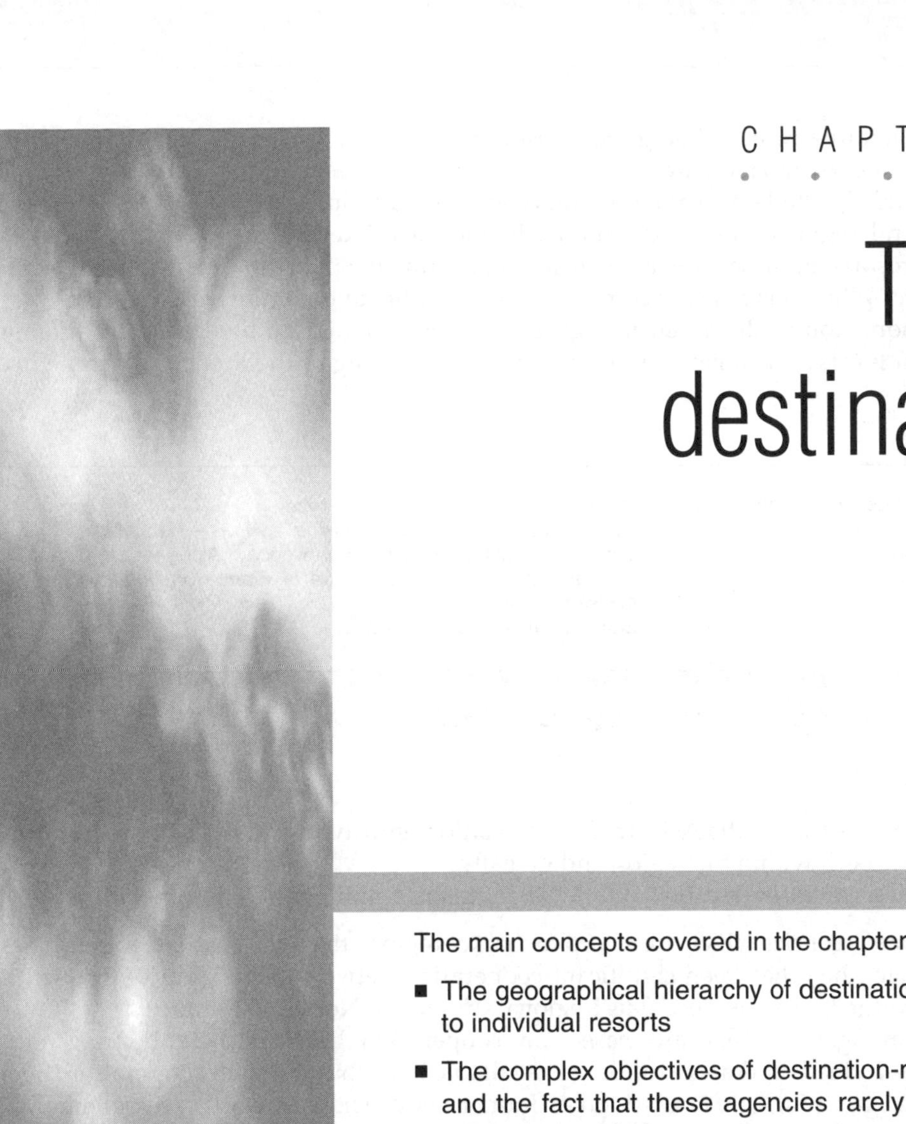

CHAPTER 16

Tourist destinations

Key concepts

The main concepts covered in the chapter are:

- The geographical hierarchy of destinations from continents to individual resorts
- The complex objectives of destination-marketing agencies and the fact that these agencies rarely own or control the product as a whole
- The fact that no direct charge is made for the use of destinations
- The role of marketing research in destination marketing.

Introduction

In this chapter, we will consider the key issues involved in the marketing of tourist destinations. The marketing of tourist destinations is perhaps the most complex form of marketing in leisure. There are a number of reasons for this complexity but there are perhaps four which are of most significance.

Destinations exist at a number of different geographical levels which are interrelated. Within the European context, some tourists can see the whole continent as a single destination, for example, 'Inter-Railers' who tour Europe on a rail ticket that allows them to travel in most European countries. Other tourists talk about a country being their destination, for example, 'this year we are going on a coach tour of Ireland'. Regions often function as destinations, such as the Lake District in the UK, the Loire Valley in France and Tuscany in Italy. Some of these regions can be natural regions that cross national boundaries, like the Alps. Finally, there are individual resorts or urban areas such as Benidorm in Spain or cities like Paris and St Petersburg. While this appears complex, it is a simplification of the true situation.

This phenomenon is illustrated in Figure 16.1, which shows all the bodies at different geographical levels, which have an interest in the marketing of the French resort of Nice:

Municipality (Local Authority)	:	Office Municipale du Tourisme = Nice
Département (County)	:	*Comité Départementale du Tourisme = Alpes – Maritimes*
Région (Region)	:	Comité Régional du Tourisme = Provence – Alpes – Côte d'Azur
National	:	*Central Government = Maison de la France on behalf of the Ministère du Tourisme*
Europe	:	European Travel Commission

Figure 16.1 The marketing of Nice at different geographical levels

In Asia, PATA – the Pacific Asia Travel Association endeavours to market the countries of Asia-Pacific both within the region and globally.

The situation can be even more complex than this in a number of ways, including:

- Transnational agencies which are set up to market regions that cross national boundaries. For example, there has been significant cooperation between Kent County Council in the UK and the Nord-Pas-de-Calais Regional Council in North East France.
- Subregional agencies that are based on cooperation between neighbouring local authorities. Indeed, in France, funding is available to encourage such cooperation. Such subregional groupings are termed 'Pôles Touristiques'. These consortia are potentially a good way of overcoming one of the major traditional problems of destination marketing in Europe, namely tourist destination boundaries where local authority boundaries do not mirror tourist perceptions.

In spite of these latter initiatives, coordination between the different geographical levels is still one of the major challenges of destination marketing across Europe.

Secondly, *the objectives of destination marketing tend to be more complicated than those for other types of marketing, reflecting the fact that most destination marketing is carried out by public-sector bodies rather than private companies*. These public bodies are often involved in destination marketing for a wide range of reasons, most of which involve tourism being used as a means to an end rather than an end in itself. Tourism is often used by these organisations to achieve a number of outcomes, including:

- Improving the image of an area in the hope that this will encourage industrialists to relocate their factories and offices to the area.
- Increasing the range of facilities and amenities that are available for the local community. Income from tourists can help keep local shops, theatres and restaurants viable when they might go bankrupt if they had to rely solely on local residents. Tourists can also help justify and fund infrastructure development that might also benefit local people

such as new roads and airports. The same argument applies to new attractions such as museums.
- Giving local residents more pride in their local area which can happen when people see that tourists want to visit their region.
- Providing a rationale and funding for improvements to the local environment.
- Trying to make the destination politically more acceptable to outsiders by giving them an opportunity to see for themselves either what the place is actually like or what the government wants tourists to think it is really like. In the former Soviet Union, for instance, tourism was used to try to give outsiders a positive view of the achievements of the political regime.

However, public bodies can have a financial vested interest in tourism for themselves, for they can earn income from tourism in a number of ways. Central government gains revenue from sales taxes and fares paid to some state-owned airlines, for example, while local authorities often gain from the charges paid by tourists to visit public-owned tourist attractions.

The *organisations who are charged with marketing destinations are largely promoting a product over which they have no direct control, and which is not a single product.*

Destinations are a composite product which is made up of a number of components, including:

- accommodation establishments
- restaurants
- bars
- theatres, cinemas and nightclubs
- transport systems such as taxis, metros and buses
- natural features like beaches and cliffs
- man-made attractions including cathedrals, theme parks and museums
- the availability of excursions to nearby attractions
- sports centres and leisure facilities
- special events.

Generally the public-sector organisations who market destinations neither own nor control the vast majority of these elements of the destination product. Yet they have to endeavour to market them as a cohesive whole.

Finally, *no direct price is charged for visiting the destination* so that standard marketing approaches to pricing are not really applicable. This is why, for example, pricing has not as yet proved a very successful way of reducing peak demand in destinations which receive more tourists than they can cope with at peak times, like Venice.

Consumers pay to use the individual components of the destination product but not for the destination itself. Day trippers, therefore, can often use a beach for a whole day and use local infrastructure such as the road network, without contributing any money to pay for the services they use.

This fact is at the root of one of the most controversial aspects of destination marketing. In other words, most destination marketing is funded by the whole community through taxes paid to public-sector bodies. Yet most of the economic benefits go to private-sector enterprises, while the consumer rarely pays the true cost of their visit. This is clearly a moral dilemma.

The lack of control over the product which most destination-marketing agencies experience, together with the absence of a pricing mechanism, has led many of these agencies to concentrate on the *promotional element of the marketing mix*. Most destination-marketing organisations are, therefore, involved in a range of promotional activities, including:

- The production of *brochures*, both promotional and informative, although both functions may be served by a single piece of print. The promotional aspect briefly involves using colour photographs and prose laden with adjectives to sell attractive images of the destination to potential customers. The informative aspect of a brochure might involve hotel lists, a directory of services available within the destination and information on travelling to the destination.

  As well as producing a general brochure to cover the whole destination, a range of other brochures may also be offered. These may cover smaller geographical entities within the overall destination region. Alternatively, they could be targeted at specific market segments such as sports enthusiasts or business travellers.
- The placing of *advertisements* promoting the merits of visiting the destination. As the budget of the relevant agencies are often limited, most advertisements are placed in the printed media, rather than the more expensive, but more effective, medium of television. Most resort advertising is seasonal, and takes place when it is thought potential visitors will be making their holiday decisions. In the UK, for example, this leads to a plethora of resort advertising in late December and January. Most of the advertisements seek to encourage potential consumers to request a copy of the destinations brochure.
- *Press and public relations* play a significant role in the marketing activities of many destination-marketing organisations. Journalists are offered free familiarisation trips to the destination in the hope that this will result in them writing favourable articles about the destination. The same is true of television broadcasters. Likewise, many destinations undertake public relations activities to improve their image with the general public. They put out press releases on a range of 'good news stories' about the destination which they send to the media which they feel are used by their target markets. For agencies, with limited budgets, this very low cost form of promotion is particularly attractive.
- Relatively little *direct selling* is carried out by destination-marketing agencies. However, such selling is often used to attract high-spending, and thus economically valuable, conference business or coach groups.
- Due to the lack of control over the destination product and pricing, *sales promotions* are used relatively little in destination marketing. However, 'added value' promotional offers may be made available, featuring elements of the destination product over which the destination-marketing agency does have control. Thus, a local authority that owns a theatre and a museum could offer reduced price entry for people who visit the destination at certain times of the year.
- Attendance at *trade fairs and exhibitions*, aimed at both the public and the tourist trade.
- Some destinations have begun to make effective use of the Internet as a marketing tool, such as Singapore.

Most of the promotional efforts of destination-marketing organisations are channelled through the *tourist information centres* which most of them operate. These centres are the public face of the agency for visitors who are already in the destination, as well as for those who are potential visitors.

In relation to the marketing mix, these centres also perform the 'place' function, in other words, distribution, albeit, usually for elements of the destination product such as hotels, rather than for the destination product as a whole.

The role of tourist information centres varies across Europe but most of them distribute brochures and respond to requests for information. They may also perform a range of other services, including:

- hotel booking
- currency exchange
- selling local excursions
- selling travel tickets.

However, the more commercial activities can bring them into conflict with local traders, who can see these public sector subsidised centres as unfair competition. It is also vital for their credibility with the business community that these centres are seen to be impartial, rather than promoting particular enterprises only. Thus they will often not recommend hotels but simply give customers a list.

Increasingly, many tourist information centres are seeking to increase their budget by engaging in more commercial activities. Some, such as the Syndicats D'Initiatives and Offices du Tourisme, in France, have membership schemes. Private businesses pay to join in the knowledge that the centre will only actively promote the enterprises which are in membership.

Some destination-marketing agencies have sought to compensate for their lack of control of elements of the destination product by fulfilling the role of *packaging the destination product*. In part they have taken on the role of tour operators in putting together package holidays based in the destination. These packages usually include hotel accommodation as their core element, while extra elements may be incorporated including excursions, entrance to attractions, travel to/from the destination, transfers within the destination and special events.

They can also be used to promote a certain image of a destination that the agency wishes to develop, such as arts and cultural breaks in industrial cities, for example. Such themed weekend breaks have become more popular in recent years. There are many types of such breaks, including:

- activity holidays such as those provided by the Loisirs Accueil agencies in France;
- breaks linked to special events such as arts festivals;
- breaks for people who want to spectate at sporting events, like the highly successful soccer weekends which are offered in Liverpool in the UK;
- themed holidays for people who want to visit areas where films or television programmes have been set.

In many European countries, in recent years, there has been a growth in *public–private sector partnerships in destination marketing*. This has occurred for a number of reasons, notably:

- the desire for a more coordinated approach to destination marketing;
- the need to use the financial resources of the private sector to supplement the limited budget available for public-sector destination-marketing organisations;
- a wish to bring private-sector marketing expertise into the field of public-sector destination marketing.

Within the UK, for example, these partnerships have often followed the American model of Visitor and Convention Bureaux. In Birmingham and Glasgow, to give but two examples in the UK, agencies exist which are funded by both local authority grants and contributions from private-sector enterprises such as hotels and attractions. However, many such partnership agencies find it difficult to consistently attract adequate private-sector funding and tend to rely heavily on the public sector for their financial stability.

A major potential role for destination-marketing agencies, which can increase their reputation with private-sector organisations is *marketing research*. As we have noted elsewhere in the book, marketing research is a vital prerequisite for successful marketing, yet it is still at an early level of development in the tourism field.

Destination-marketing agencies can play a vital role in this area because they can take an overview which an individual enterprise cannot, and because they have no commercial vested interest, they can be relatively impartial.

Good marketing research can be beneficial for destination marketing in three main ways as follows:

(i) It can help the destination-marketing agency to carry out its marketing function more effectively.
(ii) It can assist private enterprises refine their marketing in terms of their product, price, place and promotion.
(iii) It can be used to help attract entrepreneurs to invest in new projects in the destination. If reliable and detailed market research data exists, it gives these entrepreneurs the confidence to invest in a particular destination.

There are two types of marketing research, namely:

1. Quantitative – the number of visitors, when they come, where they come from, what they do in the destination, how much they spend and so on.
2. Qualitative – why they come to the destination and their opinions on the various aspects of the destination.

Traditionally, marketing research in leisure focuses on existing customers who are easier to access. However, it is increasingly being recognised that we also need to focus on those who do not currently visit the destination and find out their reasons for not visiting. Future success may well depend on turning these nonusers into users, of the destination product.

To fulfil potential benefits of marketing research, the data must be available at the appropriate geographical level. For example, data which is only available on a regional basis may be of little value to a single resort only in that region if its market is significantly different from the market of the region as a whole.

In France, marketing research data is particularly good and is managed by a national, state-controlled body, the Observatoire Nationale du Tourisme. On the other hand, in the UK, public-sector marketing research is much less developed. Whereas in France, marketing research appears to enjoy a high status, in the UK, it has, until recently, had something of a 'Cinderella' status. Marketing research has often been the first function to be cut if the tourist boards or resort marketing department budgets were under pressure.

Good marketing research is expensive but the cost of not having good data in a competitive market will, increasingly, probably be even more expensive.

Conclusion

We have seen that destination marketing is perhaps the most complex form of marketing in the leisure fields. It is largely carried out by public-sector bodies which have complex social, economic and political motives.

Destination marketing exists at a number of interrelated geographical levels and involves interrelationships between a myriad of public-sector organisations and private-sector enterprises.

Discussion points and essay questions

1. Discuss what you consider to be the three main reasons why destination marketing is such a complex activity.
2. Using examples, evaluate the role of public–private sector partnerships in destination marketing.
3. Discuss the contention that the public sector should play no role in destination marketing.

Exercise

Select a tourist destination with which you are familiar and which you are able to visit. You should investigate its current marketing situation and identify its strengths and weaknesses, together with its opportunities and threats.

You should then produce a five-year marketing strategy for the destination on behalf of the local municipality or relevant government body.

Finally, you should focus on how the strategy will be implemented, including the following issues:

- budgets and where the money will come from;
- who will be responsible for implementing the strategy;
- partnerships with public-sector organisations;
- timescales.

CHAPTER 17

Tour operation

Key concepts

The main concepts covered in the chapter are:

- The role of tour operators in the tourism system
- The highly interdependent nature of the tour operation product
- The price elasticity of the European mass FIT market
- The highly competitive nature of the European tour operation market
- Vertical and horizontal integration as growth strategies.

Introduction

Tour operators are often described as the wholesaler in the tourism system, operating between the producer and the primary product and the retailer. However, the tour operator can also be seen as a producer who takes raw materials, like hotel beds and airline seats, and processes them into a 'manufactured' product which it then sells. The tour operator, it could be argued, represents the only genuine tourist industry that is not simply a subset of another industry. They perform a unique function in the tourism system.

However, as we will see, there is nothing homogenous about tour operation, either in its nature or in its marketing function. Let us consider some of the factors that influence the approaches to marketing which are adopted by tour operators, together with some of the key issues in the practice of tour operation marketing.

The *size* of tour operators is an important factor. There are major differences in marketing between the major European mass-market large-scale tour operators, such as TUI and Thomsons who move literally millions of tourists around per annum, and the small, specialist operators, who may only handle a few hundred customers a year. This links to two other issues which relate to size and have implications for marketing, namely *ownership* and *marketing objectives*. The large tour operators are often part of big corporations with other business interests. On the other hand, the small ones are often owned by individuals or families and can often be run as a 'hobby' or part-time business. This is true, for example, of some special interest and activity holiday operators or some of the British tour operators who offer self-catering holidays in France. The two types of operator, therefore, tend to have different marketing objectives, whereas for the big operators profit maximisation is usually their main concern. These small operators are often willing to accept less than optimum profit levels, provided that the business gives them an opportunity to indulge in their hobbies or interests, whether these be cycling in Wales or enjoying the food and wine of France, for example.

There are a number of differences in the nature of the *product* offered by tour operators, including the following:

(i) Some operators offer packages featuring destinations in their own country while others offer products based on foreign destinations.
(ii) Operators can offer highly structured, all-inclusive packages where everything a holidaymaker will need is included in a single-priced package. This is the approach of Club Mediterranée. On the other hand, some companies are recognising that other customers are looking for more flexibility and they are offering much looser packages, such as fly-drive and travel-and-accommodation-only holidays, with no meals and transfers.
(iii) Many tour operators offer the services of in-resort representatives as part of the product they offer. The quality of the representative is usually considered to be a major element in the holiday experience of the customer.
(iv) Because the tour operator is a wholesaler, they are totally reliant on their suppliers for the quality of their final product and their marketing intermediaries for the messages about their product which are relayed to customers.
(v) Some operators offer a broad portfolio of products, designed to service a range of markets, while others focus on either particular types of holidays (skiing or cycling for example), or specific countries.

Ultimately, perhaps, the most interesting aspect of the tour operation product is that it is a composite product, made up of a number of elements (destination, attractions, hotels, transport and so on). In some ways, it could be argued that it is not a finished product but rather a set of opportunities for consumers to create their own self-service holiday product. A plane load of tourists travelling on the same plane to the same hotel in Crete, for example, will all use the basic product in a different way. Some will stay around the hotel pool or the local beach while others will explore the island's archaeological sites, merely using the hotel as a base. Some will go to bed early while others will wake in the afternoon and dance through the night in the local clubs. The package tour offers customers an incredible variety of possible experiences, from which the tourist chooses those which they prefer.

Price has always been a key issue in the tour operator sector. For the mass market operators in most countries, their market is highly price-elastic. These operators specialise mainly in inexpensive holidays with low profit margins, where profits come from volume rather than the margins on individual sales. Smaller and specialist operators on the other hand tend to be able to offer prices that allow for more generous margins. This is important as they do not have the volume sales to make a profit unless they can generate higher margins.

In some countries, notably the UK, last-minute discounting is now an accepted part of the market. Consumers wait until near the departure time for a particular holiday and then look for bargains from operators who are keen to ensure that no capacity is left unsold when the holiday begins.

The existence of these last-minute bargains has changed the market so that many clients do not now book their holidays until a few days before they wish to travel. This phenomena affects profit margins and makes long-term capacity planning very difficult for tour operators.

The obsession with price, most notably in some North European markets, has implications for quality. Often the last-minute bargains are in unnamed accommodation so that clients do not know where they will be staying, which gives great scope for disappointment. Likewise, if people buy purely on price, they can find themselves in places they do not like or would not have otherwise chosen.

Likewise, for the operators and supplies, low prices and discounts give little opportunity for the enhancement of quality standards.

Traditionally, the *distribution* of this tour operation product was via travel agents. However, increasingly some operators are looking to sell directly to their customers, thus saving the commission they pay to the travel agents. Technological innovations, notably the Internet, are making it easier for tour operators to communicate directly with their customers.

As far as *promotion* is concerned, tour operators still rely very heavily on their brochure, which is often a thick, glossy, full-colour catalogue, designed to persuade people to purchase the product. One trend in recent years has been the replacement of the brochure which included every product offered by a company with several brochures featuring different products, such as activity holidays, city breaks or different countries.

Advertising is also heavily used, particularly at the start of the year when consumers are deciding on their holiday plans.

Substantial use is also made of other promotion techniques, including:

(i) Press and public relations, with many operators trying to encourage travel journalists to take one of their holidays free of charge, in the hope that they will then promote them via their television programmes and newspaper articles, in a positive way, to potential customers. This relationship clearly raises some interesting ethical dilemmas.
(ii) Direct selling, largely in terms of tour operators sales staff encouraging travel-agency counter staff to sell more of their company's holidays. This activity involves giving travel-agency staff gifts and financial rewards for selling particular products.

The promotional activities of some tour operators have drawn criticism because of their apparent lack of honesty. This ranges from the inducements to travel-agency staff and the fake statements that have been found in some brochures, for example. The European Package Travel Directive was introduced, largely, to curb some of the more dubious practices in tour operation promotional activities.

There are also a number of aspects of the tour operation *market* that influence the way in which package holidays are marketed. These include:

(i) Whether the operator offers their products primarily within the domestic market or whether they also sell their holidays to people resident in other countries. In the latter case, operators have to take into account national differences in terms of consumer behaviour, business culture and statutory controls on tourism.

(ii) Consumers are not consistent in their behaviour patterns, for their decision-making has to take into account a range of factors that are always changing, such as their income, time availability, health, responsibility for caring for others, people they will be travelling with and so on. These behaviours can then change dramatically from one holiday to another. This year, a British consumer goes on holiday with their friend to Spain's Costa del Sol and has a 'hedonistic' holiday.

Next year, the same consumer goes on an educational field trip to the archaeological remains of Greece, as part of their university course. The following year, this person gets married and goes on honeymoon to Paris, with the partner. By the following year, they have a baby and stay in their own country as they are concerned that the food and sun in another country will make the baby ill.

(iii) There are a number of ways of segmenting the tour operation market, including:

- Geographical methods in terms of where people live, which helps determine which departure airports operators should offer their clients and the preferences of customers for different geographical areas. For example, some people like mountains while others prefer particular countries. Some from Northern Europe are drawn to Southern Europe because of the sun, while others from Southern Europe travel North to escape from the hot summer sun.
- Much tour operation marketing is based on demographic segmentation. For example, holidays are labelled as family holidays and singles holidays, or they are aimed at young people or retired people, for example, Club 18–30 and Saga, in the UK. Likewise, holiday advertisements can be linked to stereotypes relating to sex, such as men playing golf and women shopping.
- Psychographic segmentation is becoming increasingly important, as we recognise that people often buy holidays that relate to their everyday lifestyles. Thus we are beginning to recognise holidaymakers who are interested in healthy holidays or green holidays.
- The purpose of travel which can include religious pilgrimage, health, education, business, making friends, enjoying new experiences and relaxing, for example.

(iv) Consumers often have unreasonable expectations of what they expect a holiday to do for them. For some people, a holiday is used to recover from a bereavement or a broken relationship or to put new life into a failing marriage.

(v) It is difficult for the operator to guarantee the quality of the consumer's experience as many of the factors that shape this experience are outside the control of the operator. These include strikes and civil disorder, bad weather and the behaviour of other people who are in the resort at the same time as the operator's clients. The consumer, therefore, may hold the operator at least partially responsible for weaknesses in the product which are outside the operator's control.

(vi) The behaviour of tourists can be contradictory because they may intend to behave in a way that is socially not considered very fashionable or acceptable. They may therefore say they intend to do something which is more fashionably acceptable while in reality they will do something else. This can make it difficult for tour operation marketers to anticipate the needs and desires of their clients.

In many countries, *competition* is intense in the tour operation sector. This was not always the case, as we know in Eastern Europe, for example, where state monopolies in the past prevented any real competition developing. However, now, competition is present in almost all aspects of tour operation globally.

Tour operators, therefore, are always looking to find ways of achieving competitive advantage, including:

- Having lower prices than their competitors or offering their customers more services or benefits for the same price.
- Opening up new destinations that are not offered by their competitors. For European operators this has, in recent years, largely meant offering new long-haul destinations in Asia, Africa, the Middle East and the Caribbean.
- Pioneering new types of holidays such as particular special-interest activities that are not available from other companies.
- Seeking to become a market leader in terms of the market for particular countries.

However, it is not always easy to identify who one's competitors are in the tour operation field. For a major European operator such as TUI, who are its competitors? Perhaps they are all the other German tour operators. However it could be argued that a small operator in Bavaria offering short break domestic holidays is no real competition for a major mass-market tour operator, which focuses on outbound holidays. Perhaps its competitors are the other mass-market operators in Germany like LTU, who are targeting smaller markets with similar products.

We could also ask if some of its competitors are perhaps foreign tour operators. At first the answer might seem to be no, as relatively few foreign operators sell holidays to German clients. However, such an answer assumes that the only competitor a tour operator faces is for customers. This is not the case, as competition also exists for the supply of the raw materials that make up the package holiday. In other words, TUI will find itself competing with foreign tour operators for hotel rooms in its destinations. If it fails to win this battle, it has no product, or a lesser-quality product, with which to compete for clients in the German market.

In the most extreme cases, competition for TUI will not come from other people who offer package holidays. Instead it will come from 'substitution'; in other words, people choosing to buy a nontourism product rather than a holiday.

This phenomenon is very common in tour operation, with people in certain years, substituting something else in place of a holiday, such as the following:

- the purchase of a new car
- buying a new home
- decorating a house or carrying out some repairs or renovation work on their home.

People may also substitute several short breaks or trips to friends and relatives for a main annual holiday because of a range of reasons including lack of money, lack of time or their responsibilities and careers.

These forms of substitution are genuine competition for a tour operator, but they are forms of competition with which it is virtually impossible for tour operators to compete.

When they wish to expand, European tour operators have used a number of *growth strategies* of which the three most popular are as follows:

(i) Vertical and horizontal integration, in other words, taking over suppliers and marketing intermediaries on the one hand and competitors on the other. The leading UK tour operator, Thomson, for example, developed its own airline, Britannia, and owns its own travel chain, Lunn Poly. In addition, it has taken over a number of competitors over the years.

(ii) Buying existing well-established brands in markets which are new ones for the operator, which is seeking to grow. To take the Thomson example again, the company has purchased, in recent years, several leading brands in the market for self-catering cottages in Britain, including Blakes and English Country Cottages.
(iii) Beginning to sell one's product to people who live in other countries. While this has happened relatively little to date in the European tour operation sector, there are signs that it is beginning to happen more and more. This is a logical consequence of a situation where some national markets are becoming saturated so that international market developments may be the only realistic prospect of large-scale future expansion.

Finally, there are a number of other issues that are worth discussing briefly because of their influence on tour operation marketing. These include the following two:

1. The marketing activities of *consortia* of tour operators, of which one of the best European examples is AITO, the Association of Independent Tour Operators in the UK. This organisation represents many smaller specialist tour operators based in the UK. This consortium was set up to counter the marketing power of the major mass-market operators. By pooling resources, its members can afford joint campaigns which they could not afford to undertake alone. They claim their AITO members offer:
   - a unique range of holidays
   - financial protection
   - personal service
   - value for money
   - high standards
   - tailor-made holidays
   - a dispute settlement service.

   They also have a quality charter which emphasises that companies have to meet strict membership criteria before they can join AITO. They also ensure that their brochures are accurate and that they listen to, and take action on, feedback from their customers. Briefly, the charter says that AITO is 'committed to raising the level of environmental awareness within the industry'.
2. AITO also encourages its prospective customers to book their holiday through an independent travel agent rather than an agency owned by one of the large British tour operators. This way, AITO claims customers receive more choice, personal service and impartial advice.

Tour operators often have to respond, at short notice, to *political and economic changes* which can affect either their market dramatically almost overnight, or their ability to deliver their product as advertised. Several examples will illustrate this point as follows:

- The Gulf War in 1991 reduced the demand from Americans to visit Europe and of Europeans to visit places in the Eastern Mediterranean which were near to the conflict, such as Israel and Cyprus.
- The terrorist attacks in the USA in September 2001 which decimated the demand for air travel all over the world.
- Dramatic changes in currency-exchange rates like the devaluation of the British Pound Sterling in September 1992. Interestingly, this made visits to Britain cheaper for many foreign tourists while it made traditionally popular destinations with British visitors, like France, much more expensive, literally overnight.

Conclusion

In this chapter, we have briefly explored the key issues in the rapidly changing field of tour operation marketing and outbound tour operations in particular. It is clear that there are major differences between large mass-market tour operators and the smaller niche market operators.

Discussion points and essay questions

1. Evaluate the suggestion that the only basis of competition in the tour operation sector is price.
2. Discuss the value of the four classic methods of market segmentation to marketers within the tour-operation sector.
3. Critically evaluate the range of growth strategies which have been adopted by tour operators.

Exercise

Choose a mass-market tour operator *and* a specialist tour operator. Obtain the main brochure of each operator. For each brochure, answer the following questions, based purely on the contents of the brochure:

(i) Who is the brochure aimed at?
(ii) What major selling points does the operator claim for their product or products?
(iii) What pricing approaches is the operator using?
(iv) What is the balance between subjective comments and factual information?

Compare the two operators in terms of the answers to these four questions. Finally, you should identify weaknesses in either brochure in relation to their role as promotional tools.

The results of this project can be presented in a report and/or through an oral presentation.

CHAPTER 18

Transport

Key concepts

The main concepts covered in the chapter are:

- The different modes of transport
- Commercial versus subsidised transport operations
- State intervention in the transport market
- The complex distribution system in transport
- The nature of competition within transport.

Introduction

The transport sector is very broad in scope and approaches to marketing will vary greatly between different modes and countries. Some of the main factors that influence the nature of marketing within the sector are discussed in this chapter.

There is diversity in the *modes of transport* which all have different strengths and weaknesses as far as consumers are concerned. These include:

- air – scheduled and charter services
- rail – modern trains and historic steam railways
- sea – cruise liners, ferries, narrow boats and canal barges
- road – private cars, car rentals, taxis, long-distance coaches, local buses, bicycles, motorbikes, horse-drawn carriages
- off-road – horses, walking, cable cars, télépheriques.

Transport involves *private-, public- and voluntary-sector organisations* with their different *marketing objectives*. While private companies seek to maximise profit, state-owned operators often have broader aims including providing a service for the community. The limited number of voluntary-sector bodies in transport tend to use leisure as a means to an end rather than an end in itself. For example, most of Europe's steam railways are run by voluntary bodies who use the income from passengers to conserve the railways and maintain them.

Even within individual modes of transport, there can be distinct differences in ownership and marketing objectives. Perhaps the best current example of this is the airline business in the European context.

Many scheduled airlines in Europe are state owned or controlled, so that they are allowed to make losses. British Airways, on the other hand, is a wholly private company which has to generate profits and is thus very marketing – and market – orientated.

From a marketing point of view, an interesting point is that many charter airlines are owned by tour operators as part of their vertical integration strategies. Thus, often, they do not set their own marketing strategies, but rather play their part in the implementation of the strategies of that parent company.

This point is linked to the fact that while sometimes it is sold as a self-contained product in its own right, *transport may also be sold as part of a larger composite product*. For example, it may be combined with accommodation to form an inclusive tour. In this case, the price the consumer pays is a single price for the complete package, so that they are unaware of the amount they have actually paid for the transport element of the package.

Some transport markets are not free markets, but are state controlled in some way, so that normal concepts of competition and pricing are of little relevance. Such markets include intra-European air travel and the private-car sector due to state taxes on petrol and road use.

The *transnational nature of many transport operations* such as airlines, ferries, car hire and international rail services. This means that marketing policies have to take account of national differences in consumer behaviour, economic factors, legal regulations and operating practices.

Technological innovations can change the nature of existing transport products or create new ones. An excellent recent example of this is the Channel Tunnel which has given consumers a totally new mode of transport for crossing the English Channel/Le Manche, and given the ferries a new competitor.

The *product* offered by most modes of transport is the opportunity to be transported from one place to another at a time chosen by the consumer. But to achieve this, the product represents a sophisticated bundle of elements and characteristics. These can be illustrated, if we take the example of a scheduled airline. Its product is shown in Figure 18.1.

Increasingly, transport operators are seeking to augment their basic product with *add-on-services* that generate more income but also satisfy more of the consumers needs. For example, the French state railway, SNCF, offers a range of extra services to its passengers, including car hire, bicycle hire and accommodation inclusive packages. It also operates a range of coach excursions across France.

However, the *transport product is susceptible to changing factors outside its control which affect the quality of the product*, before it can be offered to customers. For example, airport congestion across Europe is a problem at peak times and causes delays to flights. Strikes and civil disorder can also be a problem for transport operators.

While most modes of transport are simply ways of travelling from place to place, some forms of transport can be attractions or even tourist destinations in their own right. These include the Orient Express, major cruise liners, and, until recently, Concorde.

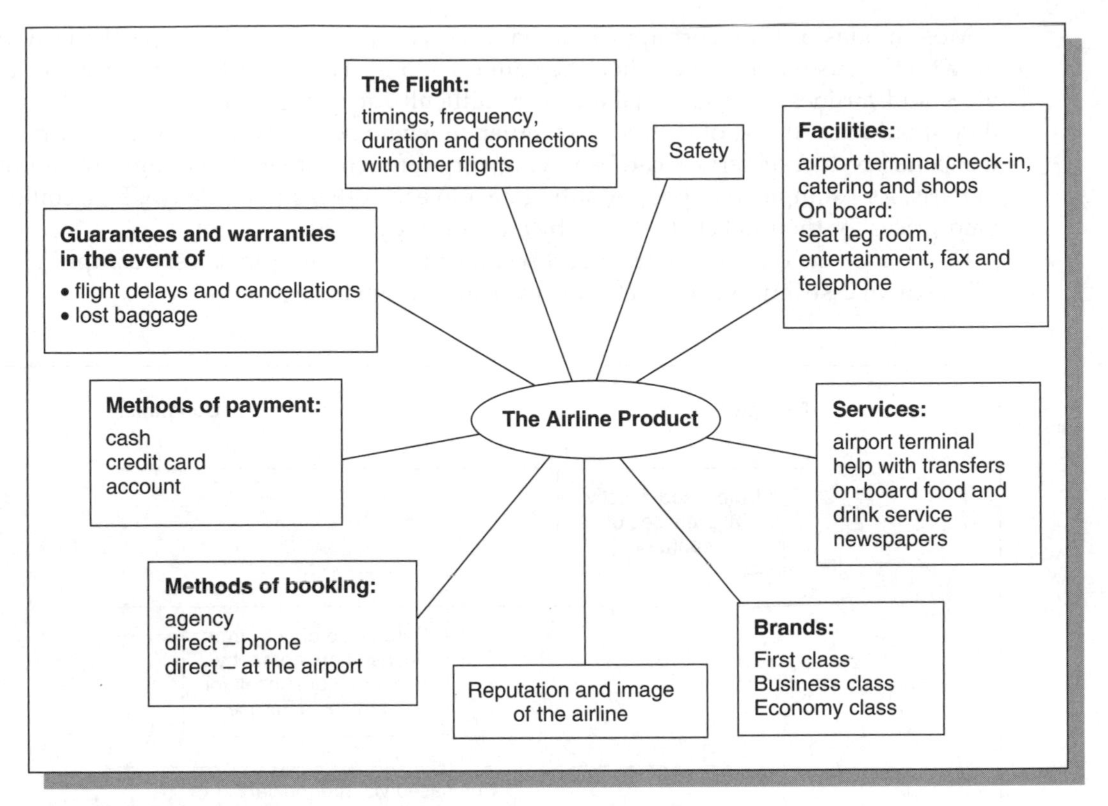

Figure 18.1 The scheduled airline product

Pricing policies in the transport sector are often influenced by *state intervention* in the market, either through statutory price-fixing and subsidies or through taxes on particular modes of transport. In sectors such as the scheduled airlines, there has been a tradition of price-fixing in relation to the state flag carriers in each country covered by a route.

However, both private and state transport operators also make use of commercial tactical approaches to pricing, such as *discounts*. If we take the airline business as an example, discounts are given to the following customers:

- franchises;
- regular customers;
- group bookings including conference delegates and people on inclusive tours;
- people taking flights at less popular times such as midday flights on popular business travel routes;
- passengers who purchase promotion and offer tickets that have strict conditions such as no cancellation refunds.

Last-minute discounting is common, as airline seats are a perishable product that has no value once the aircraft has taken off. Therefore, given this and the high fixed costs involved in operating a flight, airlines often heavily discount tickets at the last minute so that they can at least gain some revenue from the seat.

Many transport operators, particularly those in the public sector, also offer *concessions* for social reasons, to groups of customers who are thought to be disadvantaged in some way. These groups usually include the elderly and students, for example.

Most modes of transport appear to have *complex pricing structures*, particularly based on who the customer is and when they are travelling. This is particularly true of rail services and airlines. This can make it very difficult for customers to decide which ticket they should buy. It also often leads to a situation where people who are ostensibly receiving the same product or service can be paying very different prices. On a flight from London to Paris, for example, two people, sitting next to each other in Economy Class, could have paid prices for their tickets that vary by a factor of up to 700 per cent.

Distribution networks in the transport sector can be very simple or very complex.

The main distribution channels, however, are shown in Figure 18.2.

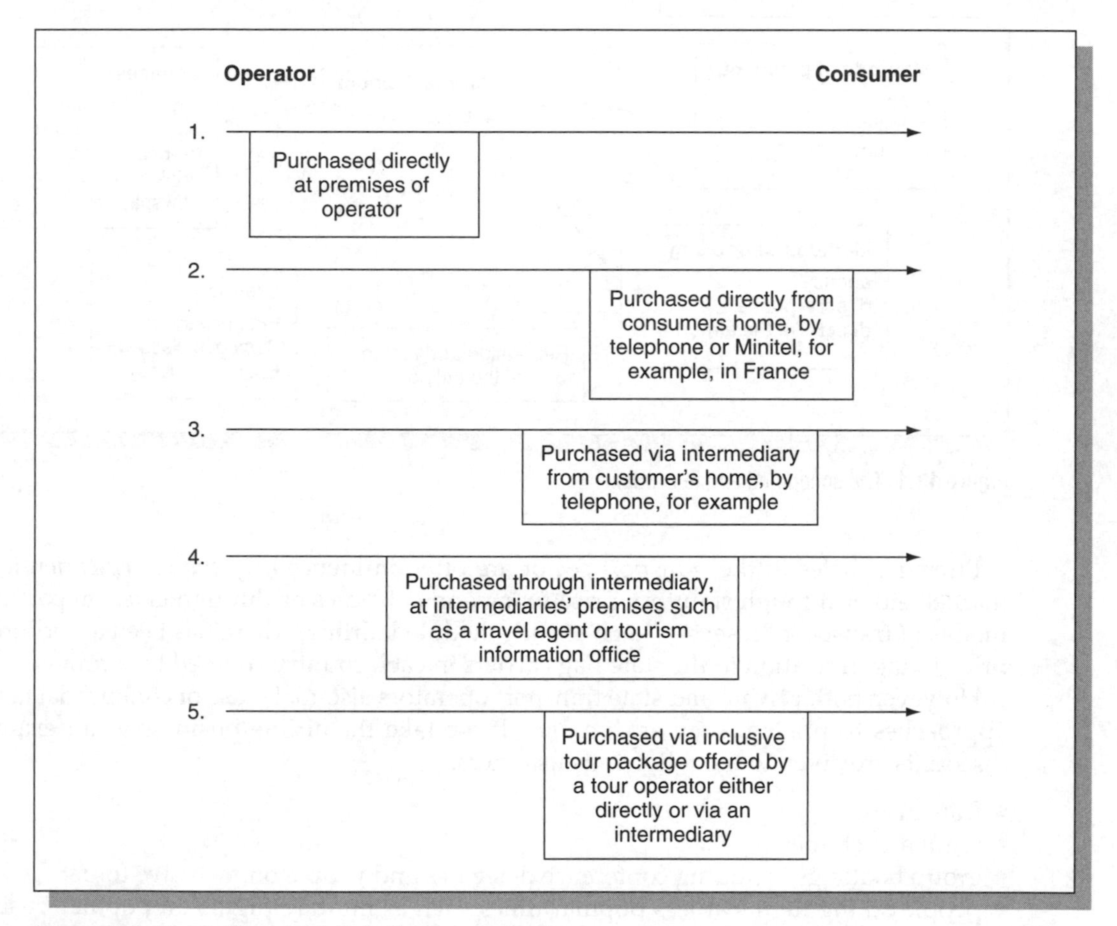

Figure 18.2 Distribution channels in the transport sector

Some airlines, for example, are now seeking to *sell directly* to their customers to save the commission they have to pay to the intermediaries. This is being made more practical by technological developments which are taking place.

The growth of the budget airlines across Europe, for example, has allowed companies such as Easyjet and Ryanair to develop large profitable businesses with the use of Internet selling.

In general, *technological innovations* are changing the nature of distribution in transport in general and airlines in particular in a number of ways, including Global Distribution Systems (GDS) and Smart Cards.

The major *promotional techniques* used by transport operators include the following:

(i) The most important piece of promotional print is the timetable, which can be difficult for the ordinary traveller to read, and is often only available to marketing intermediaries rather than customers in the case of airlines. The use of promotional brochures rather than informational publications is generally found most often in the transport sector in relation to ferry services.

(ii) In terms of advertising, television is used by major operators, particularly where new services are being launched. At the same time, considerable use is made of the printed media.

(iii) Great use is made of sales promotions, four examples will suffice to illustrate the point as follows:

- Promotional fares which are used to introduce new routes or to fill seats at quiet times. These may simply be low fares or added-value fares where one adult pays a normal fare while their partner travels free of charge.
- Frequent flyer programmes which offer a range of benefits for regular customers to encourage brand loyalty. Examples of these include American Airlines' 'Advantages' programme and the 'Frequence Plus' scheme operated by the Air France group. These frequent flyer programmes have helped the airlines to develop ongoing relationships with their regular customers.
- So-called 'piggy-back' promotions where purchasing one type of product gives consumers an opportunity to enjoy a special deal in relation to another type of product. For instance, in the early 1990s, the UK food retailer, Sainsbury's, ran a promotion with British Airways where customers who spent a certain amount of money at Sainsbury's were eligible for reduced price tickets on British Airways.
- Schemes whereby certain groups of customers such as retired people and students can buy cards which allow them to special prices. These are particularly common amongst state railways. In France, for example, SNCF has a range of cards with titles such as 'Carte Vermeil' and 'Carte Kiwi'.

(iv) Direct selling is largely restricted to relations between operators and marketing intermediaries such as travel agents, operators and major corporate clients.

The *transport market* can be segmented in a number of ways which also has an impact on the marketing function as follows:

- Geographical factors, in other words, where people live and work, as this determines the potential demand for transport on particular routes.
- Demographic factors such as age, sex and even religion. The latter is particularly relevant in relation to the type of catering offered by airlines, for instance.
- The reasons why people travel, particularly the split between business and leisure. For rail operators, the former are more likely to use first-class services while for airlines they represent the main market for 'business class' brands.
- Differences in purchasing behaviour such as how often in advance people purchase their tickets, where they buy them from and which payment method they use.
- Some people are regular users of particular transport services, while others use them rarely, maybe only once in their lives. While both sets of customers will demand safety and reliability, they will differ in terms of their main requirements of the product. Regular users will want an easy hassle-free low-key experience while the occasional user may want a more memorable experience.

Competition within the transport sector tends to be of two types, namely:

1. between different modes of transport;
2. within the same mode of transport between different operators;

Throughout the transport sector, operators seek to use the following tactics to achieve competitive advantage:

- speed, namely how quickly they can move the customer from where they are to where they want to be;
- convenience, so that the customer can travel when they want to, with the least effort possible;
- price, including the use of tactical pricing such as discounts and concessions.

However, as we saw earlier, the transport market does not allow free and fair competition in a number of ways including the following two main ways:

1. where a state operator has a virtual monopoly within one mode of transport, for example rail services in almost all countries;
2. where the state subsidises one or more operator within a market where nonsubsidised operators are trying to compete. This is the situation in the domestic airline market in France, for example, where the private airline TAT seems to compete with the state-subsidised Air France Group.

Perhaps the two most interesting examples of *competition between modes of transport* in Europe at the moment are as follows:

(i) In the business travel market, the competition between high speed trains and aircraft in relation to short-haul routes in countries like France. Competition is intense, for example, on the Paris–Lyon route between SNCF and its high speed TGV trains and domestic airlines. It appears that the train is beginning to win this battle with its ability to transport people at high speed from city centre to city centre, without the need of airline passengers to travel to and from out-of-town airports and check-in for their flight. Competition for the airlines is set to grow with the introduction of trains in France, for example, which will be capable of travelling at some 500 kilometres per hour. The only way airlines may be able to compete with this is through the airports like London City, which are based within cities and use small aircraft that need little time or runway distance to take off. However, as yet, these do not appear to be very popular with business travellers.

(ii) In the leisure travel field, the competition between Eurotunnel and the ferry companies on the routes across the English Channel/Le Manche. Eurotunnel offers speed, with a 35-minute crossing time. However, the ferries have fought back with new ships that offer shopping opportunities, sophisticated catering and are selling the time spent on board as part of the holiday, rather than merely as a mode of transport. The term 'mini-cruise' is being used to emphasise this point.

Good examples of *competition between different operators within the same mode of transport* include the following:

- car-hire companies at European airports and in city centres;
- scheduled airlines on well-used intra-European routes such as London to Paris;
- ferry companies in the Baltic and North Sea.

While competition is often beneficial for the consumer, the breaking up of state monopolies and the encouragement of private operators and competition can have a downside for the consumer.

Transport operators who wish to expand and grow, follow a variety of strategies, some of which we will now briefly discuss.

1. *Marketing consortia*, which carry out cooperative marketing activities.
2. *Strategic alliances*, particularly in the airline sector, such as the Star and One World Alliances whereby countries cooperate and share routes to optimise profitability and increase the size of their potential markets.
3. *Acquisition* or the purchase of equity in other operations, which is how the Scandinavian-based Stena group has grown to become a major player in the ferry industry in Northern Europe.
4. *Joint ventures* with other operators to create new carriers such as the abortive project to create Air Russia by British Airways and Aeroflot in the early 1990s. Joint ventures can also involve governments like the partnership behind the renowned Hong Kong Disneyland park involving Disney and the Chinese government.
5. *Franchising*, which British Airways has used within Europe to increase its influence in the marketplace. Under its franchise agreement, the franchisees operate routes in British Airways livery and fly under British Airways flight codes. Such agreements exist between British Airways and Maersk Air UK, and Manx Airlines (Europe) and Loganair.
6. Developing *ancillary activities* which either add value to or increase business for the organisation's core business. This point is illustrated by the following examples:
   - Ferry companies, like Brittany Ferries (France) and the Color Line (Norway), for example, which operate inclusive tour operations which combine ferry travel with accommodation, usually based on car travel. This clearly generates business for the ferry service.
   - Likewise, airlines which develop tour operation products based on their schedule.
7. Offering *facilities* so that modes of transport can become conference venues in their own right, rather than simply being the way in which people travel to a conference.

One interesting development of transport marketing is the increasing tendency of different modes of transport to work together. In Germany, for example, there is cooperation between airports and state rail services, while there are well-established, mutually beneficial relationships between car-hire companies and airlines.

Conclusion

We have seen in this chapter that while the various modes of transport differ greatly in their nature, there are also similarities in the ways in which they are marketed. This is particularly true of the modes which are most relevant to tourism, notably air, rail and ferry. However, we are aware that the most popular form of transport in Europe, namely the private car, has largely been excluded from this discussion. This is somewhat ironic given that the car has been at the heart of the history of leisure and tourism. In the early days, it stimulated the development of both by making new places accessible and creating new types of activity such as caravanning. Now, however, the mass use of cars is making it more difficult to maintain the quality of leisure and tourism experiences because of pollution and congestion. It could be argued therefore that there is a need to concentrate on the *de*-marketing of this particular mode of transport.

Discussion points and essay questions

1. Compare and contrast the approaches to marketing taken by railway operators, ferry companies and airlines.
2. Identify and discuss the core, actual and augmented products within the airline sector.
3. Critically evaluate the range of promotional techniques which are used in the transport sector.
4. Discuss the nature of competition within the transport sector.

Exercise

Prepare a list of all the transport operators – air, rail, sea – who are currently competing for business travellers and leisure travellers on the London–Paris route. You should then undertake the following tasks:

(a) Describe the product each one offers and identify the key differences between them.
(b) Examine the prices they are charging, including the discounts that are on offer.
(c) Evaluate their brochures and advertisements in terms of their likely effectiveness.

Finally, you should attempt to decide which of the organisations appear to have a competitive edge and explain the reasons behind your choice.

CHAPTER 19

Resort complexes

Key concepts

The main concepts covered in the chapter are:

- The relationship between resorts and destinations or attractions
- The integrated nature of the resort product
- The distinctive benefits which are sought by resort customers
- The marketing of resorts by other organisations.

Introduction

As we saw earlier in the book, the distinction between destinations and attractions is being blurred in Europe by the growth of resort complexes. These resorts offer both the attractions that motivate people to travel to visit them and the services and facilities they require. However, these resorts tend to be larger in size and area than most traditional attractions while they also differ from normal destinations in that they are in the ownership of just one organisation and are managed as a single entity.

The idea of resorts is not particularly new, with Club Mediterranée or the UK's Butlins complexes both being well over forty years old. Such resort complexes also have a relatively long history in the USA. Many American resorts are based on recreational activities such as golf, skiing or gambling. However, the Disney Organisation also pioneered the idea of theme park-based resorts through its complexes in Florida and California.

Resorts have also become increasingly common in other parts of the world, notably Sun City in Southern Africa and the Pacific Rim.

Nevertheless, Europe has, in recent years, witnessed the growth of resorts. Indeed, they have been one of the fastest growing sectors of leisure. They have been the basis of Club Mediterranée's development as one of the world's largest accommodation chains, for example. At the same time, the Center Parcs brand has expanded from its country of origin, the Netherlands, to France and the UK.

From a marketing point of view, it is important to note that the vast majority of European resorts are privately owned and their main *marketing objective* is the optimisation of profits.

We should also note that while some resorts are owned by independent companies that just own one resort, the vast majority of those found in Europe are part of chains.

The elements of the resort *product* can perhaps best be illustrated through the example of Disneyland Paris in France. This is particularly interesting as it is a resort conceived by an organisation based in the USA but located in Europe.

The main components of the Disneyland® Paris complex are:

- The main theme park, Disneyland® Paris, which is split into five different areas or 'lands', each with a different theme. There are in total thirty-nine major different rides and attractions. This has recently been expanded by the addition of a studios tour.
- An entertainment programme featuring stage shows, outdoor parades and frequent displays.
- The Disneyland® Resort, Paris. Walt Disney Studios which is next to Disneyland® Paris, allowing visitors to go behind the scenes of Cinema Animation and TV.
- Special events at certain times of the year, such as Christmas.
- A selection of on-site accommodation establishments, aimed at different market segments, all of which are themed. They range from the 'Ranch Davy Crocket' which offers log cabins and a caravan and camping site, to the luxury Disneyland® Hotel.
- There are themed catering outlets on both sites, offering sit-down meals, fast-food and take-away meal services.
- On site, there are themed shops for selling exclusive Disney merchandise.
- Leisure facilities, although these are generally located within the individual accommodation units.
- Organised activities such as the 'Character Breakfasts'.
- The brand image and reputation of Disney.
- The high quality of service for which the Disney Organisation is famed.
- Easy accessibility via specially purpose-developed road and rail systems, and coach services from Paris and the local airport.
- Opportunities for trips to the nearby city of Paris.
- Guest services like wheelchair and pushchair hire, pet-care centres and currency-exchange facilities.
- The opening days and times – Disneyland® Paris, for instance, is open every day of the year at different times according to the season.

The precise nature of the resort product depends on the type of resort it is, in other words, the Center Parcs product lays a greater emphasis on leisure facilities and recreational activities than does Disneyland® Paris.

Furthermore, we must also recognise that Disneyland® Paris is Europe's largest resort. Most others are smaller, although they offer a similar range of product elements. Whilst most resorts gear their product to the leisure user, some also offer facilities to attract the business user, namely conference rooms, in particular.

Lastly, we should recognise that some European resorts are based on the timeshare principle. Here guests buy the right to use the resort for one or two weeks every year, for as long as they want. In these cases, the marketing challenge is the sale of the weeks in the first place rather than in needing to find new customers for them each year. However, it is important that the complex is self-contained as it must function as a 'home from home' for those customers who are committed to visiting the resort year after year.

There are different approaches to resort *pricing* as follows:

- What we might term, the 'Club Med' approach of 'all-inclusive' prices where guests pay one price and that includes all or almost all of the elements of the product.
- The item-by-item approach, favoured by Disneyland® Paris, for example, where each element of the product is a separate price, and visitors buy only those elements they wish to, or can afford to, purchase.

Generally, resorts are relatively high priced to reflect the costs incurred in their development and maintenance, and their exclusivity value. However, discounts are used to attract business at the less busy times of the year.

Consumers do not always know what price they are paying for the use of the resort, as it may be part of a package holiday for which they have paid a single price.

Place or the distribution of the resort product tends to be either by direct sale or via marketing intermediaries, such as travel agents. Club Mediterranée, Center Parcs and Disneyland® Paris all offer opportunities for clients to book directly but they are also available through travel agents. Some resort operators use specialist representatives in foreign countries from which they wish to attract tourists, to help potential customers buy the product.

As far as *promotion* is concerned, most of the major resort operators have large budgets and make use of television advertising as well as widespread printed-media advertisements. Their brochures tend to be large and glossy and they make considerable use of sales promotions. Personal selling is used particularly to gain bookings from coach and tour operators, and conference organisers, in other words, those who control high value business.

Many resorts also use direct mail, based on their databases, to either attract new customers or persuade previous users to make a repeat purchase.

The resort *market* can be segmented in a number of ways, including:

- Where customers live which determines whether their catchment areas are local, regional, national and international. This obviously influences where the resort operator will concentrate most of their advertising effort.
- Where consumers are in terms of the family life cycle, including young couples, families and so-called 'empty nesters' or people aged around the early fifties whose children have left home.
- Day visitors who are simply using the nonresidential attractions on the site and those staying visitors who are also using the on-site accommodation units.
- Those visitors who want to relax and the customers who want to spend most of their holiday indulging in active pursuits.
- People who use the resort in the peak season and those who visit in the off-peak season.
- Gregarious people and those who prefer to be on their own, likewise extroverts and introverts, as some resorts suit one of these types of people while others appeal to the other types.
- Leisure visitors and business users.

The *benefits sought* by resort users vary depending on the nature of the resort in question and the personality of the particular guest. They can include the following:

- privacy or companionship;
- complete relaxation or the chance to practice a number of sports and recreational activities;
- the opportunity to enjoy a complete holiday without the need to leave the site, in other words, convenience;
- value for money at those resorts where the price is all-inclusive.

There is *competition* in the resort sector, but as the product they offer is often very different and their target markets vary, much of the competition is between resorts and other types of holiday, rather than between resorts.

For example, Club Robinson is aimed at German tourists and is for those who prefer a much more individual type of holiday than Club Mediterranée which is aimed more at French and English-speaking consumers and is based on a more communal approach to holiday-making.

As far as the nonresort competition is concerned, it depends on the type of resort, but can include the following:

- the destinations which offer a similar range of attractions and services, whether that is a seaside resort, a place with a local theme park or a skiing centre, for instance;
- attractions which offer on-site accommodation such as Futuroscope in France;
- package holidays that offer inclusive packages that include the elements that might otherwise be available at a resort such as accommodation, entertainment and activities.

In the case of theme park-based attractions, such as Disneyland® Paris, the competition may be in terms of hotels outside the resort, where customers use the theme park but not its accommodation. Clearly, this dramatically reduces the resorts' income from that which it would receive if the visitor chose to stay in one of the resort's accommodation establishments.

Many resorts are *marketed by other* organisations as well as by themselves, including:

- Tour operators for whom they are the core product in particular packages that they offer. Thus, UK tour operators promote Disneyland® Paris through their brochures purely on holidays they sell to Disneyland® Paris while the French State Railways, SNCF, also offer combined rail-resort stay packages to the French market.
- Destination-marketing agencies who use the resort as a way of attracting particular market segments to their area. Hence the local council in Nottinghamshire in the UK promotes the fact that there is a Center Parcs complex in their area.
- Accommodation establishments which include an entrance ticket to the resort, where such tickets are available as part of the package it offers to its clients, particularly in the weekend short-break market.

However, some resort operators, such as Disney, while happy to enjoy the benefits of joint marketing with other organisations, maintain strict control on the ways in which their product is packaged by these organisations. For example, they may insist on their logo being used and particular wording being used to describe aspects of the resort.

In addition to the resort chains like Club Mediterranée and Center Parcs, and the Disney Corporation, there are also many *individual, independently owned resorts* in Europe.

In the case of these resorts, it is difficult to draw a clear line between resorts and other sectors of leisure. Two examples of where the boundary can be blurred include:

- The so-called 'health farms' or health clubs, usually located in country houses or chateaux, which combine leisure facilities, recreational activities, accommodation and specialised healthy eating. There are many examples of such places in the UK including Champneys.
- Hotels which offer a wide range of leisure facilities are located in isolated localities and are largely self-contained.

It must also be recognised that not every complex that could justify the term 'resort' is run by a private-sector organisation. Some are owned by *voluntary-sector* bodies and a few are in *public ownership*.

Conclusion

Overall, resort marketing tends to be a function of both the size of organisation involved and the precise nature of the resort in question, in terms of its core product and its target market. Given the growth of resorts in Europe, it is clearly a form of marketing with which we will become even more familiar in the future.

Discussion points and essay questions

1. Choose *one* of the following resorts or resort companies and examine the nature of its product:
   - Disneyland® Paris
   - Center Parcs
   - Club Med
   - Sandals.
2. Discuss the main factors that may have contributed to the growth of resort complexes around the world in recent years.
3. Evaluate the ways in which the resort market might be segmented.

Exercise

You have been engaged as a consultant for a European-based organisation which wishes to develop a major new resort complex in Europe.

Your brief is as follows:

(i) to identify the optimum location in Europe for such a new resort complex and provide a rationale for your choice of location;
(ii) to develop an overall concept for the complex;
(iii) to create a two-dimensional plan of the proposed complex;
(iv) to suggest who would be the main target market or markets for the new complex.

Your report should be presented to your client in the form of both a verbal presentation and a written report.

CHAPTER 20

Retail travel

Key concepts

The main concepts covered in the chapter are:

- The different types of retail travel outlet
- The complex product offered by travel agents
- The growing competition for retail travel outlets, including different types of marketing activity
- The different markets served by travel agents.

Introduction

Retail travel, in other words, the travel agency sector, is the distribution element in the tourism marketing system. It is, in general, the interface between the producers – tour operators, hoteliers, airlines and transport operators, for example – and their customers.

In some countries, including Germany and the UK, the main interests of travel agents are in outbound travel, helping their own nationals travel abroad on holiday or for business. However, in other countries, such as Southern Europe, travel agents are also often involved in inbound tourism, arranging excursions and car hire for inbound tourists, for example.

In terms of *ownership and size*, travel agents tend to be of four types as follows:

1. Travel agencies which are part of chains with a number of branches in different locations in one country, which are in turn part of larger corporations which have interest outside

tourism. Such an organisation is the French travel agency group Havas Voyages, which also has substantial media interests, for example.

2. Travel agencies which are part of chains with branches in different locations, which are part of larger corporations with interests in other sectors of tourism. Examples of this in the UK include the Lunn Poly and Going Places chain which are both owned by leading UK tour operators.

   It is also possible, in relation to both of these types of chain, for them to have branches in more than one country, in other words, to be truly international. Two examples of this are Thomas Cook and Thomson Travel, which is owned by the German tour operator TUI, and American Express Travel, which is part of the credit card group.
3. Privately owned, independent travel agencies that are not chains but do own several outlets.
4. Privately owned, independent single-outlet travel agencies which are owner-operated.

There has also been a recent growth in the number of online retail travel agents such as Expedia that offer a mix of tourism and leisure products via the Internet. The use of technology has allowed these businesses to grow and has produced a significant threat to retail travel agents on the high street, who are increasingly having to compete on the level of service that they offer.

Finally, the final difference between types of travel agencies is that distinction which can be made between those which specialise in leisure tourism and those which concentrate on business tourism.

Whatever the type of agency, the *product* it offers tends to be similar. Its product is a service, or more to the point, a range of services. These include:

(i) Providing an opportunity for customers to purchase or book the product offered by tour operators, hoteliers, transport operators and theatres, for instance.
(ii) Offering advice and information both in relation to the products that are available and other matters such as currency rates, obligatory inoculations and visa requirements.
(iii) Being an outlet where consumers can obtain the brochures produced by tour operators and other producers in the tourism industry.
(iv) Collecting payment from the consumer and passing it on to the organisation offering the product (less the agent's commission).
(v) Operating as the first line of after-sales service to which problems and complaints can be referred.
(vi) Offering a range of other services such as currency exchange for the convenience of their clients.

Agents do not charge the customer a *price* for their service, usually. Their income comes in generally from the commission they are paid by the industry organisations on the sales of these organisation's products. These are expressed, usually, as a percentage of the purchase price of the product and this may range from 7 or 8 per cent to 15 per cent.

The fact that their income is dependant on commission leads to criticism that the agent may have a vested interest in not selling their client the cheapest appropriate product as this would give them a lower commission.

In terms of the third 'P' in the marketing mix, *place* is concerned, it is not in general relevant to agents for they are in the distribution element in the tourism system. However, the way in which their customers gain access to their service is literally place, in other words, the location of their retail outlet.

Some are located in the high street of major urban areas, particularly those involved in the mass market, where casual passing trade is an important element of their market. Perhaps, this is particularly relevant to the budget end of the market where people may wish to compare special offers which are available at different agencies in an urban centre.

Conversely, in the case of niche-market agents or those which offer higher priced, more specialist products, they can really be located anywhere as people will travel to them because of their expertise. Some agents seek to become the major player in a particular neighbourhood.

It has to be said that, in general, these comments are mainly applicable to Northern Europe. Given that we noted earlier that many Southern European agents also serve inbound tourists, agents in these countries are often located in the heart of the towns and cities which are most popular with tourists, to capture the passing trade.

Methods of *promotion* in retail travel tend to vary depending on the size of the organisation. Major chains of agencies tend to make use of television and press advertising, particularly at the main times of the year when people book holidays. Smaller agents on the other hand have to rely more on local newspaper advertisements.

However, there are other promotional activities which agents can undertake to raise their profile and increase awareness amongst potential customers. These include:

- Running special evenings in a local hotel, for example, to inform customers about particular types of holidays that are available through the agency. These evenings often include some drink and food, and are usually free of charge.
- Services within the agency's premises when representatives of leading tour operators are on hand to advise clients.
- Special offers, where people buying holidays receive a discount or do not have to pay a deposit. Most such offers carry conditions, however, which are often controversial such as the requirement that people buy the agent's own insurance to be eligible for these offers.

Travel agencies also tend to make great use of visual displays in their windows to tempt customers to enter their premises to see what they have to offer.

Personal selling is important for travel agents, otherwise people will simply take away brochures and eventually buy a holiday elsewhere or not buy a holiday at all.

Travel agents service a range of *markets* including:

- Those who use them simply as sources of advice and information. This is particularly true of independent travellers thinking of travelling to lesser-known destinations.
- People who wish to book travel services only such as air tickets or car hire, or who use the agency to make hotel bookings.
- Individual customers who purchase an inclusive tour, who are, in general, the bulk of most leisure travel agents' business.
- Associations and clubs who book group travel services via a travel agency.
- Companies and organisations who use the agency to manage their business tourism needs.
- Individuals who buy ancillary products from the agency such as foreign currency or travel insurance.

The aim of travel-agency marketing has got to be to ensure that the yield per consumer can be maximised by effective personal selling and offering a range of services that meet the needs of the majority of customers.

Most travel agencies rely for the bulk of their business on clients who wish to travel to other countries. In general, selling products based within their own country does not generate a substantial element of their income.

At the present time, *competition* is intense in the retail travel sector in Europe. This competition comes in two forms, namely internal and external.

By *internal competition* we mean competition between different travel agencies which takes several forms as follows:

- that between the major chains based on each one's desire to increase their share of the relevant national market;
- that between the major multiple chains as a whole and the small independent agents;
- that between all the agencies, the multiples and the independents in a particular geographical area.

The large chains tend to use their ability to offer big discounts as their way of achieving competitive advantage, which the small independents cannot afford to do. They therefore have to focus on service and building 'brand' loyalty, so that they attract repeat business.

External competition largely relates to the growth of direct selling in tourism in which products and consumers communicate directly with each other without the need of an intermediary or agent.

This communication takes a number of forms, including:

- the computer reservations systems of some hotel chains which are available via toll-free telephone numbers;
- the GDS such as SABRE, which offers services which can increasingly be accessed by business tourists;
- flight consolidators in the air-travel market who sell discounted tickets directly on behalf of airlines, but who are not travel agents in the usual sense of the word;
- airlines and tour operators which sell their product via newspaper and major advertisements, and direct booking telephone lines to their offices;
- retailers in other industries may seek to offer travel-agency services as part of their overall range of activities;
- home-based information services such as the Minitel in France and 'Teletext' in the UK;
- the media who are increasingly, in some European countries, offering advice that people would possibly have sought from travel agents.

The major competitor though is now the *online travel agencies*, such as Expedia and Lastminute.com, which offer travel-agency services, 24 hours a day, 7 days a week.

Conclusion

In some countries, such as France, travel agents have never become powerful players in tourism to the extent they have been in other countries like the UK. However, many commentators are now saying that technological innovations and changes in consumer behaviour are changing the very nature of the retail travel sector. These writers offer a vision of the future where customers prefer independent travel to package tours and have home- or office-based technology to give them access so that they can book the product they want. If this prediction proves accurate, retail travel marketing in the future will not be about achieving competitive advantage; instead it will be about marketing for survival.

Discussion points and essay questions

1. Identify the different markets which exist for the services of retail travel outlet and compare and contrast the needs of these different markets.
2. Discuss the various forms of external competition which retail travel organisations are increasingly facing and examine the approaches they might adopt in response to this competition.
3. Compare and contrast the service offered by an online travel retailer such as Expedia and a high-street travel agent in your country.

Exercise

Select a local retail travel outlet which you are able to visit and where you can arrange an interview with a manager. For your chosen outlet, you should visit and interview the manager and then undertake the following tasks:

(i) Evaluate the strengths and weaknesses of the service which it offers.
(ii) Identify its competitors and see how it might seek to gain competitive advantage over them.
(iii) Examine the current role of technology within the business and see how technological developments might affect the way it operates in the future, positively and negatively.

Arts and entertainment

Key concepts

The main concepts covered in the chapter are:

- The scope and nature of the arts
- The different marketing objectives of arts organisations in the public, private and voluntary sectors
- The arts product and the arts as a component of other leisure products
- Competition within the arts, and between the arts and other leisure activities.

Introduction

The arts are a very important subset of the leisure market and arts marketing has developed dramatically across the world in recent years.

However, before we begin to look at the practice of marketing in the arts, we must first define *the scope of the arts*. Figure 21.1 represents the view of the Arts Council in the UK as to the scope and nature of the arts.

Within these overall definitions, there are a number of other ways of classifying the arts. As these tend to affect either products or market segments, they clearly have a major influence on arts marketing. We will therefore briefly discuss them. They include:

(i) The distinction between whether the consumer is a *spectator or a participant*. For example, a person may go to a theatre to see a professional drama performance, or they may be a member of an amateur theatre company which puts on its own performance, as a hobby.

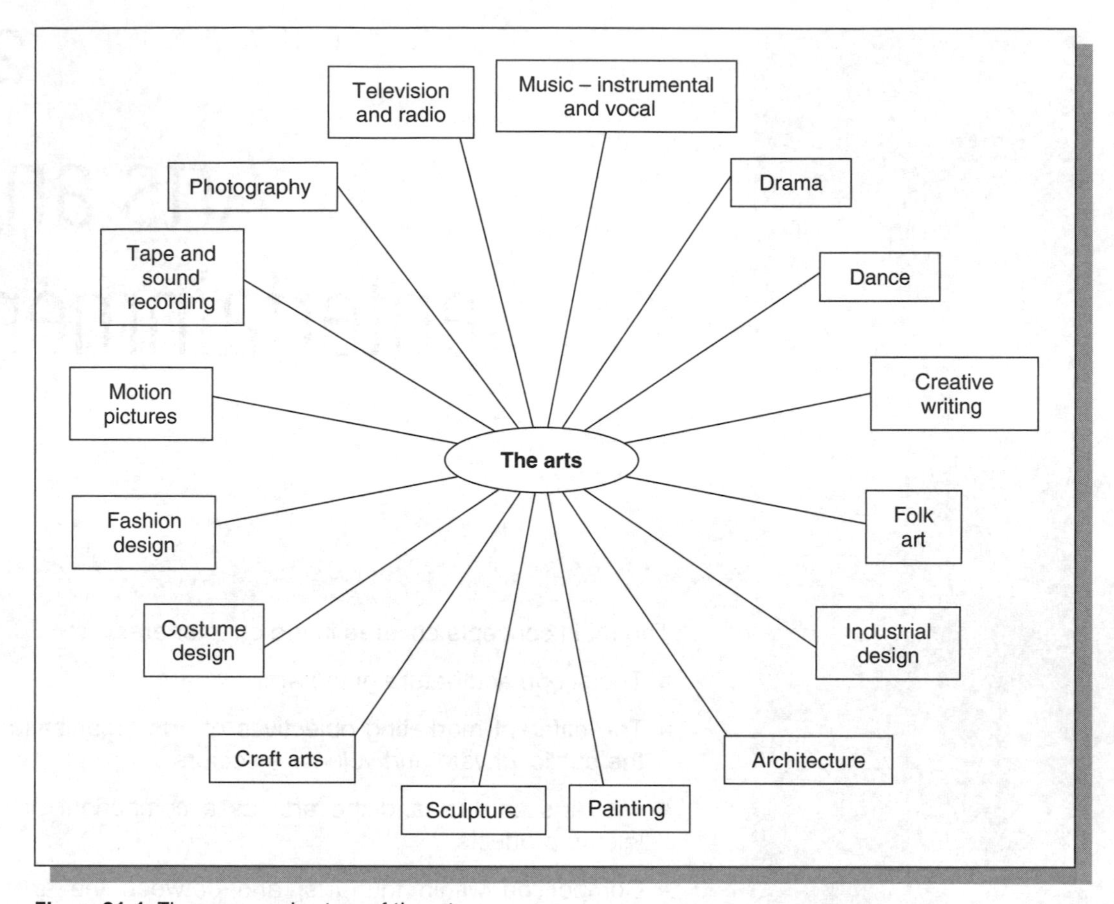

Figure 21.1 The scope and nature of the arts

(ii) The differences between *facilities and activities*, which can also be related to the difference between spectators and participants. Arts facilities include art galleries, art centres, theatres and cinemas, while arts activities include painting, making craft products, dancing and going to rock concerts or arts festivals.
(iii) Some types of arts activity are usually *organised in advance*, such as a theatre visit, while others can be *spontaneous*, such as visiting a local art gallery. This difference is partly accounted for by the fact that prebooking is normal for the former activity but not for the latter.
(iv) Arts activities can be consumed by either *groups or individuals*; for instance, attending a concert is an example of the former while painting is often a solo activity.

There are also differences in terms of *ownership and marketing objectives*. The public sector tends to be a major provider of facilities such as art galleries and theatres, which are usually subsidised. The reason for the subsidy is that there is a belief that arts facilities like these are essential for the cultural life of an area and must therefore be provided even if they lose money. The marketing of such public-sector facilities is therefore largely about increasing usage as well as ensuring whether the budget targets are met. Voluntary-sector involvement in the arts is largely in the field of activities, where the aim is to give opportunities for amateurs to develop their interest in particular hobbies. Their marketing objective is therefore often to generate enough income to allow them to carry on with their activities. Conversely, in the private sector which is strongly represented in areas like the cinema, television and music, the aim is to maximise profits and boost market share where appropriate. These differences in marketing objectives can lead to these organisations adopting different approaches to marketing. In the first two cases, there may be a tendency to concentrate on the product and hope a market can be found for it, while in the latter sector, the focus is on looking at what the market wants and developing an appropriate product to satisfy this demand.

In the public sector, arts are a crucial element in the cultural and leisure policies of central and local government. They are often, therefore, called upon to help achieve broader social objectives such as education and providing activities for young people.

There have always been some blurred lines between the arts and entertainment and sport. The arts have traditionally been seen as rather high level, 'high brow' activities that somehow uplift the soul and enrich people's lives. On the other hand, entertainment and sport are often somehow seen as activities that meet people's basic desires for amusement or exercise, but which do not merit the term 'arts'.

However, in an era when we are talking about the so-called 'postmodernism', it may well be that the demarcation lines are becoming less and less relevant. Indeed, many would now argue that entertainment and sport can equally be considered as arts, for example:

- developing and playing computer games;
- taking part in 'Karaoke' evenings in clubs and pubs;
- circuses;
- playing sports such as football and tennis, or taking part in sporting activities like skiing, for instance.

The arts *product* can take a number of forms, including the following, for example:

- a permanent facility which offers opportunities for people to look at the tangible products of the arts, such as an art gallery, or craft centre;
- a permanent facility which provides opportunities for people to participate in an arts activity, for instance, such as a dance studio or recording studio;
- a club, association or society, membership of which allows someone to indulge in a particular activity and/or have access to equipment they require to take part in an activity. This might be an amateur dramatic club, for example;
- a special, temporary event such as a concert, a theatre performance, or an arts festival.

If we take one type of product, for example, a theatre, the actual product consists of the following elements:

- its programme, in terms of what plays and other types of performances it offers;
- the building in terms of its location, seat comfort and facilities such as bars and restaurants;
- the days on which it is open and the times of its performances;
- its booking system, in terms of how customers can reserve tickets and what methods of payment are accepted;
- the theatre's image, reputation and brand name.

As well as being products in their own right, the arts can also be elements in the wider product of tourism and hospitality organisations. For example:

- Tourist destination-marketing organisations may utilise arts festivals to attract tourists to their town, city or region. France has many examples of such festivals including the annual European Street Theatre Festival in Aurillac and a Festival of Bandes Dessinées, or illustrated comic books, at Angouleme to give but two examples.

- The inclusion of arts facilities and activities in the excursion programmes offered by tour operators to holidaymakers in and around the resort where they are spending their holidays. For instance, tourists in London might be taken to the museum of the Moving Image in the city, which illustrates the history of film and television. Likewise, tourists in countries such as Greece and Spain may be offered a national 'folklore evening'.
- Many hotels now offer weekend break products based on the arts. These can include painting, crafts, art appreciation and theatre weekends.

Pricing is a complex issue in the arts, and it can also be controversial, particularly due to the role of public-sector *subsidies*. These subsidies can mean that some arts facilities and activities of high quality may be offered at no charge. This may include major art galleries, while subsidies may also mean that publicly owned facilities such as theatres may be able to offer their products at levels below the true market value. This is true of activities such as opera performances. As we will see later, this can be seen as unfair competition by commercial-sector arts organisations.

A particularly controversial aspect of such subsidies is that they are often not linked to activities which are enjoyed by people on limited incomes primarily, where subsidies could be justified by the fact that they allow less-affluent people to enjoy the art. In the case of opera, for example, where subsidies can be worth several pounds sterling per ticket sold, most customers are relatively affluent. There are, therefore, debates over the ethics of such subsidies and discussions about who should subsidise and which arts should be subsidised.

Other pricing issues in the arts revolve around concessions which are given to economically and socially disadvantaged groups such as students and the elderly, and on the other hand, discounts which are offered for purely marketing reasons. These may include the need to boost ticket sales at less busy times or the encouragement of group bookings.

Place or distribution is a relatively simple concept in the arts, with three major elements as follows:

1. the use of marketing intermediaries from which consumers can purchase tickets for performances, such as travel agents and tourist information offices;
2. direct booking with arts facilities or activity organisations by telephone or in writing;
3. where prebooking is not the norm, place can literally mean the location, where people are attracted to enter buildings or join in events, simply because they happen to be passing by at the appropriate time.

Most arts products are marketed using a limited range of *promotional techniques* because the budgets of arts organisations are often limited. The most popular methods of promotion in the arts include:

- leaflets covering individual facilities or individual special events or published programmes covering a season of plays at a theatre;
- advertising, largely in the printed media, in either local or regional newspapers or specialist periodicals;
- sales promotion offers, both added value (two tickets for the price of one for a theatre performance, for example) and discounts (£1 off a ticket for students at a cinema);
- press and public relations are also widely used, gaining favourable media coverage, that is largely free;
- sponsorship of arts organisations by organisations which raises the sponsoring organisation's profile and/or brings extra revenue.

The relatively few major transnational corporations in the arts also undertake more sophisticated advertising, such as television advertising, when a new film is released.

Some arts organisations have combined the promotion of their core business with forays into the visitor-attraction sector. This phenomenon has been clearly seen in the US film industry with studio-based attractions such as Universal Studios.

There are a number of issues relating to the arts *market* which are relevant to arts marketing. These include:

- The different-sized *catchment areas* of arts facilities and events. Some have only a local catchment area while others can be largely international, and many others lie somewhere between these two extremes. For example, many cinemas may serve a local clientele, while a major art gallery, such as the Louvre in Paris, has a truly international catchment area. The same is true of events where a small music festival may draw most of its visitors from the locality, and others such as the Salzburg Music Festival draw visitors from all over the world.
- The market can be divided into a number of different *market segments*, on the basis on a range of criteria including age, sex, income, nationality, language, place of residence, lifestyle and personality. However, the market can also be broken down into those who like to watch and those who like to participate. There is also a difference between groups and individuals in terms of consumer behaviour.
- The benefits sought by the users of arts products vary dramatically, and some of these differences are related to the existence of different market segments. Some of the most significant benefits sought include:
  - status
  - aesthetic pleasure
  - learning a new skill
  - an individual or a collective experience
  - sensual pleasure
  - hedonism
  - ego enhancement
  - increased confidence
  - health and fitness

  to name but ten from a list that probably includes hundreds. It is important to note how these benefits sought vary between different customers even in relation to purchasing what is ostensibly the same product.

For example, the benefits sought by a young couple visiting a cinema to see a film might be one of the following:

- The cinema represents a place where they can enjoy a romantic experience in the dark!
- They may be keen to gain status by being able to say they have seen a particularly fashionable film.
- Escapism from the dullness of everyday life, or fear, or the chance to learn something new, depending on the nature of the film.
- The pleasure of enjoying the snacks and drinks on sale at the cinema.
- Taking advantage of a special discount offer, perhaps with a fast-food outlet which gives away cheap cinema tickets when people purchase particular meals.

Finally, in terms of the market, the fact that while most arts involve the use of leisure time, there is also a business-related market. For example, some companies use arts activities such as opera performances as part of corporate hospitality packages for their customers. This phenomena may be developed to the point where it can form part of formal sponsorship arrangements between businesses and arts organisations.

Competition is a complex issue in the arts field. As it is a leisure activity, the real competitors are all other forms of leisure activity or opportunities for spending disposable income. This can best be illustrated by taking an example such as a cinema which specialises in family films. Its competitors might typically include:

- other cinemas in the same geographical area, with similar programmes;
- theatres in the same area, offering family shows;
- special events targeted at families, such as craft fairs;
- eating out at restaurants;
- visitor attractions which are aimed at families, such as theme parks;
- recreational activities like taking a walk in the countryside, bicycle riding or swimming;
- visiting a leisure-shopping complex;
- visiting friends and relatives;
- home-based leisure activities such as barbecues;
- home entertainment where the family stay at home and indulge in activities such as watching videos, playing computer games or simply playing games in their garden.

There are accusations that there is *unfair competition* in some areas of the arts. For example, our cinema above is privately owned, receives no subsidies and has to make a profit to survive. On the other hand, the local theatre, with which it is competing, is publicly owned and receives a subsidy so that it does not have to charge a market price for its tickets, unlike the cinema.

However, in the public sector, in particular, there is also *internal competition* where arts facilities owned by the same body may indeed be competing with each other. This may be true in relation to theatres or art galleries, for example.

Marketing activity has to be carefully planned, therefore, to ensure that the organisation is not spending money to allow it merely to compete against itself.

Finally, in relation to arts marketing, we will briefly outline several *miscellaneous issues*, relating to the marketing of arts products.

1. *Consortia* play a significant role in arts marketing, with organisations, particularly in the public sectors which have limited budgets working together to increase their combined buying power in terms of advertising campaigns and brochure production and distribution. These consortia often relate to either a particular art, such as dance or crafts, or arts organisations within a specific geographical area. However, such consortia can also be found in the commercial sector, with perhaps the best example being the Society of West End Theatres in London.
2. Many arts organisations operate on a *transnational* basis so that they have to take into account national differences in terms of consumer behaviour, business practices, legal frameworks and so on. Examples of such transnational activities include:
   - foreign tours by dance companies and rock bands;
   - the sale of television programmes to networks in other countries;
   - international record sales;
   - art exhibitions mounted by galleries in one country that take place in a foreign country.
3. The *size of marketing budgets* for arts organisations can vary dramatically from a few hundred pound sterling for a small art gallery to major film companies which may spend millions of pound sterling promoting just one film.

4. In some of the arts, there is a *tension between the art and those who practice it, and the concept of marketing*. Many people in the arts believe that marketing is harmful to the arts because it can mean having to compromise artistic principles and values to meet the wishes of consumers. This is particularly true in those art forms where professionals with a strong sense of vocation undertake performances, such as drama, dance and music.

Conclusion

Overall arts marketing is a complex but growing area of activity. Particularly in the public and voluntary sectors, it can have a very strong set of social marketing objectives. At the same time, in the private sector, one can see some of the most overtly controversial and aggressive types of marketing found in any industry.

Discussion points and essay questions

1. Compare and contrast the approaches to marketing which are taken by public- and private-sector organisations in the arts.
2. Evaluate the nature of the product within the arts sector.
3. Identify all the main forms of competition which might be faced by an individual theatre *or* art gallery, both within and outside the arts.

Exercise

Choose *one* public-sector body and *one* private-sector company, within the arts sector.

Compare and contrast these two organisations in terms of their:

(i) marketing objectives
(ii) the nature of the product offered
(iii) pricing policies
(iv) promotional techniques
(v) policy in relation to competitors
(vi) performance indicators.

You should finally attempt to explain any differences which you may identify in relation to these six issues between the two organisations.

CHAPTER 22

Recreation and sport

Key concepts

The main concepts covered in the chapter are:

- Types of recreational activity
- The different objectives of organisations in the public, private and voluntary sectors
- Recreation and sport as an element in tourism and hospitality products
- Transnational marketing in recreation and sport.

Introduction

Recreation is defined by Torkildsen (1999) as 'activities and experiences usually carried on within leisure and usually chosen voluntarily for satisfaction, pleasure, or creative enrichment'. He goes on to say that, 'it may also be perceived as the process of participation. Physical recreation is closely allied to sport.'

In this chapter, we are going to focus on the marketing of those aspects of recreation which are concerned with activities and sport, rather than the more passive forms of recreation. We will also concentrate on those forms of recreation which are most closely linked to leisure. Figure 22.1 illustrates some of the major different *types of recreational activity* that people indulge in during their leisure time.

Even this brief, selective picture illustrates the diversity of forms of recreation which explains why it is such a complex

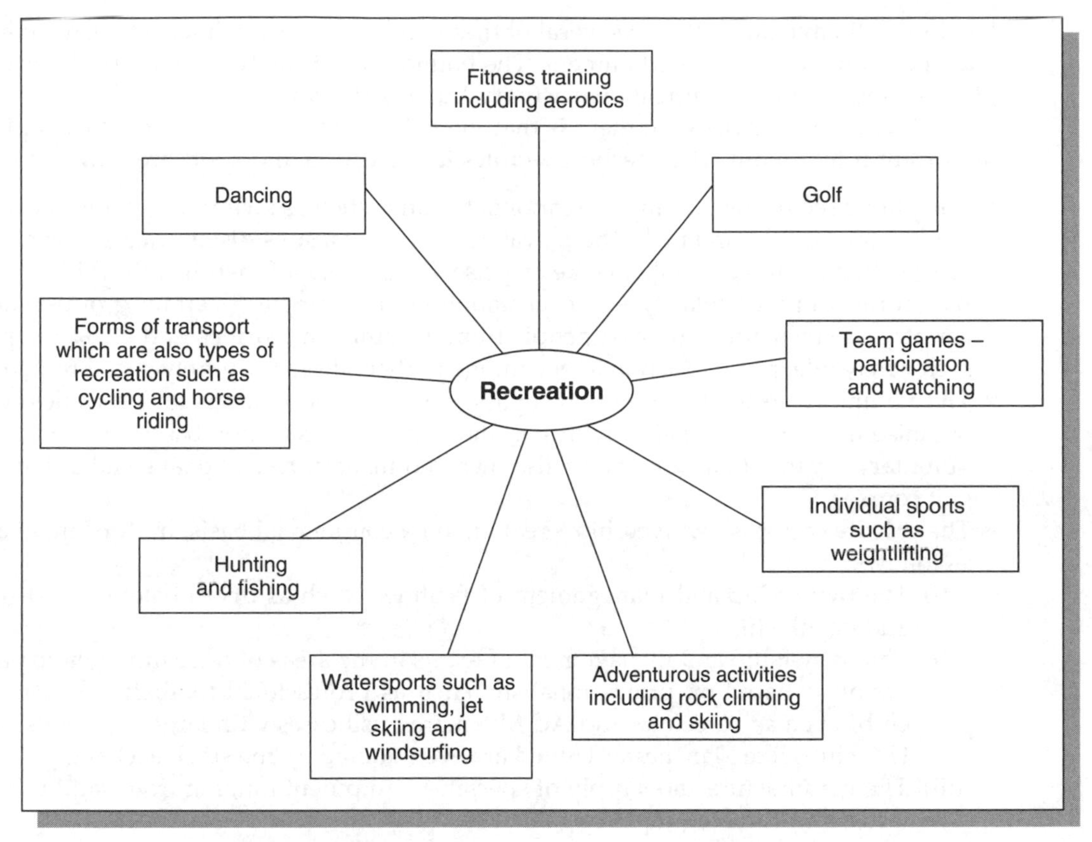

Figure 22.1 Types of recreational activity

sector as far as marketing is concerned. Some of the differences between forms of recreation which influence marketing practice in the sector include:

- Some recreational activities, such as dancing and fitness training, can be practised in people's homes or in their local area. Others require participants to travel considerable distances to the places where specialist facilities such as rock faces or water areas are located.
- Partly for this reason, some forms of recreation can be indulged in on a daily basis, while others may only be undertaken once or twice a year, on an annual holiday, for example.
- Some activities require special clothing and equipment such as skiing or golf, while others require little or none, as in the case of playing football in a public park, for instance.
- Some forms of recreation are supported by a large physical infrastructure of facilities such as golf courses, while others are not.
- Certain recreation activities can be controversial, political or even illegal in certain countries. The best example of this phenomenon is, perhaps, hunting.
- Some activities are group ones such as playing team games, while others are very much individual activities like horse riding.
- While prebooking is required for some recreational activities such as golf, it is not for others, including cycling and rock climbing.
- Recreation can be a matter of being a spectator watching others play football, for instance, or it can be about participation, in other words, playing in a football match.

Readers will have noted that in several of these aspects there are links between recreation and sport, and arts and entertainment. The boundaries of the two are blurred, for example, dancing is a type of recreational activity, but it is also an art form.

Another similarity between them is that the *public, voluntary and private sectors* play an important role in both. Their respective roles in recreation and sport are outlined below:

- The public sector owns many recreational facilities such as swimming pools and woodlands, for example, and make them available, often at a subsidised price, or even free of charge, to encourage people to take exercise, for the sake of their health. Where participation rates in particular types of recreation are low amongst certain groups, such as countryside recreation amongst people from the ethnic minorities in the UK, the public sector may take positive action to encourage participation, for purely social reasons.
- The voluntary sector tends to encompass the clubs, associations and societies, which organise many recreational activities, in those areas of recreation based on amateurism. Voluntary organisations sometimes also own and manage recreational facilities including golf courses.
- The private sector is involved in recreation, on a commercial basis, in three main areas, as follows:
  - (i) The ownership and management of facilities, such as dry-ski slopes, and fitness and health clubs.
  - (ii) The ownership and management of teams in the areas of recreation where participation is based on professionalism, such as professional football. Some football clubs such as Barcelona and AC Milan are businesses with large turnovers. In the UK, clubs like Manchester United are even quoted on the stock exchange.
  - (iii) The manufacture and supply of specialist equipment ranging from saddles to leotards, and climbing ropes to golf clubs.

Sometimes the boundaries between these three sectors can be blurred. For example, many public-sector agencies are having to become more commercial in response to reductions in their state funding. Likewise, some voluntary associations and clubs can have large turnovers on which they generate profits like private companies. Some may even be incorporated as private companies in respect of some of their activities.

Finally, it is important to note that all three sectors can be represented within one type of recreation. For example, some golf courses are owned by municipal authorities, while others are in the ownership of voluntary bodies or private companies. Furthermore, most golfers are amateurs, while a few are highly paid professionals.

Because of the diversity of the recreation sector, we will focus on just three different elements of recreation when we consider the application of the marketing mix to recreation and the recreation market. These are:

1. countryside recreation in a national park;
2. a golf course owned by a voluntary-sector golf club;
3. a major professional football club.

The countryside recreation *product* in a National Park can be both 'natural' and artificially created. Whilst much of the landscape will usually be natural, its attractions may have been enhanced by the development of picnic sites and new footpaths. Further, artificial product development may take place in the form of a new programme of guided walks. The 'product' represents a series of opportunities from which users can build their own experience, whether it be a quiet picnic near their car or a long strenuous walk. A key element of the product is its accessibility from where people live, by private car or public transport. As far as *price* is concerned, users are rarely asked to pay a direct charge for the use of the countryside for recreation purposes.

Instead, the cost of providing for their needs is usually met by taxation levied on the population in general. As prebooking is not the norm, *place* plays little real role in most countryside recreation in National Parks. As most National Parks are managed, if now owned, by the public sector, they have wider aims than simply encouraging countryside recreation. Their main responsibility is often conservation, so that frequently they have to indulge in demarketing to reduce demand and divert visitors to less popular areas to reduce pressure on the landscape.

Promotional techniques are often used in this connection to achieve this aim, through brochures, in particular, and press and public relations activities too. The limited budgets of most National Park authorities tend to result in relatively little advertising being undertaken.

As far as the *market* is concerned, several important points need to be made, as follows:

- Some National Parks, due to their remote location, have relatively small visitor numbers, while others which are nearer to urban areas have large visitor numbers (around 20 million in the case of the Peak District National Park in the UK).
- Many parks have a large local and regional market such as the Peak District, while others, particularly those in well-established tourist destinations, have predominantly national and even international markets, like those in the French Alps.
- In some parks, the majority of visitors are repeat visitors, while in others most visitors will only visit once in their lives.
- The benefits people seek from countryside recreation in a National Park can vary dramatically, as we can see from the brief list below, of different types of benefits:
  - passive relaxation or a chance to indulge in an energetic and even dangerous activity;
  - the chance to escape from others and be alone, or the opportunity to meet new people;
  - the desire to try a new experience or the attractiveness of doing something with which you do often.

The *product* which the voluntary-sector golf club offers has a number of elements, as follows:

- The golf course itself with its golf-related features such as its bunkers and other hazards, and the nature of its greens. The product also covers the environmental setting of the course and the views that are enjoyed by those playing the course.
  - the days and times on which the course is available;
  - the facilities available in the club-house such as bars and restaurants;
  - the availability of advice and coaching from a resident golf professional;
  - the image and reputation of the course locally, regionally, nationally and internationally;
  - the social life involved in playing the course and/or belonging to the club.

The *pricing* structure tends to vary between the situation where members pay to belong to the club and then pay a modest sum for each round of golf they play, and where casual players who are nonmembers are asked to pay a higher price. Some municipally owned, public-sector courses may also offer concessions to groups who are seen to be socially disadvantaged.

In terms of *place* and distribution, membership of the club is the way of gaining regular rights of access to the course, but often people have to be invited to join, rather than simply apply. Thus they need to know people who are already members. The system of distribution for players seeking a casual one-off round of golf, at such clubs, and those wishing to play on municipal courses is a simple matter of prebooking by telephone.

Promotion is often not relevant as in many cases demand outstrips supply, particularly at peak times. However, where newer courses have been established in countries like Spain and France, to help attract tourists, substantial promotional activities may be undertaken, by the golf course itself, the local destination-marketing agency or a tour operator which is selling golf packages based on the course.

The *market* for golf courses can vary dramatically. With an old, well-established, famous course in the UK, most users are the members, who live within the same region. Few nonmembers will be able to use the course, in general, except when open tournaments are underway. On the other hand, at some of the newer courses in Spain and Portugal, for instance, most users may well be foreign tourists, with relatively few local people making use of the course.

As far as the benefits sought by the consumers of golf courses and golf club services, status perhaps comes near the top of the list, in relation to the more exclusive courses. However, in general, the benefits sought include:

- relaxation in the fresh air;
- gentle exercise;
- the social life and atmosphere that is part of the golf scene;
- the chance to gain satisfaction from improving one's ability to play the game;
- an opportunity to mix business and pleasure with business people using golf as a way of doing business in a relaxed, informal atmosphere.

In many European countries, professional football is big business, with clubs having high turnovers and generating considerable profits. This is particularly true in Spain, Italy and the UK.

The *product* which is offered by a professional football club has two main elements as follows:

(i) The football team which offers, in effect, a special event product, namely a ninety-minute spectacle involving playing a competitive match against another team. However, a football match is about more than the ninety minutes of the game on the pitch. The team also offers opportunities for its fans to bask in their team's glory, or lament its failures to look forwards to the game throughout the preceding week. For a team, its image and reputation is all important to its fans, potential investors and prospective players.

(ii) The stadium, in terms of tangible features such as the quality of seating and catering facilities, together with intangible aspects such as the atmosphere.However, increasingly, football stadia are not just venues for football matches. They also act as a venue for concerts, for example.

In terms of the corporate market, football clubs often combine their two products, the team and the stadium, into a lucrative corporate hospitality product. Companies pay for facilities where important customers can be wined and dined and enjoy the match at the same time.

Prices tend to be relatively high for tickets at leading professional football matches, but there are different prices depending on where one sits within the ground. Season tickets are also offered to encourage brand loyalty and give the club cash flow at the beginning of the season. Corporate packages tend to be premium priced, particularly if the club is a famous one.

As far as *place* or distribution is concerned, prebooking by post or telephone is the norm for football match tickets, and is obligatory for the purchase of corporate hospitality packages. For matches, a certain allocation of tickets may be given to the visiting club which it will then distribute to its supporters.

In relation to football matches, *promotion* is usually a very low key. Supporters are simply regular visitors and they buy their ticket almost automatically. All they need to be given is a fixture list for the season. The match brochure or programme can be used to promote particular matches. On the other hand, the corporate hospitality market, which is very competitive, and is also a lucrative activity, merits glossy promotional brochures and a considerable amount of personal selling activity on the part of the clubs.

There are, as we have seen, a number of distinct *market segments* for a professional football club, namely:

- Local people who support the team and go to watch all its matches.
- Local people who go to some matches, particularly the most important ones.
- A small number of nonlocal supporters who will travel longer distances to watch some of its matches. This happens more in the case of the more fashionable clubs like Manchester United, or Liverpool, in the UK, for instance.
- Business people who use the matches for corporate hospitality purposes.
- Those people who use the stadium only when it is playing host to other kinds of events such as concerts.

The *benefits sought* by a football club depend on which segment one is talking about. Local supporters go to the match to see their friends, demonstrate their loyalty to the club and relax. For them the match is the focus of their trip to the ground.

Conversely, for most business users, the game is a means to an end rather than an end in itself; in other words, the match is an opportunity to impress customers and discuss business in an informal setting.

While these three examples cannot represent the whole of recreation and sport, they at least demonstrate the great variety of marketing issues found in this sector.

Competition in recreation and sport is also a complex matter, and exists at a number of levels, including that between:

(i) different providers of the same product such as golf courses or gymnasia;
(ii) different forms of recreation such as dancing, swimming and jogging for those interested in improving their health;
(iii) free or subsidised public-owned recreation facilities and commercial promotion from private-sector organisations;
(iv) active recreation and sport, and passive leisure activities such as watching television or eating out.

There can also be internal competition such as when a local council offers several types of recreation facility to its local population, and they can end up competing with each other for the local market.

Finally, we will consider a range of *miscellaneous issues* that influence the nature of marketing in recreation and sport.

1. The *marketing of recreation and sports facilities by other bodies*. Many facilities and activities are promoted by other bodies, as well as by the owners or operators themselves. For example, in the UK, the Sports Council promotes a wide range of sporting activities and facilities.

2. *Links with the marketing of tourism and hospitality*. Recreation and sports products are increasingly being used as part of broader tourism and hospitality products, as the following examples illustrate:
   - tour operators developing holidays based on recreational activities, as diverse as the following:
     - a golfing holiday in Portugal;
     - a hunting holiday in Siberia;
     - a walking holiday in the mountains of Spain;
     - a skiing holiday in the Rockies in the USA;
     - a scuba diving trip to the Red Sea;
     - a holiday based on going to see the Olympics in Athens in 2004;
   - excursions available within tourist destinations which are based on recreational activities such as golf, horse riding, and wind surfing;
   - destination-marketing agencies promoting an area on the basis of the natural and man-made resources, it offers for recreational activities, including:
     - the golf courses of Ireland;
     - the surfing beaches of the Aquitaine coast in France or Cornwall in the UK;
     - the proximity of skiing facilities to Norwegian resorts such as Voss and Lillehammer;
     - Hotels developing leisure facilities within the hotel such as swimming pools and gymnasia, to attract customers who wish to keep fit and take exercise while they are staying at the hotel;
   - the development of mass events such as the Olympic Games which attract international sponsorship and media coverage, and is one of the major events in the world;
3. *National differences in recreation and sport*. These include:
   - the popularity of different sports in different countries as golf is very popular in Scotland and Ireland, but much less so in Greece, for instance;
   - certain sports which are peculiar to individual countries or regions such as pelota in the Basque country of Spain and France and hurling in Ireland;
   - differential scales of provision from the massive football stadia in Spain and Italy to the small grounds of Scandinavia;
   - countries which have traditionally had a relatively small domestic market for recreation and sport, and those where participation rates, within the domestic market, are much higher. While this distinction was often considered to exist between Northern and Southern European countries, respectively, it is a gross over-simplification. It is often simply that the people of the varying countries have different tastes for different types of activities, but that levels of participation are, in some form of leisure activity, relatively similar overall.
4. *Transnational marketing*. While most recreation and sport marketing is domestic, there is a significant amount of transnational marketing, particularly in the field of destination marketing. These organisations involved in such marketing clearly have to take into account national differences in consumer demand, legislation and business promotions. Examples of such transnational marketing include:
   - Destination-marketing organisations in France attempting to attract UK golfers to the newly built courses of France.
   - Irish destination marketers trying to attract anglers from the UK, USA, Germany and the Netherlands.
   - The marketing of sporting events which have an international market such as the 2004 Olympics in Greece, the annual tennis championships at Wimbledon in the UK, and even the running-of-the-bulls festival in Pamplona, Spain.

5. *Consortia* can play a significant role in recreation and sport marketing, particularly in the public and voluntary sectors. These consortia can either take the form of pressure groups and lobbying bodies on behalf of a particular activity, or a loose consortium of similar types of facilities such as golf courses.

Conclusion

As we have seen, marketing in the recreation and sport sector is complex, due to a range of factors related to the nature of the product, ownership and marketing objectives, and different types of market demand. However, we have also noted that it shares some of these characteristics with the arts and entertainment sector.

Discussion points and essay questions

1. Compare and contrast the marketing objectives of public- private- and voluntary-sector organisations in the recreation sector.
2. Evaluate the differences in terms of the application of the Marketing Mix between countryside recreation and a professional football club.
3. Discuss the links which exist between recreation and leisure.

Exercise

You have been engaged as a consultant to undertake *either* of the following tasks:

(i) to encourage more people to take exercise by walking, riding and bicycling in a rural area of your choice, on behalf of a public-sector body, charged with promoting healthier lifestyles;

(ii) to increase the income of a professional football club of your choice, which owns its own stadium.

For your chosen project you should

- identify target markets;
- develop appropriate new products to meet the needs of these markets and indicate how these products could be priced to make them attractive to these markets;
- outline the main distribution channels for these products;
- produce a promotional plan, indicating what promotional techniques would be utilised to persuade target markets to purchase these products;
- highlight key implementation issues, including funding.

CHAPTER 23

Leisure shopping

Key concepts

The main concepts covered in the chapter are:

- A typology of leisure-shopping facilities
- The nature of the leisure-shopping product
- The benefits sought by leisure shoppers
- Links between leisure shopping and other sectors of leisure.

Introduction

While most shopping is utilitarian in nature, undertaken to purchase the goods which are the prerequisites for everyday life such as food and household goods, there has always been an element of pleasure shopping for nonessentials. However, it is only in recent years that we have seen the growth of a sector of leisure which is solely concerned with retailing as a leisure activity. It is not the concept of leisure shopping which is new, but its rapid expansion and the growing provision of purpose-built shopping facilities.

These *leisure-shopping facilities* come in a number of forms, as follows:

(i) *Major leisure-shopping complexes*, where all or most of the retail units sell products which are not essential to everyday life. They are purchased purely for pleasure as part of a leisure experience. An excellent example is the Albert Dock in Liverpool, UK, where it has been used to spearhead the regeneration of the economy of the city through leisure, on the model which has been used in US cities like Baltimore and San Francisco. This is interesting because the idea of leisure-shopping complexes or 'Malls' originates in North America with major centres such as the West Edmonton Mall in Canada.

(ii) *Leisure-shopping areas which are found within established tourist destinations*. These can range from the shops in UK seaside resorts selling 'rock' (candy confectionery) and novelty hats at cheap prices to the chic retail outlets of the French Riviera. This aspect of leisure shopping has a relatively long history compared to the complexes we have just discussed.

(iii) *Industrial leisure-oriented shops in existing retail areas of towns and cities* which are not major tourist attractions. They are targeted both at locals and the relatively small number of tourists that visit the place, and are usually located in the districts which are most likely to be visited by such people.

(iv) *Craft centres* which sell craft goods and may even provide opportunities for visitors to watch the product being made. These centres are particularly popular in the major coastal resorts in Europe, as well as in rural regions in many countries.

(v) *Leisure-oriented outlets which are part of visitor attractions*. For many attractions, a significant element of their income is obtained from the sale of merchandise. This is equally true whether the attraction is a major theme park like Disneyland Paris, or a museum such as the Victoria and Albert Museum in London.

(vi) *Outlets linked to home-based leisure activities*, such as garden centres and 'Do-It-Yourself' centres.

At the same time, a leisure dimension is also being added to more utilitarian retailing activity such as food purchasing and everyday clothes, as the following two examples illustrate:

1. People being encouraged to visit *food providers* as a leisure experience and buy some of their products directly. For example, in France, one can buy cheese from a farmer who makes it, and wine from the local cooperative. The pleasure is derived not just from the consumption of the product, but also from the experience of seeing where it was made and meeting the producer.
2. The phenomena of *factory shops* where producers, mostly of clothes, sell them directly from their premises. In the UK, coach trips are often organised by groups and coach operators to such factory shops. These are seen as a leisure experience as well as an opportunity to purchase clothes at below-normal prices.

Most leisure-shopping facilities are offered by the private sector whose *marketing objectives* are purely commercial. However, there is also a role for the voluntary and public sectors, whose objectives are broader than merely financial. For example, in the UK, one of the largest organisations involved in leisure retailing is the National Trust, a voluntary body. It uses the income generated from its retailing operations to fund its conservation work.

The leisure-shopping *product* varies depending on which type of leisure retailing we are considering, but in general it contains the following elements:

- the products which are on offer in terms of their design, aesthetic appearance, features, reputation and exclusivity value;
- the industrial retail outlet itself including the location, decor and reputation;
- the service element, and the attitudes and product knowledge of the staff;
- the methods of payment which are acceptable;

- the outlet's opening times in terms of how convenient they are for prospective customers;
- the areas in which the outlet is located in terms of its environment, fashionability, accessibility, car parking facilities, ambience, and the proximity of other services such as catering.

The customer pays *no price*, usually, for entering a leisure-shopping complex or an individual leisure-retailing outlet. For some people, therefore, leisure shopping is a very economical leisure experience. They gain pleasure from looking rather than buying.

Place or destination is relatively simple in the leisure-shopping sector, in general. Prebooking is not normal and therefore little use tends to be made of marketing intermediaries. In this case, 'Place' really does mean location, for it is often where the complex or unit is situated that is one of its major attractions for visitors.

The *promotional techniques* used tends to depend, as usual, on the size and budget of the organisation. A small rural craft centre may rely on simple leaflets and word-of-mouth recommendations while a major leisure-shopping complex may spend heavily on television and printed-media advertising campaigns, together with glossy brochures.

Many smaller leisure retailers rely heavily on repeat purchases, so that they need relatively little promotional outlay designed to attract new customers.

The *market* for leisure retailing can be segmented in a variety of ways but is usually based on geographical and demographic factors, including:

- where people live, as most complexes or units have local, regional, national or international catchment areas;
- stage in the family life cycle, in other words, children, couples, families and older people, for example;
- sex, as women are seen to be far more enthusiastic leisure shoppers than men, for example.

The benefits sought from leisure shopping by consumers differ between these different types of leisure shopping. However, typically they might include:

- the chance to buy a unique and unusual product that is not available elsewhere;
- the pleasure of 'window shopping' without buying anything;
- the opportunity to purchase a product directly from the producer at a lower cost than it would be available in a shop in the person's own area.

However, leisure shopping can also offer some more fundamental benefits. It is often the core attraction of trips made by people who are depressed; the so-called 'depression shopping' is becoming more widely recognised as an issue in some parts of Europe. For many people, leisure-shopping trips are social activities which involve travelling with a group of friends. This can represent a break with routine, a form of 'escapism'.

In many cases, the benefit sought is not an individual element but rather the overall experience, including:

- the journey to and from the retailing area;
- the company of friends;
- the pleasure gained from looking at goods or buying something special;
- a meal in the middle of the trip in an attractive restaurant.

Competition takes a number of forms in leisure shopping, including:

(i) Between different types of outlets and complexes within a particular geographical area.
(ii) Between similar types of outlets and complexes in a wider geographical area.

(iii) Between leisure shopping and utility shopping.
(iv) Between shopping and other forms of leisure pursuits such as gardening, reading, eating out or sporting activities.
(v) Between shopping and other forms of leisure spending on a day out, such as entrance fees to attractions, and food and drink. As we can see, the form of competition will largely depend on the type of leisure-shopping outlet or complex one is considering.

As well as marketing themselves, leisure-shopping facilities are also *often promoted by organisations in other sectors of leisure*. For example:

- The excursions organised by tour operators often feature a leisure-shopping experience. This may be a rural craft centre in Ireland, gift shops on the Costa del Sol, a garden centre in the UK, or a Christmas market in Bavaria.
- Hotels often promote leisure-shopping facilities when they are trying to sell their weekend break packages. This is true of destinations from London to Los Angeles, Paris to Istanbul, Hong Kong to Mineapolis, Dublin to Dubai.
- Transport operators such as the ferry operators offering services across the English Channel, Le Manche, who promote off-peak season shopping trips from the UK to France, for example.

These examples lead us into a broader discussion of the *links between leisure shopping and other sectors of leisure*. These links take a number of forms, including the following:

- Many accommodation establishments have installed retail outlets featuring largely up-market leisure-shopping products.
- Leisure-shopping complexes and units often enhance their attractiveness through the provision of catering facilities. Particular types of catering have become associated with leisure shopping such as 'tea rooms' or *Salons de Thé*, coffee shops, wine bars, and unusual ethnic restaurants.
- Conference social and partners programmes often include leisure-shopping trips.
- Airports, airlines, and ferry companies are developing leisure-shopping facilities of their own to increase income. This is particularly important following the loss of duty-free sales.
- Shops selling the equipment required for hobbies and recreational activities, such as painting or skiing, have grown considerably in recent years.

Consortia play a limited but significant role in some areas of leisure shopping, notably the two which follow:

1. voluntary groupings of individual retailers within individual leisure shopping areas or complexes who combine to mount joint promotional campaigns;
2. consortia of similar types of leisure-shopping outlets, such as craft centres, which aim to promote their particular type of retailing and product.

Conclusion

Overall, leisure shopping is a growing area of activity within leisure. It has strong links with other sectors in these three fields, but it also has some interesting characteristics of its own, from a marketing point of view. It seems likely that in the future it will become increasingly recognised as a separate sector within leisure.

Discussion points and essay questions

1. Identify the main types of leisure-shopping facilities which exist, and examine the differences between them.
2. Discuss the different markets that exist for leisure-shopping products and outline the benefits each of these markets might seek from leisure shopping.
3. Examine the nature of competition within the leisure-shopping sector.

Exercise

Choose an example of a leisure-shopping outlet, complex or facility which you are able to visit. You should visit your chosen outlet, complex or facility and spend some time there, looking at the product it offers and finding out the opinions of its customers. You should also endeavour to talk to the manager or owner about their marketing activities.

On the basis of evidence gained from this research, you should:

- evaluate the strengths and weaknesses of the outlet, complex or facility, from the point of view of both customers and the manager or owner;
- identify its main competitors in the opinion of both the customers and the manager or owner.

Finally, you should compare and contrast the views of customers with those of the manager or owner, in relation to these two issues, identifying, where appropriate, those areas where their opinions differ markedly.

CHAPTER 24

Restaurants and catering

Key concepts

The main concepts covered in the chapter are:

- The wide variety of types of catering
- Catering as part of leisure products
- The complex nature of the catering product
- Methods of segmenting the catering market and the benefits sought by these different segments.

Introduction

Catering is now a massive business across the world and is a crucial element in the product offered by many leading tourist destinations.

It is primarily concerned with preparing meals which are consumed either on the caterer's own premises or at the consumer's home. The catering product is a combination of tangible elements such as the food and drink, together with an intangible service element.

Traditionally, catering has been seen to be distinctly different from food manufacturing and food retailing, but these distinctions have become blurred in recent years. Some aspects of catering, such as contract catering, have more in common with the production lines of food factories than with traditional restaurants. At the same time, more and more supermarkets are selling preprepared convenient dishes to compete with 'take-away' catering outlets.

However, even within mainstream catering, there are many sub-sectors with very different characteristics, from a marketing point of view, some of which are illustrated in Figure 24.1:

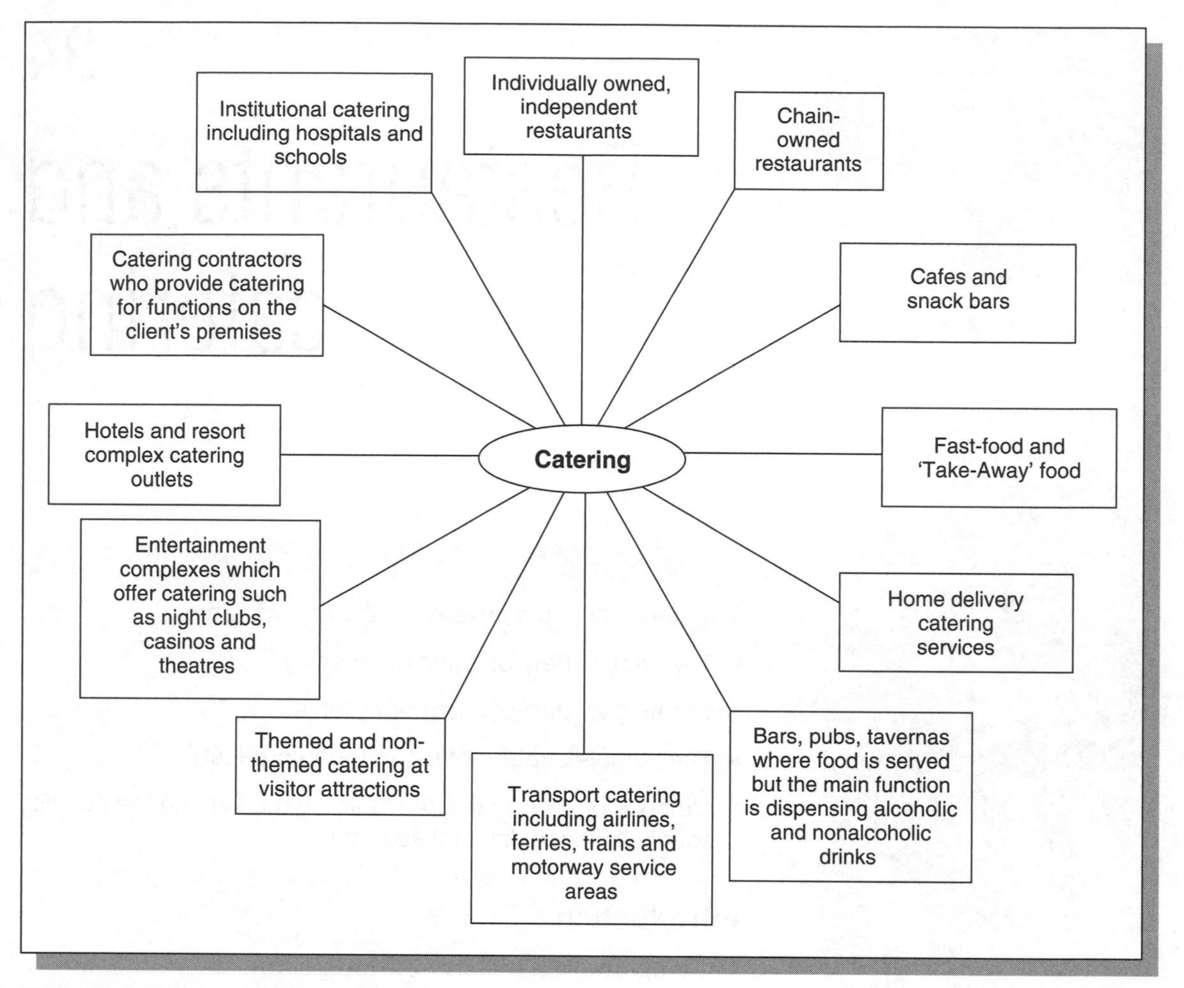

Figure 24.1 Different types of catering

Clearly, this picture is simplified and relates largely to terms which are used in the UK. However, the types of catering it outlines are generally found around the world, although the specific names may be different.

There are a number of general points that need to be made in terms of the marketing of catering in Europe that relate to *ownership and marketing objectives*. These include the following:

- Some of the major players in some areas of catering in Europe are non-European, for example, McDonald's and KFC. This had led to the introduction of American concepts of catering and service to the European market which have affected the approach of European players such as Burger King.
- While most of the catering trade is in the private sector where profits and market share are the key marketing objectives, there is a welfare element which exists in the public sector, such as schools and hospitals, which have social objectives.
- The majority of catering outlets are small businesses operating single units, while the rest are generally parts of chains which offer a standardised product in a number of locations.

There are some interesting *links between catering and tourism and leisure* which are becoming increasingly interrelated, as the two following examples illustrate:

- At many leisure facilities and visitor attractions, catering is a major element of the product on offer and contributes a significant proportion of overall income. In some cases, a particular catering outlet at an attraction can be almost as powerful a factor in a decision to visit a particular attraction as the attraction itself.
- Catering can be an attraction in its own right, encouraging people to visit a particular location, usually a famous restaurant. Certainly the quality of catering outlets has been a major element of the marketing campaign of Kinsale in Ireland. Likewise, many people choose to travel to the Lyonnais region in France, amongst other reasons, because of the restaurant of Paul Bocuse which is located there. There is also a strong link between food production, catering and tourism which is clearly shown in the case of the Bourgogne (Burgundy) region of France. People travel to this region to visit wine producers and enjoy meals in local restaurants which feature traditional local dishes made using locally produced ingredients.

Therefore, as we can see, catering is not only marketed by caterers, but also by attraction and destination marketers, for example. However, it is also marketed by *accommodation operators* for whom catering is often a major source of revenue, through in-house catering operations, such as hotel restaurants and banqueting facilities.

The general conclusion from this section of the chapter is that while catering is the core business of most catering businesses, it is an important ancillary product for other leisure organisations, which may encourage potential customers to purchase that core product.

Now that we have looked at several issues that provide the context for catering marketing, it is now time for us to begin to look at the practice and techniques involved in such marketing, beginning with the Marketing Mix.

Clearly the precise nature of the catering *product* varies depending on the type of catering, but it usually includes the following elements:

(i) A meal, in a form in which it can be consumed immediately. The meal itself, a product, is a combination of the food and the way in which it is presented visually.
(ii) The efficiency of the person serving the meal in terms of ensuring that the order is taken quickly and processed accurately to make certain that the person receives the meal they ordered. However, as well as efficiency, the service element will also be judged by the consumer on other criteria such as the member of staff's knowledge of the product and their attitude to the customer.
(iii) The decor, comfort and ambience of the catering outlet, whether it be a restaurant or a fast-food area where one collects a meal that will be consumed off the premises.
(iv) The location of the outlet which will determine the type of customers that will be attracted.
(v) The days of the week the outlet is open and its opening times.
(vi) The range of items which are offered and how clients are able to combine them through à la carte or fixed table d'hôte menus, for example.
(vii) The methods of payment which are accepted including cash, cheques and credit cards.
(viii) The product's reputation which may be reflected in a brand name, whether it is an individual high-class restaurant such as Le Manoir aux Quat' Saisons of Raymond Blanc in the UK, or a chain of restaurants such as Harvester in the UK or Flunch in France.

This list relates to mainstream catering, but there are, as we saw in Figure 24.1, more specialist forms of catering where the core product is different. For instance, we have:

- home delivery services where food is delivered to the consumer's home;
- contract catering where a catering service is provided for a client either on the client's premises or, at least, on premises chosen by the client which are now owned by the contract caterer.

Clearly in these cases, where the core product is not the standard catering product, different approaches to marketing have to be adopted.

In general, *prices* in catering are fixed and are based on the principle of cost-plus pricing. However, *discounts* are used and are usually given for one of the two main reasons, namely:

- to stimulate business at quiet times such as the early evening and also particular days, such as Mondays;
- for group bookings, where the discount is given in recognition of the volume of business.

Customers, however, do not always pay a discrete, separate price for a catering product. Sometimes it can be included in a package for which an overall price is paid. An example of this are the in-resort excursions offered by tour operators. Thus, an excursion sold as a day trip to an archaeological site in Greece might include lunch in a taverna, with a total price for the excursion of 40 Euros. However, the client will not know what proportion of this charge is specifically for the catering, rather than the other elements of the package, such as transport and entrance charges.

Lastly, prices in catering are not always true market prices, as in some European countries there are statutory regulations that control food and drink prices.

The concept of *place* or distribution is generally very simple in the catering sector. Where prebooking is the norm, reservations are usually made by telephone with the relevant outlet. However, in many cases there is no prebooking and consumers simply look for an outlet when they are hungry, and enter.

Likewise, in many cases the *promotional techniques* used by catering outlets are simple, reflecting the relatively low unit price of the product and the generally small capacity of outlets.

Most restaurants, for example, rely on local press advertisements, 'point of sale' material, such as advertising boards outside the restaurant, and the occasional 'special offer' sales promotion, together with word-of-mouth recommendation to generate most of their business.

However, the catering chains do indulge in more expensive and sophisticated promotional campaigns, involving national television and press advertising, together with sales promotions. Such promotions can be either added value (for example, two main courses for the price of one) or discounts (such as £1 off for a fast-food meal). Often these products are offered through partner businesses so that it is only the partner business customer that can benefit. Restaurants may, for example, use such joint promotions with cinemas or urban bus operators. Some of the more up-market restaurants find they do not need to do any promotion, as they are full because of their reputation and word-of-mouth recommendation, while most of the sophisticated marketing offers tend to be seen in the competitive fast-food sector.

If we turn our attention to the *catering market*, it is difficult to make generalisations both in terms of how the market segmented and what benefits consumers seek from different catering products.

In terms of market segments, Figure 24.2 illustrates how segments can differ depending on the type of catering outlet we are considering.

Type of outlet	Main segment or segmentation criteria
Famous Michelin three-star restaurant in France	• Affluent people from the region who can afford the price • Foreign tourists – business and leisure • Higher social classes • Occasional users, mainly couples
Fast food 'Fish and Chip Shop' in England	• People in lower social classes with limited income • People living within a kilometre of the outlet • Regular users • Couples, individuals and families
Greek taverna in a village	• Local people who live in the village • Greek tourists • Foreign tourists of different classes and incomes • Occasional and regular users • Families
Conference venue in Germany	• Business people – local, regional, national or international, or a mixture of all four

Figure 24.2 Segments and different types of catering outlets

There are similar differences in terms of the benefits which consumers seek from catering products, as we can see from Figure 24.3.

Clearly, the real world situation is never as simple as this for a variety of reasons. First, different consumers in a restaurant will all have their own individual sets of benefits they are seeking, and they will be different, as with the case of the different users of a Greek taverna. Foreign tourists will see a taverna as a special place that offers them a chance to glimpse the 'real Greece' and try new dishes. For locals, the visit will be an everyday activity which simply provides them with a chance to socialise with friends and eat the

Catering product	Main benefits sought
Famous Michelin three-star restaurant in France	• Reputation • Once-in-a-lifetime experience • Status • Special atmosphere • Aesthetic pleasure of a sophisticated meal
Fast food 'Fish and Chip Shop' in England	• Economy • Convenience • Reliability • Speed • Familiarity
Greek taverna in a village	• Social atmosphere • Informality • Simple food • Relaxation
Conference venue in Germany	• Chance to talk about business to other people • Novelty of trying foods not tried before • The meal is served quickly enough that the conference timetable is not disrupted

Figure 24.3 Benefits sought from different catering products

familiar foods. Likewise, in the case of the German conference venue, there is a difference between the benefits sought by the customer (the company organising and paying for the conference catering) and the consumer (the delegate who eats the food). The former sees the meal as a utilitarian activity where economy and efficiency of service are the key benefits sought. On the other hand, the consumer will see the meal as a chance to enjoy the pleasures of eating and may want to try new dishes, and so on.

There are many other benefits which different groups of consumers look for in a catering product and, in marketing terms, these benefits can be used as a basis for segmentation. An excellent example of this are those people who are interested in healthy living and want to buy catering products which help them enhance their health. This may involve them seeking low calorie or low fat meals or dishes prepared using organically produced ingredients. These people represent a particularly lucrative, identifiable, targettable market segment.

At the same time, it appears that the European catering market is becoming ever more 'internationalised'. Chinese and Indian restaurants are very popular in many European countries, as are Italian and French restaurants.

Japanese restaurants are becoming more common while much of the fast-food sector across Europe is dominated by major American competitors. However, at the same time, many European tourists who holiday in other European countries seek out food like they eat at home, while they are on holiday. Hence, the British may look for fish and chips in Fuengirola and some Germans search for Bratwurst in the Balearic Islands.

Competition in catering is generally intense, but this competition can take a number of forms as follows:

- Competition between different types of catering outlet such as independent restaurants versus outlet chains;
- Competition between different types of cuisine including Italian, French, Asian and American fast food, for example;
- Competition within sectors of the catering trade such as fast-food sector;
- Competition between the major chains in the catering business;
- Competition between catering outlets and food retailers who offer preprepared dishes such as Marks and Spencer plc in the UK and the traiteurs in France;
- Competition between all types of catering outlets in a particular geographical location.

In some cases, however, there is no competition, namely in the case of hospitals and schools catering, where there is in effect a captive market and a monopoly situation.

Finally, in relation to competition, catering can be used as a way of achieving competitive advantage by organisations in other sectors for whom catering is not their core business. Hence, many airlines promote the quality of in-flight catering when selling their business-class brands. Likewise, hotels may promote their own restaurant's quality, as a way of persuading clients to book into their hotel.

Where catering businesses wish to expand, their main *growth strategy* has traditionally been through horizontal integration, with the purchase of other existing catering outlets. At the same time, catering companies may also, obviously, create new outlets or brands. However, franchising has also started to become common, particularly in relation to international chain-owned fast-food outlets and themed restaurants. For example, the UK brand, Burger King franchises are now found in a number of other European countries, most notably France, Germany and Spain.

Technological innovations in *management information systems* are providing more data for catering marketers. Restaurant systems can provide information on indicators such as average spend per cover, customer profits, table turnover ratios and the popularity of particular menus, dishes or drinks.

Because of the level of competition in urban areas in some countries in Europe, many urban hotels in these countries no longer offer a *hotel restaurant*. This is particularly true in France, for example. There is also a phenomenon in some European countries, most notably again in France, where the restaurant within the hotel is franchised or leased to a separate operator.

Conclusion

Catering marketing is a complex matter, reflecting the diverse nature of the sector. There are clear distinctions in terms of marketing practice between independent and chain-owned outlets, and take-away and eat-in outlet, for instance.

Discussion points and essay questions

1. Compare and contrast the core, augmented and ancillary products of fast-food outlets *and* a Michelin three-star restaurant.
2. Discuss the links which exist between catering, and tourism and hospitality.
3. Evaluate the application of the four classic methods of segmenting a market to the catering sector.

Exercise

You have been engaged as a consultant by an entrepreneur, who wishes to develop a new restaurant in your local area. Your brief is as follows:

- to devise an overall concept or theme for the restaurant;
- to identify the target market or markets for the restaurant;
- to suggest an appropriate location for the restaurant;
- to advise the entrepreneur on how the proposed restaurant might differentiate itself from other restaurants in the area.

Your results should be presented in report form, supported by a verbal presentation.

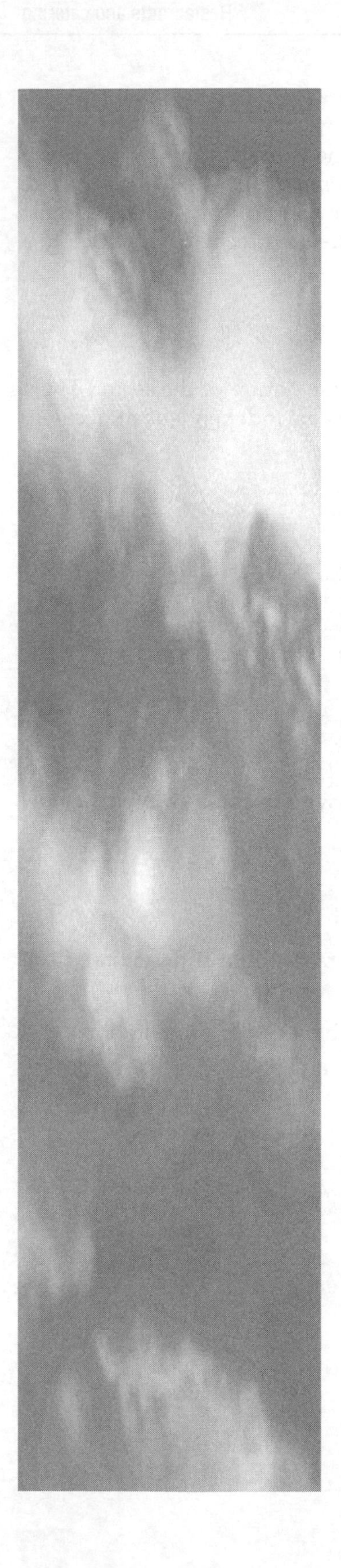

Conclusions

In the preceding chapter we have explored the key issues in marketing in the different sectors of leisure. Many differences between these sectors can be identified but there are also some general points which can be made which appear to be relevant to a number of different sectors, including:

- Organisations in the public, private and voluntary sectors have different marketing objectives. These different objectives influence marketing activity in a number of ways including their pricing policies and their willingness to cooperate with other organisations in a similar business. The existence of different types of organisation also has an impact on the nature of competition.
- The product which is offered is largely intangible, and the service element is highly important in determining the quality of the product which is enjoyed by customers.
- Tactical pricing is widely used to stimulate purchasing at times when demand is low.
- Place or distribution methods depend on whether or not prebooking is the norm. Where it is, marketing intermediaries such as travel agents are widely used, while direct sales are the standard form of distribution where prebooking is unusual or impossible.
- While large private organisations often make great use of advertising, particularly on television, smaller private companies and public and voluntary organisations often have to rely more on brochures, sales, promotions and press and public relations, together with limited advertising. Face-to-face selling is only a key element in promotional strategies generally in relation to high spending customers or individual customers who purchase large amounts of the organisation's products.
- Markets are often segmented on the basis of geographical and demographic factors, and they are frequently divided between leisure use purchasers and business people.

- Benefits sought by consumers vary between sectors but in all of them, status is an important factor.
- Competition is intense in some sectors, particularly where the product is largely provided by private companies. On the other hand, there may be little real element of competition in a market which is largely the preserve of public-sector organisations.
- In many cases, the products of one organisation in one sector are sold on its behalf by another organisation in a different sector.

This last point raises the wider issues of links between leisure. We have seen how closely these three fields can be in marketing terms. For example, tour operators sell hotel beds, hotels offer leisure facilities and leisure-based short break holidays, while resort complexes and business tourism, for instance, bring leisure together.

Unfortunately, space precludes the possibility of looking at differences between marketing practice in different countries. However, we have sought to use case studies from different countries to illustrate some of the different approaches which are taken to marketing across the world.

Nevertheless, it is reasonable to assume that marketing will be different to some extent in different countries, even within a particular sector, in response to factors such as the following:

- government legislation and policies;
- economic situations;
- patterns of consumer demand;
- business culture and practices.

These differences are a particular challenge for those organisations, in all sectors, which are involved in operating in, or selling their product to people, in other countries.

Overall, however, it appears that the main characteristics of marketing in particular sectors are fairly standard. This may be because the nature of the product, and its appeal to consumers in individual sectors is largely the same, regardless of which country we are discussing.

Having looked at marketing in individual sectors within leisure, it is now time for us to look at five topical issues in leisure marketing.

Part Six

Topical issues in leisure marketing

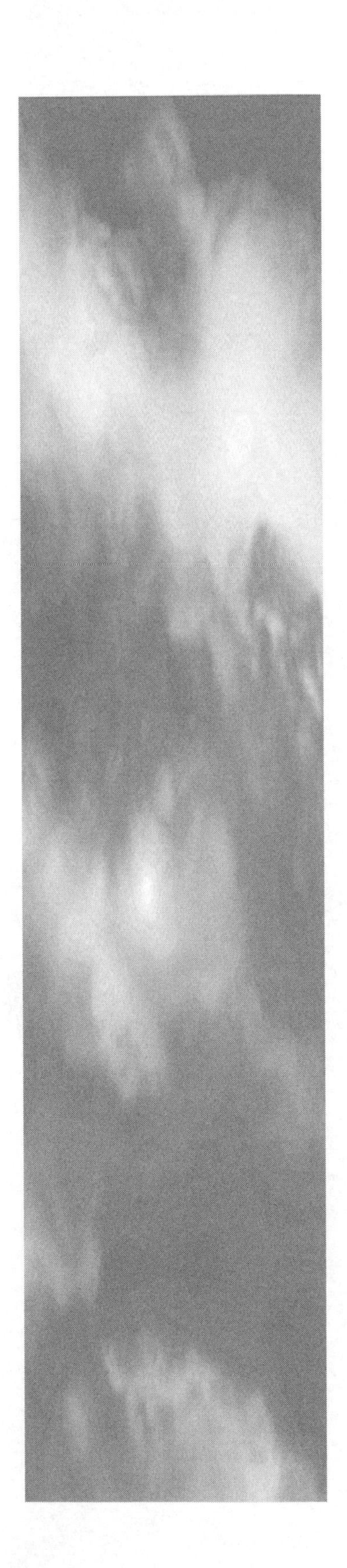

Introduction

In Part Six we focus on four issues which are particularly important topics currently in the development of marketing in leisure.

These topics are as follows:

Chapter 25 The nature of competition and the ways in which leisure organisations may seek to gain competitive advantage in their respective sector.

Chapter 26 The concept of quality and the application of traditional and emerging approaches to quality management in leisure.

Chapter 27 The twin topics of ethics and social responsibility in relation to leisure.

Chapter 28 Marketing research, which is clearly crucial at a time when the conventional wisdom says that successful marketing means being market- or consumer-led.

CHAPTER 25

Competition and competitive advantage

Key concepts

The main concepts covered in the chapter are:

- Differences in the degree of competition which exists in the market in the various sectors within leisure
- The main types of competitive advantage strategies used within leisure
- The wide range of factors which influence the competitive advantage strategies an organisation chooses to adopt.

Introduction

One of the clichés of marketing is that markets are becoming increasingly competitive, and organisations must therefore strive constantly to find new ways of achieving competitive advantage.

In leisure, these issues are particularly topical for two reasons. First, the Europe-wide recession of the early 1990s and the Asian economic crisis of 1997–1998 made many markets more competitive and this competitiveness appears to be continuing after the economies have begun to recover. Second, increased competition is being seen in sectors where it has hitherto been limited such as the scheduled airline market in Europe, due to political factors such as deregulation.

In this chapter, we examine both competition and competitive advantage strategies, in other words, we will look at the following:

(i) The *nature of competition* in leisure, given that competition is intense in some sectors, such as tour operation, but has traditionally been limited and even nonexistent in some areas such as state-owned airlines or public-sector leisure provision.
(ii) The *ways in which leisure organisations may seek to achieve competitive advantage*. We will look at what organisations in the three sectors are doing.

We should begin by noting that the ways in which an organisation seeks to achieve competitive advantage often depends on the state of the economy and market at any one time. In a period of recession, competitive advantage is often based on cost reduction and price discounting, while in times of economic prosperity, mergers, acquisitions and new product development are commonly used methods.

Competition is where two or more organisations are engaged in selling a similar product to a common target market. The customer thus has a choice of product and the competition between the organisation is to see which one can persuade the consumer to buy their particular product.

We have seen that in leisure there are great differences in terms of the degree of competitiveness which are found in the market in particular sectors.

For example, competition is intense in the mass market tour operation sector but is very low, in general, in the noncommercial theatre sector. Likewise, there is considerable competition in the market for fast food and budget hotels, but it is often less pronounced in the area of local authority provision of leisure facilities.

Furthermore, the competition can exist at a number of different geographical levels.

This can range from local competition between organisations in the same town or city, for example, in the restaurant sector, to truly global competition between organisations based on different continents, as is the case with major scheduled airlines.

However, there are also two other factors which complicate any discussion of competition in leisure, as follows:

(i) Internal competition where one part of an organisation appears to be in direct competition with another part of the same organisation. This can be true for local authority museums in the same city or for travel agents owned by one operator selling the product of a competitor operator, or for hotels in adjacent towns, owned by the same chain, chasing the same conference booking.
(ii) Competition from outside the sector altogether, or what is sometimes termed, 'substitution'. In other words, the competition for a tour operator trying to sell a holiday to a consumer may not be another tour operator, but rather another form of consumer purchase. For example, the consumer may choose, in a particular year, to substitute the purchase of a new house or car for a holiday. Likewise, for many visitor attractions, their main form of competition is not other visitor attractions, but other uses of leisure time and spending such as gardening or home entertaining.

The diversity of levels and type of competition within leisure are a reflection of differences between individual sectors within these three fields, in terms of a range of factors including the following:

- state intervention in the market through subsidies, regulation of entry into the market and the role of state-owned organisations as active players in the market;

- the number of major players who are in any one market and the extent to which they may cooperate, formally or informally, together with the possible existence of implicit or explicit price-fixing;
- the lack of a profit motive for many public- and voluntary-sector organisations within the three fields which tends to modify the concept of competition;
- professional cultures in some sectors which are based on cooperation rather than competition, such as in the case of museum curators.

Finally, it has to be noted that the lack of marketing research data, in many areas with which this book is concerned, means that many organisations' attempt to identify their competitors are based more on perception than hard facts.

We will now look at a number of *approaches to achieving competitive advantage* which have been used, or could be used, in leisure. These include:

- rationalisation and cost reduction measures
- innovations in product development
- product differentiation
- pricing policies
- improved distribution systems
- more effective promotional techniques
- relaunches and rebranding
- developing brand loyalty
- market focus
- mergers and acquisitions including vertical and horizontal integration
- strategic alliances
- franchises
- marketing consortia
- diversification into other fields that reinforce the core business
- selling corporate values to prospective customers as part of the organisation's product.

In some sectors, *rationalisation and cost reduction* have always been a popular way of trying to achieve competitive advantage. The aim is to reduce the organisation's cost base below that of its competitors, in line with the concept of cost leadership in Porter's model of generic competitive strategies. This usually involves reducing labour costs, in particular, as these are a relatively high proportion of the costs of many service industry organisations. This strategy is particularly common in times of economic recession when the lack of consumer spending power is holding down prices or even forcing discounting to take place. With such limited prospects for increasing income, reducing costs may be the only real option for managers.

However, rationalisation and cost reduction may also be used in anticipation of the arrival of a new competitor in the market. For example, the cross-channel ferry companies operating between France, Belgium, Holland and the UK undertook such action in anticipation of the opening of the Channel Tunnel.

There is always a danger of such an approach, thought, that cost reductions may lead to poorer standards of service which may cause competitive disadvantage in the longer term.

Many leisure organisations have sought to 'leap frog' over their competitors through *innovative product development*, by introducing new concepts and types of products. Examples of this in the last fifty years include the Club Med all-inclusive formula resorts, Center Parcs, the Disney theme parks and Concorde. Furthermore, if successful, this will spawn imitations so that the organisation will need to be constantly seeking new ways of keeping ahead of its competitors. Thus, Club Med now faces competition from a number of all-inclusive resorts.

Rather than one-off innovations in product development, most product-related competitive advantage strategies in leisure are concerned with *differentiating the product* of the organisation from that of its competitors. The following examples serve to illustrate this point:

(i) the services offered to business-class passengers on airlines including check-in facilities, exclusive lounges, in-flight catering and seat pitch;
(ii) the range of destinations offered by tour operators and the departure airports which they can offer their clients;
(iii) hotel chains competing in terms of hotel location and services such as leisure facilities, in-room computer link ups for business clients and the number of people the room can accommodate, for the family market;
(iv) many theme parks desire to have the latest, most attractive 'white knuckle' ride;
(v) tourist destinations that seek to develop reputations based on particular specialist aspects of their product such as Scheveningen with its casino, and those which have developed their sport facilities, like Sheffield;
(vi) the different programmes of dramas and musical events offered by theatres.

Pricing is used as a competitive advantage tool in leisure in a number of ways, as follows:

- low introductory prices for a new product entering a competitive market;
- low prices in general for organisations seeking to attract consumers for whom economy is a key benefit sought from any purchase;
- last-minute discounting to generate some income at least in the case of perishable products;
- discounting to attract particular market segments such as groups at visitor attractions and major corporate clients for airlines;
- premium pricing to differentiate the product on the grounds of exclusivity and status value.

Leisure organisations are constantly trying to *improve the effectiveness of how they distribute their product* to their potential customers. This can include the following:

- looking to use new technology to allow the organisation to communicate directly with customers, rather than through marketing intermediaries, most notably the Internet;
- developing ever more sophisticated Computer Reservations Systems (CRS) and Global Distribution Systems (GDS);
- offering more incentives for intermediaries to encourage them to sell more of the organisation's product.

Many leisure organisations spend considerable sums of money on *promotion* and it is natural, therefore, that efforts should be made to achieve competitive advantage through making promotional activities more effective. Such efforts include:

- The use of video and multimedia to portray product images to prospective customers;
- More eye-catching, imaginative advertisements;
- Joint 'piggy-back' promotions with nonleisure organisations which sell to similar target markets such as the promotions between British Airways and the UK food retailer, Sainsbury's, and between Air France and Martells Cognac in the 1990s.

Nevertheless, in spite of this it is noticeable that in areas like promotional literature, there is often relatively little differentiation in style and format between most tour operator brochures across Europe, for instance.

Relaunches are a well-established way of trying to gain or regain competitive advantage in leisure. In the UK, the old Butlin's holiday camps have been relaunched as sophisticated modern 'Holiday World's'.

On a grander scale, some seaside resorts have relaunched themselves such as Schevinengen in the Netherlands, Majorca and Benidorm in Spain and Torbay in the UK, the latter under the banner of the 'English Riviera'.

Rebranding has been also used by some organisations to respond to changes in consumer preferences. Relaunches and rebranding can help to re-invigorate an older organisation or product range but they do not guarantee success.

At a time of great competition, most organisations want to encourage *brand loyalty* for it is easier to keep customers than to try to win new ones. We have seen this particularly in the scheduled airline sector with its frequent flyer programmes. On a more modest scale, visitor attractions such as museums and theatres may also offer season tickets for the same reason.

The third of Porter's generic strategies, *market focus*, has been used successfully by some leisure organisations to achieve competitive advantage. In the UK, for example, the market has been segmented on demographic lines for this purpose with Saga focusing on older, retired customers, and Club 18–30 concentrating on younger customers in their late teens and twenties. Marketing in leisure has often focused on demographic factors as we can see from destinations which advertise themselves as family resorts and those which concentrate on couples as their main market. Those organisations seeking to adopt a market focus in the future may perhaps target those who are particularly health-conscious, for instance, or may aim to attract those who are particularly interested in new technologies such as virtual reality.

Mergers and acquisitions have long been used, predominantly in the private sector, to develop competitive advantage within leisure. This process often involves both vertical and horizontal integration. For example, the UK tour operator, Thomson, has grown by taking over other tour operators such as Horizon and Blakes Country Cottages, as well as buying up or creating suppliers and marketing intermediaries such as Britannia Airways and the Lunn Poly travel agency chain. In turn, of course, Thomson itself was ultimately taken over by the German travel group, TUI. The French Accor group has also grown through mergers and acquisitions, even outside its core business of leisure. Its purchase of the Wagon-Lits group also gave it a chain of travel agency outlets. However, mergers and acquisitions can be an expensive form of growth strategy.

In some areas of leisure, such as the airline sector, *strategic alliances* have been more popular than outright mergers and acquisitions. This may be because the capital costs involved in civil aviation are so high that acquisitions may be too costly at a time when most scheduled airlines in Europe are not making profits. However, it may also reflect state intervention in the market which can make some mergers and acquisitions particularly unacceptable to some governments when they involve foreign companies. Whatever the reason, strategic alliances have been widely used in the airline industry to achieve competitive advantage, at relatively little cost.

Strategic alliances may also exist between sectors such as hotels and airlines, or car-hire companies and airlines, or theme parks and local hotels, to give just three examples.

Another relatively inexpensive and low risk way in which some leisure organisations have sought to increase their power in the marketplace has been through *franchising*. The franchiser provides the franchisee with the right to use the franchiser's brand, together with a range of other support which might include assistance towards capital costs, marketing advice, purchasing services and so on.

However, the franchiser will also set a specification of minimum standards with which the franchisee must comply, together with standard operating procedures to ensure conformity with the overall brand. In this way, the franchise organisation can grow the brand at minimal cost and risk to itself. Most of the risk and cost is shouldered by the franchisee.

Franchises have been used extensively in the hospitality sector for example, in the case of Domino Pizza, Holiday Inn and the Campanile chain. They are also being used widely now by McDonald's. In addition, franchises can be found in the leisure sector in relation to sports facilities, for example. However, they have also now appeared in the transport sector too. For instance, in the 1990s, British Airways franchised certain independent carriers to operate in its livery and provide services under the British Airways Express brand. These carriers included Maersk Air UK, GB Airways, Manx Airlines (Europe) Ltd and Loganair Ltd.

In an era of competition and economic uncertainty, franchises can be a very attractive way of attempting to gain competitive advantage. However, franchisers have to be careful to ensure that franchises maintain their own standards, otherwise the overall reputation of the brand may suffer.

Marketing consortia have been developed widely within leisure, most commonly in the public and voluntary sectors. However, there are a number of well-known ones in the private sector too. In most consortia, partners come together to undertake joint marketing activities which they could not afford to carry out on their own. Usually the partners will share a theme. France, for example, has a number of such consortia, many of which bring together different towns and cities as partners. For example, there is an association of Roman towns and cities which produce joint brochures on the Roman monuments of the respective partner towns and cities.

Marketing consortia in the private sector are found most commonly in the hospitality sector. A good example in Europe is the Minotel Group which brings together small privately owned hotels across Europe. Then there is Best Western which is also a consortium.

However, whichever sector they exist in, consortia have the same basic concept, namely to give individual organisations power in the marketplace they could not otherwise have, through cooperation with other organisations in a similar field.

Some leisure organisations have sought competitive advantage, partly through *diversification* into other fields of activity which nevertheless reinforce their core business. An excellent example of this is the Georges Dubeouf organisation in France.

A renowned wine producer, the organisation opened a state-of-the-art visitor attraction devoted to telling the story of Beaujolais wine, at its headquarters in Romaneche-Thorins. The attraction also serves to remind visitors of the George Duboeuf brand, and there is a shop in the attraction where the customer may purchase the products of the organisation.

In other industries, we have seen a trend towards some organisations attempting to *sell their corporate ethical values* as part of their product. Some of these have been very successful, such as the UK organisation, the Body Shop, with its policy of not testing its products on animals and its involvement in aid projects in developing countries. Such organisations make customers feel good about buying their product because of the organisation's moral approach to business.

As yet, we have seen few such examples in leisure. Perhaps such examples will develop in the future, if consumer interest in ethical business and environmental issues grows in relation to leisure. We may be already seeing the start of this trend with the rise of small tour operators who claim to offer environmentally friendly holidays, particularly in the Netherlands. Likewise, with the action on environmental issues of major companies such as TUI in Germany and its partly owned partner company, Grecotel, in Greece.

Having now considered the main ways in which organisations *in leisure may seek to gain competitive advantage*, it is an appropriate time to look at how organisations choose which strategy to adopt. As we noted earlier, most organisations utilise several approaches rather than just one.

The factors influencing the approach taken by an individual organisation can include internal ones such as the organisation's history, culture and financial resources, together with external ones such as consumer behaviour and state intervention in markets. The factors will be different for each organisation and it will be a mixture of manager's perceptions and reality. Some of the most important factors are illustrated in Figure 25.1.

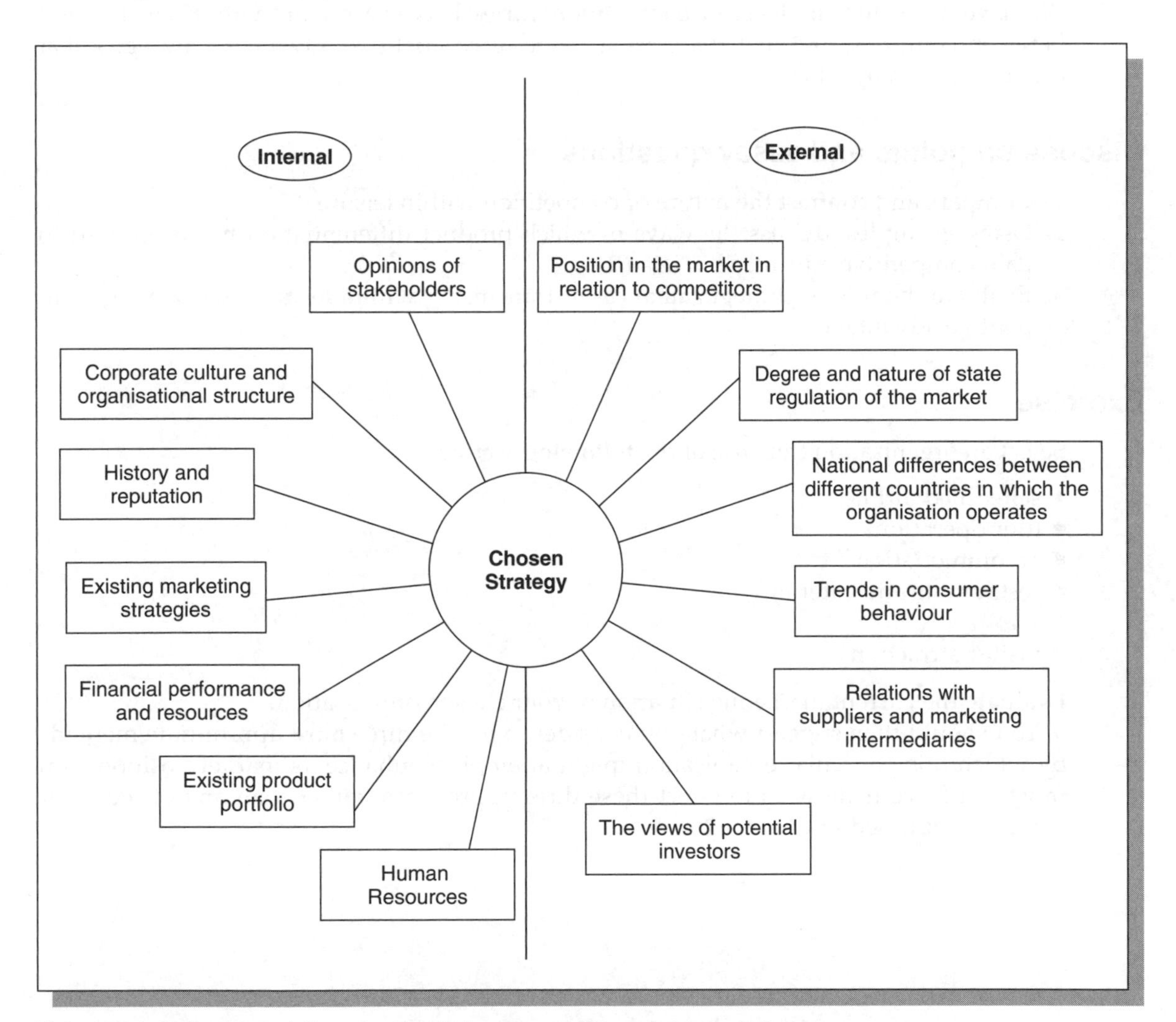

Figure 25.1 Major factors influencing the choice of competitive advantage strategies

In many respects, there are perhaps greater differences between sectors than between countries in terms of the level of competitiveness in markets and competitive advantage strategies. National differences do, however, exist in relation to levels of competitiveness in particular sectors such as the hotel market, for example. In the UK, there is virtually no regulation of hotel prices, whereas in Greece, hotel prices are partly fixed by state intervention.

In terms of competitive advantage strategies, some of the more modern approaches such as franchising, marketing consortia and strategic alliances are found more commonly in certain countries such as the UK and France, for example.

Finally, organisations wishing to expand into certain countries may be forced to adopt particular approaches simply because national laws and government policy make other approaches impractical.

Conclusion

We have seen that the level of competition varies between sectors within leisure, and between countries, and that there are a range of competitive advantage strategies that organisations may adopt.

Discussion points and essay questions

1. Compare and contrast the nature of competition within leisure.
2. Using examples, discuss the ways in which product differentiation has been used to gain competitive advantage in leisure.
3. Evaluate the role of strategic alliances *or* franchising within leisure in achieving competitive advantage.

Exercise

Select an organisation from *one* of the following sectors:

- scheduled airline
- tour operation
- accommodation
- restaurants and catering
- arts
- visitor attractions.

Evaluate the current marketing situation of your chosen organisation.

You should then suggest what you consider to be, the three most appropriate methods by which this particular organisation might attempt to enhance its market position. You must justify your decision to select these three approaches, rather than any of the other which are outlined in Chapter 26.

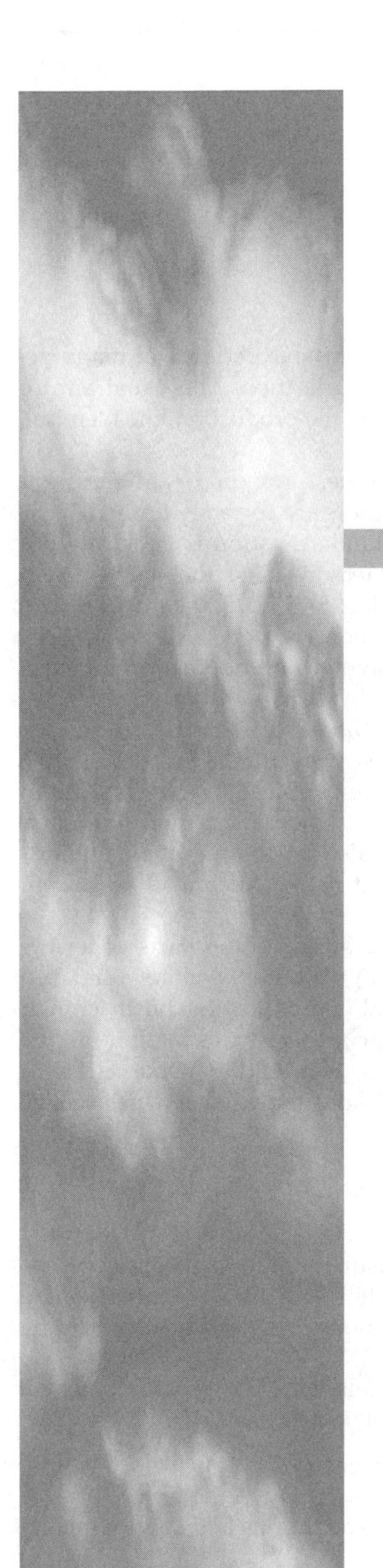

CHAPTER 26

Quality

Key concepts

The main concepts covered in the chapter are:

- Definitions of quality
- The concept of the 'service gap'
- Quality management systems
- The links between quality and the Marketing Mix
- Quality and different audiences
- Official quality standards.

Introduction

Quality has been perhaps one of the most fashionable words of marketing. However, while it is often used, it is rarely defined.

In this chapter, we will take a broad view of the concept of quality in leisure. To do this a number of issues will be examined, including:

- what the term 'quality' means in the context of leisure;
- the nature of quality in service industries;
- the different types of quality management systems that exist, including quality Control, Quality Assurance, Total Quality Control and Total Quality Management;
- quality and the marketing mix;
- official measures of quality such as ISO 9000;
- constraints on the operation of quality management systems in leisure.

There is no universally accepted definition of quality, but certain principles do appear to be quite widely agreed upon. First, the idea that quality is about those features and characteristics of a product or service that affect its ability to satisfy the needs and desires of consumers.

Secondly, there is the concept of 'fitness for purpose' whereby quality is judged in terms of the extent to which a product measures up to its expressed purpose, usually defined in terms of a set of consumer needs. Both approaches put the customer at the centre, which fits neatly with the concept of customer-led marketing which is so popular at present.

Quality and service industries

Most theory and practice in quality management grew out of the experience of manufacturing industries where the emphasis is on product standardisation. The usual aim of manufacturing companies is to have every product coming off the production line identical, with no faults.

Furthermore, this is an attainable goal, most of the time, providing that the right machinery is purchased, it is well maintained and its operators are correctly trained.

However, in service industries, such as leisure, this standardisation is generally not attainable, and it may not even be desirable, for three main reasons. First, the main element of the product is the individual who perform the service, and all staff are different. They have different abilities or attitudes, and their moods are constantly changing. Secondly, in service industries, the production process involves an interaction between consumers and staff, and the consumers are separate individuals with their own specific attitudes and expectations which they contribute to the process. Finally, most customers do not want to feel they are receiving a standardised product, with the possible exception of fast-food outlet customers and hotel-chain clients. Most customers want to feel that the product will, at least in part, be tailor-made to meet their own particular needs and desires. This customisation of the product is also important as a standardised product does not usually carry the status value that many customers seek from leisure products.

It may also be that standardisation is not an attainable aim in some parts of leisure because in these specific parts of our industries we do not give our customers a finished product. Instead, we give them a set of 'raw materials' and invite them to construct their own final product. For example, it could be argued that a tourist destination simply offers a range of attractions, accommodation, restaurants, bars and transport systems from which tourists can create their own 'do it yourself' holiday experience which will be unique.

The 'service gap'

Quality management systems in service industries like leisure tend to focus on the intangible service element of the product and the people who deliver it. Quality enhancement is often viewed in terms of reducing gaps between perceptions of service quality held by an organisation and its customers.

In 1985, Parasuraman, Zeithaml and Berry identified the following five types of potential service gaps, with which most leisure managers will probably empathise:

(i) gaps between consumer expectations and management perceptions of consumer expectations;
(ii) gaps between management perceptions of consumer expectations and service quality specifications;

(iii) gaps between service quality specifications and the service which is actually delivered;
(iv) gaps between service delivery and what is communicated about this service to consumers which will shape their expectations;
(v) gaps between consumer expectations and their perceptions of the actual quality of service rendered.

Quality management systems

Most quality management systems originated in manufacturing industries, but they can be applied to some extent in service industries such as leisure. This part can be illustrated if we look at the case of a restaurant meal in relation to the four most common types of quality management systems as follows:

1. *Quality control* – This is where the production process is monitored so that problems are eradicated before the product is delivered to the customer. This is well suited to manufacturing companies where problems are often easy to identify and there is a relatively long period between production and delivery to the customer. The equivalent in a restaurant meal situation would be an inspection of the dishes before they left the kitchen to be presented to the customer. However, while this does happen in some restaurants, the speed required to serve the dish while it is still at its best makes such careful inspection difficult. Furthermore, just because the dish looks and smells right, it does not follow automatically that it will satisfy the client. They may already have negative views about the restaurant because of its decor or how they were greeted. Or they may not like the chef's selection of vegetables, no matter how well they have been cooked. Even if quality control is possible in the case of our restaurant meal, it does not prevent waste arising in the first place, for if the dish is deemed not satisfactory, it may well be thrown away.
2. *Quality assurance* – Here the emphasis is on prevention rather than cure. The aim is to prevent the problem arising in the first place, and rather than making quality the responsibility of one or two 'inspectors', the system places the onus on each member of staff involved to get it right first time. This prevents waste and removes the need for 'inspectors'.
3. *Total quality control* – Under this system, a broader view is taken of the production or service delivery process. All possible factors that affect the final product or service are considered. In the case of our restaurant meal, this might include the quality of raw materials being provided by suppliers to the training of the kitchen staff. The aim is to ensure that by looking at these wider issues the quality of the product can be maintained and enhanced on every occasion.
4. *Total quality management* (*TQM*) – This is undoubtedly the most fashionable quality management system at present. It is predicated on the idea that quality must permeate the whole culture of an organisation and involve every employee. It argues that organisations need to strive to make continuous improvements in quality.

In other words, this approach acknowledges that quality is not an absolute standard which can ever be attained. Instead, it is a continuous journey to an ever-changing destination. In terms of our restaurant meal therefore, a 'TQM' approach would involve looking constantly at how the meal might be improved in terms of its content, presentation, delivery and price, for example.

The marketing mix and quality in leisure

We will now consider the implications of the concept of quality for the four elements of the 'Marketing mix' which marketers in leisure manipulate to achieve their objectives. We will begin with the product.

The *product* is crucial in that it is what the customer purchases in order to satisfy their needs and wants. A quality product is one which satisfactorily performs the task for which it was purchased and bestows the expected benefits on the purchaser. There are a number of ways in which quality and the product are linked in leisure, as follows:

(i) There is what we might term the quality of the designed characteristics of the product, in other words, those physical attributes of the product that have been deliberately designed. These might include the location and leisure facilities of a hotel, and the comfort and pitch of the seating in the business class cabin of an airliner.
(ii) The service element, including the service the customer receives and the attitudes and competence of the people who deliver this service.
(iii) The reliability, or lack of it, of the product. How often does the product promised to the consumer by the organisation fail to materialise. For example, it is not satisfactory to promise that a room rate includes a free morning newspaper each day if the person responsible forgets to deliver it to the room.
(iv) The issue of what happens when things go wrong, and the systems which have been put in place to correct errors. For instance, if a guest complains that they have no clean towels in their room when they first arrive, how long will the guest have to wait before fresh towels are provided.
(v) Finally, there is the image and reputation of the product in the outside world at large. This is often an important factor in the decision-making process for first-time purchasers who have no previous personal experience of the product. It is also the basis on which some organisations are able to charge premium prices for their product. This image and reputation may derive from a variety of sources including popular culture and the media, together with the views of previous customers.

There is always a rapport between quality and *price*, for quality is not an absolute. We tend to buy the level of quality we can afford so that there is a trade-off between price and quality. However, contrary to some views, which seem to equate quality with expense, quality exists at all price levels although its precise nature will vary at these different price levels. Ultimately it is quality if it meets the desires and needs of the customer.

A good example of this argument is the accommodation sector. Many overseas visitors are as thoroughly satisfied when they stay in private homes offering 'bed and breakfast' accommodation for say £30 per person per night as other people are when staying in a prestigious £300-a-night hotel in central London. The different prices will lead the customer to expect different benefits from purchasing each product but they will probably see both each as a quality product if it meets their individual needs and expectations.

However, it is important to note that the relationship between quality and price in leisure can be complicated in the following ways:

(i) No charge is made, directly, to those who use some products such as some local authority museums and most tourist destinations.
(ii) Some prices charged are not true market prices and reflect a level of public-sector subsidy, for instance many opera performances.

(iii) For many customers it is not the price that matters but rather whether they feel they have received 'value for money'. Thus, many of the most expensive visitor attractions around the world also have the highest visitor numbers.

Quality is also an issue in the *place* or distribution element of the marketing mix, as follows:

- the ease with what potential consumers are able to purchase the product, through theatre ticket agencies and travel agencies;
- the quality of service offered by the operators who distribute the organisation's product and their reliability;
- the accuracy of messages given by these agents to potential customers about the organisation's product. Inaccurate messages may, in the short-term, increase sales but in the longer term they may well lead to customer dissatisfaction and a lack of repeat purchases.

Many leisure organisations are seeking to develop tighter relationships with their distributors, partly because they are aware of these issues. However, these moves are also often a result of government legislation regarding product liability under which producers are held liable, increasingly, for the actions of their intermediaries.

There is, finally, clearly a quality dimension to the issue of *promotional* techniques, most notably brochures and advertisements, and also face-to-face selling. Quality in promotional activities in the leisure industry has often been seen in terms of the glossiness of brochures and the ability of advertising campaigns and selling to persuade people to buy a product. However, this is an industry view of quality in promotion. Consumers may see quality in a different way in relation to the promotional activities of organisations, namely:

(i) Honesty in brochures and advertisements such as claims made about the quality of beaches in resort brochures, noise levels in hotels and walking times from accommodation to beaches in tour operator's brochures. To some extent the lack of self-regulation on the part of industry has led, at least in the tour operation field, to European Commission legislation to enforce such standards of honesty on the industry. Hence, the 1990 European Union's Directive on Package Travel, Package Holidays and Package Tours.

(ii) Organisations providing advice for customers to help them enjoy the organisation's product safely. This might include, for example:
  - advice on areas of cities which should be avoided because of crime levels;
  - information about potentially hazardous activities such as scuba diving, and how those trying these activities for the first time can do so safely;
  - advice about how to avoid skin cancer;
  - suggesting people should not hire mopeds or ride horses if no safety helmets are provided.

However, such advice could obviously dissuade some customers from purchasing the organisation's product, particularly in the tour operation sector. It is unlikely, therefore, that any organisation would undertake such an approach alone. Instead it would probably only do so if competitors agreed to do likewise or there were government legislation.

Finally, *operations management* too has a vital role to play in achieving and enhancing quality. It is concerned with how the customer experience is managed on a day-to-day basis. Its contribution to quality covers a number of areas, including:

- ensuring that the organisation's products are 'user-friendly' for all groups of customers whether they are disabled people, families with children or customers who speak a different language;

- keeping customers as safe and secure as possible from potential threats ranging from fire to food poisoning;
- operating an effective complaints procedure so that complaints are quickly resolved. On occasions, it could be argued that a well-handled complaint might enhance an organisation's reputation more than would have been the case if all had gone well in the first place, when the consumer might have taken the service for granted!

It is clear therefore that quality is a team game and the responsibility of all management functions within an organisation.

Quality and different audiences – clearly the most important audience an organisation needs to address in terms of the quality of what it sells is the customer. However, there are many other audiences which have an interest in the concept of quality in relation to any organisation and its products. Each of these audiences will have their own particular interest in quality and will have different criteria for evaluating quality.

These criteria can be at odds with each other. If we look at a hypothetical example, a theme park, we can see how many different audiences there might be and what their likely definition will be of what constitutes quality at a theme park:

1. Customers who will see a quality theme park as one which is user-friendly and offers the most enjoyment for the least cost. However, customers are not a homogenous category for there are ex-customers, nonusers, first-time users and regular customers.
2. Theme park managers, on the other hand, view quality in terms of the smooth operation of the theme park together with its visitor numbers and financial performance.
3. For the staff, a quality theme park is one which provides good working conditions and where there are not too many customer complaints to handle.
4. Investors and shareholders evaluate quality as how good a rate of return on investment the theme park earns for them.
5. Suppliers might see quality in terms of a theme park that pays its bills promptly.
6. For marketing intermediaries such as coach tour operators and tourist information centres, a quality theme park is likely to be seen as one which offers generous group discounts to the operator and keeps the centre regularly supplied with brochures, respectively.
7. Government regulators who will judge quality in terms of the safety consciousness of the operator, for example.

In many sectors within leisure, a major audience which needs to be convinced about the quality of an organisation's product is the media. Guidebooks, television programmes and journals aimed at providing information and advice for leisure customers have grown rapidly in recent years. Managers, therefore, have to be aware of the need to impress this audience.

In terms of *official quality standards* public-sector bodies play an important role in quality within leisure in a number of ways. These bodies may be local authorities, national governments, the European Commission, or international bodies such as the International Air Transport Organisation (IATO). The various official standards of quality in leisure include the following:

- national government official classifications of hotel standards such as the 'star' system in France;
- the licensing of premises such as restaurants to indicate that they meet certain health standards;

- the licensing of tour operators which often is in recognition of the fact that they have adequate financial resources;
- the licensing of tourist guides where knowledge is thought to qualify them to act as guides.

As one can see, these different standards of quality all have different purposes and use different criteria. They can therefore be very confusing, particularly for the customer.

Furthermore, some of them are highly subjective, particularly hotel classification systems. Not only are the symbols different in the various countries (stars, crowns, letters of the alphabet) but so too are the criteria on the basis of which they are awarded. These criteria might include:

- price
- facilities in the hotel and/or individual rooms
- location
- services available and when they are available
- size of the establishment.

This, again, is clearly very confusing for the customer, hence the intention of the European Commission to attempt to harmonise these systems and produce a single European hotel classification system.

Public bodies may also try to improve quality through the use of voluntary codes of practice which they try to encourage organisations to follow. For example, in the UK the government's domestic tourism agency, the English Tourist Board, has introduced a voluntary code of practice for quality management at visitor attractions.

In addition to these official standards which are specific to our area, there are also official measures of quality itself which are applicable across all industries, including leisure. The most obvious example of this is ISO 9000 in the UK, the internationally recognised standard of quality. It is a documentation-driven system that has given rise to the criticism that it is more concerned with production processes than consumer satisfaction. There is also a worry that it might become a 'lowest common denominator' to which all organisations can aspire rather than a recognition of outstanding quality which only a few organisations will be able to attain at any one time.

Finally, if governments or supra-governmental bodies feel there are quality problems in particular industries, they may seek to introduce legislation to raise standards by regulation. For example, the honesty of tour operators advertising in brochures has been increased by the European Commission's Package Travel Directive.

There are a number of *constraints* which affect the ability of leisure managers to develop totally effective quality management systems. These include:

1. Those factors which while contributing to the quality of the consumer's experience are largely outside the control of the organisation. Such factors might include the following:
   - The weather which can delay flights and ruin holidays, or where it rains and sunbathing is the main aim of the customer, or where skiing is the purpose of the holiday and there is no snow.
   - The attitudes and expectations of the customers themselves. They may arrive with negative feelings because of dissatisfaction with their everyday life, or their expectation may be unrealistic. A couple may, for example, take a weekend break holiday in Paris thinking it will bring romance back into their failing marriage.
   - Industrial action which can ruin a holiday or business trip, such as the almost annual industrial action of air traffic controllers somewhere in Europe!

2. Limited financial resources with which organisations can fund product improvements. This is particularly a limiting factor where the capital cost of product improvements may be very high, such as in the hotel and airline sectors, or where the organisation is a local authority whose expenditure is controlled by central government.
3. The customer's willingness, or lack of willingness, to pay for quality. The level of quality an organisation provides must be in equilibrium with the price its customers wish to pay for the product. A guest may dream of a centrally located plush hotel suite with porters to carry their luggage, 24-hour room service and expensive complementary items which guests may take away, such as bath robes.

   However, the same individual may only be able to afford a budget, out-of-town 'motel-style' hotel with neither porter nor room service and no complementary gifts.
4. Some organisations can be constrained when they seek to be seen as providers of a quality product if their history and existing culture has given them the opposite reputation.
5. The lack of agreement on what quality achievement is and its purely subjective nature in leisure makes it very difficult to develop effective, simple performance indicators for quality in our industries.
6. The concept of quality is always changing, and today's effective quality management system will become tomorrow's obsolete system.

Quality as an explicit, defined subject within management is not an equally developed concept across the world. Yet the idea of quality is well understood in the leisure industry across much of the world, by consumers and professionals. The quality of French and Italian restaurants, Greek beaches and Irish hospitality are well known throughout Europe, while Eastern European professionals readily recognise the need to improve service quality in their countries, and Europeans are usually very impressed by service standards in Southeast Asia.

The concept of quality probably does vary from country to country. For example, healthy food in the UK may be seen as diet and low fat processed foods, while in Mediterranean countries it may be equated with fresh produce rather than processed foods. However, attitudes towards what constitutes quality in leisure are probably quite similar for certain segments which are almost global, such as international business travellers.

There can, though, be an element of patriotism involved here, which can lead to large proportions of a population taking a similar view of quality in relation to the products in their own country, most notably food, and also cultural events for instance.

Conclusion

Quality is clearly an important issue for all leisure organisations, but it is a highly subjective concept. It could be said that quality is in the eye of the beholder and every beholder sees it differently. Furthermore, the concept of quality is constantly changing and evolving. The 'benchmark' of what constitutes quality has to be continuously moved in response to the changes in consumer expectations and the ability of organisations to improve their product.

However, there is a danger that the current obsession with quality may debase the whole idea of quality, particularly if quality becomes seen as a focus for marketing hype rather than reality.

Discussion points and essay questions

1. Define what is meant by the term 'quality' and examine its application to service industries.
2. Identify the four main quality management systems and discuss their application to a leisure product of your choice.
3. Evaluate the relationship between quality and price, using examples.
4. Discuss the different 'audiences' that exist in relation to quality and consider how their concepts of quality may differ.

Exercise

Choose a leisure organisation which you consider to be of particular high quality and whose product you have never used. Identify the reasons why you hold this view of the organisation. For example:

(i) Is it because of your own experience or the experience of your friends and relatives, or have your views been influenced by the media or by the promotional activities of the organisation itself?
(ii) Is the quality reputation of the organisation a result of the nature of its product, its pricing policies, its marketing methods, its culture and history, or the quality of its suppliers?

The next stage is to find several people who have used the products of your organisation and ask them if they view the organisation as of high quality or not, based on their experience of its products.

You should then contact people within the organisation, namely its managers and staff. Ask them if they think the organisation is of high quality, and if they do you should ask them on what basis they hold this view.

You should then endeavour to identify differences and similarities in your view, that of customers and that of people within the organisation.

CHAPTER 27

Ethics and social responsibility

Key concepts

The main concepts covered in the chapter are:

- A typology of ethics and social responsibility
- The variety of ethical dilemmas and social responsibility challenges which face organisations in the different sectors of leisure.

Introduction

There appears to be a growing interest in the twin concepts of ethics in management and social responsibility in business. Perhaps, amongst other reasons, this is a result of the numerous scandals in political and economic life which characterised many countries in the 1990s.

Ethics and social responsibility are broad subjects with many elements, as can be seen from Figure 27.1. This also illustrates the fact that some ethical dilemmas and issues of social responsibility are primarily internal to organisations while others relate to the organisation's links with the outside world.

In this chapter, we will consider several types of ethical dilemmas and issues of social responsibility which are found in the various sectors of leisure. We will also consider the marketing implications of these for organisations within these sectors.

Later in the chapter we will consider how such ethical dilemmas can be seen as either threats or opportunities. Furthermore, the chapter will conclude with a brief discussion of national differences and similarities across the world, in attitudes towards ethics and social responsibility.

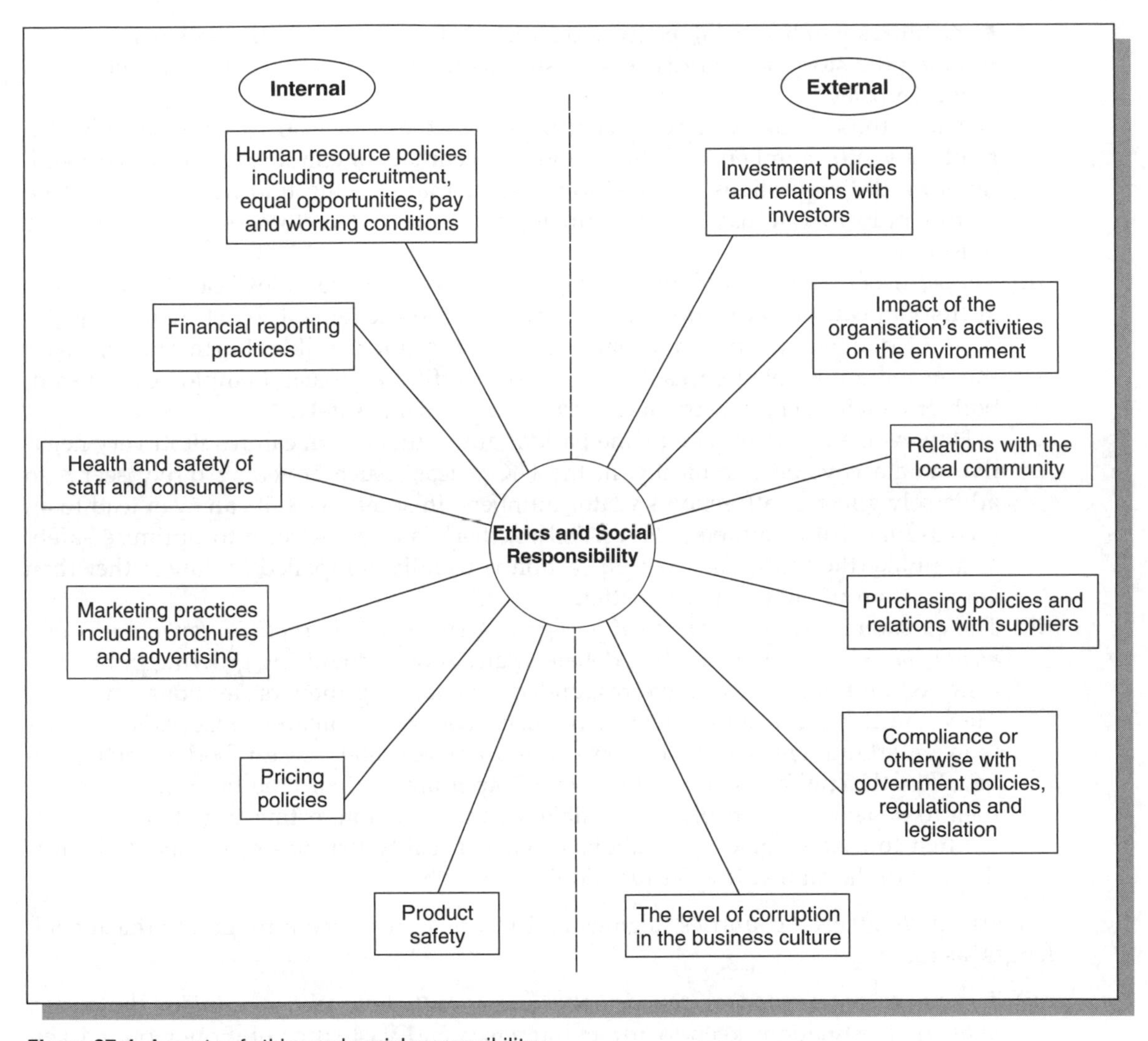

Figure 27.1 Aspects of ethics and social responsibility

By definition, the choice of issues in this chapter is selective but it does serve to illustrate the range of such issues which are encountered by managers in leisure.

It is also important to note that as ethical standards are highly personal, the choice of issues and the comments made about them are subjective and, at times, perhaps, controversial.

The broad range of ethical dilemmas and questions of social responsibility in the *visitor attractions* sector are illustrated by the following examples:

(i) In the museums sector there are the issues of how to handle *controversial and politically sensitive historical events and the ways in which the history of minority groups should be represented*. Such issues might include:
- the role of British entrepreneurs in the slave trade;
- the contribution of Turkish workers to the 'economic miracle' in Germany;
- the treatment of the Jews by the Nazis;

- the blurring of historical reality and nationalist aspirations in the Balkans;
- telling the story of minority groups such as the Basques, the Corsicans, the Lapps and Gypsies.

Tackling these issues can be a painful process that can lead to adverse publicity, reduced visitor numbers and the creation of a climate of conflict. On the other hand, ignoring these questions can lead to the story that is being told not offering a true picture of history. It may also discourage some potential customers from visiting the museum.

(ii) The *safety of theme park and amusement park rides* is a more complex issue than it might at first appear. The attraction of many rides is the excitement which requires just a tinge of danger, and in any event total safety is not possible. Furthermore, many theme and amusement parks live on narrow profit margins and employ casual staff, both of which can be constraints in terms of optimising safety.

However, an accident at a theme park or amusement park can result in very negative media coverage. Ironically, in the UK at least, such coverage rarely seems to adversely affect an attraction's visitor numbers. In some cases, it can even lead to an increase in visitor numbers! Nevertheless, there is a moral duty to optimise safety and, unlike the museums example, action is usually compelled by law, rather than being a thoroughly voluntary matter.

(iii) The *question of zoos and whether it is right to keep animals in captivity for the entertainment of visitors* is a long-standing debate. Many zoos, recognising growing public distaste for traditional zoos, have responded by changing their promotional message. They now sell the idea that their main purpose is education and conservation, rather than entertainment. As many zoo owners are voluntary-sector bodies, acting on behalf of the 'public interest', it is vitally important to their credibility that they are seen to behave in a socially responsible manner. It is interesting to note that one of the first tourism-related applications of virtual reality that has been talked about is the idea of the animal-less 'Virtual Zoo'.

Tourist destinations – countries, regions and resorts – also face a range of ethical challenges, as follows:

(i) To what extent *should those who do not gain financially from tourism subsidise the tourism industry*. Destinations keen to attract tourists spend vast sums of money on marketing and infrastructure, for example. This money usually comes from taxation which is levied on the community as a whole. Yet in many destinations, only a minority of the population will rely on tourism for their livelihood, directly or indirectly. Often relatively poor residents may find themselves subsidising the promotion of private-sector enterprises or the holiday costs of more affluent tourists. Such hidden subsidies distort the pricing system on which all private-sector marketing concepts are predicated.

(ii) The *degree to which public money is spent on tourism rather than other sectors of the economy and society* is a contentious issue. Many developing countries, and even Eastern European countries, see tourism development as a good way of achieving short-term economic development. However, money spent on tourism is clearly not available for spending on other items such as health, education and housing. The marketing implication is that local resentment towards tourists may increase as people become frustrated by the priority accorded to tourism-related government expenditure. This resentment can reduce the quality of the holiday experience and lead to a decline in visitor numbers.

(iii) Finally there is the *tension between short-term and long-term perspectives in the development of destinations*. This tension has been seen clearly in some Mediterranean and Asian countries and is currently evident in Eastern Europe. The need for the short-term benefits of tourism can lead to tourism development which is too rapid and uncoordinated. In the longer term this may lead to social and economic problems which will make the destination less attractive to tourists who may go elsewhere. The destination can then be left with huge capacity which is under-utilised.

The *accommodation* field offers many examples of ethical issues and social responsibility dilemmas, as follows:

(i) The *existence of many allegedly poor employment practices* in this sector is undoubtedly a contributory factor to the problems of recruitment and the high labour turnover that characterises the accommodation sector. Long hours, low wages, poorly developed equal opportunities, and racial and sexual harassment have all been identified within this sector. Yet employers would argue that some of this reflects consumers' unwillingness to pay a higher price for the product.

This has underpinned the opposition of many hoteliers to the ideas of the European Commission on minimum wages and maximum working hours. However, the problems are clearly about attitudes as well as money, in relation to equal opportunities, for instance. The result, from a marketing point of view, is that high turnover and low staff morale can lead to poor service and reduced levels of repeat custom.

(ii) *Purchasing policies* can pose an ethical dilemma for accommodation operators. Buying from local suppliers aids the local community and increases local goodwill. However, if local suppliers are relatively expensive, operators may be forced to buy elsewhere for financial reasons. The most severe challenge may be when local products are best in terms of quality but are more expensive than those from elsewhere. Here there is a quality–cost dilemma which may be very difficult to resolve.

(iii) The rapidly developing *timeshare sector* of the accommodation 'industry' has seen much controversy over the ethics of some of its selling methods. Images of aggressive sales people accosting people in Mediterranean resorts and using the prospect of 'free gifts' to invite people to view and buy timeshare properties is a common phenomenon across much of Western Europe.

Tour operators live in a transnational and competitive business environment, which contains many ethical dilemmas and social responsibility challenges, incuding:

(i) The issue of *how honest they should be in their promotional activities*. Tour operators in many countries have a poor reputation for honesty in their brochures, for example. Hotels have often been said to be 'just five minutes from the beach' when this would only be possible by helicopter! Some winter holiday brochures may feature photographs of the destinations taken in the summer when the temperatures are much higher and all the seasonal tourism businesses are open, and not a word may be said about the building work which may be taking place in a rapidly growing resort. Tour operators are reticent to take a lead in honesty in brochures in case they suffer competitive disadvantage if their competitors do not follow suit. However, in Europe, we have seen with the EC Package Travel Directive that such inaccuracy may result in compulsion through legislation.

(ii) *Many tour operators do not provide adequate advice for their clients on potential hazards and inconveniences* in case such information might discourage them from purchasing the product. This might cover everything from diseases that are prevalent in particular destinations to the risk of Deep Vein Thrombosis on long flights, to the annoying insects of Scotland and Scandinavia, to street crime in major cities and the lack of plugs in many Eastern European hotels! In the short term, failing to give such guidance may not be a major problem, but in the longer term it may lead to customer dissatisfaction and a loss of business.

(iii) The classic dilemma of *whether to add to the problems of already overcrowded destinations* by selling holidays to those destinations. On the one hand, a customer-led organisation should, sell these because these are the places consumers want to visit. On the other hand, continued emphasis on such destinations may destroy them in the longer term. Where then will the operators take their clients?

The *transport* sector is a rich vein of ethical challenges and issues of social responsibility, of which the following are a brief selection:

(i) The question of *'fair competition' in the airline sector* where state intervention has taken place in Europe, to protect state-owned national airlines. This is now changing as a result of 'liberalisation' introduced in European Union countries as part of European Commission competition policies. However, the supporters of state intervention would argue that it is beneficial in that it protects the strategic interest of nations concerned and safeguards nonprofitable routes. Opponents on the other hand would argue that it artificially inflates prices and leads to inefficient operations. Liberalisation is thus ushering in an era of massive change which also offers the prospects of lower fares for the consumer, and more competition.

(ii) The *debate over the use of the private car* in leisure is highly topical. The car opened up leisure opportunities for many people in the 1950s, 1960s and 1970s and it created new forms of leisure such as caravans touring. However, now the increased car ownership is harming the quality of experience as well as harming the environment. Yet we cannot bring ourselves to ban cars for they are a symbol of the basic right to freedom of movement. This dilemma is found from the clogged streets of historic cities to the narrow lanes of the countryside. Failure to tackle it effectively may result in certain congested destinations losing much of their appeal to tourists.

(iii) *Safety on ferries* is a major issue after a series of ferry disasters around the world. However, greater safety means slower turn around times in ports and higher fares at a time when competition with other modes of travel such as the Eurotunnel and air transport is at a peak. Operators, therefore, have to balance their desire to achieve greater safety with the willingness of customers or put up with the effects of such action.

The main ethical issue which is specific to *resort complexes* is the question of their relationship with the area around them. Many appear like self-contained 'tourist ghettos' which have little to do with the local economy and communities that surround the complex. This can be said of the types of complexes managed under brands like Club Med and Center Parcs. One view suggests that this isolation is good in terms of protecting the locals from the social, environmental and economic 'pollution' that tourism can cause.

Others are unimpressed, saying such isolation is socially divisive. To some extent, perhaps, it is a matter of the extent to which tourists wish to mix with the host community and feel safe in the broader destination area. It is perhaps no coincidence that many modern resort complexes that are self-contained have developed in areas where tourists may feel a little uncomfortable or unsafe at certain times.

Retail travel includes a range of ethical dilemmas and moral challenges, as follows:

(i) The *incentives which a tour operator may give travel agency staff to sell its products* can be financial or nonfinancial (a free holiday, for example). This means that the client may not receive the impartial advice they expect to receive. This situation is exacerbated in the UK, for instance, by the fact that the leading travel agency chains are owned by the major tour operators.

If this form of inducement continues, it may further convince customers that travel agents are not impartial, and in time technology will allow tourists to access products without the need for travel agents.

(ii) *Many travel agents use sales promotions with restrictive conditions* to attract customers. For example, the client purchases the travel agent's own insurance policy at the same time. This means that the client is obliged to buy the insurance, which may well be relatively expensive, to obtain the discount. This can be seen as a form of unfair, less than scrupulously honest promotion which again might reduce the reputation of travel agents as impartial intermediaries.

There are numerous ethical dilemmas within the *arts and entertainment* field, including:

(i) The issue of *subsidies* – in other words, who should fund the subsidies and who should receive them. For example, there is the debate in the UK about the validity or otherwise of subsidising a minority art form such as opera, where most opera-goers are relatively affluent, as a whole, while providing little or no subsidy to the cinema. Commercial operators who receive little or no subsidy believe such subsidies for their public-sector 'competitors' amount to unfair competition. In any event, the existence of subsidies certainly distorts pricing mechanisms within the arts and entertainment sector.

(ii) The question of subsidies is also linked to the debate about *the extent to which arts and entertainment organisations should seek to encourage participation from people who do not normally participate in, or even spectate at, arts and entertainment events*. Sometimes trying to attract such people can lead to what purists might see as a dilution or trivialisation of the pure art form. This happens, for instance, when directors attempt to increase the appeal of Shakespeare plays by staging them in the modern day and in modern dress. On the other hand, not seeking to attract new customers in this way can limit audience numbers and reduce income at a time when state subsidies are often being reduced.

(iii) *Some parts of the entertainment 'industry' are increasingly thought to be having a detrimental effect on society*. This is particularly true of television which is often accused of discouraging young people from playing outside their homes or taking part in healthy activities. It is also often blamed for violent behaviour amongst children. The influence of television is clearly spreading with the growth of satellite and cable television and computer games. This has serious implications for other sectors of leisure such as visitor attractions, for whom they represent competition.

The broad field of *recreation and sport* offers a wide range of examples of ethical issues, including:

(i) In many countries, *football is increasingly seen as a business where the owners of famous football clubs seek to use them to generate a profit*. At the same time, these clubs are also an important part of the everyday life of the people who live in that area; they are part of the social fabric and heritage of the locality. Many clubs seek to charge prices that will be high enough to secure a good rate of return on investment, while their supporters simply want to pay as little as possible to see their team play.

Customers are seen as a captive market tied to a monopolistic product so that they will pay the price demanded in return for, what is to them, a unique experience. This polarity of interest is reinforced by the, some would say immoral, fact that clubs which pay huge salaries and transfer fees for top players, yet provide relatively poor facilities for their consumers, the spectators. How many other businesses could survive if they behaved in a similar manner?

(ii) The ethical dilemma of social engineering and paternalism is evident in areas such as countryside recreation. In the UK, for instance, strenuous efforts have been made to encourage people from ethnic minorities to take part in countryside recreation. This was based on two beliefs which may or may not be true, namely:
   1. That countryside recreation is 'good for you' and is somehow an 'uplifting experience'. This view is probably not shared by everyone.
   2. That people from ethnic minorities would visit the countryside if they only knew more about it. This appears a rather patronising view that appears, in general, not to have been borne out by the results of the various marketing campaigns that have been undertaken by the relevant governmental agencies.

Leisure shopping, as we have seen, is a relatively recent arrival on the leisure scene. Nevertheless, it has already given rise to a range of issues relevant to this chapter, including:

(i) The criticism that *leisure shopping encourages people to spend money they do not have on goods they do not need*. Some commentators argue that it has fuelled the rise of materialism and the development of the all-embracing consumer society.

On the other hand, it could be argued that it is simply offering consumers a choice which they are free to accept or reject. If many choose to take up the offer of the leisure-shopping sector, who is to say it is a 'bad thing'.

(ii) In many modern mixed use developments it could be argued that *leisure-shopping complexes within such developments have helped ensure that the less affluent have been forced to move out*. In the UK, dockland development schemes in London and Liverpool, for example, have hardly any shops selling 'normal' products such as bread and vegetables. Instead they are packed with 'leisure' shops selling gifts, stationery, exotic foods and city souvenirs, usually at relatively high prices. Such shops can afford higher rents than everyday utility shops, and, in any event, developers prefer leisure shops because of their ability to attract visitors to the development. However, because they dominate retail provision, less well-off local people without access to a car cannot live in the area, for there is nowhere for them to buy the things they need for everyday life. In the long run, this means that such developments become 'leisure ghettos' with no indigenous resident population to give them a sense of continuity and purpose, and a living heart. In the end, this may reduce their attraction for visitors. Others would argue that this is simply an example of market forces in a postmodern world.

Several major ethical dilemmas are found within *the restaurant and catering* sector, namely:

(i) *Whether priority in purchasing policies should be given to products that are more animal-friendly*, such as truly free range eggs and chickens that have lived in a natural environment. These products are usually more expensive than their industrially farmed counterparts and it is a matter of will consumers care enough to pay the extra price.

(ii) *The issue of what is healthy and what customers like to eat*. Caterers have to decide if they will sell products which, while popular, are known to be harmful to people's health.

They may contain sugar or be rich in fats, for instance. Yet they are popular with customers. Surely the consumer-led approach to marketing dictates that such products should be sold, but to what extent does the caterer have a moral obligation to remind the consumer of the health implications of eating these products given that the customer may then not purchase the product?

(iii) Many would, furthermore, argue that *caterers in any location should also have a responsibility to maintain local gastronomic traditions* by offering at least some traditional local dishes, using local ingredients. However, often, customers want more international dishes. Likewise it may well be cheaper to produce the dishes using nonlocal ingredients. Should this be done, and if so, should the customer be told?

Organisations can adopt a number of responses to ethical issues ranging from denial ('it is not a problem') to full ideological conversion leading to a total change of corporate policy. Most responses lie somewhere between these two extremes. Some may see such issues as a threat and seek to nullify this threat by making changes to policies and marketing practices, so they are less vulnerable to criticism.

On the other hand, certain issues may be viewed as opportunities by some organisations, to be exploited through the development of new products, supported by a promotional campaign to inform potential customers about the stance the organisation is taking.

Leisure organisations have taken a range of proactive approaches on issues of social responsibility, including:

- The airline Virgin's legal battle with British Airways in the 1990s over what might be termed the issue of fair competition and alleged 'dirty tricks'
- Proactive action of German tour operators TUI and LTU on environmental policies
- Burger King setting out to employ more older people to counter criticisms that the hospitality sector is ageist in its recruitment policies.

However, as yet, no leisure organisation has gone as far as the 'Body Shop' in making its stance on ethical concerns, perhaps the main strand in its competitive strategy. This may change if De Bono's concept of 'sur-petition' or the selling of corporate values grows in popularity.

The decision on which stance an organisation should adopt on any particular ethical issue is determined by a range of factors including the views of major shareholders, the organisation's culture and reputation and the views of its customers. Or more accurately, perhaps, the views which managers think are held by their consumers.

There are apparently *national differences and similarities* in relation to this subject, at a number of levels as follows:

- There is a similar situation across much of the world whereby interest in ethical issues in all industries in general has risen in recent years as a result of numerous scandals.
- Debates have developed in a number of countries over a range of ethical issues and matters of social responsibility in leisure, including employment policies, transnational organisations, promotional techniques and the whole field of sustainability.

At the same time there are also differences between individual countries and blocs of countries as the following examples illustrate:

- In Eastern Europe the need to pursue short-term economic development has relegated many of the ethical issues we have explored in this chapter to matters of secondary importance.

- On most issues, concern seems greater in the Northern European countries that have traditionally been the tourist-generating countries than in those Mediterranean countries that have generally been net receivers of tourists. This may simply reflect the way tourism has developed and may change as the economies of countries like Spain, Portugal, Italy and Greece develop further and they become even greater generators of tourist trips.

Interestingly, the similarities may grow as the European Commission legislates on some of the issues covered in this chapter, and enlargement means that more and more European countries join the European Union.

Conclusion

We have seen that there are many complex ethical issues in leisure. Furthermore, they appear to be growing in importance, particularly those which we might group under the heading of 'sustainability'.

It is also clear that there are similarities between the issues faced by organisations in different sectors within our field. For example, both destinations and tour operator face dilemmas in how they should present their product to potential consumers.

As yet, very few leisure organisations appear to have been willing to take high profile stances on ethical issues. Perhaps they see this as a risky strategy, particularly if consumer interest is not high enough that such an organisation taking a proactive stance would be rewarded by increased custom.

Some would argue that either it is impossible to be highly ethical in any business or ethics are really the responsibility of government and society, not individual organisations.

Indeed if one were to argue from the point of view of customer-led marketing, it could be said that, ultimately, organisations have to respond to consumer pressure so that they should mirror the options of their customers in the ethical stance they adopt.

Whichever view one takes, it seems likely that for leisure marketers, ethical issues and questions of social responsibility will become increasingly important considerations in their working lives.

Discussion points and essay questions

1. Discuss some of the major current ethical dilemmas in one of the following sectors:
   - museums
   - restaurants and catering
   - hotel
   - recreation and sport.
2. Evaluate the action which some leisure organisations have taken on ethical issues in relation to social responsibility.
3. Compare and contrast attitudes to ethics and social responsibility between different parts of the world.

Exercise

Select *one* sector, within leisure from those covered in Chapters 14–24 inclusive.

Identify an ethical dilemma which currently exists for organisations operating within your chosen sector.

You should then:

- produce a short report introducing the dilemma and discussing its implications for organisations within your chosen sector;
- outline the range of possible stances which organisations in the sector may adopt in response to these implications;
- discuss the main factors which an organisation should take into account when deciding which stance to adopt.

CHAPTER 28

Marketing research and relationship marketing

Key concepts

The main concepts covered in the chapter are:

- The difference between market research and marketing research
- Different types of market research
- Problems with the collection and interpretation of data
- The lack of knowledge about why consumers behave in particular ways and how they make decisions
- Prerequisites for successful marketing research.

Introduction

In the era of the so-called consumer-led marketing, marketing research must, by definition, be a key topical issue. Marketing research is a particularly crucial current issue in leisure because in these three areas it is a relatively underdeveloped activity. We still know little about why consumers in leisure behave in the way they do.

This chapter is not intended to provide a guide to how to undertake marketing research in leisure. There are a number of texts which perform this task admirably, including those by Ryan and Veal, for example. Instead, it is designed to simply highlight some of the problems and topical issues involved in marketing research in our three fields. To do this it will cover the following areas:

- an outline of the rationale for marketing research and the different types of research;
- a hypothetical case study that illustrates the problems involved in the collection and interpretation of data in leisure;
- a short examination of five major current challenges in marketing research in leisure;
- a brief discussion of the factors that assist the development of effective marketing research.

Given the title and content of this book, it is appropriate that this chapter is about marketing research rather than market research. The difference between the two may seem pedantic but it is important. Marketing research is a precise, focused activity with the single aim of providing data which will be useful to help improve the effectiveness of an organisation's marketing activities. On the other hand, market research is a broader, less-focused activity, where the main aim is to gather information about a market. The former is a more applied form of research than the latter.

However, marketing people will also find market research valuable, as background information. It can often help them to frame the objectives and content of their own marketing research projects.

Marketing research is designed to allow organisations to evaluate their current performance, identify opportunities and develop products and messages to allow them to exploit these opportunities. In other words, marketing research is about improving the efficiency of the organisation's marketing activities.

In terms of what they need to know, organisations need to know about their markets, both existing and potential, and that is the main function of marketing research. Hence it is largely concerned with numerical data about its market together with the behaviour, opinions and perceptions of consumers. These issues will be explored in more detail shortly through a hypothetical example of a Mediterranean Island and the organisation responsible for marketing it. While this example is about a public-sector agency, the points are equally relevant to private-sector organisations.

However, a major distinction between marketing research and market research is that the former is not merely concerned with the consumer. It is interested in all research which might be of assistance to the marketing function. This might include information on the following:

- the activities and plans of competitors;
- changes in the macroenvironment such as new legislation, technological innovations and changes in the economic climate;
- the opinions of marketing intermediaries such as travel agents, who deal directly with the organisation's clients.

Marketing research tends to be of two types, namely:

(i) *Quantitative* research – in other words, facts and figures. This can include factual information on characteristics of the market, together with statistics on the performance of the organisation, including sales figures and market share.
(ii) *Qualitative* research, which is largely concerned with the perceptions, opinions and attitudes of consumers, about organisations, their products and their competitors.

Traditionally, it has been easier and cheaper to collect quantitative statistics than to gather qualitative data. Easier because it is simpler to count the number of times someone buys a product than it is to discover why they buy the product. Cheaper because qualitative research requires long in-depth interviews with skilled interviewers, while quantitative data can usually be gathered through short, simple questionnaires that can be undertaken by less-skilled staff.

Research data is generally compiled from two major sources as follows:

(i) Original primary research to gather new information which is not available elsewhere. This may be used, for example, by an organisation which wants to test consumer attitudes towards their own products, such as a hotel chain or an airline.
(ii) The interpretation of existing secondary research data which has been produced previously and is available to an organisation. Thus, the would-be developer of a potential new visitor attraction might use secondary data to establish whether a viable market existed for the potential attraction.

Several hypothetical examples will serve to demonstrate some of the *main potential applications of the types of marketing research*, in leisure, including:

(i) Endeavouring to discover how customers perceive a hotel in relation to its competitors in terms of a range of criteria, including its location, facilities and price. This would include where the hotel operator is needed to concentrate with its marketing, in other words, on the product or the price, for example.
(ii) A tour operator seeking to see how satisfied their customers are with the product they purchased from the operator, to identify gaps which might affect the customers' satisfaction. Research could help the operator construct a gap analysis, for a specific destination. This gap analysis would help the tour operator decide if it needed to remove the destination from its programme or use its brochure to modify customer expectations of the destination.
(iii) Research by a health club to see how customers would respond to a proposed new service.
(iv) A major restaurant chain investigating the likely impact of potential prices on its existing customers. It will need to establish how many of its customers will stop using the restaurant after a price rise.

Clearly the latter two types of research are more difficult to carry out than the former two, as they involve hypothetical events rather than real ones which have been, or are, taking place, during the research period.

Problems with the collection and interpretation of data in leisure

Most leisure managers would probably agree with the statement that marketing research is inadequate in the area. We know neither enough facts and figures about our markets nor sufficient data about the attitudes and perceptions of our consumers. However, there are some good reasons why this is the case, particularly in the tourism area.

Perhaps these can be best illustrated if we imagine a small Mediterranean Island, which is becoming a popular tourist destination. The island government now wants to develop a marketing strategy and to this end, it requires reliable, up-to-date marketing research.

It has decided to undertake a survey of visitors to find out both quantitative and qualitative information. We will shortly look at the problems they might experience in carrying out such a survey, but first let us look at this island in a little more detail.

It is about 100 square kilometres in area and has an airport and a small port which is visited by both cruise liners and a ferry from the mainland. There are also several marinas which attract pleasure craft and some isolated inlets which provide safe anchorage for such craft. The accommodation stock ranges from luxury hotels in the two well-developed resorts to farmhouses which are available for rent, campsites and even the beach where some people sleep illegally. There are many restaurants and bars, particularly in the two main resorts. In addition, the island has five beaches and several major tourist attractions including a museum, a water-based theme park and some nice old villages. There is also a small convention centre and spa, and the north of the island has a reputation for its wildlife. Finally, we should note that the island is within the European Union.

We will now look at what information the island government feels it might need to produce a marketing strategy and the difficulties it might experience in trying to collect and interpret such data.

Given the constraints of space, we will keep it simple by limiting questions to finding out the answers to just ten questions. These are as follows:

1. How many tourists does the island receive?
2. What is the purpose of their visit?
3. When do they visit the island?
4. Where do they come from?
5. How much do they spend?
6. Who are these visitors?
7. What do they do when they are on the island?
8. What do they think about the island as a destination?
9. How do they believe the island compares to its competitors?
10. Will they make a return trip to the island?

Before we look at each question in detail, it is important to start by talking briefly about methodology and particularly sampling. To gain useful answers to these questions, what percentage of the island's visitors would have to be surveyed and how would they be chosen? The island receives three million visitors a year and the cost of interviewing all of them would exceed £30 million sterling, which is ten times the island's tourism marketing budget!

For financial and logistical reasons the survey would probably have to be small, perhaps 5 per cent, but we must recognise that if we decide to interview less than 100 per cent of all tourists, we can never have the full picture.

The number of tourists

The first problem is to separate the island residents from tourists. After that it is a matter of how best to measure the tourist flows. The traditional way is through immigration controls, for example, requiring all nonresidents to complete an immigration form which is then collected on arrival in the country. However, as the island is in the European Union, it would not be normal practice any more to issue such cards to tourists who come from other European Union countries. As people from such countries represent the bulk of the island's tourist market, such a method would be ineffective.

Another method might be to use the passenger lists of the ferry and airline operators who serve the island. However, the ferries that visit such islands may only rarely have such lists and there is always the problem of separating residents from tourists. There is a further difficulty in that these people who arrive on private yachts will be excluded from such a count.

Finally, the numbers may be established by using the receipts of accommodation establishments. This is a totally flawed method for four main reasons, as follows:

(i) Many people may not stay in officially recognised accommodation. This might include sleeping on the beach and rooms in private houses. These people would thus be excluded from such a count.
(ii) Those staying with friends and relatives which in some places might constitute a significant volume of tourists. This is particularly likely to be the case on an island where there are a number of second homes owned by foreigners.
(iii) Day trippers would be excluded from the count and if the island is relatively close to the mainland, the ferries could bring significant numbers of such visitors to the island.
(iv) Some accommodation establishments may falsify and underestimate the number of tourists they accommodate to reduce their tax bills.

So far we have assumed that all the tourists are foreign, but it may well be that the island has a substantial number of domestic tourists. Measuring domestic tourism is particularly difficult because of the following characteristics of such tourists:

- they cross no national boundaries;
- they are likely to travel by private car rather than ferry or bus;
- they will not use commercial accommodation but rather the home of a friend or relative, or their own second home.

The purpose of the visit

The reasons for people visiting could be interesting in terms of helping the island government to segment its market so that it can design appropriate products. Some reasons might include business, leisure travel, whether package holidays or independent, health, study or attending special events, for example. In general, such information can only be gathered through costly face-to-face interviews.

Furthermore, these purposes are not always mutually exclusive. For instance, business people may use package holidays as an inexpensive way of travelling to the island so that they can carry out their business. We have also noted earlier in the book that there is not always a clear dividing line between business and leisure travel. Business travellers become leisure travellers when the working day is over and many business travellers take partners with them who are leisure travellers for the whole of their stay.

When tourists come to the island?

Tourism tends to have clearly defined patterns of seasonality which means that any survey designed to give an accurate overview of the island's existing market must cover the whole year. For example, most business travel will normally take place outside the summer months but most leisure travel will usually occur in these very same months. Different national markets may visit the island at different times during the summer, reflecting national differences in school holiday dates. There may also be particular times of the year when groups visit the island for specific reasons, which might include watching birds which migrate to the island in December, or attending an arts festival in February.

Where the tourists come from?

This is clearly linked to the last question to some degree as it is in general a relatively straightforward issue. However, it can be a little more complex than it might at first appear. People may make a trip to the island from a location which is not of their normal place of residence. They may be staying with friends or relatives, for example. This is important from a marketing point of view because the island government needs to know in what geographical areas to concentrate its promotional activities so that its message reaches its target markets.

Tourist expenditure

What the island government may want to know is how much money do tourists spend on the island and where do they spend it. However, it is often very difficult to differentiate money spent on the island from that spent off the island. If a tourist buys a 1500 Euro trip to the island from a German tour operator, a significant portion of this money will never leave Germany. For example, it will be used to pay for the seat on a German charter airline on which the tourist will travel.

However, if we simply focus on the money tourists spend once they have arrived on the island, there are still some problems as follows:

- Some people will claim to spend more than they do in fact spend to appear more wealthy than they are in reality.
- Other tourists say they have spent less than they have because they want to be seen as good bargainers.
- Certain tourists may simply not know how much they have spent on holiday.

However, if the island government is keen to estimate tourism impact on their economy, there are two, difficult to quantify, sets of data they need to identify namely:

- what proportion of tourist spending on the island leaves the island to pay for imports or as profits to foreign companies;
- the multiplier effect of tourist spending on the island.

A profile of the tourists

If one is trying to establish factual profiles of tourists, there are difficulties that may be encountered. Some people may lie about their age or income, for instance. There may also be problems in applying the measures of social class used on the island to visitors from other countries, where the concept of class may be different.

Products based on family life cycle can also be stereotypical and can lead to the idea that all families, for example, will require certain things which may well not be the case.

The activities of the tourists

It is usually not possible to discover tourists' activities through observation as it is very expensive. Normally, therefore, one relies on what tourists tell interviewers undertaking surveys or through self-completion questionnaires. However, tourists may not tell the truth, in other words:

- They may say they have not done certain things when they have in reality because they feel they are seen as not socially acceptable, such as indulging in casual sex or drinking heavily.

- Alternatively, they may claim to have done things which are more acceptable, such as visiting historic sites, when they have in fact done no such thing.
- Some may give totally wrong information because they have been involved in illegal activities such as hunting or child sex.

Finally, some tourists may not even remember all or even most of the things they did on holiday!

Tourist opinions of the island as a destination

Some tourists will give an unrealistically positive opinion of the island because they feel it is what those conducting the survey want to hear. Others may give a negative view not because they do not like the island, but rather because they are generally unhappy about their relationships or their life in general, for example. Generalised opinions can also mask views on specific aspects of the island which could be very useful to those responsible for marketing the island.

For example, someone who says they like the island overall may actually have been very unhappy about some aspect of the holiday such as their hotel or a particular beach. On the other hand, a tourist who in general appears to have a negative view of the island may have really enjoyed a particular leisure activity or a specific beach.

How does the island compare to its competitors?

This is difficult to ascertain for several reasons, as follows:

(i) The tourist may not have visited any of the places the island has identified as its competitors.
(ii) Identifying the competitors can be a difficult task for they will be different for each different market segment, such as business travellers, hedonists and sightseers, for instance.
(iii) Tourists' views of competitor destinations may be based on experiences which are a number of years old and are therefore out-of-date.

The likelihood of repeat visits

The response to this question may be distorted by the fact that people may, at the end of their holiday, say they are likely, or even certain, to return because they are filled with nostalgic feelings for the holiday they have just experienced. However, when they are home, and memories have faded and other destinations have targeted the same tourists with their promotional messages, the likelihood of a repeat visit in the near future is usually much reduced.

Even concentrating on just ten questions, we have seen how difficult marketing research is in the field of tourist destinations. However, it would be wrong to say that it is as difficult in all sectors of leisure. It is particularly difficult in relation to destinations because of their complexity and the fact that they are not in single ownership. In hospitality, for example, conducting research on the market is relatively easy for individual corporations such as hotel chains and fast-food outlet operators. Nevertheless, it can still be difficult to gain accurate information on these markets as a whole. Again, consumers may give misleading answers, for instance, diners may claim to eat healthier dishes than they do because such behaviour is more socially acceptable.

In spite of the advances made in marketing research in recent years, there are still *five fundamental challenges in leisure marketing research*. These are as follows:

1. *The lack of reliable research on why consumers do what they do and how they make purchasing decisions*. There is relatively little empirical research to show, for example:
   - Why people choose to visit particular visitor attractions?
   - How tourists select hotels?
   - The reasons why people choose to use one travel agent rather than another.

   The data that does exist on these issues tend to be based on small samples in one country or region, so that it is difficult to draw any general conclusions.

   In the absence of readily available, reliable such research, managers are left with only their experience and judgement on which to base their marketing decisions. Such judgements can often be inaccurate due to personal bias.

   There have also been very few comparative studies, designed to identify national differences and similarities in consumer behaviour in our field. This has made it difficult for organisations to evaluate whether or not their product may sell well in another country. At a time when many organisations in leisure are seeking to expand internationally, this gap in marketing research is a particularly topical concern.
2. *The difficult and high cost of finding out about nonusers* to discover why they are not purchasing the services provided by an organisation. This is important as most leisure organisations need to attract new customers if they are to thrive, or even to survive.

   There are several sectors where this is a major issue, namely:
   (i) Subsidised theatres where only a minority of the local population usually makes use of the theatre. Attracting more people from the local area to visit the theatre is crucial to the management of the theatre because it must be seen to be serving the whole community in order to justify the subsidy it receives.
   (ii) Seaside resorts in the UK where many British people do not visit the resort and yet little is known about why they do not make use of the resort.

   While research on nonusers is difficult, it is vital for marketers. It can help them identify different types of nonusers for whom different marketing messages need to be developed and transmitted, including:
   - Ex-users who need to be tempted back, either by being told about new features of the product or by being reassured that it has not changed.
   - Those who are aware of the product but have not yet been persuaded to buy it. They require a 'hard sell' message or perhaps a 'first-time user's special promotional offer'.
   - Those who are not aware of the product's existence, who need to be informed about the product.
3. *Problems with the identification of trends because of the lack of longitudinal studies* carried out over a lengthy period of time using a common methodology.

   This is unfortunate as trend extrapolation can be a valuable, if far from infallible, way of forecasting short-term future trends. If we cannot make such forecasts with any confidence, then our ability to undertake effective marketing planning is significantly reduced. While progress has been made on longitudinal studies in recent years, there are still too few of them, partly because of the high cost of mounting such studies.

4. *Our lack of knowledge of the behaviour of individuals.* We still tend to treat tourists and hotel users, for example, as homogenous groups who will behave in a particular way. Yet we know, from our own experience as tourists or hotel users that our individual behaviour changes over time and varies depending on circumstances. However, there is still little reliable research in leisure on the behaviour of individual consumers. The lack of such data clearly limits our ability to realistically segment markets.

   It also makes us develop stereotypes that may not reflect true behaviour. For example, we assume that some people prefer package holidays while others prefer independent travel, and that some prefer the coast while others have a preference for the countryside. Yet we have not yet proved that these people are different people.

   It may be that they are the same people doing different things at different times in response to changes in their circumstances or the 'determinants' which affect them.

   We also know relatively little about how the behaviour of individual tourists or hotel customers, for example, changes over time. For instance, many commentators say one of the problems of the previously mentioned seaside resorts in the UK is that those who visited them in previous decades are now holidaying abroad. We all tend to accept this view as a truism, yet where is the empirical evidence?

   We have to learn that markets are the result of the behaviour of individuals who are all different and who behave differently at different times. It is logical, therefore, that our research should start with the behaviour of individual consumers, rather than with markets as a whole, for the overall picture includes major variations in individual behaviour which are very important from a marketing point of view.
5. The fact that *inadequate budgets* are still devoted to marketing research in most leisure organisations. The many small operators and public-sector bodies in this field often cannot afford research while many large organisations see it as a relatively low priority, which is one of the first areas that can be cut in times when resources are severely limited. This appears to be somewhat more of a problem in some countries such as the UK, where a lack of commitment to market research in the private sector is compounded by a lack of resources for marketing research in the public sector. Thus, potential developers and marketing people find it difficult to find reliable, up-to-date, comparative data, collected and made available by the public sector, than would be the case in France, for instance. This undoubtedly is an obstacle to both the development of new products and the effective marketing of existing ones.

   Marketing research is, increasingly, an expensive activity, but one which organisations need in order to optimise their marketing. Who pays for it – individual organisations or the public sector – is a major debate but it has to be paid for somehow, or the quality of leisure marketing will suffer.

For marketing research to be successful, in other words, effective and useful for marketers, a number of prerequisites are required as follows:

(i) having clear objectives as to what it is hoped will be gained from the research;
(ii) selecting the appropriate methodology to achieve these objectives;
(iii) only collecting data which has implications for marketing action;
(iv) being able to carry out research on an ongoing basis rather than as a one-off 'snapshot' only;
(v) adequately briefing all staff involved in the research project;
(vi) providing enough resources to allow the research to be conducted professionally;

(vii) having the mechanisms to analyse all the results quickly before the research becomes outdated;
(viii) having staff with the ability to accurately interpret the results;
(ix) presenting the results in a user-friendly form for those who need to use them.

While the principles of marketing research are largely the same in leisure across the world, there have been national differences in emphasis. In countries where inbound tourism is vitally important, such as Spain and Greece, it is vital that data is gathered on the relevant foreign national markets. In countries like the UK where both inbound and outbound tourism are important, data on both types of markets are important.

There are certainly major differences in terms of the level of development and competitiveness of public-sector marketing research. As one of the case studies illustrates, France, for example, has a highly developed system compared to other states such as the UK and Portugal, for example.

One problem, however, which all states tend to experience is the difficulty of measuring domestic tourism flows. This is a serious problem in those countries where such tourism is on a particularly large scale such as the states of Eastern Europe and many Asian and African countries.

In relation to the fashionable concept of relationship marketing, the effective use of qualitative marketing research, coupled with the use of sophisticated customer databases and Internet technologies, has allowed organisations to develop relationships with their existing customers. These are in their early stages of development and include the loyalty programmes that have been developed by the airlines and major hotel groups.

The increasing emphasis on the research of customer satisfaction and purchase behaviour patterns will allow organisations to develop much more meaningful relationships with consumers in the future.

Conclusion

Marketing research is in some ways relatively underdeveloped in leisure, in comparison with some industries. This might reflect the fact that while it is modern, at least it has become a major, recognised industry in recent years. Or it may be a function of the tradition of entrepreneurship, based on hunches and judgements. However, it is more likely that it is because marketing research in our three fields is by nature very complex as we have seen in this chapter. In such a situation it is tempting to rely on judgement when data is either nonexistent or of dubious quality. However, at a time when markets are becoming evermore fragmented, consumers more sophisticated and business environments more complex, marketing research will become increasingly important. It may well be that the development of marketing research to a higher level may be the sign that leisure has at least become a mature industry.

Discussion points and essay questions

1. Discuss the different types of marketing research and identify which ones are the most difficult to undertake.
2. Evaluate the main difficulties involved in collecting and interpreting qualitative data on tourists' behaviour, perceptions and attitudes.
3. Examine what you consider to be the most important prerequisite for successful marketing research.

Exercise

Your group has been retained as consultants by a destination-marketing agency. The brief you have been given is twofold, namely:

(i) to discover the perceptions of their destination which are held by people who live in your local area;
(ii) to identify which of these people have never been to their destination and to ascertain what the destination could do to persuade these people to visit.

You should choose a destination that is reasonably well known to people in your local area.

There are four stages to the project as follows:

(i) Deciding how you will go about handling this brief and deciding what survey or surveys you need to conduct;
(ii) Designing questionnaires for your survey or surveys;
(iii) Carrying out the survey with an appropriate sample of the population in your local area;
(iv) Presenting the results to your client through a presentation and a report.

Part Seven

The wider context

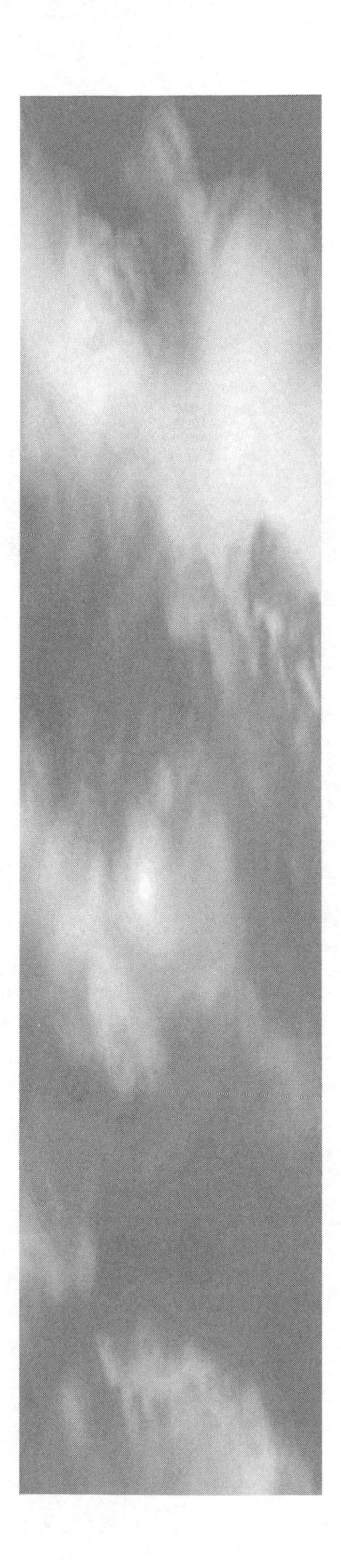

Introduction

This brief part, which consists of just two chapters, is nevertheless of great importance, for it sets the content of most of this book, in a wider context, in two respects.

First, Chapter 29 relates what we have been saying about leisure to key trends and developments in other industries and sectors of consumer society. This is highly relevant because, in many ways, what is happening in leisure is mirroring, or even following on from, what has happened, and is happening, in these other areas.

Secondly, Chapter 30 relates what is happening in leisure to developments in the world as a whole in terms of globalisation.

CHAPTER 29

Leisure and the wider consumer society

Key concepts

The main concepts covered in the chapter are:

- Similarities with other countries as a result of political, economic, social and technological change
- The continuing trend towards the concentration of ownership and transnational operation
- Similarity of trends in relation to the behaviour of consumers of leisure products and services with those in other industries.

Introduction

In this book the authors have made a number of comments about the ways in which marketing is developing in the leisure sector. These comments have covered the nature of the product, trends in the market demand and the methods of marketing which are used.

However, it is, perhaps, a significant fact that many of these comments could have been applied, with modifications, to a number of other sectors of the consumer society. What is happening in leisure is often mirroring similar developments in other industries. Indeed, in a number of cases, these developments are taking place at a slower pace than in some of these other industries.

This chapter will consider these links between trends in leisure and those in different industries. We will look at this issue under two main headings, as follows:

1. The impact of political, economic, social and technological change;
2. The structure of industries, including concentration of ownership and the growth of transnational corporations.

While comparisons can be drawn between a wide range of industries and leisure, the greatest similarities are with many other service industries, particularly perhaps the following:

- food retailing
- financial services
- media (press, radio and television)
- education.

However, similarities can also be identified with what is happening in a number of manufacturing industries, including food manufacturing and the car industry, for example.

Political change is creating new markets and new business environments for a range of industries in much the same way as it is for leisure organisations. In Eastern Europe, for example, food manufacturers are seeking to develop new markets for their products while wine and food products from Eastern Europe are increasingly finding their way into Western European retail outlets.

Likewise, the arrival of democracy in South Africa and relative peace in certain regions of the world is encouraging enterprises in a number of sectors to invest in these countries.

Finally, the Single Market and the enlargement of the European Union is also providing new opportunities for companies in a number of sectors. Privatisation and deregulation are also creating new opportunities in sectors such as the water industry where privatisation in the UK has created investment opportunities for French utilities. In many ways, *economic change* is clearly linked to political change, for many economic policies are clearly politically motivated. Differential levels of economic development between countries can stimulate the growth of branch factories in countries where costs are lower than in the company's own country. We have seen this phenomena in the car and food industry, for example. At the same time, economic growth in particular countries can make them attractive places for inward investment as their domestic markets grow in purchasing power. Conversely, economic instability and wildly fluctuating exchange rates can discourage such investment.

Social change is affecting both products and markets in a range of industries. Or perhaps it is more realistic to say that social change in markets is leading to the demand for new types of products. Examples of this include:

- Growing interest in environmental issues leading to manufacturers modifying their products in response to criticisms. Hence the removal of Chlorofluro-carbons (CFCs) from aerosol deodorants in recent years.
- Developments in the idea of healthy lifestyles which has created a demand for healthy food products such as diet foods and organic food, for example.
- The recognition of a growing youth culture on a global scale, which has led to new media and entertainment products being developed for this group of consumers.
- A desire on some people's part to retire at an earlier age than normal which has created a market for new types of personal pension products.
- The increasingly multicultural structure of many national populations has generated a need for education provision to be tailored to meet the needs of students from ethnic minority communities.

Technological change is also changing other industries in the ways it is changing leisure. Interactive television and multimedia systems are leading to the rise of 'tele-shopping'. Smart cards are being used increasingly in food retailing while virtual reality is beginning to play a significant role in education, in the training of surgeons, for example.

If we move on to the second heading, we can also see similarities between leisure organisations and other industries.

The trend towards *concentration of ownership* is being seen in most industries through globalisation. Media 'empires' have grown up like that of Signor Berlusconi in Italy, and mergers and takeovers are creating ever-larger food manufacturers. In many sectors, small independent suppliers are being squeezed by the growth of these larger players with their considerable power in the marketplace.

At the same time, we are witnessing a general growth in *transnational* corporations across the world, in a range of industries, through a variety of different mechanisms. For example:

- Some education institutions have developed strategic alliances with other institutions to offer joint courses, or have franchised their courses to certain foreign institutions, particularly in Asia.
- Services such as financial consultants, estate agencies and civil engineering companies have established branches in the newly developing markets of Eastern Europe.
- Joint ventures in the food industry have been created between partners based in two or more countries.
- Car manufacturers working together in research and development.
- Food retailing like Aldi and Netto setting up units in the UK.

The issues we have been briefly discussing in this chapter have led to a number of trends in terms of marketing in a range of industries including leisure.

In terms of the *market*, they have led to a growth in segmentation, a recognition that most markets are made of sub-groups with shared characteristics as purchasers. Identifying these segments, developing products which are tailor-made for them alone and giving them the right messages about these products is increasingly seen as the key marketing challenge in a range of international industries.

Likewise, there is a growing belief that we are seeing the slow rise of some international segments which behave similarly irrespective of their nationality. Such groups might include:

- young people and teenagers, who share similar tastes in clothes, music and food;
- those interested in living a healthy lifestyle who take regular exercise and are careful about their choice of diet;
- people who are particularly concerned with environmental issues for whom this concern manifests itself in the household products they buy, the forms of transport they use and the food they choose to eat;
- business executives who are united by their use of particular modes of communication and the management theories by which they operate.

If this trend continues, then these groups will develop into the 'global consumer'.

What makes them fascinating from a marketing point of view is that their whole lifestyle is determined by the types of factors we have outlined above. Every purchasing decision is consciously or unconsciously designed to reinforce the lifestyle, both in the consumers' own eyes and in the eyes of other people.

Clearly this offers considerable opportunities for *new product development* by international companies. This is already being seen in a number of industries, including:

- the food industry where the so-called health products such as 'bio-yoghurts' are being sold across the world to health-conscious consumers, whether they be Swedish or Spanish;
- global branded clothing products, particularly in relation to the teenage market;
- pan-European management education courses, aimed at the 'Euro-business executive' market.

The *way in which products are marketed* is also changing in a range of industries, largely in response to technological innovations. Direct marketing based on computerised databases is growing as the technology that underpins it becomes ever more efficient. This is clearly a threat to marketing intermediaries such as retailers. Technology is also leading to the growth of some forms of advertising media such as the Internet, multimedia systems like CD-ROM, and Interactive television.

This brief summary has hopefully shown that there are great similarities between trends in leisure marketing and other industries.

However, we must be careful not to exaggerate these similarities, for there are differences, and the speed at which the trends are moving also varies between the different industries.

There are some intrinsic characteristics of leisure that mean it may never be like other industries in some ways. For example, in general, the consumer still has to travel to enjoy the tourism product while in most industries the product can, in some form at least, be taken to the consumer. This point also leads to another relevant observation namely that leisure marketing is not in itself a homogenous activity. While the tourism product often requires the consumer to travel to it, many leisure products can be taken to the consumer. We must therefore recognise the differences and similarities within leisure marketing, as well as those with other industries.

However, ultimately, leisure is merely a part of our overall consumer society. It is likely, therefore, that in many ways they will mirror and influence changes in marketing practice in other industries to some extent.

Finally, we should also recognise that in this chapter we have not dis-aggregated the discussion to the level of individual countries. Yet this is important for a number of reasons, as follows:

- Countries differ greatly in terms of their business environments, so that in some countries trends that we have discussed in this chapter will be almost unknown.
- In some countries the similarities between trends in leisure marketing and marketing in other industries will be very close, while in others they will be much less obvious.
- Trends such as industrial concentration and transnational operations are much more highly developed in some countries than others.

If the reader wants to test this view, he or she should simply look at the issues we have discussed and compare, almost at random, four different countries which all share the same first letter, namely Sweden, Singapore, Saudi Arabia and Senegal.

Conclusion

We have seen that there are similarities between what is happening in leisure and developments in certain other industries.

We have now looked at the first aspect of the wider context of leisure marketing, albeit briefly and selectively. It is now time for us to look at the second element namely globalisation.

Discussion points and essay questions

1. Compare and contrast the impact of technological developments on leisure, with their impact on other industries, now and in the future.
2. Evaluate the differences and similarities in market trends between leisure and other industries.
3. Discuss the extent to which leisure organisations are using marketing techniques similar to organisations in other industries.

Exercise

Choose *one* organisation from *each* of the following industries:

(i) Leisure;
(ii) Financial services, media, education or food retailing;
(iii) Car manufacturing, food processing or textile production.

Identify the political, economic, social and technological factors which you believe will have the most important implications for your three chosen organisations over the next decade.

Compare and contrast these factors between the three organisations to see where there are similarities and differences.

CHAPTER 30

Globalisation

Key concepts

The main concepts covered in the chapter are:

- The process of globalisation in terms of demand, supply and the business environment
- Globalisation as an opportunity and a threat for European organisations.

Introduction

We must recognise that leisure organisations are global activities and transnational industries. Furthermore, there is a trend towards increased globalisation in the leisure sector.

By globalisation we mean companies that increasingly operate across the world and sell their products to a worldwide market, which in itself is becoming more homogeneous.

For two European authors, it is interesting to look at globalisation from a European perspective. Readers from other regions of the world may wish to look at it from the point of view of their own part of the world.

The position in Europe needs to be seen in the context of this process, and the concept of competition within Europe needs to be considered in relation to competition from outside

Europe. Later in this chapter we will look at the issue of competition between Europe and the rest of the world, and the ways in which they are influencing each other.

First of all, however, we will look at the *three interrelated aspects of globalisation*, namely:

1. consumer behaviour – the demand side;
2. industry structure – the supply side;
3. the business environment – the context for the relationship between the demand and supply side.

In many ways it is the latter factor, which is the driving force behind changes in the other two areas. However, it is important to appreciate that the links between all three are blurred and they are all inseparably intertwined.

Nevertheless we can identify some forces in the business environment which are driving the move towards increased globalisation.

Some of these forces, both in terms of the *macro and the microenvironment* are as follows:

(i) Technological developments such as Global Distribution Systems which are allowing companies to operate on a truly global basis. Likewise, increasingly sophisticated types of media technology such as the Internet are making it easier for consumers to gain access to products from all over the world.

(ii) Political change in a number of regions of the world such as Southern Africa, the Middle East, Eastern Europe, North America and Mexico (with the trade treaty between the USA, Canada and Mexico). In general, these changes are making it easier for companies to set up operations in these regions, and for investors to invest in new projects in such countries.

(iii) Trade treaties such as the GATT Agreement are slowly creating a 'level playing field' on a global scale where companies from other parts of the world can compete with local companies on equal terms.

(iv) Economic development in many countries outside the so-called 'developed world' is taking place often at great speed. These countries, such as those of South-East Asia, for example, are thus becoming more attractive markets for foreign companies. They are also developing their own leisure industries as their economies grow, and their companies are proving increasing competition for those from the older industrialised countries.

(v) The media is also becoming more globalised and that in turn is leading to some globalisation of social and cultural factors in the business environment. For example, interest in environmental issues is growing in many countries and the media has played a major role in this. The same is true in relation to health, for example. Likewise the globalisation of the media has also helped create some globalised social phenomena such as the international teenage culture, for instance.

(vi) The growth of competition within individual countries and the impact of domestic economic recessions in the early 1980s has led to companies looking abroad for their future growth. Globalisation through joint ventures, franchises, strategic alliances, takeovers and mergers has become the way in which many organisations have sought to achieve competitive advantage.

(vii) Management theorists, particularly those from the USA and Japan, have had their ideas widely disseminated around the world and many have been highly influential. Many companies are therefore now being managed in terms of standardised management theories, from Bradford to Bogota, and Boston to Bangkok. In theory, at least, this should make it easier for companies to undertake transnational expansion.

This brief selective list shows some of the factors which are driving the process of globalisation in leisure marketing. We can see, therefore, that globalisation is a matter of both a choice being exercised by the industries, and changes in technology and the political environment which are making it possible for them to exercise this choice.

Some commentators tell us that we are moving towards the day when we will see the birth of the *global consumer* in leisure, whose behaviour will differ little in relation to their nationality. If this is the case, it will probably be a result more of the actions of the relevant industry than a desire for such a development on the part of the consumer.

Furthermore, globalisation in leisure will also be promoted by some companies in other industries to help achieve the broader aims. For example, the media companies and information technology industry will see leisure as an area of application for their globe-shrinking new products such as smart cards and multimedia systems.

We should note that this process of globalisation is affecting many other industries apart from leisure, for some of the same reasons that we noted earlier in respect of the sector with which we are primarily concerned – for example, the food and drink industry, the entertainment business, financial services and retailing. Indeed, it could be argued that globalisation in these industries is much more highly developed than it is in leisure. Hence the growth of truly global brands such as Coca-Cola.

Clearly, in some ways, leisure has always been a global industry by its very nature, moving people from continent to continent. Some hotel chains have been global operators for many years, for example, football companies operating across national boundaries. However, the trend is now gathering pace, becoming more widespread and is encompassing leisure increasingly too.

Nevertheless, there appear to be some obstacles to globalisation, particularly in relation to national differences in consumer behaviour and government policies, for example. Patterns of demand and preferred holiday resorts can vary dramatically between different countries while some governments take a negative attitude towards the arrival of foreign companies in their national market. So the march of globalisation will continue to vary in pace between different countries, and will falter from time to time, in response to these obstacles.

If we believe that the process of globalisation will continue then from a European perspective, we have to see it as both an opportunity and a potential threat in terms of the leisure markets.

Globalisation is an opportunity for European organisations because it means opportunities for expansion and new markets to exploit. In recent years we have seen European companies growing through strategies based on becoming players on a truly global scale. Examples of these include:

- Club Mediteranées expansion in terms of its resorts in countries such as Mexico and Australia, together with its campaigns to attract customers in the US and Japanese markets;
- Accor's expansion into the USA hotel sector through its purchase of the Motel 6 chain.

However, there are clearly risks for organisations when they seek to exploit globalisation, such as British Airways' ill-fated rebranding that saw it remove the UK Union Jack from the tails of its aircraft to be replaced with artwork drawn from different countries in its global network. It is clear that this statement about being a global rather than a UK airline was not to the taste of many international as well as British customers.

This globalisation has not just been seen in the commercial sector. Government-funded destination-marketing agencies have also put some effort into marketing their product on a truly global scale.

However, we already can see *how globalisation could be a threat to Europe's leisure industry* in the following ways, for example:

- Europe is already losing its share of the worldwide international tourism market as new destinations, outside Europe, come into the market;
- the rapid expansion of American fast-food chains such as McDonald's in Europe, which have changed the catering industry in Europe dramatically;
- the interest being shown in the liberalisation of Europe's air transport industry by the lean and fit US airlines which have already survived the American de-regulation process.

Clearly these opportunities and threats are similar to those which have already been faced by other industries, particularly in the manufacturing sector. In many older traditional industries, such as steel and textiles, and newer industries like computers and audio equipment, we have seen Europe losing out to non-European countries. These countries have tended to succeed for a variety of reasons including lower prices and being more in tune with changes in consumer demand.

We must, of course, appreciate that there are inherent differences between services like leisure and manufacturing industries. However, we should recognise that some of the ways in which Europe is seeking to compete in manufacturing, product markets may offer lessons for the situation with regard to leisure. These include:

- concentrating on higher quality, premium priced products rather than competing purely on price;
- working on improving the service element of the product which is often compared unfavourably to those offered in other parts of the world, most notably South-East Asia;
- becoming better at marketing in terms of research, new product development, promotion, distribution and selling;
- anticipating changes in consumer behaviour better and adapting products quicker to meet changes in demand;
- utilising technology to improve both efficiency of operation and the service which is offered to customers;
- the coming together of European businesses in particular sectors so that their combined strength allows them to compete with non-European companies.

Conclusion

If we look to the future, we will probably see a continued move towards globalisation, which will be made increasingly possible by technological innovations. Each day we move a little closer to the so-called 'global village'.

It may well be that while we in Europe are concerning ourselves with the concept of Europeanisation, Europe will find itself being 'leap-frogged' by the process of globalisation. We must therefore always consider leisure marketing in terms of a global context rather than behaving as if somehow Europe were a closed system.

Currently, in tourism at least, globalisation appears to be moving the 'centre of growth' of the leisure market from Europe to Asia.

Discussion points and essay questions

1. Critically evaluate the extent to which the process of globalisation is making the concept of countries and even regional blocks like the European Union obsolete.
2. Discuss the opportunities and threats which the process of globalisation represents for leisure organisations in Europe, Asia and North America.

Exercise

You should choose *one* of the following sectors:

- hospitality
- recreation and sport
- tour operation
- museums.

For your chosen sector you should produce a report covering the following issues:

(i) the role of European organisations in the relevant market(s) in non-European countries;
(ii) the role of non-European organisations in the relevant market(s) within Europe;
(iii) the extent to which the relevant market(s) may be considered to be global at present.

Part Eight

Conclusions

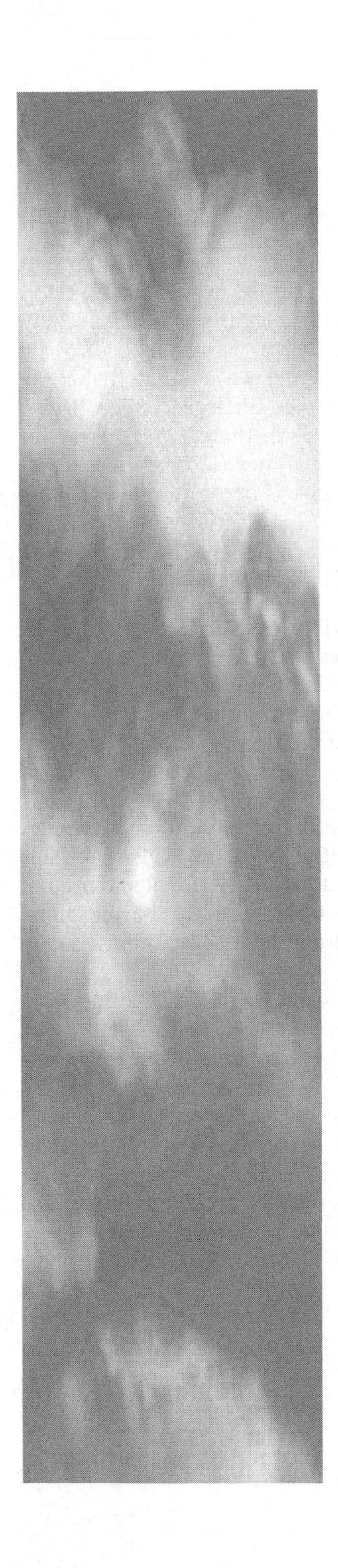

Conclusions

At the end of such a long, complex and wide-ranging text, attempting to draw conclusions is a necessary but awesome task. Perhaps the only real conclusion we can draw is that there are no generally applicable conclusions. However, this is too trite a statement, and we feel we must endeavour to pull together some broad conclusions for the benefit of readers.

Before going to outline these conclusions in some detail, we would like to begin by seeing how the book has, in our opinion, lived up to the objectives set out in the preface. However, it is for readers to decide how successful we have been in this respect, though we believe we have produced a text which is truly international in flavour, particularly through the case studies and examples that have been used. We have attempted to illustrate the many facets of leisure marketing in this far-ranging text.

In *Part 1* of the book we tried to define the *marketing concept* and considered both the philosophy of marketing and the practical application as a management discipline. In Chapter 2 we also defined the term leisure and attempted to look at the concept of leisure time and began to consider the types of organisations that offer leisure experiences.

In the early part of the book, we also saw that there are *significant differences between leisure* in terms of marketing. These differences cover products, organisations, markets and marketing techniques. Furthermore, even within each of these fields, we have seen that there can be significant variations in marketing practice. These are, perhaps, most noticeable in relation to the following criteria:

- The *marketing objectives* of organisations which tend to vary depending on whether the organisation is in the private, public or voluntary sector. This characteristic can also reinforce the differences between our three fields, for the private sector is much more powerful in tourism and hospitality than it is in many forms of leisure.

- The *size of organisations* ranging from small one-person enterprises to massive transnational corporations. Marketing in the latter type of organisation is usually well funded, heavily planned and carried out by specialist staff. In the case of small businesses, on the other hand, marketing often has limited budgets, is opportunistic rather than planned and is usually carried out by the entrepreneur themselves, who may have little or no specialist marketing expertise.

In *Part 2* we looked at *consumers, markets, industry structure* and the *business environment* of the leisure sector. While we were able to use copious examples from different countries, it was not always easy to see a great deal of homogeneity.

If we talk about markets and consumer behaviour, there is currently a generally heterogeneous situation. A French tourist, for example, still behaves differently to a British tourist. He or she is more likely to holiday in August, to stay in their own country for their main holiday and to shun the package holiday in favour of more independent forms of holidaymaking. However, we suggest that this heterogeneity is not the same as saying each country is very different.

Furthermore, we believe that trends are taking place which are making the picture more complex and perhaps leading to more homogeneity. For example:

- Certain *niche markets* or *market segments* are developing which appear to be more international in nature than we have seen previously. Examples of these include the student traveller, who travels on study exchanges and then takes side trips from their study base.

  There also appears to be shared behavioural characteristics amongst many youth travellers, in general, such as the 'hedonists' of Northern Europe. It is perhaps not surprising that the younger generation, with its greater language skills and lack of memories of wars past, is taking the lead in this trend.
- There is growth in the *business tourism* market where consumer behaviour and demand patterns appear to show less variation than is the case with leisure travel. Perhaps this is because these travellers do not choose where, when and how they travel and are not motivated by a pleasure imperative. It is largely a utilitarian activity. Furthermore, much business travel is undertaken by employees of multinational companies who are by nature more international than national in outlook.
- The continuing *globalisation* of the media is playing an increasing role in influencing consumer behaviour in leisure.
- As more and more citizens become *experienced tourists*, they are alike in seeking ever-more unusual new experiences and more flexibility from leisure providers.
- *International regulations* are slowly standardising a range of factors within members' countries which affect leisure marketing. These vary from controls on working hours to social benefits and consumer protection legislation.
- Many *new leisure activities* are sweeping across the world, usually backed by huge promotional campaigns undertaken from major transnational corporations. These include everything from computer games to karaoke!

This is just a brief, selective list but it does indicate the range of such factors that are currently influencing leisure markets.

Clearly, there are links between trends in consumer behaviour and the *supply side*. Consumers can only buy what industries offer while organisations are always seeking to vary their offers in response to changing consumer preferences.

In Chapter 4 we identified several important issues in relation to the supply side, in other words, the industrial structure of leisure. These included:

- the polarisation between small businesses and large corporations;
- the growth of transnational companies;
- the ongoing process of industrial concentration.

Chapter 5 went on to look at the *international business environment* and concluded that it is still largely heterogeneous in relation to leisure. However, again we noted trends which will lead to greater standardisation, including the following:

- technological developments which are truly global and for which geographical boundaries are of little relevance;
- political changes like the harmonisation policies of the European Commission and the introduction of market or semi-market economies in Eastern Europe;
- the process of economic globalisation;
- the growth of more and more standardised approaches to management, education and training.

In the next section of the book, *Part 3*, we examined the application of the concept of the marketing mix to leisure. This resulted in the following points being identified:

1. The *product* in all cases is intangible, a service, but it usually has tangible elements like the food in a restaurant or the seat on an aircraft.
2. The *benefits* which the product bestows on the consumer vary between different sectors within leisure.
3. The same *pricing* mechanisms are available to most organisations but some show a preference for discounting for tactical marketing reasons while others offer concessions for social reasons.
4. *Place* or distribution comes in both forms namely direct from producer to consumer and via an intermediary such as a travel agent.
5. While the range of potential *promotional techniques* is very similar for all organisations, they are used in different ways within different sectors. The main reason for this difference appears to be budgetary but there may well be others, notably the nature of the product, the size of the market and the price of the product.

In *Part 4* we looked at the *marketing planning process* in relation to leisure. Using examples, we looked at how organisations seek to answer four questions, namely:

- where are we now?
- where are we going?
- how will we get there?
- when will we know when we have arrived?

However, as was indicated in Part 4, doubts have been expressed about the validity of traditional marketing planning in leisure mainly due to the volatility of the business environment.

Nevertheless, we did see that marketing planning is used by leisure organisations, and we examined some of the issues involved in implementing such an approach.

Part 5 was where we looked at a range of *individual sectors* within leisure. This was very illuminating, for we believe that in terms of the practice of marketing there are greater differences between the sectors of leisure than there are between countries. Three examples will illustrate this point as follows:

- The *benefits sought* by those taking part in countryside recreation in Greece and Britain are probably similar but the benefits sought by Greek people from a restaurant meal or a shopping trip are likely to be very different.

- *Methods of distribution* are usually similar within the same sector in different countries, although to different degrees. For instance, most package holidays in France are sold through travel agents just as they are in the UK. However, in neither country nor in any other European country do travel agents play a significant role in the sale of tickets to visitor attractions, for example.
- The *promotional techniques* used are often similar between organisations in different countries within one sector. Airlines and hotel chains advertise widely while most museums rarely do. Tour operators across Europe tend to rely heavily on glossy brochures or catalogues, while the main promotional literature of airlines tend to be their information-packed brochures.

That is not to say, however, that there are not significant differences between countries in terms of the marketing mix in some respect. All four elements of the mix are affected by a range of factors that can create major national differences in the framework within which the marketing mix is manipulated. Many of these factors are political and governmental and include laws on advertising, price controls and restrictions, or the lack of them, on the use of marketing intermediaries.

In *Part 6* we highlighted five topical issues within leisure marketing, namely competition, quality, ethics and social responsibility and marketing research. Even in a fashion-conscious area like marketing, these five areas stand out as being ones which are particularly exercising the attention of both academics and managers.

Two interesting points emerged from our examination of these topical issues, namely:

- *they are interrelated*, in other words, quality is a way of achieving competitive advantage and green issues are an ethical challenge for leisure organisations;
- *all of them put the customer at the centre*. Organisations are interested in quality, green issues and ethics because they think these things are important to their customers. Competitive advantage is seen in terms of offering customers more benefits or different benefits to those offered by competitors. Lastly, marketing research is seen as crucial because we need to know who the customer is and what they are looking for in order to be effective and successful in marketing terms.

In the last section, *Part 7*, we sought to place leisure in a wider context. This led to some interesting conclusions as follows:

- *marketing in leisure is very similar to that in many other industries*. There are few characteristics of marketing within leisure that are not also found in at least one or two other industries;
- *continents such as Europe are no longer – if they ever were – closed systems*. It is involved in a two-way relationship with the rest of the world. Indeed some might argue that globalisation is making the concept of Europe and Europeanisation obsolete before they have even become a reality.

General conclusion

Having drawn conclusions from each section of the book, it is now time to look at more general points that have arisen from the book.

First, *marketing in leisure is a very complex and diverse field*. This diversity reflects a number of factors including:

- the differing objectives of organisations in the public, private and voluntary sectors;
- the variations in markets in terms of their size and the extent to which they are free or regulated;
- the size and resources of organisations;
- whether the organisation operates on a purely domestic level or is transnational.

Leisure marketing is increasingly becoming a global pursuit. Leisure organisations are increasingly finding themselves developing standardised marketing programmes as a result of a series of factors as follows:

- the enlargement of the European Union and the creation of a Single Market;
- the activities of transnational companies;
- management training and international education programmes which are spreading similar messages about leisure marketing from Iceland to Italy, and from the Azores to Albania;
- technological developments which are making national boundaries less and less meaningful.

This last point has also to be put in the context of the steady march of globalisation. In the emerging world order, Europe's traditionally strong position in the world of leisure is clearly threatened by the rise of new geographical areas, most notably the countries of the Pacific Rim.

Whether or not the reader believes this book has achieved its original objectives, it has, hopefully, highlighted the fact that leisure marketing is a fascinating and increasingly sophisticated field which merits more study by academics. We have not as yet even started to dig under the surface of this deep and ever-changing field. Such studies should also seek to place marketing in the context of trends in marketing in other industries.

These conclusions are part of a continuum – they reflect trends that began some time ago and will carry on in some form into the future.

Part Nine

Case studies

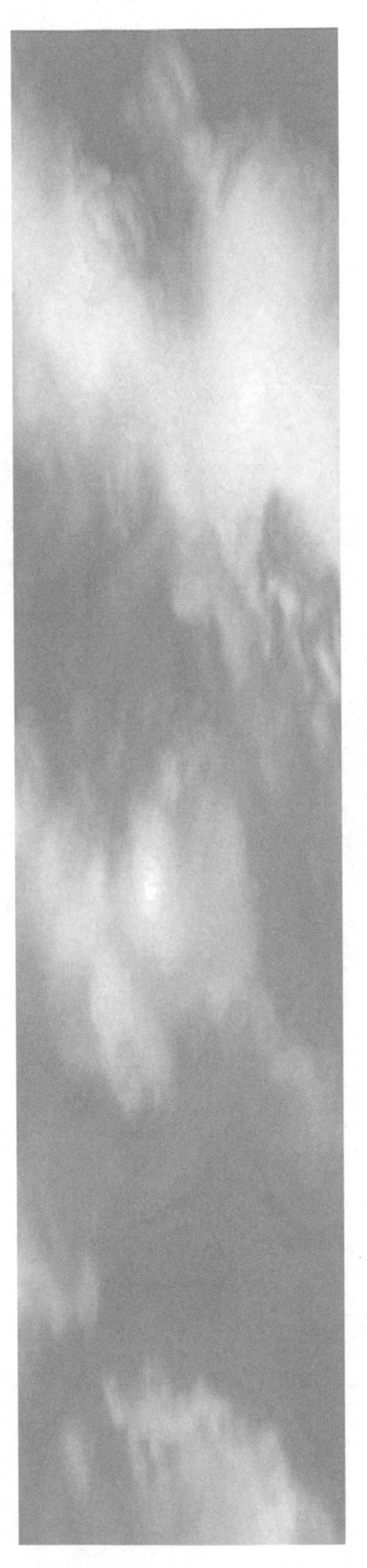

Introduction

This book has used copious examples and mini-case studies to illustrate points made in individual chapters.

However, the authors also believe that readers might find a small number of larger and broader case studies valuable.

The case studies which follow show how a number of leisure organisations currently carry out their marketing activities. These cases illustrate some interesting differences and similarities in marketing practice.

It should be noted that the material for these case studies was collected, largely during 2003 and early 2004. They must therefore be seen, like all published case studies, as snapshots in time, which will date quickly. Of course, this does not make the lessons that can be learned from them invalid.

Case study 1

The Victoria and Albert Museum (V&A)

The Victoria and Albert Museum is the National Museum of Art and Design in the UK, devoted to increasing the understanding and enjoyment of art, craft and design through its collections.

The V&A Museum was originally opened in 1852 as a Museum of Manufacturing, situated in the centre of London, in Marlborough House. The museum moved in 1857 to the fields of Brompton, where it became known as the 'South Kensington Museum'. In 1899 it was renamed 'The Victoria and Albert Museum' in honour of Queen Victoria and Prince Albert. Queen Victoria laid the new foundation stone of the new building in that year. It is not, however, a museum of Victoriana. The strength of the collections lie in the combination of great works of art with a broad range of objects of many different types and styles. It contains the national collections of furniture, silver, fashion, ceramics, glass, sculpture, watercolours, jewellery and photographs drawn from Britain and over the world, and spanning 4000 years.

Facilities

The V&A is situated in South Kensington. It is near to other major museums of London – The Science Museum and the Natural History Museum.

The main museum is situated on four floors and houses the core collections of sculpture, ceramics, furniture, glass, etc.

The guide book suggests that the visitor should walk around these galleries following colour-marked routes in the book.

The remainder of the exhibits are housed in the Henry Cole Wing, which is accessed from the ground floor. This wing of the museum houses Fine Art including an impressive collection of paintings by Constable, ornaments and English Miniatures. The museum also has the following facilities:

V&A shops

The shops sell products associated with the museum. The shop stocks an excellent range of quality gifts, stationery, books, ceramics and textiles. There is also a Crafts Council shop.

The new restaurant

Open:

Monday	12.00–17.00
Tuesday–Sunday	10.00–17.00

The restaurant is well furnished and provides an excellent range of food and drink. There is a jazz brunch on Sunday mornings.

V&A picture library

Offers pictures for loan including commercial loan.

Research services

The V&A offers an extensive range of research services and opinion services. These include:

- National Art Library – housing 1 million books – The National Collection of books on art
- Archive of Art and Design.

Study rooms

- the Print Room
- the Textile Study Room
- India and Southeast Asia Study Room
- Theatre Museum Archive and Study Room.

Branch museums

The museum has completed an extensive programme of structural repair and redecoration of Aspley House, which is situated at Hyde Park Corner. This was given to the nation in 1947 by the Seventh Duke of Wellington. It is a palatial London townhouse which houses a spectacular collection of paintings with works by Velázquez, Murillo, Correggio, Rubens and Van Duke.

The V&A also has branch museums at Bethnal Green and Russell Street, Covent Garden. Details of the branch museums are shown in Exhibit 1.1.

Exhibit 1.1

The branch museums of the V&A

1. **Bethnal Green Museum of Childhood, Bethnal Green, London**
   The national museum of childhood displays. Facilities include a shop and café. Free entrance
2. **Theatre Museum, Russell Street, Covent Garden**
   The national museum of the performing arts. Admission charges
3. **Aspley House 'Number 2 London' Hyde Park Corner, London**
   The home of the Duke of Wellington Fine collection of art, sculptures, furniture and personal relics of the Duke. Admission charges

Market position

The V&A is one of the major museums which are open to the public in London. It is also an example of a leading National Museum.

The V&A has recorded increasing numbers of visitors over a ten-year period. This growth started in 1994 when the V&A welcomed over 1.4 million visitors which was a large increase on figures for 1993.

Director of the V&A in 1995, Elizabeth Esteve-Coll, reported this success in the following statement:

> There is no doubt that members of the public are enjoying our exhibition programme, and, more importantly, are taking time to explore and get to know the permanent collections during their visits.

A profile of visitors for the period 2000–2002 is shown in Exhibit 1.2.

This exhibit shows some interesting facts in relation to the museum, as follows:

- A larger proportion of women (64 per cent in 2002) visit the museum compared to men (36 per cent in 2002). This is because of the theme of the museum which has a strong focus on design.
- The individual visitor tends to be older. This data does, of course, exclude school visits. This is probably due to the theme of the museum that attracts an older age group.
- The individual visitor comes from a high socio-economic group as a result of the theme of the museum.
- A large proportion of the individual visitors come from the UK, with a preponderance coming from London and the Southeast.
- A small percentage of the visitors came from North America (16 per cent in 2002) and Europe (12 per cent in 2002). Nine per cent of visitors came from the rest of the world in 2002.
- A large proportion of the visitors are from the white ethnic group (90 per cent in 2002).
- A large proportion of the visitors are repeat visitors who have been before (59 per cent in 2002). This shows the importance of relationship marketing in the museum strategy.

Financing the V&A museum

The museum is funded through a number of sources:

- *Government grant* broken down between building maintenance and acquisitions grants;
- *Donations from visitors* amount to over £1 m annually;
- *Development Office*: dealing with corporate Patrons and Benefactors of the V&A; raising sponsorship for the refurbishment of existing galleries and the creation of new galleries;
- *V&A Enterprises*: The trading arm of the V&A. V&AE's areas of activity include: running the two museum shops and a mail order catalogue service; licensing and development of new product lines based on objects in the collections; corporate entertaining through the Special Events Department using the V&A as a different and unusual place for corporate events such as dinners, receptions, recitals, private views of exhibitions and galleries, etc.;
- *Friends of the V&A*: The Friends – are very productive in raising funds for the museum, and pay an annual membership fee. All revenue generated is used to finance various projects

Exhibit 1.2

Summary	2000–2002	2002				2001			2002									
		Spring	Summer	Autumn	Ave	Spring	Summer	Autumn	Spring	May	June	July	Aug	Sept	Oct	Nov	Dec	Ave
GENDER	Male	33	33	34	**33**	33	33	42	39	43	27	40	29	43	39	28	36	**36**
	Female	64	66	64	**65**	67	66	57	61	57	73	60	71	57	61	72	64	**64**
AGE	To 15	9	9	9	**9**				5	11	8	5	19	6	8	5	3	**8**
	16–24	12	16	21	**16**	13	13	10	1	5	7	17	11	9	9	15	15	**10**
	25–34	15	18	19	**17**	15	24	17	11	26	11	19	11	20	22	19	14	**17**
	35–44	15	18	15	**16**	19	16	17	15	24	25	18	23	17	22	19	15	**20**
	45–54	15	18	15	**16**	23	17	24	22	16	18	27	24	24	21	18	24	**22**
	55–59	23	18	14	**18**				22	7	22	11	13	7	15	8	12	**13**
	60–64								7	10	6	1	9	7	7	9	9	**7**
	60+	7	7	10	**8**	31	28	32	21	13	12	8	10	16	6	11	10	**12**
SOCIO-ECONOMIC CLASS	AB	61	47	44	**51**	51	57	54	43	50	46	51	46	52	39	54	35	**46**
	C1	29	41	44	**38**	28	29	38	43	43	41	43	42	20	44	31	46	**39**
	C2	6	7	4	**6**	9	5	4	5	2	3	4	5	9	6	4	3	**5**
	DE	4	4	3	**4**	6	5	3	7	2	10	2	7	2	4	5	5	**5**
	Student	10	16	25	**17**	12	15	9	9	6	5	17	10	10	7	13	11	**10**
ORIGIN	London	32	24	37	**31**	29	34	33	27	28	29	28	26	29	31	25	32	**28**
	S/E	22	16	15	**18**	25	17	19	28	10	22	5	21	12	18	21	12	**17**
	Rest of UK	16	13	17	**15**	17	16	24	22	18	18	18	17	13	21	18	17	**18**
	Europe	10	13	8	**10**	9	11	8	10	7	8	17	15	9	14	10	16	**12**
	N.America	15	24	20	**20**	16	14	9	10	26	16	22	12	17	10	12	15	**16**
	Rest of World	3	12	6	**7**	5	7	4	3	12	8	11	9	16	7	7	6	**9**
ETHNICITY	White								93	94	88	89	93	89	88	93	83	**90**
	Mixed								1	1	1	4	2	1	2	1	1	**2**
	Asian								0	2	7	2	2	6	0	1	3	**3**
	Black								1	0	0	0	0	0	0	1	1	**0**
	Chinese								0	1	1	1	0	3	3	0	0	**1**
	Other								2	3	2	4	2	1	6	2	8	**2**
	Refused								2	0	1	1	0	1	1	2	5	**1**
REPEAT	First visit	34	52	45	**44**	34	39	27	35	41	29	57	50	45	45	29	36	**40**
	Been Before	65	48	55	**56**	66	61	73	65	59	71	43	50	55	55	63	64	**59**

Source: Mori Visitor Profile. The Victoria and Albert Museum

such as gallery improvements. Benefits of being a Friend include private viewings of exhibitions, a newsletter three times a year, access to Late View, exclusive use of a Friends Room and free access to all exhibitions;

- *International and American Friends of the V&A*: a new charity set up in 1993 to further work done by the UK Friends.

Current marketing issues

> Museums will stand or fall not only by their competence to care for collections, but by their ability to care for people. In other words, they need to be market-oriented if they are to survive.
>
> Cossons (1985)

The aim of the marketing and public relations department of the Victoria and Albert Museum is to position the V&A as the natural museum of choice for leisure, education and association in support of its mission.

The museum is faced with competition from all leisure activities, but must maintain an increasing annual visitor number. It is also being faced with more financial constraints, and is seeking to increase revenue wherever possible. The main issues which are facing the museum are therefore common to other visitor attractions.

The V&A building is a Grade 1 listed building. One of the main strategic issues facing the museum is how to make the building attractive to visitors, and incorporate services which will not alter the fabric of the building.

High profile public relations campaigns are an essential part of the marketing campaign. The press office are proactive, developing relationships with a range of media in support of the press strategies.

The main objectives of the current Marketing and PR are shown in Exhibit 1.3.

These objectives were derived after considering the strategic vision of the museum.

Build awareness, understanding, and influence

The marketing department of the V&A ensures that the museum has a high profile. This assures that people know about the museum and want to do something about it. This means that visitors continue to come. It also helps to support relationships with business contacts who provide an important source of sponsorship.

The museum also has strong links with the tourism and attractions industry. It has a close relationship with bodies such as the LTB (London Tourist Board), London First and VB (Visit Britain).

The V&A considers itself to be a *leisure attraction* and uses the marketing techniques which have been developed in the private-sector service industries.

It is important that media coverage of the museum is always achieved, particularly when the excellence of research, education, sponsorship, conservation and scientific development can be covered.

An example of an educational development which the V&A used to gain media coverage was the work that the museum staff have completed with teachers to develop the National Curriculum. Scientific breakthroughs can also offer the V&A the opportunity for press coverage. The V&A Science staff, for example, have worked with scientists from the neighbouring Imperial College in the area of glass conservation and have made major scientific advancements.

Special events give the V&A a particular opportunity for raising the profile of the museum. The hosting of prestigious conferences and of exhibitions are examples of special events which can be used to give the museum a media coverage.

Exhibit 1.3

Main objectives of the marketing and PR plan

1. Build Awareness, Understanding and Influence;
2. Increase Visitor Numbers;
3. Increase Revenue;
4. Improve Visitor Experience through Information.

The reopening of Aspley House to the public also gave the V&A the opportunity to target media coverage.

Exhibitions and Gallery openings provide the largest opportunity for media coverage.

The V&A plans a balanced programme of large and small, scholarly and popular exhibitions to attract a broad range of audiences, and to enhance the visitors' understanding of the museum's collections. Exhibitions planned for the next two years include:

Vivienne Westwood
Bill Brandt
Exotic Encounters: the meeting of Asia and Europe 1500–1800
International Arts and Crafts
Diane Arbus

Admission and opening Hours

Admission to the Victoria and Albert Museum is FREE. There is a charge for major exhibitions.

Opening hours
10.00–17.45 daily (closed 24, 25, 26 December)
10.00–22.00 Wednesdays and the last Friday of the month (except December)

Increasing visitor numbers

It is very important that the museum continues to increase the visitor numbers each year. There are various methods which the museum can use to help the continued increase in visitor numbers, including effective market segmentation and targeting. The museum carries out quantitative market research at the main museum and during special exhibitions to identify a profile of visitors.

The press officers who work within the marketing department have the job of maintaining a strong, open and positive relationship with the press. The majority of this work is carried out in the UK, but the press officers are also responsible for communicating with the overseas press.

Special exhibitions are often promoted overseas. The Wedgwood exhibition, for example, which took place in 1995 was launched in France. The V&A sent a Japanese speaking press officer to support a touring exhibition of Japan and to promote the V&A in London as a tourist attraction.

Work on publicity leaflets and visitor services must continue on an ongoing basis to encourage increased numbers of visitors. This material should enable the museum to develop a strong image. The use of the V&A logo, for example, in all publicity material, is a very important aspect of this work. The visitor's first impression of the museum should be favourable. The design of information desks and the training of front-line staff in this area is an ongoing marketing activity.

The museum marketing department also identifies key activities which are developed each year. This can be in the form of a joint marketing activity with other museums. The development of overseas markets for a major museum is a key area of marketing activity. The V&A is busy developing the Japanese and American markets.

The main ways that the V&A is increasing visitor numbers can be summarised as:

- Effective targeting and planning;
- Effective advertising and promotional campaigns;
- The development of new propositions.

Specific campaigns are devised for particular exhibitions. These campaigns include leaflets, promotions and ticket offers. Each exhibition will have a different market segment. An exhibition or fashion, such as the Vivienne Westwood exhibition, which is due to take place in 2004 has a younger audience target, for example, than a more traditional exhibition such as the International Arts and Crafts exhibition scheduled for 2005.

The marketing department also liaises with the *Development Department* and the *Education Department*. The Development Department has the job of financing major developments at the exhibition and obtaining major sources of sponsorship.

The Education Department is responsible for development School and academic links. It is heavily involved in developing community education programmes.

The marketing department has also used sales promotion techniques to increase visitor numbers. The *jazz brunch*, for example, was so successful as an initial sales promotion when the V&A was opened on a Sunday morning that it has remained as a permanent fixture. Exhibit 1.4 shows the key market segment that the V&A is attracting.

Exhibit 1.4

Key market segments for the V&A

1. Local and regional residents living near the museum;
2. National visitors who are visiting London on a day trip, a short or longer break;
3. Overseas visitors travelling on their own;
4. Overseas visitors travelling in a group, usually in association with a package company.

Increasing revenue

The V&A marketing aim is to increase revenue from donations and exhibition revenue. This work has been concentrated in a number of areas, including:

- focusing on special exhibitions and therefore encouraging secondary spend in café/restaurant and shop;
- working to increase donation levels;
- working in partnership with marketing and travel operations.

In addition, the PR function helps support the wider museum aim of increasing sponsorship.

Improve visitor experience through information

The V&A aims to continually improve the levels of information and service which are available in the museum. This includes improvements to desks, signposting and ancillary services such as the restaurants.

The V&A has developed a prominent presence in London with the use of leaflets and posters. This is very important because the location of the museum, which is out of the main tourist area, means that it has to attract visitors from the centre of London.

The V&A carries out extensive market research with visitors to the museum and to the special exhibitions so that improvements can be made. The front of house service staff at the museum have all been trained in customer care techniques. Every two months, all the areas dealing with visitors meet in the 'Visitor Services Group' including security staff, restaurant, education department, desk staff, buildings maintenance and cleaning staff, and marketing department.

Other activities

Friends of the V&A

Friends of the V&A is an organisation which has been set up to support the work of the museum. Friends give their time in voluntary work and financially support a wide range of projects including the purchase of objects, refurbishment of galleries and grants for research.

Friends and Patrons of the V&A and their guests can attend special events including late viewing in the museum and late lectures. Drinks and buffet suppers are also served in the restaurant to accompany these events.

Special events

The V&A is housed in a magnificent Victorian building with remarkable rooms of the period. This has allowed the museum to offer clients the opportunity of entertaining in the heart of London.

The V&A can cater for receptions, dinners, lunches, conferences and presentations of up to 700 guests. Events can be booked in a number of key locations in the museum including The Dome, which is the museum's resplendent main entrance, and The Gamble Room and the Morris Room, which is smaller and elegant. The Pirelli Garden can also be used for entertaining and can be floodlit at night.

One of the most spectacular corporate venues in the country was opened in June 1995 as a result of Apsley House reopening. Apsley House can be booked as a corporate venue.

Conclusion

The Victoria and Albert Museum is one of the national monuments in the UK. The marketing activity carried out by the museum is critical for the success and development of the museum in the future.

Discussion points and essay questions

1. Evaluate the implications of the 2002 visitor profile data for future promotional strategies that might be undertaken by the Victoria and Albert Museum.
2. Identify the main competitors for the Victoria and Albert Museum and discuss how it might seek to gain competitive advantage over these competitors.
3. Discuss the challenges which the Victoria and Albert Museum will face from future changes in the macroenvironment.

Case study 2

Disneyland Resort, Paris: The marketing mix

After a difficult beginning, Disneyland Resort, Paris, has consolidated its position in recent years as the leading tourist attraction in Europe. This is partly the result of its famous brand name, of course, but it is also due to the sophisticated, well-funded marketing activities undertaken by Disneyland Resort, Paris. These activities involve the effective manipulation of the marketing mix or Four Ps; in this case study we will explore the marketing mix of Disneyland Resort, Paris, in a little detail.

Product

The product is multifaceted to appeal to different markets and tastes. Its main components are as follows:

- *Disneyland Park*, the original core of the attraction and the part based on the classic Disney characters. It has a number of themed elements including Main Street USA, Fantasyland, Frontier Land, Adventure Land and Discovery Land. This park is made up of rides including exciting 'white knuckle' rides such as Big Thunder Mountain.
- *Walt Disney Studios® Park*, a cinema, animation and television themed park with four areas, namely Front Lot, Animation Courtyard®, Production Courtyard® and Back Lot. This park is full of special effects as well as rides.
- *Major spectacles* on site such as *'The Lion King Show'* and the *'Fantillusion® Parade'*.
- A programme of *special events and festivals* all year round, including Disney character–based events such as the Disney Cinema Parade, together with seasonal events such as the Halloween Festival.
- Opportunities, at extra cost, to *meet Disney characters* and even share a meal with them.
- *Disney Village*, a complex of shops, shows and catering outlets that is open day and night.
- *Seven themed Disney Hotels*, aimed at different markets. They range from the Davy Crockett Ranch with its 'cabins' which are targeted at self-caterers to the luxury of the full service Disneyland® hotel.
- Special *facilities for families with children* such as baby care centres, play areas and push chair hire.
- *Services for visitors with special needs* including those with mobility problems or visual impairments.
- *Golf Disney*, a 27-hole golf course near the Park.
- *Conference facilities* for business groups, under the brand name of 'Business Solutions'.

The attraction has different opening times at different times of the year. For example, in most of July and August, Disneyland Park opened from 9.00 am–11.00 pm in 2004, whereas it closed by 8.00 pm in June 2004.

As well as its own attractions, Disneyland® Resort, Paris, works with partners to promote other attractions that help reinforce its own appeal. In 2004 these other attractions included:

- the Manchester United Soccer School, football coaching services for youngsters aged between 7 and 14;
- Sea Life branded Aquarium Val d'Europe;
- La Vallée outlet-shopping 'village' selling famous brands at discounted prices;
- Themed family-oriented hotels such as the Movenpick Dream Castle Hotel;
- Excursions from the resort to Paris and Paris-discounted transport cards;
- Hertz car hire at the Disneyland® Resort, Paris, train/RER station.

Disneyland® Resort, Paris, is also keen not only to add new attractions each year to encourage first-time visitors, but also to persuade previous visitors to make another visit. For example, the Summer 2004 brochure had, on its cover, a headline note that there was a new Lion King show. However, it is interesting that other than this new feature, the brochure contained no news of other 'new' attractions at the resort.

Finally, the owners are constantly including new schemes to reduce the problem of queuing, such as the Fastpass® ticket.

Price

The Summer 2004 Official Holiday Brochure of Disneyland® Resort, Paris, showed that the owners are keen to sell 'added value' packages as well as park entrance tickets. A range of inclusive packages were on offer in summer 2004, including:

- hotel packages including two-nights accommodation with breakfast and a three-day park pass based on Disney-owned accommodation, ranging from £108 to £698 per adult depending on how many adults are travelling and when they are visiting;
- packages of a similar duration at non-Disney hotels around the resort ranged in summer 2004 from £102 to £782;
- transport-inclusive passes including the hotel/park entrance ticket as above, plus transport from the UK, for example.

In Disney-owned hotels, the prices for this ranged as follows:

- £243–1010 on Eurostar;
- £196–963, flights with Air France;
- £132–992, self-drive, via Dover-Calais ferry.

In addition, a late-booking fee of £25 was applied to all reservations made within seven days of the departure date.

The resort obviously offers a range of other services for which an extra payment is required, notably:

- Breakfasts with Disney characters which ranged from £12 for adults and £8 for children to £18 and £10 respectively.
- Pre-booked meal options, ranging from £14–19 per adult and £7 for children.

For pricing purposes, Disney classified children as being from three- to eleven-years old. In hotel-only packages, children paid from a standard £57 for the package regardless of the hotel used. These inclusive children's prices were a standard £147 regardless of the hotel used.

Place

Disneyland® Resort, Paris, distributes its products in a number of ways via travel agents, tour operators and its own website.

In its brochure it distributes its park product by working in partnership with intermediaries, including:

- local, non-Disney-owned hotels
- professional transport carriers such as Eurostar, P&O Ferries and Air France.

Their brochure encourages prospective visitors to contact their local travel agent but it also provides details of their website and the contact details for their telesales call centre, which is staffed seven days a week.

Promotion

Disneyland® Resort, Paris, obviously makes great use of a range of promotional techniques to sell itself, ranging from press and television advertising to press and public relations, and direct selling to group organisers and travel agents.

However, in its Official Holiday Brochure for Summer 2004, it also featured a number of special offers which appeared to have three main objectives, namely:

- to encourage people to book in advance, and to book early
- to increase visitor spending
- to attract off-peak season business.

Some examples of the offers may illustrate this as follows:

(i) offering four nights for the price of three for weeks in April to July and September, but not in the peak month of August;
(ii) hotel upgrades, guaranteed for those booking for June and July by 1 April 2004;
(iii) a 15 per cent discount on 'Buffalo Bill' Wild West Show, including a meal.

Each offer carries conditions as one might expect, although they are generally not too restrictive.

In addition, Disneyland® Resort, Paris, Hotel also offers special joint promotions with certain partners. For example, the Summer 2004 Official Holiday Brochure contains details of the 'Visa Privilege Programme' in collaboration with Visa credit cards. If customers used their Visa Platinum (the highest level available) credit card to pay for their Disneyland® Resort Package, they received a voucher entitling them to discounts at the Disneyland® Resort. However, the offer was only available at the more up-scale Disneyland® Resort Hotels.

At the same time, Disneyland® Resort, Paris, promotes itself in partnership with other well-known brands from Europe and the USA. Its 2004 Official Holiday Brochure, for instance, noted its 'official partners' as Coca-Cola, Esso, France Telecom, Hambro, Hertz, DBM, Kelloggs, Kodak, McDonald's, Nestlé, Vauxhall and Visa.

The brochure itself is a high quality production with the emphasis on photographs showing families enjoying the resort and park together. Interestingly, but not usually for tourism brochures in Europe, most families had only one or two children and the families were all white with no people of any other ethnic origin featured.

Finally, the brochure was detailed and clearly written and all conditions/restrictions of prices and special offers were clearly highlighted.

Conclusion

Disneyland® Resort, Paris, is a very professionally marketed, multifaceted product at the higher end of the market, price-wise. Its 2004 Official Holiday Brochure offered a wide range of packages for prospective visitors, together with many special offers. It also emphasised the resort partnerships with other leading brands, from credit card companies to airlines.

Discussion points and essay questions

1. Compare and contrast the marketing of Disneyland® Resort, Paris, with that of a major visitor attraction in your country, noting the differences.
2. Critically evaluate the potential benefits for Disneyland® Resort, Paris, of its partnerships with brands such as Visa, Vauxhall, Kodak and France Telecom.
3. Discuss the relative importance of each of the 4 Ps – product, price, place and promotion in the marketing of Disneyland® Resort, Paris.

Exercise

Select a major visitor attraction in your own country. For your chosen attraction you should produce a short report, highlighting how it could 'add value' to its core product in the way that Disneyland® Resort, Paris, does.

Case study 3
Modern art museums

In the world of leisure attractions, it seems that few have reached the scale and sophistication in marketing as that practised by many modern art museums. Public interest in recent years seems to have grown enormously around the world with new museums opening all the time and plenty of visitors wanting to visit them. In this case study, we will look at some of the leading 'brands' in the modern art museum sector, for there are now several such powerful brands.

1. *Guggenheim Museums*
   This is perhaps the world's leading brand of art museums with a history which dates back to the late 1930s. The story of this phenomenon in the art world is outlined in the following extract from one of the Guggenheim Museum's websites.

> The Guggenheim Museum began with the vision of Solomon R. Guggenheim, heir to an American mining fortune and an enthusiastic patron of the arts. In 1929, Guggenheim enlisted the guidance of German baroness Hilla Rebay, an advocate of innovative and experimental art, and was able to amass a major collection of contemporary European painting. Many of the abstract paintings in this collection became available for public view in 1939 when Guggenheim created the Museum of Non-Objective Painting, housed in a former automobile showroom in New York City. Plans for a permanent home for the collection began in 1943 and in 1959 the renamed Solomon R. Guggenheim Museum opened in the landmark Frank Lloyd Wright building on Fifth Avenue at 89th Street.
>
> Under the leadership of museum directors James Johnson Sweeney, Thomas Messer, and Thomas Krens, the collection has broadened to encompass myriad movements of Modern and contemporary art in virtually every medium. The Solomon R. Guggenheim Foundation now incorporates the important collections of several discerning patrons, including the 20th-century paintings and sculpture owned by Peggy Guggenheim, niece of Solomon R. Guggenheim; the Justin K Thannhauser collection of Impressionist, Post-Impressionist, and School of Paris masterpieces; and Guiseppe Panza di Biumo's outstanding group of Minimal and Conceptual artworks. As distinctive as the art itself – indeed, works of art themselves – are the buildings designed to house it. The name Guggenheim has become synonymous with the innovative structures by Frank Lloyd Wright in New York, by Frank O. Gehry in Bilbao, and by Rem Koolhaas in Las Vegas. Now an international constellation of museums in New York, Venice, Bilbao, Berlin, and now Las Vegas, the Guggenheim Museum brings its extraordinary collections to a worldwide audience.
>
> www.guggenheimlasvegas

Each Guggenheim has its own distinctive character and style.

The Venice museum is known as the Peggy Guggenheim Museum and is located in a historic canalside building. It has a programme of temporary exhibitions and has a large shop, which is next door to the main museum. This shop, in addition to the normal range of souvenirs, sells copies of the sunglasses and shoes which Peggy Guggenheim used to wear.

The museum is open six days a week and opens one night a week until 10.00 pm in the summer. Admissions in 2003 cost 8 Euros per adult but with free entry being offered to members of a number of bodies including Members of the Guggenheim Museum Organisation and the Freccia Alata Club of Alitalia, for example. The museum café is owned by a famous local restaurant, the 'Ai Gondolier'.

The museum building was quite small, but in 2003 a new building was opened to increase the size of the museum, details of which are included in the following extract from the museum's website.

> The expansion of the Peggy Guggenheim collection on the site of Palazzo Venier dei Leioni makes important progress this fall with the opening of a converted property on the southeast corner, at number 704 Dorsoduro, overlooking the Rio delle Torreselle.
>
> Growing attendance and manifold exhibitions, events and programmes [two or more temporary exhibitions per year, didactic activities for children, programmes for members, garden concerts, etc.] have made compelling the need to increase public space and improve visitor services at the Peggy Guggenheim Collection. The new property brings new benefits and facilities: a sculpture court [166. sq.m], an entrance foyer and checkroom facilities, a new museum shop [two rooms], exhibition space [100 sq.m.], public bathrooms [8] and improved wheelchair access.
>
> The new property provides access to the museum via a single large foyer [replacing the two small entrances currently operative], with furnishings designed and constructed by **Progretto Lissone**, which have the capacity to process the museum's 300,000 visitors per annum. The opening of the new shop enables the former shop to be converted for temporary exhibition use. Two new exhibition galleries are linked to the existing spaces and make possible larger exhibitions or concurrent small-and medium-sized exhibitions. The opening of the new entrance has seen the introduction of electronic ticketing and of a new generation of audioguides provided by 'acoustiguide'. The additional restrooms better serve the museum's visitors who have more than doubled in number over the past ten years [currently ca. 300,000 visitors per year] and facilitate access for visitors in wheelchairs.
>
> www.guggenheim-venice.it

In 1997, the Guggenheim Foundation opened a museum in Bilbao, Spain, in a joint venture with the Basque authorities to help rejuvenate the city. Horner and Swarbrooke have identified some of the key features of this museum, as follows:

- Its opening has helped Spain as a whole to further its strategy of developing other forms of tourism so as to reduce its dependence on mass market coastal tourism.
- The new museum has put Bilbao on the international tourist map as a short break destination for cultural tourists.
- The museum has helped improve the image of the city which was previously seen as a rather economically depressed and unattractive place.
- The development of the Guggenheim is an example of a partnership between the regional government of an area with a distinctive culture and an international charitable foundation.
- The motivation for attracting the Guggenheim Museum to Bilbao was clearly wider than just the desire to develop tourism in the city. It was also about projecting an image of a modern, dynamic region to the wider world.
- The design of the museum was deliberately intended to be unforgettable, to make a bold artistic statement about both the Guggenheim Foundation and the city of Bilbao.
- The museum follows the fashion of many such institutions by placing a great emphasis on income from retailing and on merchandising in general.
- As the museum evolves, it will be interesting to see what percentage of the visitors are local people and how these local people view the museum.
- It will be interesting to see how visitor numbers develop over time and to see if the Guggenheim will be able to continue to attract first-time visitors.
- It will also be fascinating to find out the extent to which the museum brings benefits to the city as a whole or whether it will remain an isolated phenomena.
- The museum appears to have been successful in spite of being isolated in a region which has experienced terrorist attacks over a period of time.
- Much of the success of the museum probably stems from the fact that it has a famous 'brand' name that is world renowned in the art museum world.
- The success is also partly due to the fact that the Guggenheim organisation is well funded and highly experienced in managing museums.

Horner and Swarbrooke, 2004

Perhaps the most innovative museum bearing the Guggenheim name is the one located in Las Vegas. This is interesting from two points of view, namely:

(i) it is located within a hotel, the Venetian Resort Hotel-Casino
(ii) it is a joint venture with the world famous Hermitage Museum in St Petersburg in Russia, and it displays some works from this great collection.

However, in 2003 the main Guggenheim museum was closed and only the 'Jewel Box' Guggenheim-Heritage Exhibition remains although this has been a success.

The Guggenheim museums are an excellent example of a major American phenomenon, well-endowed charity foundation owning and running major museums, but it is unusual in having exported its 'brand' to Europe.

2. *Tate Galleries, UK*

There are four Tate Galleries in the UK, as follows:

(i) Tate Britain, the national gallery of British Art over the past 500 years
(ii) Tate Modern, a modern and contemporary art gallery in London
(iii) Tate Liverpool, the largest modern art museum outside London
(iv) Tate St Ives, a museum of modern and contemporary art in a Cornish coastal town which is famous for its connections with British sculpture.

All Tate galleries are free due to the subsidies they receive from the UK government, but donations are accepted and indeed welcomed. The galleries offer a good education service and they all endeavour to earn more from their retail and catering activities. They are also keen to attract corporate hospitality events because of the income they generate.

3. *Museum of Modern Art (MOMA), New York*

Some argue that New York's Museum of Modern Art, with its 'MOMA' brand, created in 1929, is the foremost modern art museum in the world. It is a charitable educational that is committed to making modern art accessible to the population.

The entrance fee for visitors in 2003 was US$12, but it was free for children, and on Sundays, in the evening, the museum let people enter on a 'pay what you wish' basis. Unlike other museums, MOMA does not promote its café very strongly, although it did promote, on its website, its online retailing operation. Website information on the museum was available in late 2003 in English, French, Italian, Spanish, Japanese, German, Chinese and Korean but its audio tour was only available in English. MOMA also promoted its education service on its website together with its publications and research reviews. Overall, it seems less commercially minded and more educationally focused than the Tate and Guggenheim museums.

4. *Centre Pompidou, Paris*

This pioneering modern art centre is now over 30-years old although it underwent a major refurbishment for the millennium. A state project, it was named after the president of France, at that time a lover of modern art and culture. The Pompidou Centre is popular with Parisiens as well as tourists and is open between ten and eleven hours every day except Tuesday. The Centre places a great emphasis on encouraging children to appreciate art, with a special Children's Gallery, aimed at young people visiting with schools or their parents. It runs a lot of workshops and events for both adults and children. The dramatic building itself remains a symbol of Paris around the world.

Conclusion

Modern art museums are very popular today and are the cornerstone of the tourism product in many countries, particularly in the USA and Europe. They are often run by rich private charitable foundations or governments, and are becoming increasingly commercialised as they seek to increase their income to support their activities. It remains to be seen if this phenomenon will be a passing fashion or become a permanent feature of the leisure market.

These examples, together with the other leading modern art museums such as the Guggenheim Museum in Lisbon, seem to suggest that modern art museums today tend to:

- be located in the USA and Europe primarily;
- be owned by charitable foundations in the USA, while in Europe, the government often owns, or at least funds, most of these museums;
- place emphasis on earning extra income from retailing and catering;

- arrange temporary exhibits at these museums which can become major attractions for tourists in the cities where they are located;
- not only appeal to a range of age groups, but also place a great emphasis on education visits by school children.

Discussion points and questions

1. Discuss the advantages and disadvantages of modern art museums being owned by private charitable foundations and governments, respectively.
2. Discuss the reasons why you believe modern art museums have become so popular in recent years.
3. Discuss why you think there are relatively few modern art museums currently in Asia, South America and Africa.

Exercise

Access the website of a range of modern art museums around the world. You should then produce a report highlighting the differences between your selected museums in terms of product and price.

Case study 4

Health, leisure and tourism marketing

There is no doubt that more people than ever before are concerned about their health, most notably in the so-called developed countries. This concern manifests itself in everyday life in terms of everything from leisure club membership to the purchase of diet food and drink products.

However, in recent years, the tourism industry has recognised the growing potential of this interest in health as a potentially lucrative market to be exploited.

In this case study, we will explore the links between health, leisure and tourism by looking at:

- the health and beauty market in the UK;
- spa hotels around the world.

Health and leisure: the health and beauty market in the UK

The health and beauty market is highly developed in the UK, by international standards. An interesting report on this subject published by Mintel in 2003 analysed both the supply and the demand side of this market. From this report and the author's own research come some interesting points, notably:

(i) In the UK the concern is less with 'serious' medical health matters than with the 'softer' question of 'health and beauty'. This is in contrast with other countries, particularly the former Communist countries of Eastern Europe.

(ii) The market is generally seen to be predominantly female but there is a belief that demand for health and beauty will grow amongst men in the future.

(iii) Some elements of the market are highly seasonal, such as the desire to look good in time for Christmas and summer holidays.

(iv) In the UK market, at least, attention to health are linked closely to broader aspects of a person's personal appearance. This can include looking younger than one's age.

(v) While concerns over health are thought to be growing, a recent survey by TGI showed some interesting results, as shown in Exhibit 4.1.

According to the survey, if we look at those who 'definitely agree' with these statements, male and female interest in health issues seems actually to have fallen a little between 1998 and 2002. At the same time in any event, interest is not particularly high, with only 14 per cent of women (15 per cent of men) definitely agreeing with the statement that 'I make sure I take regular exercise'.

(vi) Nevertheless, Mintel found that at the beginning of 2003 there were a number of specialist chains meeting the needs of the UK health and beauty at the local beauty salons and health and fitness clubs. Some of these were controlled by large companies which own chains of units such as Body Care International with over 100 'Tanning Shops' and Fitness First plc and the Esporta Group Ltd. Likewise, major brand names from other industries are entering the health market, such as Virgin.

(vii) Hotels also play a large role in the UK health and beauty market, not only through services offered to overnight guests, but also through their leisure clubs which are open to local people to join. A good example of this phenomenon are the 'Living Well' clubs found in Hilton Hotels in the UK. In recent years, health and beauty facilities have become a major way in which hotel chains have sought to achieve an advantage over their competitors.

(viii) The UK has also developed a rather different form of hotel-based health and beauty concept than any other countries, namely the 'health farm'. These tend to combine beauty treatments and pampering with exercise and dieting. Some major brand names in this field include Champneys and Ragdale Hall.

(ix) In recent years, the hotels with leisure clubs and the 'health farms' have tried to evolve and rebrand themselves as 'hydros' or 'spas', the latter a term used widely around the world.

Exhibit 4.1

Trends in attitudes towards health, personal appearance and gender, 1998 and 2002 (Base: adults aged 15+)

Women	**1998**	**2002**
Definitely agree	%	%
It is important to keep looking young	15.1	13.8
It is important to me to look well dressed	18.3	18.7
Most of the time I am trying to lose weight	14.8	14.0
I should do a lot more about my health	15.9	12.7
I always think of the calories in what I eat	7.1	6.4
I make sure I take regular exercise	14.1	14.0
Men		
It is important to keep looking young	9.9	8.7
It is important to me to look well dressed	14.9	16.3
Most of the time I am trying to lose weight	6.0	4.9
I should do a lot more about my health	14.1	12.0
I always think of the calories in what I eat	3.2	3.1
I make sure I take regular exercise	15.6	14.8

(*Source*: TGI/Mintel, 2003)

(x) This is a very fashion-conscious market where treatments and therapies, together with health clubs and beauty parlours, come in and out of fashion.

Health and tourism: spa hotels and the world

It would be wrong to suggest that health-based tourism is a new phenomenon, for visiting spas, bathing for medicinal reasons, is a practice that dates back several centuries, in Europe at least.

However, the links between health and tourism today are numerous and varied, and include:

- trips taken to other countries for surgery and medical treatment to cure illness or disease;
- trips taken to other countries for cosmetic surgery;
- longer-term trips to mountain or seaside sanitoria to improve the health of patients suffering from illness exacerbated or caused by environmental problems in their own home area;
- trips designed to tackle stress and thus improve the mental and psychological health of the traveller;
- general health and beauty trips.

The concept of spas is an old one, which began with mineral waters emerging from the earth, which were meant to have beneficial effects on health. These grew into resorts where visitors came not only for health treatments but also for a good social life, entertainment and good living. In some countries, spas like these are still seen as an essential part of state health care, often being subsidised by the government and staffed by qualified medical personnel.

However, in recent years the concept of the 'spa' has also been adopted by hotels and resort complexes in many countries which have endeavoured to become like spa resorts, but on one site only and owned by one organisation only.

These spa hotels and resorts come in a variety of forms. Below, the authors offer descriptions of several of them, taken from the website of a consortium called 'Great Hotels of the World' in late 2003.

Chiva-Som International Health Resort

Chiva-Som, or 'haven of life', is situated in 2.8 hectares on the exclusive royal beach of Hua Hin. Its philosophy is to achieve harmony between the mind, body and spirit with spa treatments that are complemented by holistic and fitness treatments. The ravishing retreat is a cluster of Thai-inspired guest pavilions and rooms surrounded by waterfalls, lakes and tropical gardens, overlooking the Gulf of Thailand. Requests can be made for non-allergenic pillows or flower arrangements.

Chiva-Som presents gourmet cuisine created by a unique team of Thai and international master chefs. All the delicious, low-calorie Asian and western specialities are prepared with fresh, wholesome produce from the resort's own organic herb, fruit and vegetable gardens.

Chiva-Som's ultra modern spa boasts over 100 traditional and alternative therapies as well as luxurious beauty treatments that utilise essential oils, Thai herbs, flowers and botanicals. There are many fitness activities including t'ai chi, yoga, pilates, health and beauty workshops and holistic programmes that incorporate forms of traditional Chinese medicine. Diverse facilities include a jacuzzi, aquatic therapy pool, exercise pool, sauna, flotation room, multi-level steam room and 42 treatment rooms including outdoor massage pavilions, Thai massage pavilions, beauty rooms and five for consultations. An initial Health and Wellness consultation with a dedicated Chiva-Som professional is available to guests to help them select and design a personalised treatments programme.

The new Chiva-Som Spa Suite – This suite has been designed so that each person can experience the treatments they ideally need whilst still enjoying the Chiva-Som experience together. Simultaneously, one partner could experience a Thai Fruit Wrap whilst beside them their partner is experiencing a Thai Honey Glow. A range of refreshments including lemongrass tea, a whole menu of juices and teas, as well as a light meal may well be served to guests whilst they are totally indulged in such an intimate setting. A wide choice of music is also privately controlled within the suite, allowing couples to personalise their environment whilst relaxing and enjoying their treatments.

Begawan Giri Estate

Begawan Giri Estate is a secluded, luxury resort set amidst the serenity of Bali's famed rice fields, lush tropical greenery and mist-shrouded mountains. Spread across eight hectares of landscaped gardens are the property's five elegant residences, comprising 22 well-appointed suites, named after the elements of fire, wind, water, forest and earth. Villas occupy the western slop of the property and feature their own swimming pools, kitchen, living and dining areas. A personal butler and his/her team serve every residence. An eight-to-one staff-to-guest ration assures you of impeccable service, warm and unhurried.

The Source, Begawan Giri Estate's unique health spa, is no ordinary spa. Here, you have the natural benefits of tropical gardens, mountain air and holy spring waters. The spa maintains a holistic approach to physical and spiritual wellbeing. Body treatments such as massages, skin scrubs and other rituals are founded on ancient or traditional methods and use natural ingredients in oils, lotions and herbal preparations. You can enjoy a Balinese massage with aromatic oils, or exotic treatments such as Javanese Mandi Lulur and Bali Boreh Spice. The Source further appeals to the senses with a selection of baths and wraps created from volcanic clays, sea salts, flowers and indigenous plants. Experienced staff are on hand to pamper guests thoroughly, but the focus remains on simplicity, balance and a return to nature. Healing retreats centred around The Source are also available.

Kumarakom Lake Resort

The Spa – Kerala has a rich tradition in Ayurveda, a traditional Indian system of holistic and natural healing that has evolved over the past 5000 years. Ayurveda states that diseases are caused by disturbances in one's equilibrium, which is maintained by three dishas, Vata, Pitha and Kapha. Treatment is administered to correct the imbalanced dosha. Kumarakom's Ayurvedic health centre, Ayurmana, offers a variety of rejuvenation and healing packages. Consult the house physician to gain relief from conditions such as high blood pressure, arthritis, obesity, stress, asthma and migraine. Or, indulge in one of the health and beauty treatments such as an Essence of Earth facial. Select from a choice of sandal, basil, honey, aloe, almond, and citrus. The signature Ayurvedic Facial involves the use of a combination of fruits and rare herbs to enhance the complexion.

Little Palm Island Resort and Spa

Little Palm Island Resort and Spa is the perfect destination for those seeking a combination of tropical surroundings, deluxe accommodations, the finest cuisine and a world-class spa. Spa Terre, located on a private island, the exclusive resort caters for only 30 couples ensuring a secluded, private feeling. All thatched-roof suites boast a king-sized bed, separate living room, jacuzzi whirlpool bath and private indoor and outdoor showers. Guests can relax on their private balconies complete with oceanfront views and make good use of the bird guide and binoculars in each suite. To ensure a peaceful environment, there are no televisions, telephones or alarm clocks in the suites. Children under the age of 16 are not permitted.

Created for self-indulgence, Spa Terre is one of only 13 in the USA that features Indonesian rituals including the Javanese Lulur Royal Treatment and the Bali Sea Ritual. These are the perfect choices for those who want to combine a celebration of tradition with a memorable spa visit. The philosophy behind this unique spa is to provide guests with a cross-cultural experience. Asian cultures have a strong influence because of their long tradition of using healing spices and flowers as remedies.

The signature treatment is the Balinese Massage, which combines a variety of techniques and tempos including acupressure to invigorate the muscles and increase blood circulation. Other popular choices include a Milk and Honey Body Treatment and Table Thai Massage.

Le Montreux Palace

Set close to the lake, the glorious Montreux Palace overlooks the mighty Alps to the south. Built in 1906, the hotel is a gem of art nouveau architecture at its most inspired and provides a vibrant Belle Epoque ambience of style and grace. The setting is quite simply perfect, whether guests simply want to relax or to enjoy a wealth of cultural and sporting experiences. With remarkable panache, Le Montreux Palace and its first-rate term manage to combine the good taste of a bygone age with the comfort and amenities required to meet today's high expectations. In October 2002, the hotel opened a state-of-the-art Amrita Wellness Centre specialising in massages and other treatments to aid relaxation.

The exclusive, state-of-the-art Amrita Wellness complex offers an idyllic setting on the shores of Lake Geneva with breathtaking views over the lake and Alps. It follows an integrated approach that combines fitness, relaxation, treatments and nutrition advice. Amongst the signature treatments is the Ayurvedic massage, which provides deep relaxation, detoxification and rejuvenation. It includes a gentle full body massage with a herbal oil according to your consultation, followed by a Shirodhora [the flow of sesame oil to the forehead]. Also an aid to deep relaxation, the Amrita foot and legs treatment includes a revitalising foot scrub, a gentle massage with essential oils for the legs and feet followed by a foot wrap with mineral extracts.

The Western Cape Hotel and Spa

The exclusive five-star Western Cape Hotel and Spa is situated on the Arabella Country Estate next to Southern Africa's largest and most beautiful natural lagoon. The resort offers a safe and secure, unsurpassed lifestyle experience that blends integrally with the surrounding protected biosphere environment.

As the premier spa and wellness location in South Africa, the Altira SPA features several luxurious regenerative and therapeutic treatments. These comprise high-quality advanced skin and body therapies. Indulge physically and mentally, and learn the meaning of self-nurturing. A qualified spa team is dedicated to excellence and customer service, and is served by the latest equipment and technology. Try the unique treatment of Rassoul, a ceremonial interpretation of health, skincare and beauty from the ancient Orient. The basis of Rassoul is the integration of different elements: water, fire, earth and light. For a more specialised choice, opt for the Multivitamin Power Treatment that targets the various causes of premature ageing. Alternatively, select the Ancient Sea Mineral Vichy for total relaxation and detoxification.

Le Royal Meridien Beach Resort and Spa

Le Royal Meridien Beach Resort and Spa lies on a pristine stretch of sand on Jumeirah Beach overlooking the clear, blue, warm waters of the Arabian Gulf, where modern sophistication and ancient civilisation blend together. Set in landscaped gardens, it is a true oasis with heated outdoor swimming pools and a Roman fantasy spa inside. Le Royal Meridien was voted as 'The Best Spa' and 'The Best Hotel Design Project' in the Middle East. It was also highly commended in 'The Best Environmentally Friendly Hotel' and the 'Best Restaurant Innovation'.

The Caracella Spa is situated in the royal tower, in a naturally lit atrium and has six therapy rooms with treatments including massage, body wraps, facials, seaweed therapy, balneotherapy, aromatherapy and beauty treatments to soothe body and soul. There are five Hammam pools ranging between 18 and 38 °C [60–106 °F] housed in a Roman-themed bathing room decorated with murals, to de-stress, unwind and enhance circulation and well-being. Plus, there is a sauna, steam room and jacuzzi. The toning cellulite treatment is hands-on, relaxing and totally luxurious. This involves body brushing to stimulate the circulation, then a mixture of algae and detoxing pure lime and juniper essential oils are massaged over the body. The guest is wrapped in foil, which warms the system and helps to absorb the nutrients and flush out waste. During the treatment, there is a scalp and foot massage and, after showering, a back massage.

Paraiso de la Bonita Resort and Thalasso

Set within its own ecological reserve on Mexico's Mayan Riviera, Paraiso de la Bonita is the first thalassotherapy spa resort in Mexico and only the second of its kind in Latin America. The 3000 sq. ft. Bali Suite, the créme de la créme of the resort, is decorated with antiques and fabrics from Indonesia. Designed and built by a Mexican architect, the resort features traditional Mayan decorations including Manoseado plastered walls, colonial archways, decorative ironwork and mosaic walkways, along with added influences from other continents.

Created exclusively for relaxation, Paraiso de la Bonita's Thalasso Centre features an impressive range of innovative therapies and the very latest in beauty treatments including Thalassotherapy. This luxurious spa includes a hydrotherapy treatment area with hydro-massage, jet baths, showers and a hydrotherapy pool. All the treatments are performed using seawater, which is pumped directly from the ocean. Lymphatic Drainage, Sport and Swedish massages are all available. Couples can enjoy a relaxing massage session in their own private room if they prefer.

From this brief selection of spa resorts around the world, we can make several general points, namely:

- some focus wholly on health as the core of the product while for others, such as the Le Meridien in Dubai, health and beauty is an important addition to the normal services of a conventional high quality business hotel;
- many of the spa hotels link health to beauty and also the desire to be in beautiful locations with the ability to observe wildlife and so on;
- a number of spas stress the idea of taking guests 'back to nature' but offer all the modern luxuries and services expected by the affluent tourist;
- many spas promote 'holistic approaches' to health which are mystical and almost seen as religious. They often try to tempt 'western' tourists with the suggestion that they will discover 'secrets' from ancient, predominantly Asian, cultures;
- spas are often luxurious and emphasise their exclusivity;
- most spas focus on both physical health and mental well-being and relaxation, seeing the two as inextricably linked;
- a number of spas explicitly make the connection between healthy eating and healthy living, and some stress the organic nature of the food served in their restaurants;
- some spas make an overt link between health and romance with some, even being adult or couples only to enhance the romantic nature of the experience.

However, as the number of spa hotels and resorts grows, they are continually searching for ways to differentiate themselves from their competitors so they may gain competitive advantage. This differentiation can be based on a number of different characteristics, notably:

- their target market – families, couples, trendy people, particular nationalities;
- their locations – rural, mountain, coastal, jungle;
- their treatments – the range and types on offer;
- their ethos or philosophy – holistic, 'new age', environmentally friendly, natural.

In terms of marketing, these spa resorts are an excellent example of the concept of psychographic segmentation. They are clearly aimed at consumers with particular lifestyles and personalities.

Their promotion is often highly aspirational and targeting the ego of the potential customer. For example, entries of a number of spa hotels on the 'Great Hotels of the World' consortium website talk about the resort as follows:

- 'appealing to a discriminating, international clientele seeking seclusion, relaxation, fine dining, and attentive services' (La Sumanna, French West Indies);
- 'Classified as a heritage property . . . the resort offers a fairytale setting on the banks of the picturesque (lake) which is swept by the intoxicating fragrance of spices' (Kumarakom Lake Resort, Kerala, India);
- 'Chiva-Som, or haven of life . . . . (aims) to achieve harmony between mind, body and spirit with spa treatments that are complemented by holistic and fitness treatments. The ravishing retreat is a cluster of Thai-inspired guest pavilions' (Chiva-Som International Health Resort, Thailand).

Conclusion

Health is a growing concern amongst people all over the world, in general, today. However, it is only in the most developed economies that it has yet become a well-established element of the leisure and tourism markets.

In terms of leisure and tourism industry provision, health is often viewed in different ways between countries and cultures, and is often linked with beauty and personal appearance, as well as being concerned with either physical or mental health, or both.

Health, and leisure and tourism are also at the forefront of development in marketing theory in terms of being an example of modern psychographic segmentation, for example.

It is also a good illustration of the growing 'internationalisation' of the leisure and tourism markets in two main ways, namely:

- the use of health and beauty by Asian destinations, for example, to attract European and American tourists;
- the emphasising of treatments originating in foreign countries – Swedish and Thai massages, for example – as if these are better than domestic treatments.

Finally, it seems likely that health, leisure and health-based tourism will continue to grow in the foreseeable future, and that it will slowly spread to more and more countries of the world.

Discussion points and exercises

1. Discuss the reasons why many commentators may feel the interest in health and beauty will grow in the future.
2. Critically evaluate the products and services offered by the spa hotels featured in this case study and discuss the extent to which they encourage healthy living.
3. Discuss the ways in which health tourism may develop around the world over the next ten years or so.

Exercise

You should choose a health and fitness club *or* a spa hotel. For your selected club or hotel, you should endeavour to carry out a SWOT Analysis for it and suggest strategies it may wish to pursue in the future to achieve competitive advantage.

Case study 5

Manchester United: Marketing the brand

Soccer today is big business worldwide and nowhere is this fact more clearly illustrated than in the case of Manchester United Football Club. Today this team is a world-famous brand and marketers are constantly seeking ways of raising the profile of the brand ever further and using it to increase income for the company that owns the football team. In this case study we will explore some of the ways in which Manchester United is marketed, as a brand.

It is important to recognise that Manchester United is a public limited company, or plc, which was first launched on the London Stock Exchange in 1991. It is, therefore, answerable to its shareholders and has to be successful financially.

Currently, Manchester United is perhaps the most successful team in any sport in the world, with supporters all over the planet.

The organisation has been very successful at exploiting the brand, as can be seen from the following examples taken from the official club website:

(i) A major on-site shop or 'Megastore' which also sells a huge range of merchandise online.

(ii) An 'Official Membership Scheme', 'One United' which is described in the following terms on the website:

Formation

You can become a *Match Member* for £22. As a Match Member you will get the chance to apply for match tickets plus loads of exclusive benefits. Alternatively you can become a non-ticket Member for £11, and still get some exclusive United benefits.

We also offer *Junior Match Memberships* for £14 which are specially tailored according to age group, either under-10s or 11–16s. Alternatively you can become a non-ticket Junior Member for £11 and get the same benefits as the Adult Members.

When you sign as a *Match Member* or *Junior Match Member* of *One United* Adults and Juniors both get:

- The chance to apply for home game match tickets
- Exclusive Members' Review magazines
- One United Membership Card for the 2003/2004 Season
- Free admission to home reserve games
- The chance to watch the team train for free at Old Trafford
- Exclusive members-only competitions to watch the team train at Carrington
- Vote for your Player of the Year and win the chance to present the trophy to the winning player
- Automatic entrance into 2 prize draws to be a club mascot.

Plus, Adults get:

- The chance to win match tickets and travel to Champions League away game
- Members only Yearbook and Premier League Guide
- If you take out car insurance with Manchester United Insurance we'll take the price of your club membership off your premium (UK only).

And Juniors get:

- An exclusive Superstars book of United Player profiles
- A members-only Man Utd poster
- A United Activity Book (under-10s only)
- A Members-only Yearbook (11–16s only).

Member

If Match Membership isn't right for you, we also offer the chance to join as a Member, or, if you are under 16, a Junior Member for £11. As a Member or Junior Member you won't be able to apply for match tickets, but you'll still get some exclusive benefits, including the following:

- One United Membership Card for the 2003/2004 Season
- Exclusive Members' Review end of season magazine

- Vote for your Player of the Year and win the chance to present the trophy to the winning player
- Free admission to home reserve games
- The chance to watch the team train for free at Old Trafford
- 10% Megastore and Red Cafe discount
- 50% Old Trafford Museum and Stadium Tour discount
- If you take out car insurance with Manchester United Insurance, we'll take the price of your Adult Membership off your premium (UK only).

Membership
Whichever type of membership you choose you'll automatically become an E-Member for free. As well as the basic E-Membership package you'll get E-Membership Plus, giving you access to all the latest match info and club news as it happens.

As soon as you get your membership number you'll be able to visit ManUtd.com, register and start enjoying your E-Membership benefits. So, as well as everything you receive when you sign as a Match Member or a Member, you'll also get the following:

- Exclusive members only weekly e-newsletter
- Access to Freeview online video content (MU.tv Channel 1)
- Up-to-the-minute e-views from Fergie
- The inside track with player interviews
- An Old Trafford stats pack
- Exclusive members-only online news and *views@www.Manutd.com*.

www.manutd.com/supportersunited

(iii) MUTV, the club's official satellite channel which is a joint venture with Granada and British Sky Broadcasting.
(iv) MU Finance, a branded operation which offers everything from home and travel insurance to mortgages to savings schemes.
(v) A range of relationships with well-known companies such as online betting with Ladbrokes and holiday bookings via Travelcare Direct. These relationships are mutually beneficial to both Manchester United and its partner brands.
(vi) MU Mobile, which brings Manchester United features to the phones of the fans including news flashes, ticket information, the manager's pre-match press conferences, special ring tones and lyrics, and so on.
(vii) Corporate hospitality facilities at the stadium.
(viii) Running trips for fans to away games in the UK and abroad.

All of these activities are clearly about exploiting the club brand for financial gain.

However, the club has also used the power of its brand to help good causes. For example, it has been a supporter of the UNICEF campaign to end child exploitation.

Manchester United has, over the years, developed awareness of its brand around the world through tours and the exploitation of the fame of its players such as David Beckham. Indeed, the majority of Manchester United fans now probably live outside the UK.

The club has also sought to raise its international profile, and boost its income, through its highly publicised marketing alliance with the US baseball team, the New York Yankees, which was created in 2001.

However, when a club like Manchester United has worked so hard to create a successful brand, it has to protect this brand, not only for its supporters, but more importantly for its shareholders. With this in mind, Manchester United has had to handle some major public relations challenges in recent years, including:

- the Club's decision several years ago not to take part in the FA Cup, in the UK, so it could focus on overseas competitions, which gave rise to negative reaction in the UK;
- the news that its star player, David Beckham, was moving to Real Madrid in 2003, which gave rise to the fear that this might raise the profile of the Real Madrid brand internationally, particularly in Japan, at the expense of Manchester United;
- the controversy surrounding Rio Ferdinand and a drugs test in 2003.

All such image and public relations issues are important for a public limited company because they can affect share prices and the value of the company.

As if evidence were needed that soccer clubs are first and foremost just businesses in today's world, stories which appeared in the media in September 2003 provided it. The BBC news website reported that:

Manchester United has played down a press report that three foreign billionaires may launch bids to buy the club.

The Observer newspaper reported that three wealthy potential buyers had separately sounded out City advisors over whether a takeover bid would be successful.

The would-be buyers have not been identified, but are thought to include a Russian, a European, and a businessman of Middle Eastern origin.

They have been advised that the Premiership club would cost about £600 m ($960 m) and that most of its existing shareholders would be willing to sell at the right price.

They have also been told that Manchester United – already among the most financially successful clubs in the English game – could become even more profitable, the Observer reported.

But Manchester United said it had had no contact with any potential buyer. The Observer report comes two months after the surprise £150 m takeover of Manchester United's Premiership rivals Chelsea by Russian Billionaire Roman Abramovich. Speculation that Manchester United could become a takeover target has been brewing since a separate group of wealthy investors began building up stakes in the club earlier this year. Manchester United's global profile, boosted by its consistently strong performance on the pitch and its roster of star players, is higher than any other football club's.

But with profits of £32 m on revenues of £146 m in its most recent financial year, the club is ranked as a medium-sized listed firm.

news.bbc.co.uk

The team is now beginning to make headlines as much for its business activities and its shareholders as for its activities on the soccer pitch.

Many fans of football in the UK are concerned about the growing commercialisation of their favourite clubs which they feel is leading to their interests being ignored and the clubs being run for the benefit of the investors. There are also those who are worried that a few high profile rich clubs will dominate soccer in the UK while other clubs go bankrupt.

However, the opponents of this trend towards seeing soccer clubs, in the UK and elsewhere, as businesses appear to be fighting a losing battle. This trend has already been seen in baseball in the USA, and is even being seen in rugby in the UK. It seems like an inevitable development as are the increasing links between sporting brands and other major consumer brands which seek to benefit from the glamour of the sports club brands through sponsorship and partnerships. For example, Manchester United is sponsored by Vodafone, the mobile phone giant.

Finally, sporting clubs like Manchester United have become truly global brands and have been successful at using the process of globalisation for their own benefit.

Conclusion

Manchester United is, perhaps, the most successful sports club in the world with a brand which is recognised across the globe. At the same time, many fans of UK soccer feel more and more isolated from their favourite teams as they become brands managed by marketers for the benefit of investors rather than fans. This trend, no matter how unpopular it may appear, looks set to continue and likely to affect other sports too. Meanwhile Manchester United will wish to continue to perform well both on and off the field to prevent it losing ground to its competitors at home, and abroad.

Discussion points and questions

1. Discuss the reasons why some soccer clubs have become major internationally recognised brands and others have not.
2. Discuss the factors that could harm the reputation of a brand like Manchester United and reduce its commercial appeal to investors.
3. Critically evaluate the idea that the growth of branding and commercialisation in soccer in the UK is a threat to the future of the sport.

Exercise

Select a sports team or club. For your chosen organisation you should devise a plan designed to help raise its profile, create a strong brand and then exploit this brand for financial gain.

Case study 6
Sofitel hotels and resorts

Sofitel is the premium hotel brand of the leading global hotel chain, Accor. It is a luxury hotel product that seeks to offer personalised rather than standardised experience for guests. This case study, based on its 2003–2004 directory, looks at the Sofitel brand and how it is marketed as part of the Accor family of brands.

The first point to note is that, in the glossy and expensively produced 2003–2004 Directory, there were 189 Sofitel Hotels and Resorts listed, distributed around the world as follows:

Europe	99
South America	14
The Caribbean	6
North America	10
Africa	14
Middle East	16
Asia	21
Australasia and the Pacific Islands	9

The location of many Sofitel hotels reflect the fact that it is a French company, with linguistic links to the Old French Empire and the current overseas territories of France, including its heavy presence in Morocco, Vietnam and French Polynesia, for example.

It is also interesting to note that seventy-five of its hotels are located in mainland France itself, in other words, nearly 40 per cent of all its hotels.

Sofitel hotels tend to be in two types of location as follows:

- cities where the main clientele will be business people but with some leisure market;
- resorts in leisure tourism destinations, which may also attract some convention and incentive travel business.

Some indication of the future direction of the brand can be gained from the fact that of the next eight Sofitel units due to open, all of them bar one are in leisure tourism destinations, with three being in Egypt.

The Directory sets out what Sofitel believes distinguishes it from other luxury hotel brands, as the following extracts show:

'Every Sofitel is unique, revealing the soul of the destination.'

'Sofitel embodies the very best of France in the elegance of its interior design, the warmth of the welcome, the sophistication of the service and the exceptional cuisine.'

'Sofitel guests are discerning voyagers who admire both culture and luxury, have a natural curiosity, particularly of fresh ideas and emerging trends.'

'Sofitel, relegates standardised luxury to the past. One will never mistake the Sofitel hotel in Bangkok for establishments in say, New York or London.'

'Sofitel has quite literally redefined the world of luxury hotels.'

'Sofitel puts a human face on professionalism and efficiency.'

'[with the staff] their singular skill lies in anticipation and attentiveness at every instant, never giving way to either the obsequiousness of another era or inappropriate familiarity.'

It is all about blending the best of traditional service with modern ideas.

The size and facilities of the hotels tend to vary depending on their location and target markets, understandably, as the following few examples illustrate:

(i) Sofitel Thalassa Miramar, in the stylish French resort of Biarritz, has a thalassotherapy and fitness centre, and offers cookery lessons given by the chef. This fits the image of Biarritz as a coastal resort, attracting upmarket clients concerned about their health. It also reflects the popularity of thalassotherapy in the French market.

(ii) Sofitel Lyon Aéroport, France, is located within the actual airport building to make it as convenient as possible for its customers who are normally airline passengers in transit.

(iii) Sofitel Capsis Palace Hotel, Greece – a large property set on its own private peninsula with private beaches and even its own zoo!

It also claims to have more meeting rooms (110) than any other Mediterranean hotel.

(iv) Sofitel Venezia, Italy, where the hotel is located directly on one of the major canals in this unique city.

(v) Sofitel, Bucharest, Romania, which is located in the World Trade Centre complex, reflecting the fact that most of its clientele will be business people.

(vi) Sofitel Santos Costa do Savipe, Bahia, Brazil – an 'all suites' hotel with exotic vegetation surrounding it and watersports available nearby.

(vii) Sofitel Nicolas de Ovondo, Dominican Republic – a historic building near all the main museums and named after its architect and the island's third governor.

(viii) Sofitel Christopher, St. Barthelemy – a small 42-bed colonial-style hotel with views of desert islands, a tropical garden and a barbecue restaurant.

(ix) Sofitel Thalassa Mogador, Morocco, which has its own water sports centre, a fitness centre and Thalassotherapy Institute.

(x) Sofitel, Royal Golf el Jadida, Morocco, is located on a prestigious golf course and offers a free shuttle bus to the airport.

(xi) Sofitel Old Cataract, Aswan, Egypt – a legendary nineteenth-century hotel with a famous bar overlooking the River Nile, and connections with Agatha Christie, the crime novelist.

(xii) Sofitel, Hurghada, Egypt – a Red Sea coast resort on the edge of the desert with a private beach, children's club, open-air theatre and discotheque, together with facilities for attractions such as horse riding and archery.

(xiii) Sofitel Royal Angkor, Cambodia – the nearest hotel to the Angkor temple, a World Heritage site, according to UNESCO.

(xiv) Sofitel Palm Resort, Malaysia – near an airport, a resort hotel surrounded by lush tropical gardens and a 54-hole golf course. The hotel has a business centre and an exotic spa.

(xv) Sofitel Reef Casino, Cairns, Australia, with its own nightclub and direct access to the Reef Casino.

(xvi) Sofitel Marura, Bora Bora, French Polynesia, built on an island which is a divers' paradise, the hotel, it is claimed, was built following Dino de Laurentis' initiative for the film, *'The Hurricane'*. The hotel also offers daily entertainment and excursions.

(xvii) Sofitel Zhengzhan, China, next to the provincial government offices, has a beauty salon, nightclub and 'Karaoke' facilities.

Leisure facilities play a large part in all the hotels, both those within the hotel and those nearby that are accessible to guests.

Location is also a crucial issue in every hotel description whether this means on a beach, in a historic town centre or near to an airport or convention centre.

A significant amount of detail in each directory is also devoted to the restaurants in the hotel. These tend to fall into several types, as follows:

- French cuisine restaurants which tend to dominate in France, French-speaking countries and the USA.
- Restaurants based on local cuisine in the destination which tend to be particularly common in countries like Italy, China and the Middle East as a whole.
- 'International' cuisine restaurants in many destinations without widely recognised reputations for their national cuisine.

As far as the accommodation is concerned, the rise of nonsmoking rooms is an interesting issue, with the popularity of such rooms available tending to vary markedly between countries. For example, in terms of city business hotels in selected cities, the popularity of nonsmoking rooms available is as follows:

Beirut	0%
Dubai	0%
Jakarta	0%
Budapest	0%
Rio de Janiero	0%
Tokyo	12%
Zhengzhan	13%
Lima	15%
Shanghai	17%
Jeddah	24%
Lisbon	32%
Vienna	47%
London	52%
Copenhagen	56%
Brussels	65%
Chicago	89%
New York	91%

The 0 per cent figures may reflect the lack of such rooms or the lack of information provided about them in the Directory.

There are also great differences in the proportion of rooms which have been specifically adapted for travellers with disabilities between the countries. In most countries, the proportion of such rooms is well under 1 per cent but again this may reflect hotels not submitting this information for inclusion in the Directory.

An interesting aspect of the Directory is that in a directory of luxury hotels there is a separate supplement entitled 'Awards, Stars, and Caps 2003–2004' which highlights the best hotel restaurants. The 2003–2004 supplement contained twenty-five such restaurants, of which 60 per cent were in France.

The Directory also includes details of other promotional initiatives designed to attract business to Sofitel hotels as follows:

- Sofitel leisure short break promotions such as the 'Sofitel Dream Package';
- the 'Sofitel Privilege Card' a brand loyalty reward scheme; one is free but there is also an 'Exclusive Gold Card' offering substantial benefits, which cost 230 Euros in 2003;
- 'Sofitel in the Skies' allowing guests to earn benefits from the frequent flyer programmes of ten leading airlines;
- a partnership with Europcar car hire, so guests have their car delivered to the hotel, as well as receiving a 10–15 per cent discount on rates;
- the dedicated Sofitel.com online reservation service.

At the end of the directory, as well as on the first page, the customer was told about the link between Sofitel and the broader Accor 'family' of brands. The text featured all the Accor brands, including other hotel brands, as well as the travel agency, casinos and meal voucher businesses. It claimed that Accor is much more than a group, it is a state of mind. The directory said 'Accor is there to accompany you worldwide, throughout your journeys and your professional life'. It also noted Accor's support for the ethical tourism charter, supported by the French Ministry of Tourism. Finally, the directory gave details of the group-wide loyalty programme, 'Compliments from Accor Hotels', which also covers Sofitel.

Conclusion

Sofitel, while part of a huge tourism and hospitality corporation, Accor, has managed to create a clear brand identity for itself at the luxury end of the market. Its hotels are very individual and are located in both business and leisure destinations. They work hard at combining their French image with the locality in which they are situated. They also appear to be changing over time and becoming more leisure-oriented and more global in coverage.

Discussion points and questions

1. Compare and contrast Sofitel with other luxury hotel brands in the international tourism market.
2. Discuss the advantages and disadvantages of Sofitel being part of a large diverse hospitality and tourism corporation such as Accor.
3. Discuss the problems involved in developing a global luxury hotel business.

Exercise

Access the Sofitel online reservation service and that of several other luxury, mid-market and lower market brands. Compare each site in terms of ease of use and produce a report outlining your findings, noting particularly if the quality of the site reflects the quality of the hotel or not.

Case study 7

'Souljourn' USA: 'Guiding the world to the best of Black culture'

This interesting organisation describes itself as a 'multi-dimensional media company that preserves Black culture by promoting travel and cultural tourism'. It goes on to say that today 'vibrant African communities stand across the world as a result of our ancestors. Souljourn will shed light on the best of Black communities for all travellers to experience and enjoy'.

Souljourn, in 2003, offered guides to four US cities, namely Atlanta, Chicago, Los Angeles and New York.

The Souljourn guide to Los Angeles

Published in 2002, this 700 page guidebook had a subheading setting out its aim as 'Guiding the World to the Best of Black Culture'. Its editor went on to say more about the guide by saying 'Here are the sites, the scenes and the secrets of Los Angeles, ready to welcome you for whatever pleasure, with Souljourn as your guide, you'll be welcomed here. Enjoy the history. Remember the legacy. Take the journey'.

The guide had a number of distinctive features, as follows:

- A two-page section at the beginning in which the authors dedicate the guide to Nat King Cole, with a two-page history of his life. It ends 'this powerful and graceful entertainer, epitomised everything that Black Hollywood is today, potent, resilient, beautiful, determined, and most of all, proud'.
- An acknowledgement section that featured dozens of people from staff in the Mayor's Office in Chicago and the Harlem Hospital to American Airlines and Western Union.
- All the photographic images were of black people, understandably, even in the advertisements.
- The authors point out that many of the original settlers of Southern California were of African descent.
- The guide draws attention to the fact that in recent decades wealthy Black business owners, media personalities and professionals have occupied 'palatial homes' in fashionable neighbourhoods.
- It mentions when talking about where to stay that 'staying with families and friends is a time-honoured Black tradition' and gives advice to those thinking of staying with friends and relatives in Los Angeles.
- When talking about commercial accommodation, the guide recommends readers to approach the African-American Association of Innkeepers for advice. It also recommends hotels 'which are either located near areas that are predominantly African-American or they are those that are frequently utilised for family reunions, banquets or parties'.
- Naturally, this guide highlights Black-owned businesses to its readers including health food shops, a comedy club, shops and sports venues.
- There is a page-long list of Black-owned or controlled newspapers, radio stations and television companies, with fifteen entries.
- A six-page list of events and festivals of particular interest to African Americans.
- A list of Black churches of different denominations.
- A 'shopping Black' section featuring everything from collectables to clothing to fashion accessories.
- A museum listing museums and galleries focusing on African and African-American art.
- A three-page section on landmarks and historic sites, including tours of Black neighbourhoods.
- A section on restaurants with a strong emphasis on soul food.
- A two-page guide to significant events in Afro-American history in Los Angeles from 1781 to 1998.
- A short editorial on 'Magic Johnson Theater' – a multiplan cinema fronted by legendary Black basketball player, Magic Johnson. The cinema champions the cause of African-American films.

- Itineraries to visit places outside Los Angeles which have been influenced by Black people.
- A page of advice for budget travellers, headed 'A Day of Black Culture' for under US $25.
- A section about Black businesses noting they had grown by more than 50 per cent in the USA between the early 1990s and 2002.
- A page of editorial about how Black people can trace their roots.
- A competition with prizes of holidays to Atlanta, Chicago, Los Angeles and New York.

The whole tone of the guide is very positive and uplifting and it is clearly heavily focused on the specific needs and interests of Black travellers.

However, it is important to note that much of this guide would be of value to any visitor to Los Angeles, regardless of their ethnic origin.

The writers also clearly are aiming this guide at all those with an interest in Black culture, regardless of their ethnic origin.

This guide is far removed from the situation in Europe where the provision of specialist travel publicity for Black people are very rare. Indeed, the European tourism industry, to judge from its brochures as well as from the mainstream travel media, seems disinclined to even include images of Black people or any other ethnic group. Given that Europe is multicultural, this is very disappointing and a concern which the industry should address.

Conclusion

This guide book is a clear illustration of the fact that in the USA the Black traveller is a well-established market segment; it also suggests that non-Black tourists might also be interested in discovering Black culture in Los Angeles, as well as in Atlanta, Chicago and New York. This is in sharp contrast with Europe, where the various ethnic minority groups in different countries do not seem to have developed to anything like the same extent as Black people have in the USA. Surely it is only a matter of time before this situation changes in Europe.

Discussion points and essay questions

1. Discuss the benefits of publicity such as 'Souljourn' for Black travellers in the USA.
2. Critically evaluate the way in which the mainstream tourism industry in your country meets the needs of people from different ethnic origins in your country.

Exercise

You should select an ethnic minority group within our own country. You should then endeavour to produce a guide book about your city/region/country, which highlights the role of this ethnic group and its culture, in the city/region/country.

Case study 8

Hilton Head Island, USA: The leisure island for golf and leisure shopping

Introduction

Hilton Head Island is the largest of the sea islands along the South Carolina coast in the United States. Europeans first travelled to the island over 500 years ago, although Native Americans had lived on the island prior to this. The island is called Hilton Head Island because it is named after an English sea captain, William Hilton. He was commissioned by a group of planters from Barbados to set sail to find new lands where sugar and indigo could be planted. He landed on the island in 1663 to be greeted by the Spanish-speaking Indians and he soon claimed the island for the British Crown. The island soon developed, and by 1860 there were twenty-four plantations that grew cotton, indigo, sugar cane and rice. These were populated by slaves and their overseers. The civil war and the abolition of slavery changed the role of the wealthy plantation owner forever, and the island fell back into obscurity. The population during the 1940s and 1950s began to recognise that the natural beauty of the island, and particularly the beautiful sea pines, could offer great opportunities for the development of leisure businesses.

Charles Fraser was the first man to fully realise this potential when he developed the first plantation on the west of the island – the Sea Pines plantation. Another important milestone was the completion of the James Byrnes Bridge in 1982 which linked the island to the mainland for the first time. Since the building of the bridge, the development of the island as a leisure centre has been rapid.

Hilton Head Island today

Hilton Head Island is approximately 12 miles long and 5 miles wide and the beaches are wide, beautiful and surround the whole island. The recent development of the island means that there is no recognisable town centre, but it is composed of a number of plantations that have steadily built up.

Around 30 000 people live on the island permanently, but approximately two million tourists visit the island every year. This means that a large number of hotels, resorts and timeshare operations have grown up on the island to serve these transient visitors.

Hilton Head Island is now a major leisure centre in the United States. The main attractions of the island are based around the plantations that have been developed since the Sea Pines plantation was established. The plantations that now exist are shown in Exhibit 8.1.

Exhibit 8.1

The plantations of Hilton Head Island

Sea Pines
Wexford Plantation
Shipyard Plantation
Long Cove Plantation
Palmetto Dunes Plantation
Port Royal Plantation
Indigo Run Plantation
Palmetto Hall Plantation
Hilton Head Plantation.

Each of these plantations has road access from highway 278 that runs across the island, but they are in effect *cul de sacs* which have controlled access.

Access to Hilton Head Island is by road from the mainland from the Beaufort and Savannah regions. There is also a small airport on the island with planes arriving from major US areas including the major city of Charlotte.

The climate of the island is very good with year-round sunshine and a warm climate with small amounts of rainfall.

Exhibit 8.2 shows some facts and figures about the island. It can be seen from this that the island has based its development on the effective exploitation of the natural features of the island, in association with the development of planned leisure activities such as gold and shopping.

Exhibit 8.2

Facts about Hilton Head Island today

- Approximately 30 000 permanent visitors
- Approximately 2 million visitors per year
- Accommodation consists of approximately 3000 hotel rooms and 7000 villas and homes to rent
- Approximately 300 restaurants, pubs, cafes and bistros with every world cuisine on offer and fish a speciality
- Leisure activities based on the outdoors, nature, golf (25 major courses) and leisure shopping. Other popular activities include cycling, horse riding and walking

(*Source*: Hilton Head Island Tourist Information)

The island planners have restricted the development of high-rise buildings and have not permitted street lighting which means that the island has a very 'nature' feel despite the presence of cars.

Golf on Hilton Head Island

There are twenty-five major golf courses on the island, which means that it is a paradise for golfers. A list of these courses is shown in Exhibit 8.3.

These courses are considered to be amongst the best in the country, and several of the courses are considered to be amongst the best in the world by professional golf players. The opportunity to play golf on the island goes hand in hand with the opportunity to see professional golfers play. The major event of the year is the PGA Tour (Heritage) which is held on the Sea Pines course in the Spring.

The golf courses are a good mixture of private and nonprivate courses. It is also possible to take golf lessons on the island to improve performance. These lessons are held regularly at many of the courses and are usually run by PGA-certified instructors.

The combination of the beautiful outdoor scenery and good weather, coupled with well-developed tourism infrastructure, has meant that Hilton Head Island has become a world renown golfer's destination. The development of high-quality hotels, resorts and shopping malls has also added to the overall leisure opportunities that exist on the island.

Exhibit 8.3

Major golf courses on Hilton Head Island

- County Clubs of Beaufort
- Country Clubs of Hilton Head
- Crescent Pointe Gold Club
- Eagle's Pointe Gold Club
- Executive Golf Club
- Golden Bear Golf Club
- Hidden Cypress Gold Club
- Hilton Head National
- Island West Golf Club
- Old Carolina Golf Club
- Old South Golf Link
- Okatie Creek Golf Club
- Oyster Reef Golf Club
- Palmetto Dunes/Fazic
- Palmetto Dunes/Jones
- Palmetto Hall/Arthur Hill
- Palmetto Hall/Robert Cupp
- Port Royal Plant/Barony
- Port Royal Plant/Planter's Row
- Port Royal Plant/Robber's Row
- Rose Hill Country Club
- Sea Pines/Harbour Town
- Sea Pines/Ocean Course
- Sea Pines/Sea Marsh
- Shipyard Plantation.

Leisure shopping on Hilton Head Island

Leisure shopping has become well recognised in recent times as a leisure activity. The recognition that shopping can be a source of relaxation with the opportunity of talking to others while doing the chores was recognised a long time ago. The motivations for shopping are many and have been characterised by Dholakia (1999) as being 'as interactions with family, utilitarian in shopping as pleasure'.

Although shopping is largely associated with women (South and Sptize, 1994) there is a growing trend for other members of the family such as adults and children to engage in leisure shopping, particularly for nonessential items (Malcolm, 1987).

The different types of shopping venues that have been developed more recently have encouraged individuals to engage in leisure shopping experiences particularly for nonessential items. A reduction in working hours, rising disposable incomes and increasing ownership of cars have all fuelled the development of new shopping venues. Mixed leisure, recreation and shopping developments have grown in most developed economies to respond to this type of activity. Different types of shopping destination were defined by Mintel (2002b) as being: *Retail Parks, Shopping Centres, Regional Shopping Centres, Factory/Designer Outlets*.

Destination shopping

Destination shopping is where the individual travels to a specific retail location for an extended shopping experience. This is usually in the form of a shopping outlet that is out of town and incorporates other leisure activities. The idea that a location can develop as a shopping destination in its own right is a recent phenomenon, and one could argue originally an American invention. Hilton Head Island has developed as an important destination for leisure shopping experiences against the backdrop of a wider selection of leisure experiences.

The Official Shopping Guide to Hilton Head Island gives the visitor an extensive number of options for their leisure shopping experience during their visit to the island. Information about the shopping experiences on the island is also given on the Internet at www.hiltonhead.com/guides.

Some of the shopping centres that are available on the island are shown in Exhibit 8.4.

Some of the shopping centres offer a variety of leisure opportunities. Pineland Station shopping centre, for example, offers a very upscale shopping experience with dining and arts outlets.

Conclusion

Hilton Head Island has developed as a purpose-built leisure experience since the early development of the first Sea Pines Plantation. A summary of the leisure experiences that are on offer on the island are shown in Exhibit 8.5.

These developments coupled with careful planning to underpin the tourism development has provided the island with good tourism revenues from both national and international visitors.

Exhibit 8.4

Shopping centres on Hilton Head Island, US

• Retail Parks/Shopping Malls	The Mall at Shelter Cove
• Factory/Designer Outlets	Tanger 1 and 2 Retail Outlets
• Destination Shopping	The Plantation resorts each of which has their own shopping centre
• Speciality Shops	Day Spas, Antique collection stores, Pet stores, Clothing and Accessories

Exhibit 8.5

Leisure experiences on Hilton Head Island

- Beautiful outdoor beach locations and other natural sights such as wildlife areas
- Full range of tourism infrastructure including hotels, resorts and restaurants
- A full range of leisure activities
- A golfer's paradise
- A full range of shopping experiences including factory outlets, factory malls and speciality stores.

Discussion points and essay questions

1. Discuss the opportunities that the development of an integrated leisure experience can offer to destination managers.
2. Critically review the place of either sporting activities such as golf or shopping experiences as the basis for the economic development of a place, region or country.

Essay questions

1. Critically appraise the role of women and children in the explosion of leisure shopping development.
2. Critically assess the advantages and disadvantages that may result from the development of destinations on the basis of created leisure experiences rather than cultural and historical sights.

Case study 9

Las Vegas: The world of casinos and themed hotels

Las Vegas is one of the icons of the global tourism industry, literally an oasis of leisure and entertainment in the desert.

History

Founded at the beginning of the twentieth century as a result of railway building, the 'city' was a small backwater until the 1930s. In 1931, Nevada legalised casino gambling, and this, together with the building of the Hoover Dam nearby, provided the stimulus for the growth of Las Vegas.

Legal gambling and prohibition soon put Las Vegas on the American tourist map in the prohibition era. Indeed, it was largely money from 'bootlegging' and gangsterism that appears to have funded the building of the first luxury casinos in Las Vegas in the 1940s.

Legendary gangster Bugsy Siegel was a prime mover in the development of Las Vegas, with the Flamingo casino, although the budget overspent on the project led to him being murdered in 1947 by organised crime interests.

For the next twenty years the 'mob' controlled the development of Las Vegas and presided over the greatest hotel-building boom ever seen in the USA. Between 1951 and 1958 alone, eleven major new hotel-casinos opened in the city.

The association with gangsterism gave Las Vegas a tarnished, lurid image in the US media but it was also a place of glamour and high spending excess.

The 1950s and 1960s were also a 'golden age' for entertainment in Las Vegas, principally due to the activities of the so-called 'Rat Pack' featuring Frank Sinatra, Dean Martin and Sammy Davies Junior. At this time, Las Vegas was perhaps the best place in the world to see top-class comedy and popular music acts.

In 1966, eccentric billionaire Howard Hughes arrived in the city and began to invest heavily in the resort. This stimulated another building boom, with twelve new hotel-casinos being built between 1968 and 1973.

In the 1970s, the image of Las Vegas improved with the arrival of 'legitimate' hotel chains such as Hilton and Holiday Inn.

By the 1980s, Las Vegas was free of significant 'mob' influence and a new era began in which efforts were made to change the image of the city, from a place for gambling and sex to an entertainment destination.

This new era was ushered in at the end of the 1980s by the development of the 'Mirage' complex by Steve Wynne. As well as gambling, this US $650 million hotel-casino had a strong emphasis on theming and fantasy. Other themed casino-hotels opened throughout the 1990s.

Between 1990 and 2000, more than thirty new hotel-casinos were opened, or were due to open, including projects costing more than US $nine thousand million.

Today, Las Vegas is trying to modify its image even further and wishes to be seen as a family entertainment centre, for the first time ever.

Las Vegas today

A few statements illustrate Las Vegas' continued success today, notably the fact that:

- it is the only city in the world with more than 100 000 hotel rooms;
- Las Vegas is the fastest growing city in the USA with a population which is growing at a rate of around 4000 people per month;
- there are more shows every day in Las Vegas than anywhere else on earth.

The 'Time Out – Las Vegas' guide, published in 2003, gives an indication of the range of leisure opportunities available in Las Vegas. For example, it listed:

- 38 major hotel-casinos
- 13 nonresidential casinos
- 122 restaurants
- 43 bars
- 56 shows and reviews in casinos
- 14 adult entertainment venues.

This, of course, is a selection, not a complete listing. Let us now look at some aspects of the Las Vegas packet.

(i) *Casinos* – Gambling is available in Las Vegas 24 hours a day, on an incredible scale. For instance, the Manderly Bay Hotel-Casino has 12 500 square metres of gambling space and most major hotels have over 2500 slot machines. Many casinos have minimum stake rules with figures of US $20 or more which is not unusual. In addition to the hotel-casino, many neighbourhoods have their own local casinos which are a leisure facility, primarily for local residents.

(ii) *Themed hotels* – Many of the leading hotel-casinos are heavily themed, creating a fantasy atmosphere. For example, there is:
- Manderly Bay with its South Sea Island theme;
- Mirage, themed on a Polynesian village, with a Dolphin habitat, 'volcano', 'rainforest atrium' and 20 000 gallon aquarium;
- Paris Las Vegas with its half-size replica of the Eiffel Tower and French-speaking staff;
- Venetian, complete with sanitised canals and gondoliers;
- Luxor, including a recreation of Tutan Kharmouns tomb;
- New York, New York, featuring replications of everything from Times Square to Central Park, and the 'Coney Island Experience', an entertainment complex;
- Circus Circus, with a circus within the hotel;
- Excalibur, encompassing 'recreations' of King Arthur's Court and Sherwood Forest;
- Hard rock, with its rock memorabilia and swimming pool where music can even be heard underwater.

(iii) *Casino entertainment* – Big name artists provide the entertainment in the major casinos, with a bewildering variety of shows on offer, any night, including in 2003:
- the Penn and Teller magic show at the Rio
- the Chippendales, male strippers, also at the Rio
- the Celine Dion show at Caesar's Palace
- Michael Flatley's 'Lord of the Dance' spectacular at the Venetian
- the *'O' Cirque de Soleil* show at the Bellagio
- the 'Catch a Risky Show' comedy show at the Excalibur
- the mimical 'Mamma Mia' at the Manderly Bay.

(iv) *The buffets* – low cost 'all-you-can-eat' buffet, offered generally by the casinos to encourage customers not to leave the casino. In 2003, lunch buffets could cost as little as US $7. As everything else in Las Vegas, buffets are on a grand scale with that at Circus Circus serving 10 000 diners a day, for example.

(v) *Leisure shopping* – After a slow start, Las Vegas is now a major leisure shopping centre, with major motels and 'in-hotel' arcades of designer label shops. However, as a warning to potential gamblers, there are also many 'pawn shops' where impoverished gamblers sell their belongings to raise cash.

(vi) *The sex industry* – Las Vegas has always been noted for its role in the 'adult entertainment industry'. Nevada as a whole has more than thirty legal brothels. None are actually in Las Vegas but prostitution is widespread. However, the 2003 'Time Out' guide to Las Vegas did list two 'sex superstores' and fourteen adult entertainment venues, including two 'swingers clubs'.

(vii) *Special events* – Throughout the year, Las Vegas hosts a range of special events and festivals designed to attract visitors, targeting different market segments. The 2003 calendar included everything from the World Series of Poker to a Gay Pride Festival, and Funky Halloween Ball to the Viva Las Vegas Rockabilly Convention, and Shakespeare in the Park to the Greek Food Festival.

(viii) *Weddings* – Weddings have been big business in Las Vegas for decades due to the easy-going marriage laws. In 2002, nearly 120 000 weddings took place in Las Vegas. However, marriage, Las Vegas style, usually involves a novelty element, usually in the 'venue' which can include a helicopter flight and the 'deck' of the Star Trek starship 'Enterprise'. Most hotels have themed wedding chapels and at the 'Graceland' wedding chapel people can be married by an Elvis Presley impersonator.

(ix) *Side trips and excursions* – While the local tourism industry prefers that tourists stay within Las Vegas, the city is a good touring centre for some spectacular sites, notably:

- The Grand Canyon, which can be visited by sightseeing aircraft, bus and train at prices of up to US $200 and more.
- The Hoover Dam, less than an hour's drive from Las Vegas.
- Death Valley National Park, one of the hottest and driest places on earth.
- Zion National Park in neighbouring Utah.

(x) *Museums and art galleries* – Las Vegas has never marketed itself as a cultural destination in the classic sense. However, in recent years, as it has endeavoured to project a more optimistic and family image, some notable new museums and art galleries have opened. Firstly, there are major works galleries in some hotel-casinos, most notably the Bellagio Museum of Art and the Guggenheim–Hermitage Exhibition in the Venetian. However, at the same time, it is interesting to note that the full-scale Guggenheim Museum in the Venetian known as the 'Big Box' closed in 2003.

Major 'museums' in Las Vegas include Madame Tussaud's Wax Museum and Guinness World of Records museum, as well as a range of other attractions with themes ranging from Star Trek to Chocolate, Elvis Presley to Liberace.

The Las Vegas experience has a number of other miscellaneous elements which are worthy of mention, including:

- the architecture which is often daring and imaginative, and at the same time very kitsch;
- everything is on a grand scale with hotels, for instance, having more than 3000 rooms, and even 5000, in one case;
- often the most expensive suites in a hotel are not for open sale; instead they are often given only as 'comps', free of charge to VIPs and 'high roller' gamblers;
- gambling begins at the airport, on arrival, and up to departure, with slot machines in the airport itself;
- demand varies dramatically by days of the week and hotel prices can vary dramatically between, for instance, a Tuesday and a Saturday;
- the famous or infamous '*strip*', the main boulevard where most of the 'action' is located, particularly along a seven kilometre section. The popularity and rates of hotels are often determined by whether or not they are located on 'The Strip'.

So far we have focused on the leisure market, but much of the success of Las Vegas is based on *conventions*, many of which bring thousands of delegates to the city. Many of these events take place at the Las Vegas Convention Center, the largest convention venue, currently, in the world.

Corporation delegates often stay in hotels away from the 'Strip', which are part of major brands such as Marriott. They provide a major element of visitor expenditure in Las Vegas, particularly in the evenings, when the day's business is over.

The marketing of Las Vegas

Even with all its attractions, Las Vegas would not be such a success if it were not for the work of its destination-marketing organisation, the Las Vegas Convention and Visitor Authority. This organisation, funded by local tax income, initiates a wide range of activities to market the city. It has a particularly effective press and public relations operation which sends out press releases on everything from special offers to new airline routes to Las Vegas. There is also an excellent website.

Once tourists arrive in Las Vegas, the authority there has a large information centre, although in 2003 this was only open from Monday to Friday.

Current development

Investment and product improvement in Las Vegas is constant and on a massive scale. At the time of writing, for example, the new, improved Las Vegas Monorail was due to open in 2004, while the US $2000 million Las Vegas mega-resort was scheduled to open its doors during 2005.

Conclusion

Las Vegas is an unlikely tourist destination in an isolated and an inhospitable location. It owed its early growth to lax controls on prohibition, gambling and weddings. However, its contrived success to the resort is its constant re-invention of itself and of huge private-sector investment in product development. It is now entering a new era as a more sophisticated, family-oriented resort, but it looks set to continue to be one of the best-known brands in destination marketing and an icon of world tourism.

Discussion points and essay questions

1. Compare and contrast Las Vegas and Dubai in terms of their present and target markets, trying to explain the differences.
2. Discuss the reasons behind the creation, growth and continued success of Las Vegas as a tourist attraction.
3. Critically evaluate the idea that Las Vegas has no real competitors, either within the USA or internationally.

Exercise

Using the Las Vegas Convention and Visitors Authority website, access the latest data for the Las Vegas market. From this data, write a report which:

- identifies the key points about the current market for trips to Las Vegas;
- identifies and explains trends in the Las Vegas market over the past five to ten years.

Case study 10

New niche markets in the leisure industry: The boutique hotel, the clubbing holiday and the music festival experience

Introduction

There are signs in the leisure sector that consumers are seeking out increasing numbers of niche products and services to satisfy their demands. A niche product or service is one that is focused very much on a very particular market segment who is demanding a very specific set of benefits.

This is a very different market from the mainstream products and services that target large groups of customers with products and services that have mass market appeal. We will refer to three examples of niche markets in the leisure sector in this case study, to illustrate some of the key factors in these specialist markets. The examples which we use are:

- the boutique hotel
- the clubbing holiday
- the music festival experience.

The boutique hotel

The emergence of the boutique hotel as a phenomenon has been one of the most interesting developments in the hospitality sector of the leisure industry. Key features of the boutique hotels include:

- a smaller hotel with a more intimate feel
- an emphasis on designer fixtures and fittings and appropriate electronics
- each hotel seen as having an individual identity despite the presence of a 'soft brand' in some circumstances
- a focus on modern styles using key designers to develop the concepts
- personalised service but the hotels do not always have full service facilities such as restaurants and bars.

The first entrepreneur to launch boutique hotels was Ian Schrager, who used celebrity architects and interior designers such as Phillippe Starck. Other examples of operators who have entered the boutique hotel market are shown in Exhibit 10.1.

It can be seen from Exhibit 10.1 that the majority of the boutique hotel operators originated in the US, although the Malmaison brand originated in the UK. Ian Schrager is an entrepreneur who has led in the development of boutique hotels. He is an entrepreneur who had worked in the media industry previously and had therefore built up an impressive knowledge of individuals in this sector and their requirements when booking a hotel. Ian Schrager has developed properties across the world including ones that have opened in Los Angeles, New York, London and Miami. His concept for the hotels depends on:

- smaller properties;
- cheaper materials such as cotton, linen and slate used in imaginative ways by sophisticated designers;
- the design of the hotels is based on the lifestyles that the guests are trying to lead, rather than expensive fittings and large rooms.

The target market for Ian Schrager hotels is the person who works in the music and media industries. Many of the customers are high profile. This is a market that Ian Schrager knows well and so it has allowed him to develop highly targeted hotel offerings. One of the issues for the boutique hotel operators will be how sustainable the current trend is for these types of properties, and whether the entry of more mainstream hoteliers into the market will change the overall development patterns for this types of properties. What is clear is that this type of specialist hotels is proving very popular with a targeted group of customers who want a targeted offering.

Exhibit 10.1

Leading boutique operators

Operator	Region present	Head Office	Number of properties
Ian Schrager	US and UK	New York	12
Kimpton	US	San Francisco	35
Joie de Vivre	US	San Francisco	21
Boutique Hotel Group	US	New York	6
W (Starwood)	US and Australia	New York	17
Malmaison (Rezidor Hospitality)	UK	Glasgow	5
Firmdale	UK	London	5
Myhotel	UK	London	2
South Beach Group	US	Miami	6
Art'Otel (Park Plaza)	Germany, Hungary, UK	Amsterdam	5

(*Source*: Mintel, 2002a, based on company data)

The clubbing holiday

The clubbing holiday had its roots in the early development in the 1980s of such destinations as Ibiza, where the development of San Antonio was largely on the basis of all-night clubbing, parties and the music scene. Since this time, 'clubbing' has become a global phenomenon which has been fuelled by:

- a growth in the global music industry and universal themes in music such as garage and dance;
- the increasing propensity of young people to travel independently to large music venues that offer particular experiences;
- the emergence of international DJs such as Fat Boy Slim who fuelled the interest in dance music composed for the clubs;
- the growth of large superclubs that used branding to develop their global businesses. This included such names as Ministry of Sound and Manumission;
- the growth of designer drugs.

Holiday companies have provided 'clubbing' packages to enable the UK clubber to have holidays with a strong focus on music, clubbing and partying. Holiday companies (such as Club 18-30) have developed special brands to develop the business which was estimated to be in the region of £18,00,000 million in 2002 (Mintel, 2003).

Destinations such as Ayia Napa in Cyprus and San Antonio in Ibiza have developed their destination infrastructure to particularly support this new 'clubbing' market segment. Cities such as London (UK), Reykjavik (Iceland) and Amsterdam (Holland) have developed a 'clubbing' scene to underpin tourism development.

It is important for these destinations to be aware of drugs such as Ectasy, which became a strong feature of the clubbing scene despite legislation that attempted to control this development.

The 'clubber' tends to start their visits to suitable venues in their local region and there has been a growth in the number of clubs in particular cities to satisfy this demand. Clubs such as the Ministry of Sound, and the Republic, have developed these markets.

Clubbers then begin to look for short break holidays to major cities in the world and longer holidays to enable them to meet up with like-minded individuals from across regions of the world, such as Europe. The balance is struck between the attraction of 'clubbers' and other market segments such as couples and families. Rowdiness and bad behaviour from drunken clubbers can cause the reputation of a particular destination to be ruined if careful management and control is not exercised.

The development of the clubbing business from the UK is shown in Exhibit 10.2. It can be seen that certain cities in the country have developed particular reputations for the development of existing clubs and experiences. Cities overseas in different countries have also targeted the 'clubber' as a result of the development existing at club venues. The development of the clubbing holiday to major European destinations has also provided a significant contribution to revenues for some major European tour operators. These operators have developed specific brand identities to underpin this market development.

Exhibit 10.2

Clubbing Venues in the world and UK providers

UK destinations

- London
- Bournemouth
- Brighton
- Glasgow
- Leeds
- Sheffield

City destinations

- Amsterdam – Holland
- Barcelona – Spain
- Berlin – Germany
- Paris – France
- Reykjavik – Iceland

Worldwide destinations

- Ibiza – Spain
- Majorca – (Magaluf) Spain
- Crete – (Malia)
- Rhodes – (Falaraki)
- Cyprus – (Ayia Napa, Kavos)
- Gran Canaria
- Tenerife

UK providers of clubbing holidays

- Club 18-30
- 2 Twentys
- Escapades
- Freestyle
- Global Clubber
- Ministry of Sound Holidays
- Thomas Cook
- First Choice
- Airtours – MyTravel
- TUI UK
- STA Travel

(*Source*: Mintel, 2003)

The music festivals experience

Introduction

There has been a trend across the world towards an interest in global music of various forms. It appears that it is not enough simply to listen to the music any more. Music lovers now have a growing desire to attend music concerts and festivals to experience authentic music styles at first hand in their local setting. The growth of the international music festival has been seen as a recent opportunity for many destinations in the world, particularly if they are trying to boost their tourism revenues from inbound tourists.

The international music festival

Individuals who are interested in particular styles of music can now travel to a range of music festivals across the world at specific times of the year. Destination and events managers have worked hand in hand to develop music festivals that are often based on the local style of music. The aim of these festivals is usually to bring people together from regions, nations or the world, who can either perform or make up the audience. The larger the festival, the more likely it is to attract people from other countries to visit and therefore act as a generator of tourism revenues. Certain destinations have developed a long tradition of holding music festivals on an annual basis which also regularly attracts repeated customers because of the relationships that develop between performers and their audience. Examples of major music festivals in the world can be seen in Exhibit 10.3.

It can be seen that many destinations in the world have chosen to develop annual music events, usually on the basis of a local style of music.

Exhibit 10.3
Music festivals in the world

• *Nepal*	Jazzmandu two weeks jazz event designed to boost tourism April. www.kathmandujassfestival
• *US*	Festival de Louisiane five-day cajun and zydeco festival in Louisiana April. www.festivalinternational.com
• *Madagascar*	Donia five-day music festival on Nosy Be Island May; Carnival style pageant
• *Morocco*	Gnauua Festival three-day music festival in Essaovira June. www.festival-gnauua.co.ma
• *Serbia*	Guca three-day brass music festival www.guca.co.yu
• *Africa*	Awesome two-day music festival embracing different music styles including gospel and mbaquanga September
• *Canarias*	Womad a four-day music event held in Las Palmas November. www.womad.org
• *Colombia*	Cali Fair Salsa music festival. One week commencing on December 25. www.feriadecali.com
• *Mali*	Festival of the Desert a festival of world music 2 days – early January. www.festival-au-desert.org

(*Source*: Daily Telegraph, 2004)

Conclusion

We have seen in the three mini-case studies that there are signs that consumers are beginning to choose focused niche products and services in the leisure industry that offer specialist offerings. These needs and wants can be exploited but often means that marketers have to think of leisure as being a holistic experience where overlapping organisations from different sectors have to work together.

Discussion points and essay questions

1. Critically analyse the reasons for the fact that increasing numbers of consumers are demanding specifically designed niche products in the leisure sector.
2. Discuss the view that the development of niche leisure products has emerged as a result of the emergence of global consumers.
3. Assess the damage that can occur to tourism as a result of the development of a destination as a 'clubbers paradise'.

Exercise

Choose one place that has decided to target the 'clubber' as a key part of their destination-marketing strategy. Explore the methods that have been used to promote the destination.

Assess any possible negative impact that this might have brought to the destination.

Case study 11

International film and the tourism industry

Introduction

The growth of the film industry and the emergence of blockbuster films has had a significant influence on the leisure industry in a number of ways. The first way has been in the growth of the cinema and movie channels, and at home cinema systems that have meant that it is now possible to produce a film that has an international appeal. The film industry has also created economic growth for particular areas in the world that have concentrated on film production and the associated services that surround the film industry. The area of Hollywood and Beverly Hills, California, is an example of this type of concentrated development.

This case study is about the growth of tourism that has originated from the film industry. The case study considers different aspect of tourism development that can originate as a result of the film industry or their creation of films with an international cult status.

The film industry as a destination or visitor attraction

The concentration of the film industry into certain areas of the world has allowed organisations such as film and TV studios and destination managers to create visitor attractions that can attract tourists. The best example of this is the Hollywood and Beverly Hills areas in California, US, which have become a living museum of the American film industry.

Hollywood, Beverly Hills and Sunset Boulevard

The Hollywood area of California has developed a prosperous film industry over a long period of time and, as a result, has become a major tourist destination for visitors who are interested in the film industry, in general. The famous Sunset Boulevard was built as a route between the film studios that had developed in Hollywood and the residential neighbourhoods of Los Angeles such as Beverly Hills, Bel-Air and Malibu Colony, where the stars, film directors and associated personnel built their homes.

This area is now a major destination where visitors can do a whole programme of activities including:

- visits to various film studios including Warner Brothers (of Friends and ER fame) and MGM studios;
- tours around the stars' homes, on a conducted tour taking to areas of Hollywood and Beverly Hills;
- Sunset Boulevard itself in order to visit major attractions such as clubs, music and comedy venues, and restaurants which the stars are known to frequent;
- visits to sights further away that have been used as locations in famous films. An example of this are the beaches that were used in the film *Jaws*, and in the television series *Baywatch*.

Other areas of America have also focused their tourism development on the basis of the film industry. An example of this is the area of Mississippi that has developed a Mississippi Film Tourism Map that has been developed as a result of significant filming and postproduction activities that has taken place in the area.

A press release for this new venture (as shown in Exhibit 11.1) that is under development of a Film Enterprise Zone was launched in January 2003.

Other areas of the world are also developing visits to film production facilities as an important part of their destination development. The Indian film industry (Bollywood as it has become affectionately known) has developed a significant film industry that is now one of the largest in the world that makes over 800 films a year in many exotic locations. Some of the film studios are now opening up their doors to visitors in some locations in India. The film and studio facilities in their own right therefore offer many opportunities in terms of destination and visitor attraction development.

Exhibit 11.1

Mississippi Film Office unveils first Mississippi Film Tourism map (press release January 2003)

JACKSON, Miss – In celebration of its 30th birthday, the Mississippi Film Office, a bureau of Mississippi Development Authority's (MDA) Division of Tourism is unveiling the state's first Mississippi Film Tourism Map at an 11.00 am press conference on Monday January 13, in the Supreme Court Chamber of the New Capitol. This press conference will launch *Mississippi Film Week*, a weeklong celebration of the Mississippi Film Office's 30th birthday. It will also provide attendees with an insight into Mississippi's accomplishments in film over the past 30 years.

'The Movie Map of Mississippi celebrates film locations across the state and through the years', said Ward Emling, manager of the Mississippi Film Office. 'It provides a clear picture of the statewide impact of the film industry and will provide a base for tourism development in the countless communities that have hosted film production over the years. And it notes well those Mississippians who have played a role in this industry.'

The Mississippi Film Office was created on January 17, 1973. Beginning with *Thieves Like Us* (1973) more than 40 films, 21 documentaries, two television series, 24 television programmes, and countless short films have been filmed in Mississippi. Since its creation the film office has assisted directors in showcasing the works of such Mississippians as Larry Brown, William Faulkner, John Grisham, Beth Henley, Willie Morris, Thomas Hal Phillips, Eudora Welty and Tennessee Williams, amongst others.

Film production in Mississippi has accounted for more than $100 million dollars in direct expenditure over the years and has generated hundreds of thousands of paychecks to Mississippians. The production of *A Time to Kill* alone extended 10 000 checks. 'We have seen that film production is economic development' said Robert J. Rohrlack Jr, executive director of MDA. 'The Mississippi Film Office is committed to creating a competitive film industry here that will continue to bring solid growth to our state.'

The week's activities will include Monday's press conference launching the week's events, a ribbon cutting for Mississippi's first Film Enterprise Zone in Canton on Wednesday, and a birthday party on Friday morning in the Rotunda of the New Capitol. Communities across the state will be showcasing made-in-Mississippi films throughout the week. Local Convention and Visitors Bureaus can be contacted for more information on Mississippi Film Week movies. All events are free and are open to the general public.

The development of destinations as film locations and the opportunities for tourism development

The filming of major blockbuster films in exotic and interesting destinations has become a major part of the film industry. This is because it is very important for the film industry to produce films that have a special interest and theme that appeals to the film viewer of any age. The location of the film, as well as the theme, provides an important platform for the successful film. Film directors are therefore constantly looking for interesting themes for films, and existing and different locations to film in to keep consumer interest high. A recent development in the tourism industry has been the desire of the film viewer to see the actual locations in which major films have been shot or visit smaller attractions that are associated with the characters that have been seen in the film. It seems that it is not sufficient for the film viewer to simply see the film – they have to actually visit the site where it was filmed to explore the atmosphere of the film. This is particularly important for films that develop a massive cult status.

We can consider four destinations that have attracted film makers to shoot major films that have achieved cult status, and as a result have developed the number of tourists who visit after the film has been shown. These four examples are major blockbusters but it is also important to remember that there are many examples of smaller budget films and television programmes that have brought notariety to particular geographic areas.

The first of these destinations is Scotland.

Scotland – beautiful landscapes and haunting locations

Films shot here include *Braveheart*, *Rob Roy* and *Loch Ness*, which all featured the natural environment and historic settings. The film *Trainspotting* was a hard-hitting urban film that many thought created bad images of Scotland.

Implications

Many of the images created in the blockbuster films of wild scenery and historic monuments have been used in the promotional campaigns that have been developed for the Scottish Tourism Industry. The myth surrounding the *Loch Ness* Monster that has been shown in numerous films including *Loch Ness* has grown visitor numbers to the area.

New Zealand – unusual scenery and exotic settings

Films shot here include *Lord of the Rings* and *Kaho Na Pyar Hai* (India).

New Zealand has many very special sites and has attracted major film makers on to locations to produce major blockbusters. The most famous of these was *The Lord of the Rings* by J.R.R. Tolkien, which was shot over wide areas of New Zealand in dense forests and world-class rapids. Matamata, Tangariro National Park, Queenstown and Methuen were used as locations for the film. The castle near Methuen became a very familiar site in the film.

The Lord of the Rings trilogy was one of the most ambitious filming projects ever and *The Fellowship of the Ring* released in 2001 achieved cult status. *The Two Towers* was released in 2002 closely followed by *The Return of the King* in 2003. The Indian film industry also decided to shoot the major blockbuster *Kaho Na Pyar Hai* in New Zealand and this film also achieved cult status in India.

Implications

There were many benefits that resulted from these two major filming projects using New Zealand as their major location. These included:

- the transport of personnel and crews associated with the filming projects. This brought major benefits to the New Zealand tourism industry. Small air operators, for example, transported film crews to different locations in New Zealand for the filming and continue to offer air tours to the most inaccessible sites;
- the New Zealand tourism industry has experienced a significant influx of inbound tourism since the release of the films. This includes tourists from all areas where the two films were screened. Many small excursion operators and tourism enterprises offer tours around the most significant sites in New Zealand;
- New Zealand is able to use the significant public relations advantages that the success of the films create once they become major blockbusters. This offers many advantages with customers and tourism intermediaries such as tour operators.

The Government invested heavily in projects to promote New Zealand as a tourist destination following the release of the film. The New Zealand tourists broadbranded the country as the home of the Lord of the Rings and it is estimated that the resulting campaign reached 200 million people worldwide.

The official website promotes a variety of tours to the locations ranging from half-a-day to three-week tours to Middle Earth.

Thailand – the backpacker's dream

The beach

The film adaptation of Alex Garland's novel *The Beach* starring Leonardo Di Caprio was filmed on location in Thailand during 1999 and the film was subsequently released in the UK, US, Japan and Australia in February 2000.

The film tells the story of a young American's doomed backpacking trip to a remote island in Thailand, and achieved cult status, particularly amongst the young, in many different international settings.

The film was shot in many isolated and beautiful areas of Thailand including Phi Phi Leh near Phuket (the beach), Kho Yai National Park, Krubi and Phuket. Many of the scenes in the film were shot on public land, so it was possible for many people to watch the filming and even in some cases become film extras during the actual filming.

Implications

The filming of *The Beach* in Thailand offered many advantages to the Thailand tourism industry as follows:

- The images in the film portrayed a beautiful and authentic location particularly to young international travellers. The Tourism Authority of Thailand (TAT) carried out an extensive marketing campaign for Thailand which corresponded with the release of the film.
- The country experienced a growth in tourism after the film was shown, and although because many of the visitors were independent travellers, it was often difficult to measure increased expenditure in the country.
- There were worries that there was substantial erosion that occurred on the beaches that were used as the location for the film following the filming period and the monsoon season in 1999.
- There is still significant interest in Thailand as a destination for young independent travellers. A search on the Internet shows that there are many sites where people share photographs and experiences related to *The Beach*. Thailand is still firmly on the itinerary list for the serious young backpacker.

The United Kingdom – glittering spires and Victorian stations

Harry Potter

The *Harry Potter* novels written by J.K. Rowling have become one of the most famous sets of books in the world. The making of the films on the basis of the novels was completed by the American film giant Warner Brothers, and they now have an area of their Warner Brothers tour in Los Angeles dedicated to the Harry Potter films showing sets, costumes and props. The films had a huge budget and were released as follows:

Harry Potter and the Sorcerer's (US)/*Philosopher's* (UK) *Stone* (2001)
Harry Potter and the Chamber of Secrets (2002)
Harry Potter and the Prisoner of Azkaban (2004)

The film was shot in many important locations in the UK which have significant historic interest including:

- Alnwick Castle Northumberland
- Bodleian Library, Oxford
- Christchurch Oxford
- Gloucester Cathedral
- Goathland Station, N Yorkshire
- Kings Cross Station, London
- Australia House, London
- Lacock Abbey, Wiltshire
- London Zoo
- Bracknell, Berkshire
- Durham Cathedral.

Harry Potter and the Goblet of Fire is the final film in the series.

The growth of tourism to the UK as a result of the cult status that the films have achieved has been a major contributor to the recovery of the tourism business in the UK, following the reduction in the number of visitors following the outbreak of foot and mouth disease in 2001.

Implications

There have been many benefits that have accrued to the tourism industry in the UK as a result of the Harry Potter films and the cult status that they achieved. These include:

- The Visit Britain organisation was provided with the logo and licence for a year by Warner Brothers following the release of the film. They then produced a movie map *'Harry Potter and the Philosopher's Stone: Discovering the Magic of Britain'* which showed eight locations from the film and 32 attractions around Britain associated with related themes such as Witches, Wizards, reptiles, ghosts and steam trains. These were distributed in 27 NTA offices overseas and on the website www.travelbritain.org/moviemap.
- The promotion of the film also allowed small tourism operators to develop businesses on the basis of the film. Luxury Vacations Ltd, for example, a small tourism operator, developed specialist tours for visitors who wanted to view some of the film locations. They consider that film tourism has provided them with a big boost to their business and tourism to Britain in general. An example of one of their tours is shown in Exhibit 11.2.

Exhibit 11.2

Luxury vacations UK

Discover the *Real Magic* of Britain with a wonderful tour visiting the film locations of movies shot in Britain including: *Elizabeth, Robin Hood – Prince of Thieves, Iris Murdoch* and many more.

Day 1 Arrive London, transfer to your chosen hotel.

Day 2 Tour of London including: Buckingham Palace, St. Paul's Cathedral, Westminster Abbey, Big Ben and the Houses of Parliament, Kensington Palace, Trafalgar Square, Piccadilly Circus, The Changing of the Guards, Tower Bridge, The Tower of London including the Crown Jewels, Visit Kings Cross Station, used to film the departure of the *first young wizards as they gather on Platform 9 3/4 ready to board The Hogwarts Express.*

Day 3 Visit Oxford, one of the most famous university cities in the world, with its wonderful architecture, rivers and dreaming spires. We can see *Oxford's* most famous college buildings and discover some of the City's secrets. Visit Christ Church College and its Great Hall, used as a double for *Hogwarts School.* Lewis Carroll, the author of *Alice's Adventures in Wonderland* took inspiration from the same College where he attended. The Library and the Divinity School are used to recreate some interiors at Hogwarts.

A short drive from Oxford is one of the country's largest private homes, the ever so grand *Blenheim Palace.* We see the state apartments, Italian gardens and parkland. Lunch in a country pub and then on to the glorious *Cotswolds* to see fairy tale gardens and villages.

Day 4 Drive through the rolling hills of the Wiltshire countryside. Visit *Bath, a world heritage city* with more listed buildings than London. Visit the Roman Baths Museum with plunge pools and hot springs.

Visit Lacock Abbey. Although the Abbey was converted into a private residence in 1539, it still retains much of its medieval character, which *provided locations for various interior scenes at Hogwarts School.*

Visit *Wardour Castle*, unusual hexagonal ruins of this 14th century castle stand in beautiful landscaped gardens by Lancelot 'Capability' Brown. The *Castle featured in the movie Robin Hood – Prince of Thieves.* Visit Gloucester Cathedral – the cloisters are regarded as one of the most beautiful architectural gem in Britain and form the backdrop for several important scenes in Harry Potter.

Return to London Heathrow Airport via Stonehenge, Salisbury and Windsor Castle.

Tour Route

The fascinating film locations of Harry Potter along with the elegance of Bath and London.

Other locations: *Alnwick Castle*, Northumberland, the second largest inhabited castle in England has featured regularly in film and television productions over the years including: *Elizabeth* and *Robin Hood-Prince of Thieves.* The Castle grounds are used as *Hogwarts' exteriors. Goathland Station*, North Yorkshire, the station which has barely changed for 150 years, made a perfect double as *Hogsmeade Station* in *Harry Potter.* These locations can be incorporated into *England Explored Tour* or *Britain Discovered Tour.*

(*Source*: www.luxuryvacationsuk.com)

It is likely that the interest in the Harry Potter films will continue to boost tourist visits to the UK in the foreseeable future.

Conclusion

Film tourism has provided significant opportunities for destination managers. The filming of a major blockbuster film in a particular place will make a significant contribution to economic development of the region. Some key factors which destination managers have to consider are as follows:

- the attraction of major film makers to their particular destinations;
- the development of a strong link between film tourism and destination management;
- developing an understanding of consumer behaviour in relation to films and the media;

- development of the marketing planning processes that will underpin the image positioning and promotion strategies of particular film locations;
- consideration for future possible developments in film tourism.

Discussion points and essay questions

1. Explore the reasons why film viewers increasingly want to travel to the film locations to develop authentic experiences.
2. Discuss the economic advantage that destination managers can gain from the development of film tourism.
3. Critically analyse the way in which film tourism brings together different elements of the leisure industry.

Exercise

Choose one country that has developed tourism revenues as a result of film tourism. Critically appraise the promotional strategy that underpinned this development.

Case study 12

The growth of the online retail travel market

Introduction

The use of technology and the Internet opened up the opportunity for companies to develop online booking systems that would bypass the more traditional methods of booking such as the retail travel agents. The growth of this sector can be investigated with reference to the Porter's five forces model, shown in Exhibit 12.1.

It can be seen from the diagram above that the growth of online travel booking originated from a subtle mixture of supply- and demand-led factors as follows.

Supply-led factors

- the consolidation of the travel industry and the emergence of large suppliers;
- the emergence of powerful technologically based systems such as GDS (global distributions systems) and microsoft technology;

Exhibit 12.1

The growth of online travel booking

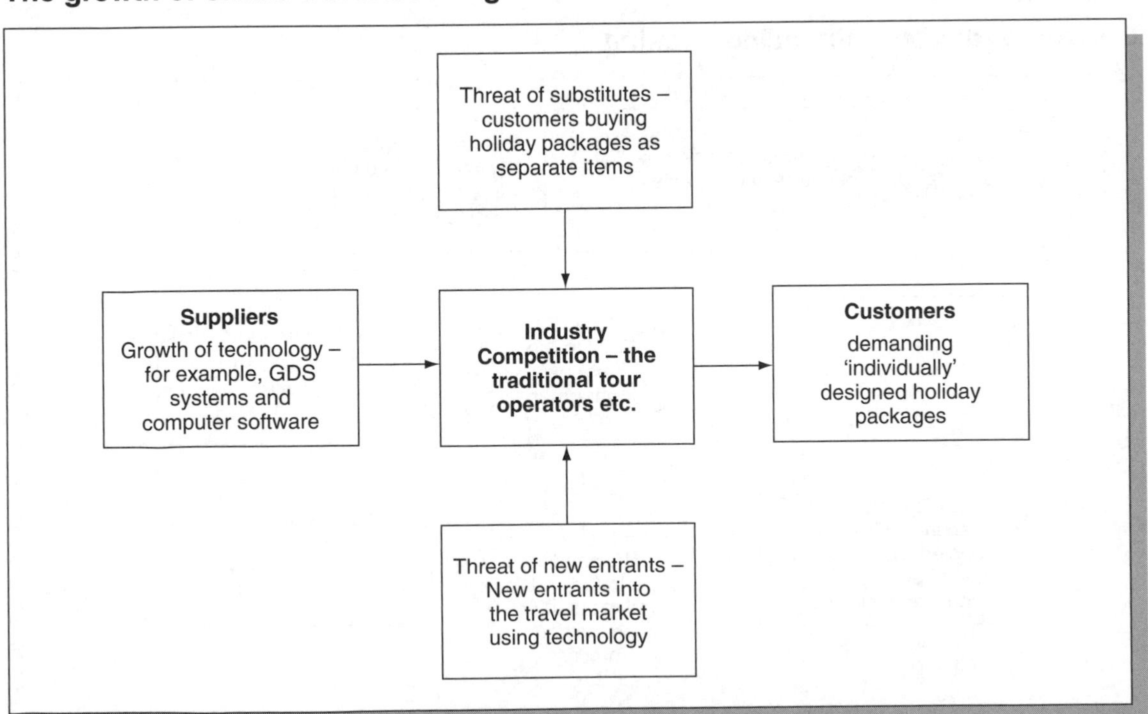

- oversupply in certain segments of the industry as a result of falling demand as a result of new suppliers and economic factors such as recession.

Demand-led factors

- a growth in international travellers and tourists who want a standardised offering;
- the desire of consumers to engage in technologically based purchase systems such as the Internet;
- the desire of consumers to book individual components of a holiday separately and put together their own 'package'. This has been attributed to the development of the postmodern movement;
- the move of the holiday into the 'bargain basement' area of consumers consciousness. The desire for last-minute bargains and heavily discounted products and services has fuelled the development of online offerings that can offer hard discounts.

The growth of online bookings

There has been a growth in online bookings for travel although estimates for the percentage of online bookings vary according to the source. It is estimated in the USA, for example, that about 10 per cent of all travel in the USA was booked online and this is predicted to raise to 14 per cent by 2005. (Travel Industry Association for Americas – TIA in O'Connor, Mintel 2003). Most commentators argue that spending on travel online will increase over the next ten years, particularly as high-speed Internet systems such as Broadband become popular in consumer's homes. The online travel industry will have to overcome the disadvantages that the consumer currently sees with online booking which are shown in Exhibit 12.2 below.

It can be seen from Exhibit 12.2 that the consumer has certain doubts in relation to online travel in 2004. These doubts of security, cash transactions and an apparent lack of brand identity all lead the consumer to feel insecure about online booking.

The low speeds associated with many Internet systems currently installed in homes may add a final level of frustration that forces the consumer to look to the high street for travel booking. This may change as online travel organisations with strong brand identities become better established and worries about credit card booking on the Internet are dissipated. Higher-speed Internet systems such

Exhibit 12.2

Consumer doubts with online booking

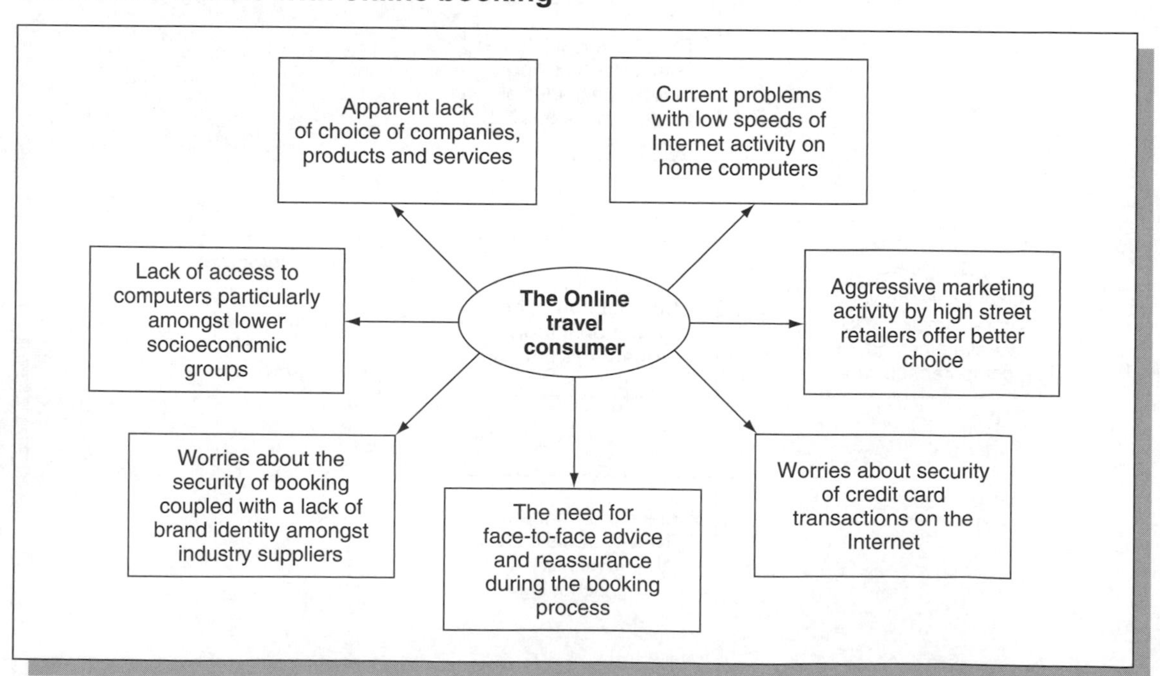

as Broadband will also make online booking more convenient for the consumer.

Online travel – the growth of the giants

The companies that have begun to exploit the online travel market are large companies that can afford the investment in the required technology and expertise. Many of the organisations shown in Exhibit 12.3 were formed in America, although European companies have begun to emerge in recent years.

The travel suppliers such as major airlines and hotel groups have begun to hit back at the new online travel companies by the establishment of their own online consortia to take bookings for particular airline seats, hotels or travel packages. Examples of these consortia are shown in Exhibit 12.4.

The future of online travel booking

It seems likely that there will be an increase in the number of travel products and services that are booked online. Although it seems likely that many of these will be in the hands of independent companies or online consortia set up by the airlines and hotel groups, there is a considerable opportunity to small entrepreneurial travel companies who want to exploit the Internet to gain interest and bookings.

The era of the giants could well give way to a plethora of small specialist online retailers.

Discussion points and essay questions

1. Explore the reasons for the growth of online bookings in the travel industry.
2. Critically appraise the reasons why a consumer may not choose to book a holiday online. Discuss the ways in which an online travel company could alleviate the issues that you have raised.
3. Critically evaluate the lessons that the growth of online travel booking has for other areas of leisure marketing.

Exhibit 12.3

The main online travel companies

Expedia	Founded in Washington US in 1996. It offers a wide selection of products and services in the USA, UK, France, Germany, Australia, Canada and Italy. Uses superior technology to dominate the on-line travel market
Travelocity	Founded in 1996. Headquarters in Forth Worth, Texas. A child of the Sabre Corporation and uses Sabre CDS. It offers a wide range of products and services to all clients who are individuals or businesses
Priceline	Founded in Norwalk, Connecticut, the company was the originator of the 'name your own price' business model. It relies on price sensitive customers and excess capacities in the industry
Hotels.com	It offers a discount hotel room service. Started as a consolidator and moved to the internet in 1995
E-bookers	Originated in the UK based travel agency Flightbookers and launched in 1999. It now has a presence across Europe and has negotiated deals with major airlines. Also offers hotels, car-hire packages and holiday insurance
Lastminute.com	It operates in a range of European and other countries (Australia, South Africa and Japan). Offers last minute deals with the idea of matching excess supply to demand in the market place

(*Source*: Adapted from O'Connor, 2003 in Mintel)

Exhibit 12.4
The main travel supplier alliances

	Launch date	Owned by	Characteristics
Orbitz	2001	United, Delta, Continental, Northwest and American	Major focus on US airline sales
Hotwire	2000	United Airlines, American Northwest, Continental, US Airways, America West Texas Pacific Group	Discount air tickets, hotels and car rental
Opodo	2002	Aer Lingus, Air France, Alitalia, Austrian Airways, British Airways, Finnair	Discounted air fares with hotels and car hire
Travelweb	2002	Hilton, Hyatt, Marriott, International, Six Continents Hotels, Starwood Hotels and Resorts, Worldwide and Pegasus	Chain hotel bookings

(*Source*: O'Connor 2003, Mintel)

Case study 13

Tour operators' brochures and advice for tourists about safety

In recent years the issue of the advice which tourists receive from a variety of sources has become a subject of considerable debate in many countries where outbound tourism is a common phenomenon. There are several reasons for this, notably:

(i) The series of high-profile problems that have increased fear of travelling since the late 1990s, namely:
- terrorist attacks against aircraft and against tourists in countries as diverse as Egypt and Indonesia
- high-profile attacks on backpackers in Thailand and Australia to give but two examples
- the publicity given to the risk of Deep Vein Thrombosis (DVT) on long-haul flights
- the outbreak of SARS that affected countries as far apart as China and Canada in Spring 2003.

(ii) The fact that more and more tourists are travelling to long-haul destinations which are often very different to their own country and culture, with potential risks of which they are unaware.

(iii) A number of tragic incidents involving individual tourists which have received widespread publicity, including everything from watersport accidents to being attacked by wild animals.

(iv) Some tourists are now taking part in activities which are intrinsically more risky than lying on a beach or lounging by the pool, such as diving, parachuting, white-water rafting and so on.

(v) The apparently growing willingness of tourists to take legal action against those tour operators who they feel have not made them fully aware of the potential risks involved in their chosen vocation.

It is not surprising therefore that there has been, and continues to be, a major debate going on about the amount of information a tourist needs about potential risks and their safety, and about from where they should obtain the information.

These sources of information include:

- the tour operators' brochure, given the power of the brochure in influencing tourists' purchase decisions and the fact that it is the tour operator who is the actual producer of the vacation package product itself;
- travel agents, except an increasing number of people, are now choosing to book direct without using agents;
- governments, given that most now offer their citizens a service by which they warn their own population of the risks involved in travelling to particular countries. However, governments are often accused of being over-cautious in their advice to the detriment of the tour operators' sales;
- guide books, but these are often out-of-date or very vague in their advice;
- the media, probably a very influential source of information for tourists, but they tend to oversensationalise stories and seek out 'shock-horror' stories.

It seems an inescapable fact that, in relation to the package travel market at least, the tour operators' brochure has to play a major role in sensitising tourists to the problems they may face in a particular destination. However, as a source of valuable information, the brochure has great disadvantages. Most notably, the fact that it is written months or even years before the vacation is actually taken and so may well give an out-dated picture, given the rapidly changing nature of some risks.

Furthermore, tourists use brochures to choose holidays not to learn about all the things that could go wrong on their holiday. This is particularly true when the warnings are often vaguely worded and in small print at the end of the brochure.

On the other hand, it is difficult to criticise tour operators for they, in any business, would feature prominent warnings about the risks involved in buying their product, in a brochure designed to sell these products.

At the same time, there is a growing view that tourists too have a responsibility for their own safety and for informing themselves to reduce the dangers they may face on vacation. There is also a view that, often, it is the tourists' own inappropriate behaviour which can turn a small potential risk into a tragedy.

Nevertheless, it is still clear that tour operators have a responsibility to make tourists aware of issues concerning their safety in their holiday destination. Indeed, in some countries, this responsibility has been enshrined in legislation.

In this case study, therefore, we will look at how some leading UK tour operators deal with this issue, particularly in relation to long-haul destinations and places which are very different to the tourists' own country, in recent brochures.

1. *Tradewinds Dubai 2004* – This brochure contained a page of very detailed advice in four sections headed, 'travel advice', 'in resort advice', 'flight information', and 'general information'. This covered a wide range of matters, not all of which related to tourist safety. However, it appeared that most of this information was very general rather than being specific to Dubai. Indeed it looks as if this page was standard and not at all specifically related to Dubai as there was a section on 'in the tropics' and advice about hurricanes.

   The advice was also quite generalised and, for example, directed tourists to consult doctors about health requirements at the Foreign and Commonwealth Office of the UK government regarding safety problems in the destination. However, this is probably wise as both types of issue can change rapidly and brochures can therefore become dated quickly. No specific information was provided for Dubai although the brochure did mention that building work was going on in the city which could have 'some visual impact'.
2. *Travel 2 Southern Africa, 2003–2004* – A detailed brochure with lots of information on the destination. It contained quite detailed information about vaccinations and the effects of too much exposure to the sun. Given that South Africa has a certain reputation for crime levels in some areas, it advises its clients 'If attention is drawn by your hotel guide to a local dangerous area, follow the advice'. It also says 'In Southern Africa, it is sensible to take the same precautions you would if travelling in any metropolitan city across the world'. Tourists are also advised to consult the Foreign and Commonwealth Office for further advice, provided by the government. The brochure also offers advice on extreme weather in certain places such as cyclones as well as the presence of malaria, or not in each game reserve.
3. *Thomson Faraway Shores, 2004* – This brochure covers many different countries around the world. It includes some country-specific advice on each destination of which the following is an example:
   - Climate – The climate is tropical. In June to November, heavy rainfall and high winds may occur. Hoteliers are generally well prepared for the occasional hurricanes that can develop.
   - Health and Hygiene – The Caribbean is a developing region. It is therefore important that you take care to minimise the risk of holiday sickness. Pregnant women, the very young and old are particularly affected by stomach upsets. You should discuss your travel plans with your GP well before departure. Please also look out for additional information provided by Thomson during the in-flight video and on arrival in resort. Hot sun combined with alcohol and new foods can cause stomach upsets so bring remedies from home. Drinking bottled water and avoiding ice will help avoid problems. All Thomson hotels in the Caribbean have signed up to an approved food management programme which ensures the highest standards of health, hygiene and food safety. Under the programme, food and water supplies are treated regularly and hotel staff undergo rigorous hygiene training. Please see the Safety First section in the A–Z guide for important travel advice.
   - Health and Safety – for health and safety reasons we do not recommend the excursions sold by beach vendors. All Thomson excursions have been fully inspected and meet all health and safety requirements.

   Thomson Faraway Shores, 2004

   Interestingly this advice says a lot about hygiene problems and stomach upsets and also warns of the potential risks of buying excursions from beach vendors. Some may argue this latter advice is motivated by commercial self-interest in that they wish the tourist to buy the Thomson excursions instead but there are undoubtedly problems with trips offered by unregulated operators. In addition to this specific destination advice, the brochure contains more general advice in a 'Safety First' section at the end of the brochure.

4. *Premier Asia, 2004* – The brochure contains detailed general advice sections on 'healthcare and vaccinations' and 'safety and security'. This includes risks such as Deep Vein Thrombosis and hygiene standards in destinations. It also reminds tourists that, 'Cities the world over have their less salubrious areas'. These can sometimes be found in central locations and may be in close proximity to tourist areas. This brochure also has detailed sections on each specific destination. The Bangkok section talks about how pollution is being reduced but does not talk about the incidence of sex tourism in the city, except by saying 'its steamy (in more ways than one)' and its 'extremes of nightlife'. The section on South Africa does recognise the reputation of the country for crime in some areas but says 'Although some concerns about crime have been expressed, in reality, incidents in tourist areas are infrequent, and if you take proper care, it is no more risky than other destinations'.
5. *Libra Holidays, 2004* – The different brochures of this company included little advice relevant to specific destinations but they had two pages of detailed advice. As well as the usual advice offered, some interesting advice about safety in hotels, in some detail, included the following: *Personal Safety* – Wherever possible, you should make use of any safety deposit boxes that are available in your accommodation. Always remember to lock your door at night and when you go out during the day in the same way that you would at home. Most hotels and apartments do not employ a lifeguard.

   Please ensure that children and non-swimmers are supervised at all times and observe the pool rules at your accommodation. We do not recommend any diving, however if you wish to dive, please check that the water is deep enough and that the property allows diving. You should also exercise caution around the pool areas since pool surrounds are often slippery when wet and you should not enter the pool after drinking alcohol.

   If you are travelling with young children, make sure they are not left unsupervised on balconies. Keep balcony furniture away from the railings so that they are not encouraged to climb up.

   Few hotels and apartments are legally obliged to install 'toughened' or safety glass in their windows, doors, and glass cabinets etc. Please take particular care when walking through patio doors. It can be difficult to spot if they are closed in bright sunlight.

   Identifying stickers should be in place on patio doors and other large glass doors. If they are missing, please bring this to the attention of your representative. Some hotels and apartment lifts do not have internal doors. This means that the inside of the lift is exposed to the lift shaft. If you hotel or apartment has this type of life, make sure that you stand clear of the wall and never allow children to travel inside any lift without an adult.

   Please read carefully all fire safety information which is available in your hotel or apartment.

   On arrival, always familiarise yourselves with the nearest fire exits to your room or apartment.

   Libra Holidays Brochure, 2004
6. *Virgin Worldwide, 2004* – This brochure contained general advice but it also noted which vaccinations were recommended in each of its destinations at the time the brochure went to press. It also gave readers information on how to access the Foreign and Commonwealth Office travel safety information. This advice was in a section in normal size print, headed 'the very important not so small print'.
7. *Jewel in the Crown Holidays, Goa 2003–2004* – This specialist brochure contained a lot of detailed information on Goa but says little about potential risks and safety issues except the currents that can make swimming in the sea difficult or dangerous. Of one ferry journey it says 'we crossed on the ancient Goan ferry . . . any UK Health and Safety Officer would have had a fit'. Perhaps this lack of detailed advice on safety and problems reflects the fact that Goa is relatively safe or that Jewel in the Crown clients are quite sophisticated travellers who are aware of the safety issues involved in visiting a destination like Goa.
8. *Bales Inspirational Journeys, 2004* – The Bales brochure contained a section of general advice entitled 'Ensuring your Safety'. It also said the company was working with hotels to implement UK health and safety standards in the accommodation in their brochures. Specific

health advice was given for each destination and the telephone number of a clinic which offers specialist advice on health and travel was given, as were details on the Foreign and Commonwealth Office website. Another section of the brochure contained information on the health problems associated with high altitudes, albeit in very small print. Finally the brochure promised that 'more comprehensive literature regarding health and safety will be enclosed with your final travel documentation and we strongly urge you to read this prior to your departure', although this again was in small print.

9. *Thomas Cook Signature, 2003–2004* – The brochure had several pages of detailed advice, including the following paragraphs, albeit in very small print at the end of the brochure.

    Health, Safety and Security Abroad
    The safety standards and regulations which apply overseas are those of the country you visit. Often they do not reach the same levels as in the UK. Because of this, general standards of safety, hygiene, fire precautions and so on can be of a different standard to those which we expect in the UK. The authorities in the country concerned may not have enough power or resources to monitor and enforce standards. As a result, please be careful when you are in unfamiliar buildings or surroundings.

    Do not let non swimmers or children jump into a swimming pool without first checking the depth and how to get out. Please get to know your escape route in case of fire. Upset stomachs can happen in many areas often caused by the change of climate or ice-cold drinks and not as a result of local hygiene or food preparation. Any change to your diet may cause an upset stomach and the local water may not help. You should be sensible especially with raw food, drinking water and ice in drinks. You can reduce the risk of bites from insects by using repellents and covering up whenever possible – especially during the evening and at night.

    We take the safety of our customers very seriously. If the Foreign Office advises that you should not visit a particular country, we will tell you and try to arrange another holiday for you. Crimes against people and property are a fact of life throughout the world and you have the same responsibility for your own safety as you do at home. In some places the local police may not be very cooperative or interested when you report theft or need insurance confirmation so take care of your property.

    Thomas Cook Signature Brochure, 2004

    The 'Worldwide' brochure also included advice on the specifically recommended vaccinations for each destination.

10. *Travel and Latin America, 2003–2004* – The two pages of general information in this brochure had sections on the risk of altitude sickness and general health concerns. It also noted that travellers to Brazil require a certificate confirming they have been vaccinated against Yellow Fever. However, in the general information section, there did not appear to be specific advice about the dangers of crime in the big cities, although this is perceived to be an issue in some big South American cities.

11. *Latin America Travel, 2003–2004* – This brochure contained two pages of general information which included the following quite detailed safety-related advice:

    Health
    No compulsory health requirement is currently in force when travelling to the countries featured in this brochure, although many countries require passengers to hold valid yellow fever certificates if you are arriving from either Peru or Bolivia. The Department of Health recommends protection against yellow fever, tetanus, polio, hepatitis A and typhoid, and produces a useful booklet entitled 'Health Advice for Travellers' (T5), which is available free from your doctor, ABTA travel agent or our offices. We must emphasise that as requirements may change at short notice, you are responsible for ensuring that you take advice from your GP or appropriate medical authority.

    Political Situation
    Some Latin American countries have in the past experienced instability but it is fair to say that the countries we feature all now enjoy a settled political climate. Substantially increased foreign investment and closer association with the European Community indicate a consolidation of this stability.

    Personal Security
    Your holiday will be one to remember for all the right reasons providing common sense is exercised throughout and normal caution is taken. All over the world, and not only in our

featured countries, poverty and urban development lead to social problems. Tourists are rarely affected but when they have been an element of predictability was usually involved.

Jewellery and unnecessary luxury items should be left at home, and if such items much be taken, they should not be flaunted in a manner that could be regarded as provocative.

Hotel safety deposit boxes are nearly always available and should be used. The Foreign Travel Advice Unit may have issued information about your destination. You are advised to check on BBC2 (Ceefax) page 470 onwards, or on the Internet under http://www.fco.gov.uk/.

Alternatively you can contact ABTA on 0901 2015050 (calls charged at 50 p/minute).

Latin America Travel, 2003–2004

The authors surveyed over fifty brochures for this case study of which the above were merely a selection. From this whole survey a number of points can be made, as follows:

- Coverage of safety-related issues is usually contained in a nondestination-specific 'general information', usually at the end of the brochure, and often in smaller print than the rest of the brochure.
- Relatively little destination-specific advice was provided in the brochures.
- Some risks were either not mentioned or heavily played down, notably terrorism and crime, as well as the relatively high risk of using public transport in some developing countries.
- Sensibly, many brochures refer their customers to doctors or the UK government Foreign and Commonwealth Office Travel Advice for up-to-date advice given how rapidly things can change in destinations.

Conclusion

In recent years, there has been growing pressure on the tourism industry to provide more safety-related advice for tourists. However, it is clearly difficult for tour operators, for example, to find a balance between providing safety advice, raising awareness of issues and trying to actually sell their products. This was clearly seen in the brochures we surveyed where such advice is often relegated to the back of the brochure and presented in very general, nondestination-specific form. Nevertheless, tour operators are trying to raise their customers' awareness of potential problems more and more and, presumably, there is also a responsibility on tourists to take some responsibility for their own safety too.

Discussion points and questions

1. Critically evaluate the suggestion that tourists should take responsibility for their own safety and not rely on advice from tour operators.
2. Discuss the reasons why more and more tour operators are putting safety advice in their brochures.
3. Discuss the role of travel agents and the government in advising tourists on safety issues.

Exercise

Obtain a selection of tour operators' brochures for different types of holidays and a variety of destinations.

Compare and contrast the nature and volume of safety advice offered in the brochure, noting differences, and suggest the reasons that may lie behind these differences.

Case study 14
Leisure travel magazines and the Islamic tourism market

Very rarely do English language tourism textbooks or journals focus specifically on the Islamic market as a distinctive market. However, there is a rapidly growing market for vacations in the Islamic world. This growth is reflected in the existence of leisure travel magazines to mirror those of Europe and the USA, such as Conde Nast and Wanderlust. The authors thought it would be useful to analyse two such Islamic travel magazines.

1. *Islamic Tourism, Autumn 2003* – This 84-page magazine appears to be published four times a year with a cover price of around five US dollars (in Dubai at least). The magazine was only started in 2001 and is published in the UK, although printed in Beirut, and it has offices in Cairo, Berlin, Dubai, Amman, Casablanca and Malaysia. The magazine is clearly designed to appeal to Moslems of all nationalities, and the following extract from the editor's introduction to the eighth issue illustrates its mission a little:

> The eighth issues . . . are concrete examples of what we intend to do for tourism and a good indication of things to come. Islamic Tourism has been borne out of a clear foresight of the need for a bridge between East and West in a world where we find polarisations and tensions on all levels of global relations. . . . we are determined to persist with our effort in providing a forum for tourism in the Muslim world and to encourage tourism between Muslim countries as well as between these countries and the rest of the world.
>
> Islamic Tourism, Autumn 2003

The text is in Arabic and English equally and this eighth issue chosen at random contained the following articles:

- an article on the potential for river tourism in Iraq along the lines of that seen on the Rhine and Danube. The article has many suggestions for how such tourism could be developed, but in ways that ensure that 'Islamic social values and morals [are] . . . upheld so that Muslims, as well as foreigners, can enjoy Iraq's natural beauty without embarrassment'. The article ends with some inspiring words, namely 'River tourism may seem like a *Fata Mogana* in today's Iraq, but without hope nothing is achieved. Aren't we planning to make Iraq an international tourist destination?'
- an article on the River Thames in the UK which is introduced by reference to the writings about the river by Arab poets, who had never seen it, in the 1920s;
- an article on Andalucia, focusing on the heritage of eight hundred years of Islamic history and influence in the region;
- an article on a major campaign launched by the Indian tourism industry to attract visitors from the Arabian Gulf. The article noted that the country received around 100 000 visitors from this region in 2003;
- an article which promoted Djibouti in East Africa, which has almost wholly a Muslim population, even though French is the most widely spoken language;
- an article on the Pakistan city of Lahore, described as 'the cultural hub of the modern Islamic state of Pakistan', offering a bundle of surprises, not least a lively film industry ('Bollywood'), fashion, and cuisine. There is a description of several of the most important mosques in the city;
- an article on health tourism in Jordan including the Dead Sea and various individual baths and spas. The article included a section talking about new investment in health tourism facilities around the Dead Sea and its general;
- an article about Ramadan in Egypt, explaining a little about how it is celebrated in Cairo;
- an article by a London-based freelance journalist talking about the future potential of Iraq as a tourist destination once peace and stability has returned.

As well as features, the issue also contained news items, particularly about a major tourism trade fair and exhibition, the Mediterranean Travel Fair which took place in Cairo in September 2003, and the Third International Hospitality Forum, held in Amman, Jordan, in September 2003. It also gave a list of travel industry trade fairs and details of the East Mediterranean International Travel and Tourism Exhibition, due to be held in Istanbul in February 2004, and was expected to attract 800 exhibitors and 120 000 visitors. The issue also contained a number of advertisements, notably the following:

- The Aden Hotel in the Republic of Yemen
- India Tourist Board
- Daallo Airlines (Djibouti)
- Air Djibouti (Djibouti)
- Hilton Park Sudan and Khartoum Hotels, Sudan
- Arab News Network
- Arab-British Chambers of Commerce
- Lebanon-Ministry of Tourism.

Overall, the magazine was glossy with many full-colour photographic articles and was well written and very informative.

Interestingly, the pages in Arabic contain articles which appear to be slightly different from those in the English section. The English section contains many news items, including:

- four pages of news about hotels, primarily in the Gulf States. Interestingly, most of the hotels mentioned were owned by Western chains and their managers were generally Europeans;
- a page of news about Ramadan and the special services being offered to guests during Ramadan by Ritz-Carlton Hotels, together with a special Ramadan offer promotion from Inter-Continental Hotels;
- finally closing its tourism promotion office in Kuwait but opening a new one in Dubai, together with others planned for Damascus and Cairo;
- the fact that received 10 470 tourists from Kuwait in 2002, an increase of 41 per cent over 2001;
- a European couple getting married underwater in Egypt;
- Jordan attracting tourists for luxurious spa tourism holidays;
- the new tourism projects under construction in Dubai;
- special promotions from Hertz on car hire;
- news of new routes, marketing activities and new aircraft from Kuwait Airways, Oman Air and Qatar Airways;
- adventure tourism including Arab mountaineers, Russian hikers and the Crown Prince of Dubai attending an equestrian event in Ireland.

This issue contained eighteen pages of advertisements, most of which were for accommodation, including a two-page advert and editorial for the Hilton Kuwait Resort, with its Thai restaurant. It also featured two unusual elements, namely:

- a page of cartoons, in English;
- a page of consumer tests on cameras.

2. *Gulf Traveller, December 2003* – Also 84 pages, this magazine was published in Kuwait and cost around four US dollars in Dubai at least. Its sub-heading was 'The Arab World's Travel and Tourism Magazine', and it appears to have been created in 2000. Most of the text was in English but there were sixteen pages in Arabic in the issue we analysed.

The editorial in this issue was a plea for the various national airlines of the Gulf region to think about the potential benefits of combining to create one powerful airline.

The articles in this issue were as follows:

- one about Aswan, described as 'The Jewel of the Nile'
- an article on eco tourism opportunities in Jordan
- a two-page guide on how to choose accommodation in general
- a double-page piece about the 46th National Day celebrations in Malaysia and the stepping down of Dr Mahathir Mohammed as Prime Minister
- four pages about Hong Kong, including advice on attractions for children
- two pages about the Music Fountain Monument in Kuwait
- a major feature on Sri Lanka
- a one-page guide to rail travel in Europe
- four pages about Pisa and its Leaning Tower
- a four-page feature on the attractions of Bosnia and Herzegovina, with its population where Muslims are the single largest religious group
- two pages about food safety and hygiene.

The general production standard was high and the magazine was in full colour.

Of the two issues, 'Islamic Tourism' was much more focused on matters of concern to Islamic tourists, unsurprisingly, while 'Gulf Traveller' was more designed to meet the needs of both Islamic and Western tourists. 'Gulf Traveller' was much the strongest in terms of news features and also contained some very basic advice sections for inexperienced travellers.

Both magazines were not quite as glossy or substantial as the major European or American leisure travel magazines and are very recent creations compared to these 'western' travel magazines. The editorials of both Islamic World magazines are more serious than those found generally in European and American journals, one showing a strength of having a mission to spread understanding between cultures while the other pleads for a Gulf region-wide airline.

The growth of leisure tourism in Islamic countries is important for the global tourism market because of its volume, but also because Islamic tourists have particular needs, in terms of their religion, for example, which hotels need to be aware of.

Secondly, for many Middle Eastern destinations, where terrorist activities have reduced visits by Western tourists, fellow Moslem tourists can be a very significant market as they tend to be more sympathetic to those destinations than non-Islamic tourists.

These magazines also show that Moslem tourists are also interested in visiting non-Moslem countries, and are doing so in every greater numbers.

Conclusion

Travel magazines promoting travel as a leisure and lifestyle activity have grown in popularity in many countries in recent years. Their emergence in the last few years in the Islamic world is clear evidence of the growth of the tourism markets in these countries. However, as we have seen in these two examples, the extent to which these magazines focus specifically on Islamic tourists vary. 'Islamic Tourism', as its name suggests, is heavily oriented to the Moslem tourist while the 'Gulf Traveller' is broader and more general in its approach and could appeal easily to both Moslems and non-Moslems in the cosmopolitan world of the Gulf States.

Discussion points and questions

1. Discuss the ways in which you think a magazine aimed at the Islamic tourism market might differ from magazines such as 'Conde Nast' (USA) and 'Wanderlust' (UK).
2. Critically evaluate the idea that leisure travel and lifestyle magazines have a major influence on tourist behaviour.
3. Discuss the reasons why leisure travel magazines may not always be the best source of advice for tourists contemplating on taking a particular type of vacation or travelling to a specific destination.

Exercise

Obtain several leisure travel magazines from your own country (if there are no such magazines in your country you should endeavour to explain this situation).

For your chosen magazines you should analyse their content and suggest at whom you think they are aimed. You should then try and decide which you think would be most/least useful for tourists looking for holiday ideas and explain and justify your views.

Glossary

The following glossary of terms is important for the following reasons:

- As marketing has become a more popular topic, marketing terms have been used more widely and perhaps increasingly with less clarity. It is vital, therefore, for the authors to define key words and phrases in terms of what they have been taken to mean when they have been used in this book.
- The meaning of some relevant terms varies between different countries and some terms may not be known to readers in some countries.
- At a time when marketing in leisure has an increasingly global dimension, there is no widely available published glossary of relevant terms.

It is clear that most of the terms used in marketing are English or, perhaps, more accurately, American. However, many relevant words also exist in other national languages.

Acorn
A method of clarifying residential neighbourhoods on the basis of who live there for use in direct mail or marketing research.

Advertising
Paid-for types of communication, designed to influence the attitudes and behaviour of the public as a whole or particular sections of people.

Allocentrics
A term coined by Plog (1977) for customers who are adventurous, outward-looking and like to take risks.

Anosff's matrix
A model developed by Igor Ansoff that suggests four different marketing strategies which organisations can adopt.

Arts
Creative activities carried out for commercial gain or personal pleasure.

Boston Consulting Group Matrix
A technique designed to show the performance of an individual product in relation to its major competitors and the rate of growth in its market.

Brand
Kotler and Armstrong (2004) define a brand as 'a name term, symbol, or design, or combination of them, intended to identify goods or services of one seller or group of sellers, and to differentiate them from those of competitors'. Well-known brands in leisure include Disneyland, Center Parcs, Club 18–30 and Big Mac.

Brand loyalty
The propensity or otherwise of consumers to continue to purchase a particular brand.

Business environment
The business world in which an organisation lives and the factors within it that influence the organisation's products and marketing activities.

Business mix
The overall balance of the different types of markets and products of an organisation.

Business tourism
Tourist trips that take place as part of people's business occupational commitments largely in work time, rather than for pleasure in people's leisure time.

Cash cow
A product that generates a high volume of income in relation to the cost of maintaining its market share.

Catchment area
The geographical area from which the overwhelming majority of a product or organisation's customers are drawn.

Chain
A term used to describe an organisation which owns a number of hotels, restaurants or travel agencies, for example, that offer a generally standardised product.

Commission
Money paid to an external agent who assists the organisation in selling a product, usually expressed as a percentage of the price paid by the customer.

Competition
The process by which organisations attempt to gain new customers from other organisations whilst retaining their existing customers.

Computer Reservations Systems (CRS)
Computer-based systems used widely in tourism and hospitality for making and recording bookings and payments made by customers.

Consumer
The person who uses a product or service. *See also* Customer.

Consumer behaviour
The study of why people buy the products they do and how they make decisions.

Cost leadership
A competitive advantage technique identified by Porter (1980) in which organisations attempt to produce a product at a lower price than their competitors.

Customer
The person who purchases a product or service. This term is often used interchangeably with the word 'consumer', but they can be different. For example, in business tourism, a company pays for the travel services but it is its employee who uses (or 'consumes') the services. *See also* Consumer.

Demand
The quantity of a product or service that customers are willing and able to buy at a particular time at a specific price.

Demarketing
Action designed to discourage consumers from buying particular goods or services.

Demography
The study of population structure including age, sex, race and family status.

Destination
The country, region or locality where a tourist spends their holiday.

Determinants
Factors which determine whether or not a tourist is able to take a holiday and, if so, then the type of holiday they are able to take.

Direct marketing
Selling directly from producer to customer without the aid of marketing intermediaries such as retailers or agents.

Discounts
A reduction in the list price of a product designed to encourage sales.

Disposable income
Money remaining after essential expenditure has been subtracted from a person's income.

Distribution
The process by which products are transferred from producers to consumers. *See also* Place.

Diversification
An extension of an organisation's activities into new markets.

Domestic tourism
Tourism where the residents of a country take holidays wholly within their country of residence.

Ethics
The moral values and standards that guide the behaviour of individuals and organisations.

Family life cycle
The stages through which people pass between birth and death that influence their behaviour as consumers.

Fast food
A form of hot food that can be prepared and served in a very short time.

Feasibility study
A study which is carried out to test the potential viability of any proposed development project or new product. A feasibility study will usually examine both the financial viability of the project or product as well as try to establish the size of its potential market.

FIT
Fully inclusive tours.

Four Ps
The elements of the marketing mix, namely produce, price, place and promotion.

Franchising
The process by which an organisation agrees to permit another organisation to sell its product and use its brand name in return for payment.

Green issues
A commonly used but rather ill-defined term used as an umbrella for a range of issues relating to the physical environment. These may range from pollution to recycling, wildlife conservation to 'global warming'.

Gross Domestic Product (GDP)
The total value of a nation's output of goods and services produced in one year.

Growth market
A market where demand is growing significantly.

Heterogeneous
A market, product type or industry sector that contains nonidentical elements that differ significantly from each other.

Homogeneous
A market, product type or industrial sector that contains elements which are wholly or largely identical.

Horizontal integration
The process by which organisations take over organisations who are, or could be, competitors.

Hospitality
In this context, hospitality is used in the way it is used in the USA, namely as an umbrella term for the whole hotel and catering field.

Intangibility
The characteristic of service products by which they lack physical form and cannot be seen or touched.

International tourism
Tourism where the residents of one country take business or leisure trips which have their destination in another country.

JICNARS
Joint Industry Committee for National Readership Surveys.

Launch
The introduction of a new product or service into a market.

Leisure
According to Collin (1994) leisure is 'free time' but it is also seen by some as an industry, or set of industries, providing products for consumers to use in their leisure time.

Leisure shopping
Leisure shopping is different to ordinary shopping in that it involves consumers choosing to shop as a leisure activity rather than treating it as a necessary task. It also implies that the products they buy will be chosen purely for the pleasure involved in their consumption rather than for their utilitarian value.

Lifestyles
The way of life adopted by an individual or community.

Market
A market is those consumers who currently are, or might potentially be, purchasers and/or users of a particular good or service.

Market focus
This is a term coined by Porter (1980) whereby an organisation seeks competitive advantage by focusing on one specific market segment and trying to become the market leader within this particular segment.

Market leader
The product which has the largest share of an individual market.

Market positioning
The position in the market of a product as perceived by customers in terms of variables such as price, quality and service.

Market share
The proportion of sales in a market achieved by a product or organisation.

Marketing
There is no single definition of marketing but a range of different definitions are offered at the beginning of the book.

Marketing audit
An analysis of the current performance of an organisation's marketing activities.

Marketing consortia
These are formal or informal groupings of organisations who cooperate in mutually beneficial marketing activities.

Marketing intermediaries
Intermediaries are organisations who provide the interface between producers and consumers. They are the retailers in the distribution system, for example, travel agents in the field of tourism.

Marketing Mix
This term refers to the four marketing variables or techniques which organisations manipulate in order to achieve their objectives, namely product, price, place and promotion.

Marketing plan
A written statement of an organisation's marketing aims and the ways in which those aims will be implemented.

Marketing planning
This is the process through which organisations plan and implement their marketing strategies.

Marketing research
Research which is designed specifically to help an organisation increase the effectiveness of its marketing activities.

Media
This term has two meanings in the context of this book. First, it relates to the news communications media in society, including newspapers, magazines and television, for example. But one can also talk specifically about advertising media, in other words, the media where advertising can be placed. These include the four previously mentioned plus cinema and poster sites, for instance.

Mission statement
A brief simple phrase or sentence which summarises the organisation's direction and communicates its ethos to internal and external audiences.

Model
A representation that seeks to illustrate and/or explain a phenomenon.

Motivators
The factors which motivate consumers to buy a particular type of holiday.

Niche marketing
This is where an organisation targets its product specifically at a particular market segment which is numerically much smaller than the size of the total market.

Off-peak
A period when demand for a product is habitually lower than at other times which are termed peak times.

Outlet
A place where products or services are sold or distributed to customers.

Pan-European
Phenomena which share similar characteristics across Europe as a whole.

Perception
The way in which people interpret the data which is available to them about a product or organisation.

Perishability
A characteristic of leisure products whereby they have limited lives, after which they no longer exist and have no value. An example is a seat on a particular flight which ceases to exist as a product that can be sold when the aircraft departs.

Personal selling
This is defined by Kotler and Armstrong (2004) as an 'oral presentation in a conversation with one or more prospective purchasers for the purpose of making sales'. Such selling is found in leisure, for example, where hotel staff try to persuade conference buyers to use their hotels as conference facilities, for example.

Place
An element of the marketing mix which is concerned with distribution and the ways in which consumers may gain access to products. *See also* Distribution.

Point of sale
Dibb et al. (2001) define this as 'sales promotion methods that attract attention, to inform customers and to encourage retailers to carry particular products'. While this definition relates primarily to manufactured goods, it is also found in leisure, for example, in window displays in travel agents' premises.

Postmodern
A sociological theory that has major implications for the study of consumer behaviour based on the idea that in the industrialised nations the basis on which people act as consumers has been transformed in recent years. The impact of postmodernism in tourism is discussed in *The Tourist Gaze* by John Urry, for example.

Press and public relations
A range of activities usually involving the free use of the media designed to raise awareness and/or enhance the image of an organisation or product amongst the population, in general.

Price
An element of the marketing mix concerned with the money which the customer pays in exchange for a product.

Primary data
The data collected by direct original surveys and observations.

Private sector
Those organisations in a market or industry which are owned by individuals or groups of individuals and are motivated by commercial objectives.

Product
What an organisation offers to satisfy customers' wants and needs.

Product differentiation
A term coined by Porter (1980) which describes a technique whereby organisations can seek to gain competitive advantage by offering a product which has features not available in the offerings of competitor organisations.

Product life cycle
The concept by which a product has a 'life' in that it is born, grows and eventually dies.

Product portfolio
This term refers to the range of products offered by a single organisation at any one time.

Product positioning
The process by which an organisation seeks to give a particular impression of its products to potential consumers in order to encourage them to purchase these products.

Product–service mix
Renaghan (1981) defined this term as 'the combination of products and service aimed at satisfying the needs of the target markets'.

Promotion
This is an element of the marketing mix and refers to all the different techniques which are used to communicate the attributes of the product to potential customers to persuade them to buy it. This includes advertising, brochures, sales, public relations and personal selling.

Psychocentrics
A term coined by Plog (1977) for inward-looking, less adventurous consumers.

Psychographic
The analysis of people's lifestyles, perceptions and attitudes as a method of segmentation.

Public sector
Those organisations which are owned and managed by either central or local government. They are generally not commercially motivated and act on behalf of the community as a whole.

Qualitative research
Research concerned with customers' attitudes and perceptions which cannot be quantified.

Quality
The features and standards of a service.

Quantitative research
Research which is concerned with data which is measurable and can be expressed numerically.

Recreation
Defined by Torkildsen (2001) as 'activities and experiences usually carried on within leisure and usually chosen voluntarily for satisfaction, pleasure, or creative enrichment'.

Relaunch
The reintroduction of a previously available product or service into a market, usually following modification.

Repositioning
The process by which organisations attempt to change the image of a product in the minds of consumers with a view to improving the product's reputation with consumers.

Resort complex
A self-contained site, usually in single ownership, which provides all or most of the products and services required by a tourist. They tend to combine attractions with support services such as accommodation and catering. Examples include brands such as Club Med and Center Parcs.

Sales promotions
In general, these are short-term tactical offers designed to stimulate demand. This often takes the form of either price discounts or added value (giving consumer more for the same price).

Secondary data
Data which comes from existing sources such as reports and databases rather than being collected by original research.

Segmentation
The practice of dividing total markets up into subgroups which have similar characteristics.

Service gap
A term used by Parasuraman et al. (1985) to describe the potential gap which can exist between expectations of a service and the reality of the way in which the service is actively delivered.

Services
Products which are intangible processes designed to meet consumer needs.

Social marketing
Marketing in noncommercial organisations where the objectives are social rather than commercial.

Sponsorship
A phenomenon whereby an unrelated organisation provides material or financial support for another organisation's activities or products in return for some benefit, which might include raising the awareness of the organisation's products amongst the latter organisation's market.

Strategic
Thinking or action which is longer term, broad in scope and generally at the macrolevel.

Strategic alliances
A competitive advantage tool which involves working with other organisations in a close relationship for mutual benefit. Such alliances are a common feature of the modern airline industry, for example.

Strategic business unit (SBU)
A self-contained subdivision of an organisation concerned with a particular product or set of products.

Subsidy
Financial support provided by an organisation to improve the financial performance of the organisation which receives the subsidy or to allow customers to afford to buy a product they could not otherwise afford to buy.

Suppliers
The organisations which provide the supplies or 'raw materials' from which suppliers can produce products. For example, hotels are suppliers for tour operators by providing the accommodation element of their package holiday product.

Sustainability
The concept of using resources to meet our needs in a way that will not threaten the ability of future generations to do the same.

SWOT analysis
A technique used by organisations to assess their urrent marketing situation. It involves analysing the organisation's current internal strengths and weaknesses, and identifying specific external opportunities and threats in its business environment.

Tactical
Thinking and action which is short term, narrow in scope and at the microlevel.

Target marketing
Marketing activity aimed at a particular subgroup within the population.

Theme park
A type of attraction, usually in single ownership, which is largely based on a central theme, for example, Disneyland Paris and Legoland.

Timeshare
A type of accommodation where customers pay a lump sum and in return receive the right to use a unit of accommodation for specific times in the year.

Total Quality Management
A fashionable management approach to quality which emphasises that quality is the responsibility of all staff and that quality is about constantly seeking to improve performance.

Tour operator
Organisations which assemble 'package holidays' from components provided by other sectors such as accommodation operators and transport organisations. They then sell those packages to consumers, often through travel agents.

Tourism
The activity in which people spend a short period of time away from home for business or pleasure.

Tourist
A consumer of tourism products.

Transnational corporations
Organisations which operate across national boundaries.

Travel agents
The retailer in the tourism system, selling the products of organisations within tourism to consumers.

Unique selling proposition (USP)
A feature that is so unique that it distinguishes one product from other products.

Upmarket
Products aimed at the more expensive, high status, higher quality end of the market.

Vertical integration
The process by which an organisation takes over other organisations involved in a different stage of production or distribution from itself; for example, where a tour operator takes over a travel agency and/or an airline.

Visitor
A widely used term in the visitor attraction field for someone who makes a visit to an attraction. It recognises that not all visitors are tourists in the technical sense of the term, in that they are not all spending at least one night away from home. Indeed, most customers at attractions are not tourists but excursionists or day trippers.

Visitor attractions
A single site, unit or entity which motivates people to travel to its location to see, experience and participate in what it has to offer. Attractions can be natural or manmade, physical entities or special events.

Voluntary sector
Organisations which are composed of volunteers who join together to achieve a shared objective or work on a common interest. Examples include the National Trust and many steam railway operators in the UK.

Word of mouth
This is where consumers who have experienced a product or service pass on their views about this product or service to other people.

Bibliography and further reading

Andraeson, A.R. (1965) *Attitudes and Consumer Behaviour: A Decision Model in New Research in Marketing*, in Preston, L. (ed.) Institute of Business and Economics Research. University of California, Berkeley.

Andraeson, A.R. and Kotler, P. (2003) *Strategic Marketing for Non-Profit Organisations*. Prentice-Hall, Englewood Cliffs, NJ.

Anholt, S. (1993) 'Adapting Advertising Across National Frontiers', *Admap*, October, pp. 16–17.

Ansoff, H.I. (1980) *The New Corporate Strategy*. John Wiley & Sons, New York.

Ansoff, H.I. (1988) *The New Corporate Strategy*. John Wiley & Sons, Chichester.

Archdale, G. (1994) 'Destination Databases: Issues and Practices', in Seaton, A.V. et al. (eds) (1990). *Tourism: The State of the Art*. John Wiley & Sons, Chichester.

Ashworth, G.J. and Goodall, B. (1990) *Marketing Tourism Places*. Routledge, London.

Ashworth, G.J. and Voogd, H. (1990) *Selling the City: Marketing Approaches in Public Sector Urban Planning*. Belhaven, London.

Ayton, P. (1994) 'Spending Time'. *Leisure Management*. February, pp. 24–26.

Bateson, J.E.G. (1977) 'Do We Need Service Marketing?' *New Insights Report*. Marketing Science Institute, Boston, November, pp. 77–115.

Bateson, J.E.G. (1991) Managing Services Marketing. *Text and Readings*. 2nd Edition. The Dryden Press, USA.

Bateson, J.E.G. (1995) *Managing Services Marketing: Text and Readings*. 4th Edition. Dryden Press, Fort Worth.

Bateson, J.E.G. and Douglas Hoffman, K. (1999) *Managing Services Marketing: Text and Readings*. 4th Edition. The Dryden Press, USA.

Boniface, P. (1995) *Managing Quality Cultural Tourism*. Routledge, London.

Booms, B.H. and Bitner, M.J. (1981) 'Marketing Strategies and organisation Structures for Services Firms', in Donnelly, J. and George, W.R. (eds) *Marketing of Services*. American Marketing Association, Chicago, pp. 47–51.

Bould, A., Breeze, G. and Teare, R. (1992) 'Culture, Customisation and Innovation: A Hilton International Service Brand for the Japanese Market', in Teare, R. and Olsen, M.D. (eds) *International Hospitality Management*. Pitman Publishing, London.

Boyer, M. and Viallon, P. (1994) *Communication Touristique*, Presses Universitaires de France.

Bramham, P., Henry, I., Mamm, H. and Van der Pool, H. (eds) (1993) *Leisure Policies in Europe*. CAB International, Wallingford.

Brent-Ritchie, J.R. and Goeldner, C.R. (1994) *Travel, Tourism and Hospitality Research: A Handbook for Managers and Researchers*. John Wiley & Sons, New York.

Brightbill, C.K. (1963) *The Challenge of Leisure*. Prentice-Hall, New York.

Brightbill, C.K. (1964) *Recreation*, 57, January, p. 10.

British Tourist Authority (1995) Visits to Tourist Attractions.

Bull, A. (1995) *The Economics of Travel and Tourism*. 2nd Edition. Longman, Melbourne.

Burns, P.M. and Holden, A. (1995) *Tourism: A New Perspective*. Prentice-Hall, Hemel Hempstead.

Burton, R. (1995) *Travel Geography*. 2nd Edition. Pitman, London.

Buttle, F. (1986) *Hotel and Food Service Marketing: A Managerial Approach*. Cassell, London.

Cadotte, E.R. and Turgeon, N. (1988) 'Key Factors in Guest Satisfaction'. *The Cornell Hotel and Restaurant Administration Quarterly*. Vol. 28, No. 4, February, pp. 44–51.

Calantone, R.J. and Mazanec, J.A. (1991) 'Marketing Management and Tourism'. *Annals of Tourism Research*. Vol. 18, No. 1, pp. 101–199.

Campbell-Smith, D. (1986) *Struggle for Take-Off: The British Airways Story*. Hodder & Stoughton. Coronet Books, Sevenoaks.

Carroll, L. (1865) *Alice's Adventures in Wonderland*. 1st Edition. First Presentation Copy. Macmillan, London.

Chain Reaction (1995) *Business Traveller*. July, pp. 22–26.

Chartered Institute of Marketing (1984) *Definition of Marketing*. Chartered Institute of Marketing, Cookham.

Chisnall, P.M. (1985) *Marketing: A Behavioural Analysis*. 2nd Edition. McGraw-Hill, Maidenhead.

Clark, T. and Clegg, S. (1998) *Changing Paradigms, the Transformation of Management Knowledge for the 21st Century*. HarperCollins, London.

Collin, P.H. (1994) *Dictionary of Hotels, Tourism and Catering Management*. P.H. Collin, Teddington.

Connell, J. (1994) 'Guide to Hospitality Marketing Literature and Intelligence'. *Insights*. September, pp. 129–142.

Cooper, C., Fletcher, J., Gilbert, D. and Wanhill, S. (1998) *Tourism: Principles and Practice*. 2nd Edition. Pitman, London.

Corporate Hospitality (1995) *Leisureweek*. 30 June.

Cossons, N. (1985) 'Making Museums Market Oriented', in *Scottish Museums Journal*. Museums are for People. HMSO, Edinburgh.

Coulson-Thomas, C. (1986) *Marketing Communications*. Heinemann, London.

Cowell, D.W. (1984) *The Marketing of Services*. Heinemann, London.

Crompton, J.L. (1979) 'Motivations for Pleasure Vacations'. *Annals of Tourism Research*. Vol. 6, No. 1, pp. 408–424.

Cross-Channel Tourism (1993) New Travel and Tourism Markets No. 2. Headland Business Information.

Crossley, J.C. and Jamieson, L.M. (1988) *Introduction to Commercial and Entrepreneurial Recreation*, Sagamore, Champaign, III.

D'Arcy, Masius, Benton and Bowles (1989) *Marketing: Communicating with the Consumer*. Mercury Books/CBI, London.

Daily Telegraph, Saturday, 6 March 2004. Music Festivals to enjoy.

Davidson, R. (1992) *Tourism in Europe*. Pitman, London.

Davidson, R. (1994a) 'European Business Travel and Tourism', in Seaton, A.V. et al. (eds) *Tourism: The State of the Art*. John Wiley & Sons, Chichester.

Davidson, R. (1994b) 'Themed Attractions in Europe'. *Insights*, May, pp. A159–A166.

Davidson, R. (1994c) *Business Travel*. Pitman, London.

Day, G.S. (1990) *Market Drawn Strategy: Processes for Creating Values*. Free Press, London.

Dewailly, J.M. and Flament, E. (1993) *Geographie due Tourisme et des Loisirs*. SEDES, Paris.

Dhalla, N.K. and Yuspeh, S. (1976) 'Forget the Product Life Cycle Concept'. *Harvard Business Review*, January–February, pp. 102–112.

Dholakia, R.R. (1999) 'Group Shopping: Key Determinants of Shopping, Behaviours and Motivations'. *International Journal of Retail and Distribution Management*. Vol. 27, No. 4, pp. 154–165.

Dibb, S., Simkin, L., Pride, W.M. and Ferrell, O.C. (2001) *Marketing: Concepts and Strategies*. 4th European Edition. Houghton-Mifflin, Boston, New York.

Douglas, S. and Wind, Y. (1987) 'The Myth of Globalisation'. *Columbia Journal of World Business*. Winter, pp. 19–29.

Driscoll, E. (1995) 'Fire and Ice'. *Business Traveller*. May 1996, pp. 51–54.

Drucker, P.F. (1969) *The Practice of Management*. Heinemann, London.

Drucker, P.F. (1985) *Innovation and Entrepreneurship*. Heinemann, London.

Dumazedier, J. (1967) *Toward a Society of Leisure*. W.W. Norton, New York.

Economist Intelligence Unit Limited (1992).

Economist Intelligence Unit Limited (1992) E.I.U. Special Report No. M141.

Economist Intelligence Unit Limited (1993) E.I.U. Special Report No. R451. Tour Operators and Travel Agents in the Single Market.

Economist Intelligence Unit Limited (1994) E.I.U. International Tourism Reports, No. 3.
Economist Intelligence Unit Limited (1995) E.I.U. International Tourism Reports, No. 1.
Economist Intelligence Unit Limited (1995) E.I.U. International Tourism Reports, No. 1, 2 and 3.
Eiglier, P. and Langeard, E. (1981) 'A Conceptual Approach of the Service Offer'. Working Paper No. 217. April. Aix-en-Provence.
Euromonitor (Annual) *European Marketing Data and Statistics*. Euromonitor, London.
Euromonitor (Annual) *European Travel and Tourism Marketing Directory*. Euromonitor, London.
Euromonitor (1994) European Domestic Tourism and Leisure Trends.
European Domestic Tourist and Leisure Trends (1994) Travel and Tourism.
Euromonitor European Marketing Data and Statistics (1995) 30th Edition, London.
European Marketing Pocket Book (1995) NTC Publications. Henley-on-Thames.
Eurostat. Statistics in Focus – Regions. 1995–2001.

Foxall, G.R. and Goldsmith, R.E. (1994) *Consumer Psychology for Marketing*. Routledge, London.
Frontiers, Henley Centre/Research International 1991/92.

Getz, D. (1990) *Festivals, Special Events, and Tourism*. Van Nostrand Reinhold, New York.
Gilbert, D.C. (1991) 'An Examination of the Consumer Decision Process Related to Tourism', in Cooper, C. (ed.) *Progress in Tourism, Recreation and Hospitality Management*. Vol. 3. Belhaven, London.
Gold, J.R. and Ward, S.V. (eds) (1994) *Place Promotion: The Use of Publicity and Marketing to sell Towns and Regions*. John Wiley & Sons, Chichester.
Goodale, T. and Godbey, G. (1988) *The Evolution of Leisure*. Venture Publishing, State College, PA.
Goodall, B. and Ashworth, G. (1990) *Marketing Tourism Places: The Promotion of Destination Regions*. Routledge, London.
Gotti, G. and van der Borg, J. (1993) CISET – 'Centro Internazionale di Studi sull'. Economia Turista no. 11/93. Tourism in Heritage Cities.
Gratton, C. (1993) A Perspective on European Leisure Markets. ILAM Guide to Good Practice in Leisure Management. Release 2.
Gratton, C. (1994) The Single Internal Market, European Integration and the Development of International Leisure markets and Transnational Leisure Corporations. Conference Paper.
Greaves, S. (1995) 'Fired Up but Freezing Iceland'. *Conference and Incentive Travel*. June, pp. 33–38.
Grönroos, C.L. (1980) 'An Applied Service Marketing Theory'. Working Paper No. 57. Swedish School of Economics and Business Administration. Helsinki.
Grönroos, C.L. (1990) 'Marketing Redefined'. *Management Decision*. Vol. 28, No. 8.
Guido, G. (1991) 'Implementing a Pan-European Marketing Strategy'. *Long Range Planning*. Vol. 24, No. 5, pp. 22–33.
Hall, D.R. (ed.) (1991) *Tourism and Economic Development in Eastern Europe and the Soviet Union*. Belhaven, London.
Hall, C.M. (1992) *Hallmark Tourist Events: Impacts, Management, and Planning*. Belhaven, London.
Halliburton, C. and Hunerberg, R. (1993) *European Marketing: Readings and Cases*. Addison-Wesley, Wokingham.
Hammill, J. (1993) 'Competitive Strategies in the World Airline Industry'. *European Management Journal*. Vol. 11, No. 3, September, pp. 332–341.
Haylock, R. (1994) 'Timeshare: The New Force in Tourism', in Seaton, A.V. et al. (eds) *Tourism: The Start of the Art*. John Wiley & Sons, Chichester.
Herbert, D.T., Prentice, R.C. and Thomas, C.J. (eds) (1989) *Heritage Sites: Strategies for Marketing and Development*. Avebury, Aldershot.
Holloway, J.C. and Robinson, C. (1995) *Marketing for Tourism*. 3rd Edition. Longman, Harlow.
Homma, N. (1991) 'The Continued Relevance of Cultural Diversity', *Marketing and Research Today*. November, pp. 251–258.
Horner, S. and Swarbrooke, J. (1996) *Marketing Tourism, Hospitality and Leisure in Europe*. International Thomson Business Press, London.
Howard, J.A. and Sheth, J.N. (1969) *The Theory of Buyer Behaviour*. John Wiley & Sons, New York.

Ilam (1992) *Guide to a Good Practice in Leisure Management*. 2nd Edition. Longman, Harlow.

James, W.P.T. (1989) *Healthy Nutrition*. WHO Regional office for Europe, Copenhagen.
Jefferson, A. and Lickorish, L. (1988) *Marketing Tourism*. Longman, Harlow.
Judd, R.C. (1968) 'Similarities and Differences in Product and Service Retailing'. *Journal of Retailing*. Vol. 43, Winter, pp. 1–9.

Kantner, R.M. (1984) *When Giants Learn to Dance*. Simon & Schuster, New York.

Kantner, R.M. (1989) *When Giants Learn to Dance*. Simon & Schuster, New York.

Kashani, I. (1989) 'Beware the Pitfalls of Global Marketing'. *Harvard Business Review*. September–October, pp. 89–98.

Kotler, P. (2000) *Marketing Management*. The Millennium Edition. Prentice-Hall, New Jersey.

Kotler, P. (2003) *Marketing Management*. 11th Edition. Prentice-Hall, New Jersey.

Kotler, P. and Andraeson, A.R. (1996) *Strategic Marketing for Non Profit Organisations*. 5th Edition. Prentice-Hall, Englewood Cliffs.

Kotler, P. and Armstrong, G. (2004) *Principles of Marketing*. 10th Edition. Pearson Education, Upper Saddle River, New Jersey.

Kotler, P., Haider, D.H. and Rein, I. (1993) *Marketing Places*. Free Press, New York.

Kotler, P., Armstrong, G., Swinden, J. and Wong, V. (1999) *Principles of Marketing*. 2nd European Edition. Prentice-Hall, Englewood Cliffs.

Krippendorf, J. (1999) *The Holiday Makers: Understanding the Impact of Leisure and Travel*. Butterworth-Heinemann, Oxford.

Lannon, J. (1992) 'Asking the Right Questions: What Do People Do with Advertising', Admap, March, pp. 11–16.

Lanquar, R. and Hollier, R. (1989) *Le Marketing Touristique*. 3rd Edition. Presses Universitaire de France, Paris.

Larrabee, E. and Meyersohn, R. (eds) (1958) *Mass Leisure*. The Free Press. Glenco, IL.

Law, C.M. (1993) *Urban Tourism: Attracting Visitors to Large Cities*. Mansell, London.

Laws, E. (1990) *Tourism Marketing: Service and Quality Management Perspectives*. Stanley Thornes, Cheltenham.

Laws, E. (1995) *Tourist Destination Management – Issues, Analysis and Policies*. Routledge, London.

Leadley, P. (1992) *Leisure Marketing*. Longman/ILAM, Harlow.

Lendrevic, J. and Lindon, D. (1990) *Mercator*. 4th Edition. Dallas, Texas.

Levitt, T. (1960) 'Marketing Myopia', *Harvard Business Review*. July–August, pp. 45–46.

Levitt, T. (1972) 'Production Line Approach to Services'. *Harvard Business Review*. September–October, pp. 41–45.

Levitt, T. (1983) 'The Globalisation of Marketing'. *Harvard Business Review*. May–June, pp. 92–102.

Levitt, T. (1986) *The Marketing Imagination*. Free Press, New York.

Lewis, R.C. and Chambers, R.G. (2000) *Marketing Leadership in Hospitality*. 3rd Edition. Van Nostrand Reinhold, New York.

Littlejohn, D. and Beattie, R. (1992) *The European Hotel Industry – Corporate Structures and Expansion Strategies*. Butterworth-Heinemann Ltd in Tourism Management, March 1992.

Lundbery, J.D.E. (1990) *The Tourist Business*. 6th Edition. London.

Malcolm, A. (1987) *'Teen-age Shopper: Desperately Seeking Spinach'*. *New York Times*, 29 November.

Manser, N.H. (1988) Marketing Terms: *Chambers Commercial References*. W.R. Chambers Ltd, Edinburgh.

McCarthy, E.J. (1960) Basic marketing: *A Managerial Approach*. Irwin, Homewood.

McDonald, M.H.B. and Morris, P. (2000) *The Marketing Plan*. Butterworth-Heinemann, London.

Middleton, V.T.C. (1994) *Marketing in Travel and Tourism*. 3rd Edition. Butterworth-Heinemann, Oxford.

Middleton, V.T.C. and Clarke, J. (2001) *Marketing in Travel and Tourism*. 3rd Edition. Butterworth-Heinemann, Oxford.

Mintel (2002a) *Boutique Hotels – Global*. April.

Mintel (2002b) *Leisure Shopping – UK*. July.

Mintel (2003) *Clubbing Holidays*. July.

Moriarty, S.E. and Duncan, T.R. (1990) 'Global Advertising: Issues and Practices'. *Current Issues and Research in Advertising*. Vol. 13, Nos 1 and 2. J.H. Leigh and C.R. Martine (eds) Division of Research, School of Business Administration. The University of Michigan.

Munzinger, U. (1988) 'Advantage/AC-J' International Advertising research Case Studies, ESOMAR Seminar on International marketing research, 16–18 November.

Nakhhoda, J. (1961) *Leisure and Recreation in Society*. Kitab Mahal, Allahabad, India.

Nash, J.B. (1960) *Philosophy of Recreation and Leisure*. William Brown, Dubuque, I.A.

Neumeyer, M. and Neumeyer, E. (1958) *Leisure and Recreation*. Ronald Press, New York.

Ohmae, K. (1982) *The Mind of the Strategist: Business Planning for Competitive Advantage*. Penguin Books, London.

Packard, V. (1957) *The Hidden Persuaders*. Longmans Greenland Co., London.

Palmer, A. (2001) *Principles of Services Marketing*. 3rd Edition. McGraw-Hill, Maidenhead.

Parasuraman, A., Zeithmal, W.A. and Berry, L. (1985) 'A Conceptual Model of Service Quality and Its Implications for Future Research'. *Journal of Marketing*. Vol. 49, No. 4, pp. 41–50.

Parker, S. (1971) *The Future of Work and Leisure*. Mac Gibbon and Kee, London.

Pearce, W. and Butler, R.G. (1992) *Tourism Research: Critiques and Challenges*. Routledge, London.

Peters, T. and Austin, N. (1985) *A Passion for Excellence*. Collins, Glasgow.

Peters, T. and Waterman, R.H., Jr (1982) *In Search of Excellence*. Harper & Row, Scrantan, US.

Pieper, J. (1952) *Leisure the Basis of Culture*. New American Library, New York.

Piercy, N. (1991) 'Developing Marketing Information Systems', in Baker, M. (ed.) *The Marketing Book*. 2nd Edition. Butterworth-Heinemann, Oxford.

Piercy, N. (2002) *Market led Strategic Change: A Guide to Transforming the Process of going to Market*. Butterworth-Heinemann, Oxford.

Plog, S. (1977) 'Why Destination Areas Rise and Fall in Popularity', in Kelly, E. (ed.) *Domestic and International Tourism*. Institute of Certified Travel Agents, Wellesley, MA.

Plog, S. (1991) *Leisure Travel: Making it a Growth Market Again*. John Wiley & Sons, New York.

Poon, A. (1993) *Tourism, Technology and Competitive Strategies*. CAB International, Wallingford.

Porter, M.E. (1980, 1983) *Competitive Advantage – Creating and Sustaining Superior Performance*. Free Press, New York.

Porter, M.E. (1986) *Competition in Global Industries*. Harvard Business Press, Boston, USA.

Prompl, W. and Lavery, P. (eds) (1993) *Tourism in Europe: Structures and Developments*. CAB International, Wallingford.

Py, P. (1992) *Le Tourisme: Un Phenomene Economique*. La Documentation Francaise, Paris.

Reid, R.D. (1989) *Hospitality Marketing Management*. 2nd Edition. Nostrand Reinhold, New York.

Renaghan, L.M. (1981) 'A New Marketing Mix for the Hospitality Industry', *Cassell Hotel and Restaurant Administration Quarterly*. April, pp. 31–32.

Rink, D.R. and Swan, J. (1979) 'Product Life Cycle Research: A Literature Review', *Journal of Business Research*. September, pp. 219–242.

Ross, F.G. (1998) *The Psychology of Tourism*. 2nd Edition. Hospitality Press, Melbourne.

Rushton, A.M. and Carson, M.J. (1985) 'The Marketing of Services', *European Journal of Marketing*. March, Hospitality Press, Melbourne, p. 23.

Ryan, C. (1991) *Recreational Tourism: A Social Science Perspective*. Routledge, London.

Ryan, C. (1995) *Research Tourist Satisfaction: Issues, Concepts and Problems*. Routledge, London.

Sasser, W.E., Olsen, R.P. and Wycoff, D.D. (1978) *Management of Service Operations: Text and Cases*. Allyn and Bacon, Boston, Massachusetts.

Scholes, K. Paper (1991) Development in Local Government. *Occasional Paper and Conference Paper*. Sheffield Hallam University, Sheffield.

Seaton, A.V. (ed.) (1994) *Tourism: The State of the Art*. John Wiley & Sons, Chichester.

Segal-Horn, S. (1989) 'The Globalisation of Service Firms', in Jones, P. (ed.) *Management in the service industries*. Pitman, London.

Sharpley, R. (1999) *Tourism, Tourists, and Societies*. 2nd Edition. Elm, Huntingdon.

Shaw, S. (1999) *Airline Marketing and Management*. 4th Edition. Ashgate, Aldershot.

Shaw, G. and Williams, A.M. (2002) *Critical Issues in Tourism: A Geographical Perspective*. 2nd Edition. Blackwell, Oxford.

Shostack, G.L. (1977) 'Breaking Free from Product Marketing'. *Journal of Marketing*. Vol. 41, No. 2, American Marketing Association, April, pp. 73–80.

Sinclair, M.T. and Stabler, M.J. (1991) *The Tourism Industry: An International Analysis*. CAB International, Wallingford.

Slattery, P., Freehely, G. and Savage, M. (1995) Quoted Hotel Companies: The World Markets 1995. March. Kleinworth Benson Research.

Smith, S.L.J. (1995) *Tourism Analysis*. 2nd Edition. Longman, Harlow.

Solomon, M.R. (1991) *Consumer Behaviour*. 3rd Edition. Prentice-Hall, Englewood Cliffs, New Jersey.

Solomon, M.R. (1996) *Consumer Behaviour*. 3rd Edition. Prentice-Hall, Englewood Cliffs, New Jersey.

Soule, G. (1957) 'The Economics of Leisure'. *Annals of the American Academy of Political and Social Science*, September.

South, S.J. and Sptize, G. (1994) 'Housework in Marital and Non-Marital households'. *American Sociological Review*. Vol. 59, pp. 327–347.

Stone, M. (1990) *Leisure Service Marketing*. Croner, Kingston upon Thames.

Swarbrooke, J.S. (1994a) 'The Future of Heritage Attractions'. *Insights*. January, pp. D15–D20.

Swarbrooke, J.S. (1994b) 'Greening and Competitive Advantage'. *Insights*. May, pp. D43–D50.

Swarbrooke, J.S. (1994c) Conference Paper: 'Greening and Competitive Advantage in the Hospitality Industry' in *Proceedings of the Hospitality Marketing Conference, Gloucester and Cheltenham College of Higher Education*. Pavic, Sheffield. September.

Swarbrooke, J.S. (1999) *The Development and Management of Visitor Attractions*. 2nd Edition. Butterworth-Heinemann, Oxford.

Swarbrooke, J.S. (2002) *The Development and Management of Visitor Attractions*. 3rd Edition. Butterworth-Heinemann, Oxford.

Swarbrooke, J. and Horner, S. (1999) *Consumer Behaviour in Tourism*. Butterworth-Heinemann, Oxford.

Teare, R., Mazanec, J.A., Crawford-Welch, S. and Calver, S. (1994) *Marketing in Hospitality and Tourism in Consumer Focus*. Cassell, London.

Tellis, G.H. and Crawford, C.M. (1981) 'An Evolutionary Approach to Product Growth Theory'. *Journal of Marketing*, No. 4, pp. 125–132.

The Boston Consulting Group Inc. (1970) *The Product Portfolio*, Boston, Massachusetts.

Theobold, W. (ed.) (1998) *Global Tourism: The Next Decade*. 2nd Edition. Butterworth-Heinemann, Oxford.

Toop, A. (1992) *European Sales Promotion: Great Campaigns in Action*. Kogan Page, London.

Torkildsen, G. (2001) *Leisure and Recreation Management*. E & FN Spon, London.

Torkildsen, G. (2001) *Leisure and Recreation Management*. Spon Press, London.

Tourism Planning and Research Associates (1993) *The European Tourist: A Market Profile*. Tourism Planning and Research Associates, London.

Tourism Research and Marketing (1994) *Theme Parks*. UK and International Markets, October.

Urry, J. (1995) *Consuming Places*. Routledge, London.

Urry, J. (2002) *The Tourist Gaze: Leisure and Travel in Contemporary Societies*. 2nd Edition. Sage, London.

Usinier, J.C. (1993) *International Marketing: A Cultural Approach*. Prentice-Hall International, Hemel Hempstead.

Uysal, M. (ed.) (1994) *Global Tourist Behaviour*. International Business Press, New York.

Van, K.F. (1993) European Community Law Series, Number 6, Tourism and the Hotel and Catering Industries in the EC. Athlone Press, Canada.

Vandermerwe, S. (1989) 'Strategies for pan-European Marketing'. *Long Range Planning*. Vol. 22, No. 3, pp. 45–53.

Vandermerwe, S. and L'Huillier, M.A. (1989) 'Euro-Consumers in 1992'. *Business Horizons*. January–February, Vol. 32, No. 1, pp. 34–40.

Veal, A.J. (1997) *Research Methods for Leisure and Tourism: A Practical Guide*. 2nd Edition. Pitman, London.

Voase, R. (1995) *Tourism: The Human Perspective*. Hodder and Stoughton, London.

Wackerman, G. (1993) *Tourisme et Transport*. SEDES, Paris.

Wahah, S., Crompton, L.J. and Rothfield, L.M. (1976) *Tourism Marketing*. Tourism International Press, London.

Wheatcroft, S. and Geekings, J. (1995) *Europe's Youth Travel Market*. European Travel Commission, Brussels.

Williams, A.M. and Shaw, G. (1998) *Tourism and Economic Development: Western European Experiences*. 3rd Edition. Belhaven, London.

Witt, S.F. and Moutinho, L. (1995) *Tourism Marketing and Management Handbook*. Student Edition. Prentice-Hall, London.

Witt, S.F. and Witt, C.A. (1992) *Modelling and Forecasting Demand in Tourism*. Academic Press, London.

Wolfe, A. (1991) 'The Single European Market: National or Euro-brands?' *International Journal of Advertising*. Vol. 10, No. 1, pp. 49–58.

Yale, P. (1995) *The Business of Tour Operations*. Longman, Harlow.

Index